D1483805

READINGS IN ECONOMETRIC THEORY AND PRACTICE
A Volume in Honor of George Judge

CONTRIBUTIONS
TO
ECONOMIC ANALYSIS

209

Honorary Editor:
J. TINBERGEN

Editors:
D. W. JORGENSON
J.J.-LAFFONT

NORTH-HOLLAND
AMSTERDAM • LONDON • NEW YORK • TOKYO

READINGS IN ECONOMETRIC THEORY AND PRACTICE

A Volume in Honor of George Judge

Edited by:

W. E. GRIFFITHS
University of New England
Armidale, NSW
Australia

H. LÜTKEPOHL
Christian-Albrechts-Universität
Kiel
Germany

M. E. BOCK
Purdue University
West Lafayette, IN
USA

1992

NORTH-HOLLAND
AMSTERDAM • LONDON • NEW YORK • TOKYO

ELSEVIER SCIENCE PUBLISHERS B.V.
Sara Burgerhartstraat 25
P.O. Box 211, 1000 AE Amsterdam
The Netherlands

Library of Congress Cataloging-in-Publication Data

Readings in econometric theory and practice : a volume in honor of
George Judge / edited by W.E. Griffiths, H. Lütkepohl, M.E. Bock.
        p.   cm. -- (Contributions to economic analysis ; 209)
    Includes bibliographical references and index.
    ISBN 0-444-89574-4 (hardback : alk. paper)
    1. Econometrics.   I. Judge, George G.   II. Griffiths, William E.
III. Lütkepohl, Helmut.   IV. Bock, M. E. (Mary Ellen)   V. Series.
HB139.R43   1992
330'.01'5195--dc20   92-15019
                                                               CIP

330.015195
R287

ISBN: 0 444 89574 4

INTRODUCTION TO THE SERIES

This series consists of a number of hitherto unpublished studies, which are introduced by the editors in the belief that they represent fresh contributions to economic science.

The term "economic analysis" as used in the title of the series has been adopted because it covers both the activities of the theoretical economist and the research worker.

Although the analytical methods used by the various contributors are not the same, they are nevertheless conditioned by the common origin of their studies, namely theoretical problems encountered in practical research. Since for this reason, business cycle research and national accounting, research work on behalf of economic policy, and problems of planning are the main sources of the subjects dealt with, they necessarily determine the manner of approach adopted by the authors. Their methods tend to be "practical" in the sense of not being too far remote from application to actual economic conditions. In addition they are quantitative.

It is the hope of the editors that the publication of these studies will help to stimulate the exchange of scientific information and to reinforce international cooperation in the field of economics.

The Editors

PREFACE

The purpose of this book is to honor George Judge and his many, varied and outstanding contributions to econometrics, statistics, mathematical programming and spatial equilibrium modeling. George Judge was born on May 2, 1925, he obtained his B.S. from the University of Kentucky in 1948, and his M.S. (1949) and Ph.D. (1952) from Iowa State University. His first position was as Assistant Professor in the Department of Agricultural Economics at the University of Connecticut (1951–55). From there he went, as Professor, to the Department of Agricultural Economics at Oklahoma State University (1955–58); he was a Research Fellow in Economics at Yale University in 1958–59, and was Professor of Economics and Agricultural Economics at the University of Illinois from 1959 to 1986. He moved to his present position of Professor in the Department of Agricultural and Resource Economics at the University of California, Berkeley in 1986. He has also held visiting positions at London School of Economics, University of California at Berkeley, Purdue University, University of Georgia and Institut National de la Statistique et des Etudes Economiques, Paris. He is a Fellow of the Econometric Society and has served on the editorial boards of several of our leading journals.

During his long and distinguished career, George has published over 60 research papers and 11 books. In each of his chosen research areas he has made a significant and lasting impact. He was first to apply the limited information maximum likelihood estimator to what was then the new area of simultaneous equations modeling and estimation. In subsequent applications he integrated this new methodology with the decision modeling necessary for econometric results to be used in an economic framework. His work in the 60s on partial and general equilibrium models for price and quantity allocation over time and space provided the foundation stone upon which today's research is based. Related work involved solutions for mathematical programming problems, applications of and estimation techniques for Markov processes, and the use of programming techniques for econometric estimation. All this work was new, innovative and forward looking. It provided inspiration and direction for many future researchers.

A long-standing practice in much applied econometric research is to try a multitude of models until we find one 'that works', one where all the statistical measures of performance are favorable. Unfortunately, such favorable performance measures can often be a measure of the researcher's perseverance, rather than a measure of how good the model actually is. They ignore the preliminary testing procedures that lead to the final model selection. George's research contributions in the 70s and 80s have done much to alert the profession to these dangers. He has derived the properties of many pre-test estimators and has suggested other alternative biased estimators that belong to the Stein and Bayesian families of estimators.

George Judge's research contributions have been great. However, to mention only his research contributions is to leave much unsaid. As a colleague, he is dynamic and stimulating. He has a real talent for motivating those around him so that they too share in his vision, enthusiasm and productivity. Much of his time is given unselfishly to young researchers who are trying to establish themselves. We editors can attest to the enormous positive impact he has on our lives and we feel sure our words would be echoed by his other friends and colleagues. This collection of papers is an opportunity for us and others to say thank you.

The papers in the volume have been grouped into four parts, each part representing an area in which George has made a significant contribution. The authors have all benefited in some way, directly or indirectly, through an association with George and his work. The three papers in Part I are concerned with various aspects of pre-test and Stein-rule estimation. Part II contains applications of Bayesian methodology, new developments in Bayesian methodology, and an overview of Bayesian econometrics. The papers in Part III comprise new developments in time-series analysis, improved estimation and Markov chain analysis. The final part on spatial equilibrium modeling contains papers that had their origins from George's pioneering work in the 60s.

We would like to thank North-Holland for giving us the opportunity to honor George in this way. To those who used their valuable time refereeing the papers, we also say thank you.

William Griffiths
Helmut Lütkepohl
Mary Ellen Bock

CONTENTS

LIST OF CONTRIBUTORS

Aigner, Dennis J.	University of California, Irvine, CA, USA
Beesley, P.A.	University of New England, Armidale, NSW, Australia
Bera, Anil K.	University of Illinois, Champaign, IL, USA and Indiana University, Bloomington, IN, USA
Bernstein, David	Massachusetts Institute of Technology, Cambridge, MA, USA
Bohrer, Robert	University of Illinois, Champaign, IL, USA
Chalfant, James A.	University of California, Davis, CA, USA
Doran, H.E.	University of New England, Armidale, NSW, Australia
Fomby, Thomas B.	Southern Methodist University, Dallas, TX, USA
Friesz, Terry L.	George Mason University, Fairfax, VA, USA
Ghali, Khalifa	Faculté de Sousse, Sousse, Tunisia
Giles, David E.A.	University of Canterbury, Christchurch, New Zealand
Griffiths, W.E.	University of New England, Armidale, NSW, Australia
Hill, R. Carter	Louisiana State University, Baton Rouge, LA, USA
Lee, Tsoung-Chao	University of Connecticut, Storrs, CT, USA
Lütkepohl, Helmut	Christian-Albrechts-Universität, Kiel, Germany
MacAulay, T.G.	University of Sydney, Sydney, NSW, Australia
Machado, José A.F.	Universidade Nova de Lisboa, Lisbon, Portugal and University of Illinois, Champaign, IL, USA
Mellin, Illka	University of Helsinki, Helsinki, Finland
Nagurney, Anna	University of Massachusetts, Amherst, MA, USA
Racine, Jeff	York University, Toronto, Ont., Canada
Teräsvirta, Timo	Research Institute of the Finnish Economy, Helsinki, Finland
Ullah, Aman	University of California, Riverside, CA, USA and University of Western Ontario, London, Ont., Canada
Wallace, Nancy A.	University of California, Berkeley, CA, USA
Yancey, T.A.	University of Illinois, Champaign, IL, USA
Zellner, Arnold	University of Chicago, Chicago, IL, USA

I. PRE-TEST AND STEIN-RULE ESTIMATION

Readings in Econometric Theory and Practice
W. Griffiths, H. Lütkepohl and M.E. Bock (Editors)
© 1992 Elsevier Science Publishers B.V. All rights reserved

CHAPTER 1

THE EFFECTS OF EXTRAPOLATION ON MINIMAX STEIN-RULE PREDICTION *

R. Carter Hill

Economics Department, Louisiana State University, Baton Rouge, LA 70803, USA

Thomas B. Fomby

Economics Department, Southern Methodist University, Dallas, TX 75275, USA

The purpose of this paper is to evaluate the performance of a variety of improved estimators under an out-of-sample mean square error of prediction criterion. Estimators that are minimax with respect to the criterion function are compared to estimators that are minimax with respect to other loss functions as well as several other biased estimators. Out-of-sample mean square error improvement is sensitive to multicollinearity conditions in both the sample data and out-of-sample regressor values. This multicollinearity difference is characterized by differences in characteristic root spectra, data ellipsoid rotation and distance between regressor means.

1. Introduction

The purpose of this paper is to consider the performance of a variety of improved estimators for the classical normal linear regression model when the measure of performance is *out-of-sample* mean square error of prediction and where the data are multicollinear. In particular we consider the performance of several Stein-like estimators that combine sample and non-sample information in a way that dominates ordinary least squares (LS) when certain design related conditions are met. Furthermore, we define data extrapolation

* The authors would like to thank Minbo Kim and Shengyi Guo for their valuable research assistance on this research project. The authors received useful comments from Roger Koenker, Mary Ellen Bock and Jim Chalfant. Any errors are, of course, the responsibility of the authors. Fomby is grateful for the partial financial support provided by the Federal Reserve Bank of Dallas while this research was in progress, especially during the summer of 1989. Of course, the opinions expressed herein are those of the authors and should not be attributed to the Federal Reserve Bank of Dallas or the Federal Reserve System.

in the multivariate context so that we can examine the effects on prediction when the out-of-sample data are different from the data used for parameter estimation. Data extrapolation takes into account not only distance between two data sets but also the directions of the major and minor axes of the data ellipsoids and the amounts of variation in each direction.

Our work may be thought of as extensions of several works. Friedman and Montgomery (1985) discuss the performance of two biased estimation procedures, ridge regression and principal components regression, with respect to out-of-sample mean square error of prediction when the data are multicollinear. They develop conditions under which ridge and principal components regression can improve upon the least squares estimator. Unfortunately, the conditions they develop depend upon the true but unknown parameters of the regression model and are not made operational. It is well known that usual procedures for operationalizing these biased estimators lead to rules that are not better than LS over substantial portions of the parameter space.

Hill and Judge (1987) examine the performance of a variety of Stein-like estimation rules with respect to in-sample mean square error of prediction. Hill, Cartwright and Arbaugh (1991) examine the performance of Stein-like and ridge rules when forecasting within the context of marketing data. Their results reveal that out-of-sample mean square error of prediction gains can be substantial when non-minimax rules are used. Zellner and Hong (1989) use Bayesian Shrinkage rules to forecast international growth rates.

The plan of the paper is as follows: In Section 2 we present the statistical model and describe the alternative estimators we will consider. In Section 3 we define multivariate measures of data extrapolation and use these concepts in designing a Monte Carlo experiment, described in Section 4. We then use this experiment to explore estimator performance. In Section 5 we report the results of our Monte Carlo experiment and Section 6 contains concluding remarks.

2. The Statistical Model and Estimators

Consider the linear statistical model

$$y = X\beta + e \tag{2.1}$$

where y is a $(T \times 1)$ random vector, X is a $(T \times K)$ non-stochastic matrix of rank $K \leqq T$, β is a $(K \times 1)$ vector of unknown parameters and e is a $(T \times 1)$ vector of random disturbances distributed as $N(0, \sigma^2 I)$.

The vector of regression parameters is unknown and it is our purpose to estimate β using an estimator δ under a weighted squared error loss measure

$$L(\beta, \delta, Q) = (\delta - \beta)'Q(\delta - \beta) \tag{2.2}$$

where Q is a positive definite and symmetric matrix. The sampling performance of δ is evaluated by its risk function

$$R(\beta, \delta, Q) = E[L(\beta, \delta, Q)]. \tag{2.3}$$

The most common choices for the weight matrix Q in (2.2) are $Q = I$, which defines the risk of estimation to be the mean square error, and $Q = X'X$ which corresponds to in-sample mean square error of prediction risk. As we are interested in out-of-sample mean square error of prediction we let X_0 be an $(m \times K)$ matrix of regressor values of rank K such that $m \geq K$. The corresponding values of the dependent variable are

$$y_0 = X_0\beta + e_0 \tag{2.4}$$

where $e_0 \sim N(0, \sigma^2 I_m)$ and $E[ee_0'] = 0$. The weight matrix for (2.2) we wish to consider is $Q = X_0'X_0$ so that

$$R(\beta, \delta, X_0'X_0) = E(\delta - \beta)' X_0'X_0(\delta - \beta)$$

$$= E(X_0\delta - X_0\beta)'(X_0\delta - X_0\beta)$$

$$= E(\hat{y}_0 - Ey_0)'(\hat{y}_0 - Ey_0) \tag{2.5}$$

which is the out-of-sample mean square error of prediction.

For the linear statistical model (2.1) the BLU and MVU estimator is

$$b = (X'X)^{-1}X'y \sim N(\beta, \sigma^2(X'X)^{-1}).$$

The estimator

$$\hat{\sigma}^2 = (y - Xb)'(y - Xb)/(T - K) = s/(T - K)$$

is MVU for σ^2 and $s/\sigma^2 \sim \chi^2_{(T-K)}$. Under the loss measure (2.2) the risk of b is

$$R(\beta, b, Q) = \sigma^2 \, \text{tr}(X'X)^{-1}Q.$$

2.1. General Families of Minimax Estimators

The estimators of primary interest which we will consider are special cases of two classes of general minimax estimators. The first class of estimators we consider is that offered by Judge and Bock (1978, p. 234). A family of estimators which are minimax with respect to $R(\beta, \delta, Q)$ has the form

$$\delta(b, s) = \left[I_K - h\left(\frac{b'Bb}{s} \right) C \right] b \tag{2.6}$$

where B and C are known and chosen so that $Q^{1/2}CQ^{-1/2}$ and $Q^{-1/2}BQ^{-1/2}$ are positive definite matrices that commute with each other and with $Q^{1/2}(X'X)^{-1}Q^{1/2}$, where $Q^{1/2}$ is a positive definite and symmetric matrix such that $Q^{-1/2}QQ^{-1/2} = I$. Here the function $h(u)$ is chosen to be a/u (Judge and Bock, 1978, p. 235) and a is a constant which for minimaxity must obey

$$0 < a < 2 \left[\frac{\text{tr } C(X'X)^{-1}Q - 2\lambda_{\max}\left(C(X'X)^{-1}Q \right)}{(T - K + 2)\lambda_{\max}(C'QCB^{-1})} \right] \tag{2.7}$$

where $\lambda_{\max}(\cdot)$ is the maximum characteristic root of the matrix argument. In addition to condition (2.7) on the constant a, the number of regressors K must be greater than 2 if (2.6) is to be minimax.

The second general minimax class of estimators with respect to $R(\beta, \delta, Q)$ that we will consider can be thought of as an extension of the first, and has been developed and explored by Mittelhammer and Young (1981) and extended by Mittelhammer (1985).

Let $R\beta = r$ represent a set of $J \leq K$ independent linear restrictions on β. The restricted least squares (RLS) estimator is

$$b^* = b - (X'X)^{-1}R'\left[R(X'X)^{-1}R' \right]^{-1}(Rb - r). \tag{2.8}$$

The general minimax estimator that combines the sample and non-sample information $(R\beta = r)$ is

$$\delta^*(b, s) = \left[1 - \frac{as}{(r - Rb)'\left[R(X'X)^{-1}R' \right]^{-1}(r - Rb)} \right](b - b^*) + b^*. \tag{2.9}$$

Sufficient conditions for minimaxity are $J > 2$ restrictions, and

$$0 < a < \frac{2}{T - K + 2} \left[\frac{\operatorname{tr}\{ [R(X'X)^{-1}R']^{-1} R(X'X)^{-1}Q(X'X)^{-1}R' \}}{\eta_L} - 2 \right] \qquad (2.10)$$

where η_L is the largest characteristic root of the matrix in braces $\{\}$.

To provide some intuition about the estimator $\delta^*(b, s)$ in (2.9) we will derive it via an empirical Bayes approach suggested by Judge, Hill and Bock (1990). The J independent linear restrictions $R\beta = r$ can be written

$$R\beta = R_1\beta_1 + R_2\beta_2 = r \qquad (2.11)$$

where R_1 is $(J \times J)$ and nonsingular, β_1 is $(J \times 1)$, R_2 is $J \times (K - J)$ and β_2 is $(K - J) \times 1$. The decomposition (2.11) is always possible, though some rearrangement of the parameters may be required (Mantell, 1973). Then we can solve for β_1 as $\beta_1 = -R_1^{-1}R_2\beta_2 + R_1^{-1}r$ and write

$$\beta = \begin{bmatrix} \beta_1 \\ \beta_2 \end{bmatrix} = \begin{bmatrix} R_1^{-1}r \\ 0 \end{bmatrix} + \begin{bmatrix} -R_1^{-1}R_2 \\ I_{K-J} \end{bmatrix} \beta_2$$

$$= h_0 + H\beta_2. \qquad (2.12)$$

To incorporate the restrictions (2.12) using the Bayesian approach we specify β_{20}, a prior mean for β_2, and we adopt Zellner's (1986) "g-prior" for β, $\pi(\beta \mid \beta_{20})$,

$$\pi(\beta \mid \beta_{20}) = N[h_0 + H\beta_{20}, \tau^2 S^{-1}], \qquad (2.13a)$$

where $S = X'X$. Written in another way

$$\beta = (h_0 + H\beta_{20}) + v, \quad v \sim N(0, \tau^2 S^{-1}). \qquad (2.13b)$$

Using the data alone we can estimate β using

$$b = (X'X)^{-1}X'y = \beta + \epsilon, \quad \epsilon \sim N(0, \sigma^2 S^{-1}). \qquad (2.14)$$

Combining (2.13) and (2.14) we see that the marginal distribution of b given β_{20}, $M(b \mid \beta_{20})$, is

$$M(b \mid \beta_{20}) = N[h_0 + H\beta_{20}, (\tau^2 + \sigma^2)S^{-1}]. \qquad (2.15)$$

Then we can write the joint p.d.f. of b and β, given β_{20}, as

$$\begin{bmatrix} b \\ \beta \end{bmatrix} \sim N\left\{ \begin{bmatrix} h_0 + H\beta_{20} \\ h_0 + H\beta_{20} \end{bmatrix}, \begin{bmatrix} (\sigma^2 + \tau^2)S^{-1} & \tau^2 S^{-1} \\ \tau^2 S^{-1} & \tau^2 S^{-1} \end{bmatrix} \right\}. \tag{2.16}$$

Using usual operations with the multivariate normal distribution, we can determine that the conditional posterior distribution of $(\beta \mid b, \beta_{20})$ has mean

$$E(\beta \mid b, \beta_{20}) = (h_0 + H\beta_{20}) + \frac{\tau^2}{\tau^2 + \sigma^2} [b - (h_0 + H\beta_{20})]$$

$$= b - \frac{\sigma^2}{\tau^2 + \sigma^2} [b - (h_0 + H\beta_{20})]. \tag{2.17}$$

Following the empirical Bayes approach we will obtain an approximation of the posterior mean by replacing the unknown parameters in (2.17) using estimates obtained from $M(b \mid \beta_{20})$ in (2.15). From (2.15),

$$(b - h_0) = H\beta_{20} + \epsilon^*, \quad \epsilon^* \sim N(0, (\sigma^2 + \tau^2)S^{-1}) \tag{2.18}$$

so that an estimate of β_{20} is

$$\beta_2^* = (H'SH)^{-1}H'S(b - h_0). \tag{2.19}$$

It is not hard to verify that β_2^* is the usual restricted least squares estimator (2.8) of β_2 and that $b^* = h_0 + H\beta_2^*$. Furthermore, consider the quadratic form

$$v_1 = (b - b^*)'S(b - b^*) \sim (\sigma^2 + \tau^2)\chi_{(J)}^2.$$

Since $v_1/(\sigma^2 + \tau^2) \sim \chi_{(J)}^2$, then $E[(\sigma^2 + \tau^2)/v_1] = E[1/\chi_{(J)}^2] = (J - 2)^{-1}$ and an unbiased estimator of $(\sigma^2 + \tau^2)^{-1}$ is

$$(\sigma^2 \hat{+} \tau^2)^{-1} = (J - 2)/v_1. \tag{2.20}$$

Finally, on the right hand side of (2.17) replace β_2 with β_2^*, $(\sigma^2 + \tau^2)^{-1}$ with (2.20) and σ^2 with the best invariant estimator $s/(T - K + 2)$ to obtain the empirical Bayes estimator

$$\beta_{EB} = b - \frac{(J - 2)s}{(T - K + 2)v_1}(b - b^*) = \left[1 - \frac{as}{v_1}\right](b - b^*) + b^* \tag{2.21}$$

where $a = (J - 2)/(T - K + 2)$. Note that (2.21) is identical to (2.9). The choice of $a = (J - 2)/(T - K + 2)$ produces an estimator that is minimax with respect to $Q = X'X$, or in-sample mean squared error of prediction.

2.2. Rules that Shrink toward the Origin

In the absence of any specific non-sample information that y and X are closely related, it is customary to use the null hypothesis that $\beta = 0$ as non-sample information to be combined with the data for Stein-rule estimation. Using the family (2.6) with $C = I$ and $B = X'X$ or using (2.9) with $R = I$ and $r = 0$ leads to the simple James-Stein (1961) estimator

$$\delta_1(b, s) = \left[1 - \frac{as}{b'X'Xb}\right]b \tag{2.22}$$

where for minimaxity $K > 2$ and

$$0 \leqq a \leqq \frac{2}{T - K + 2}\left[\frac{\operatorname{tr}\left[Q(X'X)^{-1}\right]}{\lambda_{\max}(Q(X'X)^{-1})} - 2\right] = a_{\max}. \tag{2.23}$$

In practice the positive rule variant of δ_1 is used, so that the shrinkage constant $[1 - as/b'X'Xb]$ is set to zero if it becomes negative. If $Q = I$, $X'X$ or $X_0'X_0$ the upper-bounds for a are $a_{\max} = (2/(T - K + 2)) \cdot (\lambda_K \operatorname{tr}(X'X)^{-1} - 2)$, where λ_K is the smallest root of $X'X$, $(2/(T - K + 2)) \cdot (K - 2)$ and

$$(2/(T - K + 2)) \cdot \left[\frac{\operatorname{tr}\left[(X_0'X_0)(X'X)^{-1}\right]}{\lambda_{\max}(X_0'X_0(X'X)^{-1})} - 2\right]$$

respectively. We will refer to this estimator as the "Stein-rule" in the rest of this paper.

Another estimator that shrinks toward the origin is obtained from the family (2.6) using $B = (X'X)(X_0'X_0)^{-1}(X'X)$ and $C = (X_0'X_0)^{-1}(X'X)$. Consequently this estimator has the form

$$\delta_2(b, s) = \left[I_K - \frac{a \cdot s \cdot (X_0'X_0)^{-1}X'X}{b'X'X(X_0'X_0)^{-1}X'Xb}\right]b \tag{2.24}$$

and is minimax with respect to $Q = X_0' X_0$ if $m \geq K \geq 3$ and

$$0 \leq a \leq \frac{2(K-2)}{T-K+2} = a_{max}. \tag{2.25}$$

This estimator was designed so that the upper-bound on the constant a would not depend on the design characteristics of X or X_0 under quadratic loss with $Q = X_0' X_0$. There is of course no reason why this rule should perform particularly well under other loss functions as $X_0' X_0$ diverges from I or $X'X$. Berger (1976) produces an estimator with a similar flavor for the case when $Q = I$ (in the sense that a_{max} does not depend on the sample design) and consequently δ_2 is Berger-like in that regard and we will call δ_2 the "Berger-rule".

To obtain the positive-part variant of the Berger-rule we employ the general framework employed by Judge and Bock (1978, pp. 238–240). Their general class of minimax estimators is δ (suppressing the arguments) given in equation (2.6). Now define $\omega = P'Q^{1/2}\beta$ where $Q^{1/2}Q^{1/2} = Q$ and $P'Q^{1/2}CQ^{-1/2}P = \mathrm{diag}(c_1, c_2, \ldots, c_K)$ and $P'P = I$. Then an estimator of ω is

$$\hat{\omega} = P'Q^{1/2}\delta = P'Q^{1/2}\big[I - h(u)C\big]b$$

$$= P'Q^{1/2}\big[I - h(u)C\big]Q^{-1/2}PP'Q^{1/2}b$$

$$= \big[I - h(u)P'Q^{1/2}CQ^{-1/2}P\big]w$$

$$= \big[I - \mathrm{diag}(c_1 h(u), \ldots, c_K h(u))\big]w$$

where $u = b'Bb/s$, $h(u) = a/u$, and $w = P'Q^{1/2}b$. The positive-part variant of $\hat{\omega}$ is obtained as

$$\hat{\omega}^+ = \big[I - \mathrm{diag}(c_1 h(u), \ldots, c_K h(u))\big]_+ w$$

where $[\cdot]_+$ has any negative diagonal element set to zero. Then the general positive-part variant of δ is $\delta^+ = Q^{-1/2}P\hat{\omega}^+$. The positive-part variant of the Berger-rule is produced by choosing B and C as noted above.

In addition to these minimax rules we will consider also two commonly used variants of ridge regression. This class of estimators was proposed by Hoerl and Kennard (1970a,b) and has the form

$$\hat{\beta}(k) = \big[X'X + kI\big]^{-1}X'y \tag{2.26}$$

where k is a scalar constant. Conditions exist on the constant k so that if $Q = I$ the risk of $\hat{\beta}(k)$ is smaller then the risk of the LS estimator. Unfortunately the conditions for risk improvement depend on the unknown regression parameters and usual procedures for operationalizing ridge regression select k-values after data analysis so that risk improvement is not guaranteed. Nonetheless ridge regression remains a popular biased estimation procedure. We will use the non-iterative version of the Hoerl-Kennard-Baldwin (1975) procedure as described by Gibbons (1981). The value they use for k is $\hat{k}_{HKB} = K\hat{\sigma}^2/b'b$. Secondly, we consider the empirical Bayes method for determining k of Sclove (1973) as described in Amemiya (1985). Here the constant k is chosen to be the value $\hat{k}_{SCLOVE} = \hat{\sigma}^2/\hat{\sigma}_\beta^2$ where $\hat{\sigma}^2$ is the maximum likelihood estimator of σ^2 and $\hat{\sigma}_\beta^2 = (y'y - T\hat{\sigma}^2)/\text{tr } X'X$.

2.3. Rules that Shrink toward the Sample Mean of y

One special case of (2.9) that is of interest is to limit the null hypothesis of zero values to the slope parameters. That is, let $R\beta = r$ impose the restrictions that $\beta_2 = \beta_3 = \cdots = \beta_K = 0$ so that the restricted least squares estimator of the intercept is $\bar{y}$, the sample mean. In a prediction context this non-sample information is much more reasonable than the restriction that $\beta = 0$, since in the absence of any particular structural information one would suppose that future values of the dependent variable would be like past values and nearer the mean of y than the origin. This choice of shrinkage point has been advocated by Lindley (1962) and consequently we will call the resulting estimator the "Lindley-rule".

2.4. Rules that Shrink toward the Principal Components Estimator

Denote by $V = (v_1, v_2, \ldots, v_K)$ the $(K \times K)$ matrix whose columns v_i are the characteristic vectors of $X'X$. Then $V'V = VV' = I$ and $V'X'XV = \Lambda = \text{diag}(\lambda_1, \ldots, \lambda_K)$, where $\lambda_1 \geq \lambda_2 \geq \cdots \geq \lambda_K$ are the ordered characteristic roots of $X'X$. Using the V-transformation we can rewrite (2.1) as

$$y = X\beta + e = XVV'\beta + e = Z\theta + e, \tag{2.27}$$

where $Z = XV = (z_1, \ldots, z_K)$ is the $(T \times K)$ matrix of principal components, with $z_i = Xv_i$ and $z_i'z_i = \lambda_i$ and $\theta = V'\beta$. The reparameterized model (2.27) is the principal components regression model. The least squares estimator of θ is

$$\hat{\theta} = (Z'Z)^{-1}Z'y = \Lambda^{-1}Z'y \sim N(\theta, \sigma^2\Lambda^{-1}).$$

When the original X matrix is multicollinear, as economic data often are, the characteristic roots of $X'X$ may differ substantially in magnitude, with one or more roots being near zero. This means that in the reparameterized statistical model (2.27), the $\hat{\theta}$ covariance matrix

$$\Sigma_{\hat{\theta}} = \sigma^2 \Lambda^{-1} = \sigma^2 \ \text{diag}(1/\lambda_1, \ldots, 1/\lambda_K)$$

may contain some large values, indicating that some parameters θ_i are imprecisely estimated as a consequence of the multicollinearity in the data.

In order to improve the precision of estimation it has been suggested that one or more of the z_i's in (2.27) be deleted, the remaining model is then estimated by least squares and estimates of the β parameters obtained by inverse transformation. That is, partition $Z = (Z_1 : Z_2) = X(V_1 : V_2)$, where Z_1 represents the components to be retained and Z_2 those to be deleted. The resulting linear statistical model is $y = Z_1\theta_1 + Z_2\theta_2 + e$, where θ_1 and θ_2 are conformable partitions of θ. If we delete the variables relating to θ_2, then $\hat{\theta}_1 = (Z_1'Z_1)^{-1}Z_1'y \sim N(\theta_1, \sigma^2(Z_1'Z_1)^{-1})$. The principal components estimator of β is $b^* = V_1\hat{\theta}_1$, and is equivalent to the restricted LS estimator of β in (2.1) with the sample specific restrictions $R\beta = V_2'\beta = 0$ (Fomby et al., 1978). However, from an operational standpoint the question of which components to delete remains to be answered. Either deleting components (i) with small characteristic roots or (ii) by pre-testing the implied hypotheses, leads to estimators for θ and β that under a squared error measure have risk larger than the LS estimator over portions of their respective parameter spaces (Judge et al., 1985a, pp. 41–81).

The principal components restrictions $V_2'\beta = 0$ can be combined with the sample data by using the estimator (2.9), as long as the number of restrictions is greater than 2 ($J \geq 3$) and condition (2.10) is satisfied. The resulting estimator takes advantage of the in-sample relationships between the explanatory variables that exist in a risk improving way. A conjecture about this estimator is that it should perform relatively well when the in-sample data is very collinear *and* the out-of-sample data has the same collinearity pattern. The adage that collinearity doesn't matter may well be altered to recognize that collinearity can lead to substantially improved prediction, relative to LS, when the pattern doesn't change.

For the purposes of comparison we will consider one non-minimax principal components rule. Mundlak (1981) proposed a procedure for selecting which components to delete that is a sequential version of the pre-test estimator based on the Classical F-test of the hypothesis that $\theta_2 = 0$. Mundlak finds the largest set of indices, say, ϕ^*, such that the hypothesis $\theta_2 = 0$ is not rejected. As such, the procedure results in a sequence of nested tests. To provide a basis for partitioning Z, Mundlak using the fact that $u = (1/J)\Sigma_{i \in \phi} t_i^2$ where $t_i^2 = \hat{\theta}_i^2/(\hat{\sigma}^2/\lambda_i)$ is the square of the t-statistic and J equals the number of elements in ϕ. He then orders the t_i^2 from largest to smallest and selects ϕ^* such that J is as large as possible (J^*) and $u^* = 1/J^*\Sigma_{i \in \phi^*} t_i^2 < F_{(\alpha, J^*, T-K)}$. The risk for the resulting multi-stage pre-test estimator is unknown and is not likely to have the same sampling properties as those of the usual pre-test estimator which is based on a single hypothesis test. This estimator has been examined within the context of in-sample mean square error of prediction by Hill and Judge (1987) and was found to have undesirable sampling properties.

2.5. Estimators that are Minimax when $Q = X'X$

Another rule we wish to investigate is the limited translation estimator proposed by Stein (1981). To motivate this estimator consider the trans-formed variant of (2.27), consider

$$y = Z\theta + e = Z\Lambda^{-1/2}\Lambda^{1/2}\theta + e = W\gamma + e, \tag{2.28}$$

where $W'W = \Lambda^{-1/2}Z'Z\Lambda^{-1/2} = I_K$, $\gamma = \Lambda^{1/2}\theta$ and the LS estimator of γ is $\hat{\gamma} = W'y \sim N(\gamma, \sigma^2 I_K)$. The parameter vector γ can be estimated using the James-Stein (1961) estimator, its positive-part variant (Baranchik, 1964) or the generalized version (Judge and Bock, 1978), applied directly to model (2.1). These estimators work by shrinking all the elements of $\hat{\gamma}$ toward the origin by a common shrinkage factor and then transforming the estimates back to the θ and β spaces. While the resulting estimator may have lower risk for the complete parameter vector, the risk for some components of γ may be large and the total risk gain over the LS estimator will be small unless the true value of γ is near zero.

Furthermore, this estimator violates an intuitive principle when shrinking values of $\hat{\gamma}$ To see this, note that shrinking all values of $\hat{\gamma}$ by a constant fraction, say c, yields $\gamma^* = c\hat{\gamma} = c\Lambda^{1/2}\hat{\theta}$, so $\gamma_i^* = c\hat{\gamma}_i = (c\lambda_i^{1/2})\hat{\theta}_i$. If all the $\hat{\theta}_i$'s were equal, the largest $\hat{\gamma}_i$'s would be shrunk by a greater absolute amount toward the origin than the small ones, despite the equal variability of the $\hat{\gamma}_i$'s. Because $\hat{\gamma}$ is unbiased, this does not seem reasonable. To mitigate these characteristics an estimator is desired for which the degree of shrinkage can be determined separately for each component of the parameter vector.

Proceeding with this objective, Stein (1981) proposed a truncated analog of the Efron and Morris (1972, 1973) limited translation estimator that is based on order statistics. This estimator may be defined element-wise as

$$
\delta_i^{(q)}(\hat{\gamma}) = \left[1 - \frac{(q-2)\sigma^2 \min\{1, w_{(q)}/|\hat{\gamma}_i|\}}{\sum\limits_{j=1}^{K} \left[\min(\hat{\gamma}_j^2, w_{(q)}^2) \right]} \right] \hat{\gamma}_i \qquad (2.29)
$$

where q is a large fraction of K, $w_i = |\hat{\gamma}_i|$, and $w_{(1)} < w_{(2)} \cdots < w_{(K)}$ are the associated order statistics. This estimator of γ is minimax, under squared error loss, if $q \geq 3$. If $q = K$ this estimator is the traditional James-Stein (1961) estimator $\delta(\hat{\gamma}) = (1 - (K-2)\sigma^2/\hat{\gamma}'\hat{\gamma})\hat{\gamma}$, whose proportional shrinkage is noted above. To make (2.29) operational a way must be chosen for determining q, the basis for partitioning the parameter space. Following Dey and Berger (1983), we replace σ^2 by $s/(T - K + 2)$ and q by the value $q^* \geq 3$ that maximizes $(q - 2)^2/\sum_{j=1}^{K} \min(\hat{\gamma}_j^2, w_{(q)}^2)$. In practice the positive-part variant is always used.

The new Stein estimator (2.29) "works" by shrinking each component $\hat{\gamma}_i$ toward zero. For a given choice of q, however, if $|\hat{\gamma}_i|$ is large relative to $w_{(q)}$ it will be shrunk by a smaller amount than if $|\hat{\gamma}_i|$ were small relative to $w_{(q)}$. This is intuitively pleasing since estimators that agree with the implicit prior that $\gamma = 0$ are shrunk by more than coefficients whose estimates are large and do not agree with the prior. Thus the estimator is well suited for the problem under consideration. Recall that $\hat{\gamma}_i = \hat{\theta}_i \sqrt{\lambda_i} \sim (\theta_i \sqrt{\lambda_i}, \sigma^2)$. If multi-collinearity is severe and $\lambda_i \to 0$ then $\gamma_i = \theta_i \sqrt{\lambda_i} \to 0$ as well, so that zero is a good prior and the corresponding estimates will be shrunk substantially. For other components of γ, which correspond to θ_i's that can be estimated more precisely, the prior value of zero is not a good one, and as desired, on the average the estimator (2.29) will shrink the associated estimates less. The actual estimator we consider is translated back into the β space.

Alternatively, following Judge et al. (1985b) we may extend the Stein (1981) and Dey and Berger (1983) approach and introduce the option of partitioning the parameter space into three subsets. Consequently, we preserve the Mundlak (1981) alternative of truncating the parameter space by setting some parameters to zero, and then using the new Stein rule on the remaining components. We do this by ordering the elements of $\hat{\gamma}$ and omitting the p variables with the "smallest" absolute estimates. Then using the new Stein estimator (2.29), the fraction q of the next smallest estimates are shrunk toward zero by more than the others. This risk improvement, given the ordering of the variable is

$$\sigma^4 E \left[\frac{(q-2)^2}{\sum \min(\hat{\gamma}_j^2, w_{(q)}^2)} \right] - \left(\sum_{j=1}^{P} \gamma_j^2 - p\sigma^2 \right), \tag{2.30}$$

(Judge et al., 1985b). We will select p and q jointly by maximizing

$$\hat{\sigma}^4 \left[\frac{(q-2)^2}{\sum \min(\hat{\gamma}_j^2, w_{(q)}^2)} \right] - \left(\sum_{j=1}^{P} \hat{\gamma}_j^2 - 2p\hat{\sigma}^2 \right). \tag{2.31}$$

In contrast to the Stein estimator (2.29), by this method one simultaneously selects the appropriate model and estimates the unknown parameters.

3. Multivariate Data Extrapolation

In the simple linear regression model $y_t = \beta_0 + \beta_1 x_t + e_t$ we know that variance of the forecast error of the LS predictor of $E(y_0 | x_0)$ is

$$E[\hat{y}_0 - (b_0 + b_1 x_0)]^2 = \sigma^2 \left[\frac{1}{T} + \frac{(x_0 - \bar{x})^2}{\sum_{t=1}^{T} (x_t - \bar{x})^2} \right], \tag{3.1}$$

where $\bar{x} = \sum_{t=1}^{T} x_t / T$. The further x is extrapolated away from $\bar{x}$, the larger the variance of the forecast error.

In the multivariate context the effects of extrapolation on the least squares predictor have been studied by Fomby and Hill (1990). Partition X and X_0 as

$$X = [j_T \ X_1] \quad X_0 = [j_m \ X_2]$$

where j_m is an ($m \times 1$) vector of ones. Transform X_1 and X_2 into deviation from the mean form

$$X_1^* = M_1 X_1, \quad \text{where } M_1 = I_T - j_T j_T' / T$$

$$X_2^* = M_2 X_2, \quad \text{where } M_2 = I_m - j_m j_m' / m.$$

Let $\bar{x}_1$ and $\bar{x}_2$ denote the $(K - 1) \times 1$ vectors of column means of X_1 and X_2 and their difference by $d = \bar{x}_2 - \bar{x}_1$. Fomby and Hill (1990) show that the prediction risk (2.5) of the LS estimator is

$$R(\beta, b, X_0'X_0) = \sigma^2 \left[\frac{m}{T} + \text{tr } V_1'V_2 \Lambda_2 V_2'V_1 \Lambda_1^{-1} + md'V_1'\Lambda_1^{-1}V_1 d \right],$$

(3.2)

where V_j is the matrix of characteristic vectors of $X_j^{*'}X_j^{*}$ corresponding to the roots $\lambda_{j,1} > \lambda_{j,2} > \cdots > \lambda_{j,K-1}$, $j = 1, 2$; Λ_j is the diagonal matrix of characteristic roots $\lambda_{j,k}$. Expression (3.2) reveals that the LS prediction risk depends on (1) the error variance σ^2; (2) the sample sizes m and T; (3) the in-sample and out-of-sample multicollinearity as measured by Λ_1 and Λ_2; (4) the relative rotation of the in-sample and out-of-sample data ellipsoids as measured by V_1 and V_2 and (5) the angles between the difference in means vector d and the major and minor axes of the in-sample data ellipsoid reflected in V_1. See Fomby and Hill (1990) and Fomby, Hill and Johnson (1984, Chapter 13) for the complete geometric interpretation.

If the in-sample and out-of-sample data have data ellipsoids with parallel major and minor axes then $V_1 = V_2$ and $V_1'V_2 = I_{K-1}$. We call such data *rotationally equivalent*. If the in-sample and out-of-sample data exhibits identical multicollinearity then $\Lambda_1 = \Lambda_2$ and the data is *variationally equivalent*. If the data are *rotationally and variationally equivalent* then

$$R(\beta, b, X_0'X_0) = \sigma^2 \left[\frac{m}{T} + (K - 1) + md'V_1'\Lambda_1^{-1}V_1 d \right] \qquad (3.3)$$

and, given in-sample multicollinearity, Λ_1, the prediction risk depends *only* on the distance between data means d and its orientation relative to the in-sample data. This case reflects the conventional wisdom that multi-collinearity does not affect the ability to predict as long as it "stays the same".

How these extrapolation factors affect the performance of the biased estimators in Section 2 is the research objective of this paper. The Monte Carlo design described in the next section reflects this interest.

4. Design of the Monte Carlo Experiment

In this sampling experiment we wish to consider the performance of the estimators of β discussed above under varying degrees of in-sample multicollinearity, specification error, and extrapolation. To start then, consider the following general framework for specifying X and X_0. Let U_1 be a $T \times (K-1)$ matrix of standardized variables such that $U_1'U_1 = I_{K-1}$ and the sample mean of each column of U_1 is zero, so $U_1'j_T = 0$ where j_T is a $(T \times 1)$ vector of ones. Define $X_1 = U_1 \Lambda_1^{1/2} V_1'$ so $X_1'X_1 = V_1 \Lambda_1 V_1'$. By choosing $\Lambda_1 = \text{diag}(\lambda_1, \ldots, \lambda_{K-1})$ and V_1 orthogonal we define a matrix X_1 with specific variability characteristics. Note that $X_1'j_T = V_1 \Lambda_1^{1/2} U_1'j_T = 0$ so these design variables have zero mean. Define $X = [j_T \ X_1]$ so

$$X'X = \begin{bmatrix} T & 0' \\ 0 & X_1'X_1 \end{bmatrix}.$$

Now let $\Lambda_2 = \text{diag}(\gamma_1, \ldots, \gamma_{K-1})$, V_2 be an orthogonal matrix and d a $(K-1) \times 1$ vector. Let U_2 be an $m \times (K-1)$ matrix $(m > K-1)$ such that $U_2'U_2 = I$ and $U_2'j_m = 0$. Define

$$X_2 = U_2 \Lambda_2^{1/2} V_2' + j_m d'$$

and

$$X_0 = [j_m \ X_2].$$

Note that $X_2'X_2 = V_2 \Lambda_2 V_2' + mdd'$ since $U_2'j_m = 0$, and $X_2'j_m = md'$ so

$$X_0'X_0 = \begin{bmatrix} m & md' \\ md & V_2 \Lambda_2 V_2' + mdd' \end{bmatrix} = \begin{bmatrix} m & md' \\ md & X_2'X_2 \end{bmatrix}.$$

Given these specifications, the mean square error of out-of-sample prediction for LS is

$$R(b, \beta, X_0'X_0) = \sigma^2 \text{ tr } X_0'X_0(X'X)^{-1}$$

$$= \sigma^2 \left[\frac{m}{T} + \text{tr}(X_2'X_2)(X_1'X_1)^{-1} \right]$$

$$= \sigma^2 \left[\frac{m}{T} + \text{tr}(V_2 \Lambda_2 V_2' V_1 \Lambda_1^{-1} V_1' + mdd' V_1 \Lambda_1^{-1} V_1') \right].$$

$$(4.1)$$

Note that if $d = 0$ then (4.1) becomes

$$\sigma^2\left[\frac{m}{T} + \mathrm{tr}\left(V_2\Lambda_2 V_2' V_1 \Lambda_1^{-1} V_1'\right)\right]$$

and thus the mean square error depends on σ^2, m, T and rotation and variation. If $d = 0$ and X_1 and X_2 are rotationally equivalent ($V_1 = V_2$) then (4.1) becomes

$$\sigma^2\left[\frac{m}{T} + \mathrm{tr}\,\Lambda_2\Lambda_1^{-1}\right]$$

and the mean square error is determined by σ^2, m, T and variational differences. Finally, if $d = 0$ and X_1 and X_2 are rotationally and variationally equivalent then the mean square error of out-of-sample prediction is $\sigma^2[m/T + (K-1)]$.

Using these general guidelines we specify $T = 12$, $K = 4$, $m = 6$,

$$U_1 = \frac{1}{\sqrt{4}}\left\{\begin{bmatrix} 1 \\ -1 \\ 1 \\ -1 \end{bmatrix} \otimes I_3\right\}, \qquad V_1 = I_3,$$

$$\Lambda_1 = \begin{bmatrix} 4 & & 0 \\ & 4 & \\ 0 & & 4/\kappa_1^2 \end{bmatrix},$$

where κ_1 is in fact the condition number of $X_1'X_1$, that is the square root of the ratio of the largest to smallest characteristic root, where

$$X_1 = U_1\Lambda_1^{1/2}V_1 = \left\{\begin{bmatrix} 1 \\ -1 \\ 1 \\ -1 \end{bmatrix} \otimes \begin{bmatrix} 1 & & 0 \\ & 1 & \\ 0 & & 1/\kappa_1 \end{bmatrix}\right\}.$$

Consequently $X = [j_{12}\ X_1]$ and

$$X'X = \begin{bmatrix} 12 & 0 \\ 0 & \Lambda_1 \end{bmatrix}.$$

Then let

$$U_2 = \frac{1}{\sqrt{2}} \left\{ \begin{bmatrix} 1 \\ -1 \end{bmatrix} \otimes I_3 \right\},$$

and $V_2 = I_3$.

In order to control the amount and direction of out-of-sample variability we define two out-of-sample characteristic root spectra:

$$\Lambda_2^{(1)} = \text{diag}(2, 2, 2/\kappa_2^2),$$

$$\Lambda_2^{(2)} = \text{diag}(2/\kappa_2^2, 2, 2).$$

Here κ_2 is analogous to κ_1, the condition number of $X_2' X_2$, $\Lambda_2^{(1)}$ produces an out-of-sample data scatter that is rotationally equivalent to the in-sample data scatter. That is, the major and minor axes of the two data ellipsoids are oriented in the same direction. Using $\Lambda_2^{(2)}$ creates a dramatically different situation, namely that the major axis of the out-of-sample data scatter is parallel to the *minor* axis of the in-sample data scatter *and* orthogonal to the major axis of the in-sample data scatter. Visualize data ellipses that are "at right angles" to one another.

The direction and amount of distance between the in-sample and out-of-sample means is defined to be either $d^{(1)} = (\Delta\ 0\ 0)'$ or $d^{(2)} = (0\ 0\ \Delta)'$, where Δ takes the values $\Delta = 0, 1, 2, 3$. Choosing $d^{(1)}$ translates the out-of-sample data scatter along the *major* axis of the in-sample data ellipsoid where $d^{(2)}$ moves the out-of-sample data along the minor axis of the in-sample data ellipsoid.

By combining $\Lambda_2^{(i)}$ and $d^{(j)}$, $i, j = 1, 2$; we define four extreme data configurations, using $X_2^{(i,j)} = U_2 \Lambda_2^{(i)} V_2' + j_6 d^{(j)'}$ and $X_0^{(i,j)} = [j_6 X_2^{(i,j)}]$:

case 1: $\Lambda_2^{(1)}$, $d^{(1)}$

case 2: $\Lambda_2^{(2)}$, $d^{(1)}$

case 3: $\Lambda_2^{(1)}$, $d^{(2)}$

case 4: $\Lambda_2^{(2)}$, $d^{(2)}$

In cases 1 and 2 the out-of-sample data ellipsoid is translated out the major axis of the in-sample data ellipsoid. In cases 3 and 4 the translation is out the minor axis. In cases 1 and 3 the orientation of the out-of-sample data ellipsoid is the same as the in-sample data and in cases 2 and 4 the out-of-sample data ellipsoid is rotated relative to the in-sample ellipsoid in such a way that the orientations of the major and minor axes are reversed. Case 4 represents the most unfortunate setting for LS prediction.

The advantage of this design is its simplicity and ease of interpretation. Its disadvantages include a limited number ($K = 4$) of regressors. This will limit the benefits of the Stein-like rules, which are known to perform well with larger K. Secondly, the form of collinearity we induce is restricted from the point of view of representing the broad patterns found in economic data. The condition numbers κ_1 and κ_2 take the values 1, 10 and 30.

For the results we report the parameter vector β is chosen as $\beta = L \cdot c$ where c is a 4×1 vector all of whose elements are $1/2$ (thus the parameter values are all equal) so that $c'c = 1$. Then the scalar L, which is the length of the β vector is varied. The length the parameter vector takes are $L = 0, 1, 2, 5, 10$. As L increases, the specification error, as measured by the non-centrality parameter $\beta'R'[R(X'X)^{-1}R']^{-1}R\beta/2\sigma^2$, associated with the prior information $R\beta = 0$, increases. Also as L increases the signal-to-noise ratio increases as measured by the population $R^2 = \beta'X'X\beta/(\beta'X'X\beta + T)$. For the design matrices and parameter orientations we consider the population R^2 varied from $R^2 = 0$ when $L = 0$ to $R^2 = 0.33$ when $L = 1$ to $R^2 = 0.67$ when $L = 2$, $R^2 = 0.92$ when $L = 5$ and $R^2 = 0.98$ when $L = 10$.

For each specification of X, X_0 and β, 500 samples were constructed for y and y_0 by adding to $X\beta$ and $X_0\beta$ vectors of independent disturbances from $N(0,1)$ distribution. Computations were carried out by the SAS software and the RANNOR random number generator.

The results of the sampling experiments are reported in the next section.

5. Results of the Monte Carlo Experiment

The simulation results are reported in Tables 1–5 which contain the empirical out-of-sample prediction risks for the various estimators. Across the top of the tables the parameter L denotes the length of the parameter vector, and recall that all parameter values are equal. Down the left-hand-side of the table the parameter d is the distance between the means of the explanatory variables. In the tables the risk of the LS estimator is reported in nominal values and the risks of the remaining estimators as percents of the LS risk.

Table 1 contains the results for the "base" case in which both the in-sample and out-of-sample data are orthonormal before an intercept variable is added. In Case 1 the extrapolation of the data is achieved by

Table 1

Out-of-Sample Empirical Risks of Prediction
Case 1: $\kappa_1 = 1$, $\kappa_2 = 1$

d	Estimator	$L = 0$	$L = 1$	$L = 2$	$L = 5$	$L = 10$
0	LS	1.930	1.930	1.930	1.930	1.930
	Berger ($X_0'X_0$)	0.560	0.860	0.969	0.995	1.000
	Mundlak	0.067	1.585	3.280	1.124	1.000
	Ridge-HKB	0.311	0.720	1.223	1.306	1.114
	Stein (I)	1.000	1.000	1.000	1.000	1.000
	Lindley (I)	0.699	0.876	0.984	0.995	1.000
	Stein ($X'X$)	0.456	0.855	0.969	0.995	1.000
	Lindley ($X'X$)	0.699	0.876	0.984	0.995	1.000
	EXTSTEIN	0.570	0.953	1.264	0.995	1.000
1	LS	3.270	3.270	3.270	3.270	3.270
	Berger ($X_0'X_0$)	0.813	0.927	0.982	0.997	1.000
	Mundlak	0.052	1.988	3.716	1.153	1.138
	Ridge-HKB	0.208	0.676	1.260	1.364	1.000
	Stein (I)	1.000	1.000	1.000	1.000	1.000
	Lindley (I)	0.673	0.859	0.988	1.000	1.000
	Stein ($X'X$)	0.477	0.927	1.006	1.003	1.000
	Lindley ($X'X$)	0.673	0.859	0.988	1.000	1.000
	EXTSTEIN	0.587	0.972	1.315	1.003	1.003
2	LS	7.980	7.980	7.980	7.980	7.980
	Berger ($X_0'X_0$)	0.959	0.994	1.000	1.001	1.001
	Mundlak	0.069	1.709	2.652	1.236	1.000
	Ridge-HKB	0.149	0.675	1.323	1.445	1.194
	Stein (I)	1.000	1.000	1.000	1.000	1.000
	Lindley (I)	0.645	0.876	1.004	1.008	1.005
	Stein ($X'X$)	0.486	0.914	1.025	1.013	1.008
	Lindley ($X'X$)	0.645	0.876	1.004	1.008	1.005
	EXTSTEIN	0.612	0.950	1.387	1.013	1.008
3	LS	14.990	14.990	14.990	14.990	14.990
	Berger ($X_0'X_0$)	0.973	0.993	1.000	1.000	1.000
	Mundlak	0.067	1.602	3.410	1.304	1.000
	Ridge-HKB	0.115	0.638	1.262	1.368	1.144
	Stein (I)	1.000	1.000	1.000	1.000	1.000
	Lindley (I)	0.631	0.851	0.974	0.997	1.000
	Stein ($X'X$)	0.480	0.850	0.970	0.997	1.000
	Lindley ($X'X$)	0.631	0.851	0.974	0.997	1.000
	EXTSTEIN	0.583	0.953	1.309	0.997	1.000

In this and subsequent tables, LS risks are numeric and the remaining risks proportions of LS risk.

translating the out-of-sample data ellipsoid out along the "major" axis of the in-sample data ellipsoid, the axis corresponding to the first nonconstant regressor, and the major and minor axes of the data ellipsoids are oriented in the same direction. When the data are orthonormal this, of course, does not matter. The first observation we make is that the risk of the LS estimator is clearly affected by the extrapolation of the out-of-sample data ellipsoid. The greater the distance between the in-sample and out-of-sample regressor means, the greater the LS risk. Also the risk of LS estimator is constant for all values of L and thus changing the signal-to-noise ratio has no effect on this minimax estimator. In passing we note that when out-of-sample collinearity is made more severe relative to that of the in-sample data, the risk of LS declines. It is easier to predict out-of-sample when the out-of-sample data are "concentrated".

The first biased estimator we comment on is the Berger-like estimator, denoted BERGER, which is designed to be minimax with respect to the out-of-sample mean square error of prediction loss ($Q = X_0'X_0$). This estimator does indeed dominate the LS estimator in this Monte Carlo setting and when L is small the risk gains are not negligible. Recall that this Berger-like rule shrinks parameter values towards the origin so that as L increases the specification error implicit in this assumption increases. Thus when the parameter vector length is small the prior is not badly specified and the risk gains are substantial. We do not report any of the Stein-like estimators that could be designed to be minimax with respect to out-of-sample mean square error as they differ from LS in only a few cases. When the minimaxity condition is satisfied these rules do provide modest risk gains over LS for small values of L.

The Mundlak principal components estimator, denoted MUNDLAK, deletes principal components on the basis of t-tests and is essentially a classical pre-test estimator. In the case reported in Table 1 the data are orthogonal and deleting principal components is an error, except at the origin when the parameter values are all zero. This is reflected in the empirical risk of the MUNDLAK rule. Note that its risk starts out very small at the origin (when its "prior" is correct), risk rises above that of LS, reaches a maximum and then declines to that of LS. The risk declines because as the specification error increases the t-tests on the significance of the principal components lead to no components being deleted.

The ridge rule that we report is that of Hoerl, Kennard and Baldwin (noniterative version) and is denoted RIDGE-HKB. The risk of this biased rule is small at the origin ($L = 0$) where the implicit prior of ridge regression, that all parameter values are zero, is correct. However as the specification error in these restrictions increases, the risk of this ridge rule rises above that of LS and, over the range of our data, stays above it. Clearly one would not use ridge regression, or principal components regression, when the data are orthonormal. The result is provided for reference.

We report the results of two estimators that are designed to be minimax under squared error loss ($Q = I$); the usual Stein rule, STEIN (I), that shrinks all parameter estimates proportionally to zero, and the Lindley rule, LINDLEY (I), that shrinks all estimates except the intercept towards zero so that forecasts, in-sample and out-of-sample, are shrunk towards the sample mean of the in-sample y values. The risk of STEIN (I) is constant as the minimaxity condition fails and it reverts to LS. The minimaxity condition fails despite the fact that the nonconstant regressors are orthogonal because the addition of the intercept variable affects the characteristic roots of the complete $X'X$ matrix. The Lindley (I) rule offers a risk gain over LS which is greater than that of BERGER when $d \geq 1$.

We then report the results of three estimators designed to be minimax against mean squared error of in-sample prediction ($Q = X'X$). The Stein/Empirical Bayes estimator STEIN ($X'X$) and the LINDLEY ($X'X$) rule. These two estimators are not minimax with respect to the out-of-sample prediction loss function under consideration, but, nevertheless, dominate LS under current conditions by a substantial amount when L is small (so that their specification error is small). Note that STEIN ($X'X$) dominates LINDLEY ($X'X$) at small L values as it imposes one additional nearly correct constraint in this region of the parameter space, and it is also superior to BERGER at small L values as it shrinks the parameter estimates more than the conservative, minimax Berger-rule. Finally we report the extended Stein (EXTSTEIN) estimator of Judge et al. (1985b) which truncates the parameter space based on an estimate of the risk function and then shrinks the remaining estimates differentially. This estimator will behave like the Mundlak principal components rule in many cases but it is more conservative as it bases its deletions on estimated risk. Its risk function has the characteristic pre-test estimator shape in this orthonormal case.

Finally we note that the "minimax" principal components/Stein estimator we examined behaved just like the Lindley rule given our experimental design so we do not report it. Also not reported is the Dey/Berger rule that shrinks estimates differentially. In the setting of our Monte Carlo experiment it behaved just like the STEIN ($X'X$) estimator. We did not report the results of the Sclove empirical Bayes estimator. It seems to do well when collinearity is severe but is very poor when the data is well-behaved and at low R^2 values. We will now compare these base results to other cases.

Table 2

Out-of-Sample Empirical Risks of Prediction

Case 1: $\kappa_1 = 10$, $\kappa_2 = 1$

d	Estimator	$L = 0$	$L = 1$	$L = 2$	$L = 5$	$L = 10$
0	LS	49.950	49.950	49.950	49.950	49.950
	Berger $(X_0'X_0)$	0.972	0.991	0.999	1.000	1.000
	Mundlak	0.089	0.166	0.301	0.464	1.149
	Ridge-HKB	0.819	0.829	0.850	0.910	0.962
	Stein (I)	0.820	0.907	0.967	0.994	0.999
	Lindley (I)	1.000	1.000	1.000	1.000	1.000
	Stein $(X'X)$	0.451	0.665	0.866	0.976	0.994
	Lindley $(X'X)$	0.599	0.701	0.848	0.971	0.993
	EXTSTEIN	0.575	0.679	0.663	0.763	1.121
1	LS	50.230	50.230	50.230	50.230	50.230
	Berger $(X_0'X_0)$	1.001	0.991	0.998	1.000	1.000
	Mundlak	0.022	0.201	0.450	0.544	1.263
	Ridge-HKB	0.816	0.830	0.860	0.930	0.973
	Stein (I)	0.829	0.914	0.969	0.994	0.999
	Lindley (I)	1.000	1.000	1.000	1.000	1.000
	Stein $(X'X)$	0.471	0.688	0.875	0.977	0.994
	Lindley $(X'X)$	0.624	0.720	0.856	0.972	0.993
	EXTSTEIN	0.580	0.698	0.714	0.769	1.190
2	LS	56.810	56.810	56.810	56.810	56.810
	Berger $(X_0'X_0)$	0.990	0.997	1.000	1.000	1.000
	Mundlak	0.066	0.302	0.645	0.749	1.211
	Ridge-HKB	0.801	0.832	0.884	0.967	0.994
	Stein (I)	0.839	0.915	0.971	0.995	0.999
	Lindley (I)	1.000	1.000	1.000	1.000	1.000
	Stein $(X'X)$	0.494	0.714	0.889	0.981	0.996
	Lindley $(X'X)$	0.634	0.723	0.869	0.976	0.994
	EXTSTEIN	0.615	0.723	0.764	0.808	1.164
3	LS	64.440	64.440	64.440	64.440	64.440
	Berger $(X_0'X_0)$	0.987	0.998	1.000	1.000	1.000
	Mundlak	0.091	0.489	1.047	0.785	1.177
	Ridge-HKB	0.767	0.814	0.894	0.985	0.998
	Stein (I)	0.837	0.920	0.972	0.995	0.999
	Lindley (I)	1.000	1.000	1.000	1.000	1.000
	Stein $(X'X)$	0.493	0.722	0.896	0.981	0.995
	Lindley $(X'X)$	0.633	0.749	0.889	0.978	0.994
	EXTSTEIN	0.598	0.754	0.812	0.862	1.177

In Table 2 we report the results for Case 1, in which the major and minor axes of the data ellipsoids are oriented in the same directions and extrapolation is along the major axis of the in-sample data ellipsoid. The condition numbers are $\kappa_1 = 10$ and $\kappa_2 = 1$ so that there is moderate collinearity in-sample and the data are orthogonal out-of-sample. Note first that the LS risks are increased because of the in-sample collinearity which is different than the out-of-sample collinearity and that as the distance between in-sample and out-of-sample regressor means increases, the LS risk increases too. In this setting, with different condition numbers in the data, the BERGER estimator is minimax but the gains over LS are very small even when $L = 0$. This, unfortunately, is the consistent pattern over all cases with collinearity different in-sample and out-of-sample. The MUNDLAK estimator is better than LS at all values of L except $L = 10$ ($R^2 = 0.98$). The risk of MUND-LAK will eventually return to that of LS at some larger value of L, which we did not explore. The ridge estimator of HKB also is good in this setting and has risk lower than LS over the range of the data we examined. STEIN (I) is superior to LS but not quite as good as RIDGE-HKB and LINDLEY (I) equals LS. The estimator STEIN ($X'X$) is superior to RIDGE-HKB at low L values but the ridge rule is slightly better at large L values. This will be a repeating theme. STEIN ($X'X$) is superior to LINDLEY ($X'X$) at low L values and they have very similar risks at larger L values. The estimator EXTSTEIN behaves like MUNDLAK but is not as good at small values of L as it is more conservative. This also means that it is not as bad as MUND-LAK at intermediate L values, before MUNDLAK becomes identical to LS once again. Note that the risk of MUNDLAK crosses the risk of LS twice when $d = 3$.

In Table 3 the results for Case 1 with $\kappa_1 = \kappa_2 = 10$ are reported. In this case both the in-sample and out-of-sample data have the same, moderate, collinearity patterns. Note first of all that the LS risk is not impacted by the multicollinearity since it is identical in-sample and out-of-sample. The same result holds when both condition numbers are 30 so that collinearity is severe. But this happy result only holds because the data ellipses are rotationally equivalent and the extrapolation is along the major axis of the in-sample data ellipsoid. The relative performances of the estimators in this case are about the same as when the data is orthonormal (Table 1). What is surprising is that despite the presence of moderate, or severe collinearity, the MUNDLAK estimator does not perform well. The truncation rule TRUSTEIN performs much better than MUNDLAK in this setting. When the patterns of collinearity are such that it does not harm LS predictions then the MUNDLAK rule does not forecast well in general. Note in this case, too,

Table 3

Out-of-Sample Empirical Risks of Prediction

Case 1: $\kappa_1 = 10$, $\kappa_2 = 10$

d	Estimator	$L = 0$	$L = 1$	$L = 2$	$L = 5$	$L = 10$
0	LS	1.930	1.930	1.930	1.930	1.930
	Berger $(X_0'X_0)$	0.560	0.839	0.964	0.995	1.000
	Mundlak	0.067	-1.337	2.927	1.233	1.036
	Ridge-HKB	0.720	0.824	0.974	1.109	1.062
	Stein (I)	0.824	0.933	0.984	0.995	1.000
	Lindley (I)	1.000	1.000	1.000	1.000	1.000
	Stein $(X'X)$	0.456	0.824	0.964	0.995	1.000
	Lindley $(X'X)$	0.699	0.839	0.969	0.995	1.000
	EXTSTEIN	0.570	0.881	1.010	0.943	1.031
1	LS	3.270	3.270	3.270	3.270	3.270
	Berger $(X_0'X_0)$	0.813	0.911	0.976	0.997	1.000
	Mundlak	0.052	1.859	3.590	1.474	1.043
	Ridge-HKB	0.624	0.755	0.997	1.235	1.128
	Stein (I)	0.829	0.954	0.994	1.000	1.000
	Lindley (I)	1.000	1.000	1.000	1.000	1.000
	Stein $(X'X)$	0.477	0.920	1.015	1.006	1.003
	Lindley $(X'X)$	0.673	0.835	0.988	1.006	1.003
	EXTSTEIN	0.587	0.951	1.128	0.972	1.031
2	LS	7.980	7.980	7.980	7.980	7.980
	Berger $(X_0'X_0)$	0.959	0.986	0.999	1.001	1.001
	Mundlak	0.069	1.649	3.544	1.984	1.015
	Ridge-HKB	0.580	0.772	1.058	1.315	1.182
	Stein (I)	0.835	0.965	1.001	1.004	1.003
	Lindley (I)	1.000	1.000	1.000	1.000	1.000
	Stein $(X'X)$	0.486	0.912	1.046	1.019	1.010
	Lindley $(X'X)$	0.645	0.856	1.028	1.021	1.010
	EXTSTEIN	0.612	0.940	1.203	1.006	1.021
3	LS	14.990	14.990	14.990	14.990	14.990
	Berger $(X_0'X_0)$	0.973	0.992	1.000	1.000	1.000
	Mundlak	0.067	1.579	3.660	1.708	1.008
	Ridge-HKB	0.528	0.707	1.001	1.224	1.123
	Stein (I)	0.831	0.943	0.988	0.999	1.000
	Lindley (I)	1.000	1.000	1.000	1.000	1.000
	Stein $(X'X)$	0.480	0.850	0.985	1.001	1.001
	Lindley $(X'X)$	0.631	0.838	1.009	1.008	1.003
	EXTSTEIN	0.583	0.939	1.141	1.001	1.010

Table 4

Out-of-Sample Empirical Risks of Prediction

Case 1: $\kappa_1 = 30$, $\kappa_2 = 1$

d	Estimator	$L = 0$	$L = 1$	$L = 2$	$L = 5$	$L = 10$
0	LS	438.050	438.050	438.050	438.050	438.050
	Berger $(X_0'X_0)$	0.997	0.999	1.000	1.000	1.000
	Mundlak	0.090	0.110	0.180	0.193	0.294
	Ridge-HKB	0.970	0.970	0.972	0.976	0.983
	Stein (I)	0.811	0.901	0.964	0.994	0.998
	Lindley (I)	1.000	1.000	1.000	1.000	1.000
	Stein $(X'X)$	0.451	0.659	0.861	0.975	0.994
	Lindley $(X'X)$	0.595	0.695	0.843	0.969	0.992
	EXTSTEIN	0.575	0.665	0.619	0.562	0.646
1	LS	429.690	429.690	429.690	429.690	429.690
	Berger $(X_0'X_0)$	1.000	0.999	1.000	1.000	1.000
	Mundlak	0.020	0.069	0.206	0.284	0.349
	Ridge-HKB	0.970	0.971	0.972	0.977	0.984
	Stein (I)	0.821	0.906	0.965	0.994	0.998
	Lindley (I)	1.000	1.000	1.000	1.000	1.000
	Stein $(X'X)$	0.471	0.672	0.865	0.975	0.994
	Lindley $(X'X)$	0.620	0.712	0.846	0.969	0.992
	EXTSTEIN	0.580	0.682	0.644	0.640	0.702
2	LS	451.360	451.360	451.360	451.360	451.360
	Berger $(X_0'X_0)$	0.999	1.000	1.000	1.000	1.000
	Mundlak	0.065	0.101	0.214	0.288	0.396
	Ridge-HKB	0.970	0.971	0.974	0.980	0.986
	Stein (I)	0.832	0.903	0.965	0.994	0.998
	Lindley (I)	1.000	1.000	1.000	1.000	1.000
	Stein $(X'X)$	0.495	0.684	0.865	0.975	0.994
	Lindley $(X'X)$	0.633	0.703	0.844	0.969	0.992
	EXTSTEIN	0.615	0.689	0.683	0.638	0.715
3	LS	464.010	464.010	464.010	464.010	464.010
	Berger $(X_0'X_0)$	0.998	1.000	1.000	1.000	1.000
	Mundlak	0.098	0.210	0.343	0.322	0.402
	Ridge-HKB	0.967	0.969	0.974	0.982	0.987
	Stein (I)	0.831	0.909	0.967	0.994	0.998
	Lindley (I)	1.000	1.000	1.000	1.000	1.000
	Stein $(X'X)$	0.496	0.688	0.873	0.976	0.994
	Lindley $(X'X)$	0.634	0.725	0.857	0.971	0.993
	EXTSTEIN	0.602	0.703	0.693	0.652	0.727

Table 5

Out-of-Sample Empirical Risks of Prediction

Case 2: $\kappa_1 = 10$, $\kappa_2 = 10$

d	Estimator	$L = 0$	$L = 1$	$L = 2$	$L = 5$	$L = 10$
0	LS	49.460	49.460	49.460	49.460	49.460
	Berger $(X_0'X_0)$	0.995	0.998	1.000	1.000	1.000
	Mundlak	0.089	-0.157	0.272	0.450	1.150
	Ridge-HKB	0.822	0.830	0.848	0.906	0.960
	Stein (I)	0.820	0.907	0.966	0.994	0.998
	Lindley (I)	1.000	1.000	1.000	1.000	1.000
	Stein $(X'X)$	0.451	0.664	0.865	0.976	0.994
	Lindley $(X'X)$	0.599	0.699	0.847	0.970	0.992
	EXTSTEIN	0.575	0.677	0.657	0.760	1.122
1	LS	49.750	49.750	49.750	49.750	49.750
	Berger $(X_0'X_0)$	0.997	0.999	1.000	1.000	1.000
	Mundlak	0.022	0.192	0.423	0.533	1.266
	Ridge-HKB	0.819	0.831	0.858	0.925	0.971
	Stein (I)	0.829	0.913	0.968	0.994	0.999
	Lindley (I)	1.000	1.000	1.000	1.000	1.000
	Stein $(X'X)$	0.471	0.687	0.874	0.977	0.994
	Lindley $(X'X)$	0.624	0.719	0.855	0.971	0.993
	EXTSTEIN	0.580	0.695	0.710	0.766	1.192
2	LS	56.310	56.310	56.310	56.310	56.310
	Berger $(X_0'X_0)$	1.000	0.999	1.000	1.000	1.000
	Mundlak	0.066	0.295	0.622	0.736	1.212
	Ridge-HKB	0.804	0.833	0.883	0.963	0.992
	Stein (I)	0.839	0.915	0.971	0.995	0.999
	Lindley (I)	1.000	1.000	1.000	1.000	1.000
	Stein $(X'X)$	0.494	0.713	0.888	0.980	0.996
	Lindley $(X'X)$	0.635	0.722	0.867	0.976	0.994
	EXTSTEIN	0.615	0.722	0.760	0.807	1.166
3	LS	63.960	63.960	63.960	63.960	63.960
	Berger $(X_0'X_0)$	0.998	1.000	1.000	1.000	1.000
	Mundlak	0.092	0.484	1.030	0.778	1.179
	Ridge-HKB	0.769	0.815	0.893	0.983	0.997
	Stein (I)	0.837	0.920	0.972	0.995	0.999
	Lindley (I)	1.000	1.000	1.000	1.000	1.000
	Stein $(X'X)$	0.493	0.721	0.895	0.981	0.995
	Lindley $(X'X)$	0.633	0.748	0.888	0.978	0.994
	EXTSTEIN	0.598	0.753	0.810	0.861	1.179

that STEIN $(X'X)$ is superior to RIDGE-HKB but that neither is superior to LS over the entire parameter space. There are, however, substantial gains when the nonsample information employed is nearly correct, near $L = 0$.

Table 4 contains the results for Case 1 when there is severe collinearity in-sample ($\kappa_1 = 30$) and the out-of-sample data is orthogonal. Here we note that the LS risks are much larger and that the truncation rules MUNDLAK and EXTSTEIN do very well over the range of the experiment. The performance of the other rules is essentially the same as in the other cases.

Finally, in Table 5, we report the results of Case 2 when the condition numbers of the data are 10 both in-sample and out-of-sample, implying that the collinearity is moderate. In Case 2 the data ellipsoids are rotated so that the major and minor axes are reversed. Extrapolation is achieved by translating the out-of-sample data ellipsoid along the minor axis of the in-sample data. Contrast these results to those in Table 3 and you will see that despite the fact that the characteristic roots are identical in-sample and out-of-sample the fact that the data ellipsoids are rotated means that the LS risk is affected by collinearity. The relative perfomance of the estimators is the same as in Table 3 however.

The results for cases we have not reported are subsumed by those we have reported. Qualitative relationships remain the same for similar condition number configurations. Cases 3 and 4 in which the out-of-sample data is translated along the minor axis of the in-sample ellipsoid increases the risk of the LS estimator drastically but does not change relative estimator performance from Cases 1 and 2. For example, when the ellipsoids are rotated the same and the condition numbers are both equal to 10 (compare to Table 3), if the extrapolation is along the minor axis the LS risk is 144.61 when $d = 1$, 593.60 when $d = 2$ and 1345.43 when $d = 3$.

6. Concluding Remarks

In this paper we have examined the performance of a variety of minimax and non-minimax biased estimators when the objective is out-of-sample forecasting. We have described the nature of the extrapolation problem in a multivariate context and used that analysis in designing an appropriate Monte Carlo experiment. We have identified the following patterns in our results:

(1) The nature of extrapolation certainly affects the ability of the LS and all other estimators we examined to predict out-of-sample. When the out-of-sample data ellipsoid is rotated relative to the in-sample ellipsoid and/or

when the out-of-sample ellipsoid is translated along a minor, rather than the major axis of the in-sample data, then LS and other forecasts are adversely affected by in-sample multicollinearity. On the other hand, when the out-of-sample collinearity is identical to the in-sample collinearity and extrapolation is along the major axis of the in-sample data ellipsoid then in-sample collinearity has little effect on out-of-sample predictive ability. Actually, increases in out-of-sample collinearity *improves* the forecasting ability of LS and the other estimators.

(2) Estimators designed to be minimax out-of-sample provide little, if any, improvement over LS if collinearity in-sample is different from collinearity out-of-sample. This is a negative finding and due, we believe, to the inherent conservatism of the minimaxity concept. The Berger-like rule we examined is "immune" to collinearity by construction yet offered little gains in situations when LS did not do relatively well already. The Stein-like rules we considered that were minimax with respect to out-of-sample mean squared error of prediction usually failed to differ from LS, though when they did some gains over LS were realized.

(3) The conventional biased estimators we examined were a pre-test principal components estimator due to Mundlak and the well known ridge estimator of Hoerl, Kennard and Baldwin. These rules performed approximately as expected with one exception. Specifically, neither estimator performs well when the data are orthogonal *or when the least squares prediction risk is unaffected by the severity of collinearity* (see remark 1). The latter remark is a surprise. If the in-sample data is collinear we expected these rules, especially MUNDLAK, to perform well regardless of the nature of the out-of-sample data. This, however, was not the case as the principal components and ridge rules were inferior to LS when the in-sample collinearity was matched by the out-of-sample collinearity and extrapolation was along the major axis of the in-sample data ellipsoid. In other cases these estimators performed well relative to LS over much of the parameter space we examined.

(4) The Stein-like rules designed to be minimax under squared error loss performed better than LS when they differed from LS, but this was infrequent.

(5) The Stein-like/empirical Bayes estimators that are minimax under squared error of in-sample prediction loss are the best of the shrinkage rules that do not reduce the size of the parameter space. These rules provide significant risk gains over LS when the non-sample information that is incorporated is nearly correct, here when the length of the parameter vector L is near zero. These rules are not minimax under the current objective

function, but in the cases we examined have risks that do not exceed the risk of LS or exceed it by very little.

(6) The adaptive estimator EXTSTEIN that chooses a set of principal components to delete based on an estimate of in-sample prediction risk improvement over LS, and then shrinks the remaining coefficients differentially, behaves very much like a conservative pre-test estimator. It performs well in our experiments, and less well, under the same sets of circumstances, as the Mundlak principal components rule.

All of these results are, of course, limited by the scope of our numerical experiments. The equal parameter configuration is very favorable to the ridge estimators and detrimental to the differential shrinkage rules TRUSTEIN and EXTSTEIN. The small dimension of the parameter space limits the amount of improvement offered by the biased estimators. The patterns of collinearity we have examined are very restrictive since only one dimension of ill-conditioning is allowed. More general intercorrelations will be more realistic representations of economic data.

More research should be devoted to the type and degree of extrapolation typical of economic data used in applied work. We used the extreme cases that are not, we suspect, representative of most economic data. Monte Carlo work must be done within the context of "real" data and parameter configurations to determine which, if any, of these rules will be useful in real problems with nonsample information that is correct in varying degrees. The latter point reflects the need to choose more appropriate non-sample information to incorporate with the Stein-like rules than the "null" prior that all parameter values are zero.

References

Amemiya, T. (1985), *Advanced Econometrics*, Cambridge: Harvard University Press.

Baranchik, A.J. (1964), *Multiple Regression and Estimation of the Mean of a Multivariate Normal Distribution*, Technical Report No. 51, Department of Statistics, Stanford University, Stanford, CA.

Berger, J. (1976), "Admissible Minimax Estimation of a Multivariate Normal Mean under Arbitrary Quadratic Loss", *Annals of Statistics*, 4, 223–226.

Dey D.K. and J.O. Berger (1983), "On Truncation of Shrinkage Estimators in Simultaneous Estimation of Normal Means," *Journal of the American Statistical Association*, 78, 865–869.

Efron, B. and C. Morris (1973), "Limiting the Risk of Bayes and Empirical Bayes Estimators – Part II: The Empirical Bayes Case," *Journal of the American Statistical Association*, 68, 117–130.

Fomby, T. and R.C. Hill (1990), "A Principal Components Representation of Least Squares Prediction Risk and Some Paradoxes," working paper, Economics Department, Southern Methodist University, Dallas, TX 75275.

Fomby, T., R.C. Hill and S.R. Johnson (1978), "An Optimality Property of Principal Components in the Context of Restricted Least Squares," *Journal of the American Statistical Association*, 73, 191–193.

Fomby, T., R.C. Hill and S.R. Johnson (1984), *Advanced Econometric Methods*, New York: Springer Verlag.

Friedman, D. and D. Montgomery (1985), "Evaluation of the Predictive Performance of Biased Regression Estimators," *Journal of Forecasting*, 4, 153–163.

Gibbons, D.G. (1981), "A Simulation Study of Some Ridge Estimators," *Journal of the American Statistical Association*, 76, 131–139.

Hill, R.C., P.A. Cartwright and J.F. Arbaugh (1991), "The Use of Biased Predictors in Marketing Research," *International Journal of Forecasting*, 7, 271–282.

Hill, R.C. and G.G. Judge (1987), "Improved Prediction in the Presence of Multicollinearity," *Journal of Econometrics*, 35, 83–100.

Hill R.C. and R.F. Ziemer (1984), "The Risk of General Stein-like Estimators in the Presence of Multicollinearity," *Journal of Econometrics*, 25, 205–216.

Hoerl, A. and R. Kennard (1970a), "Ridge Regression: Biased Estimation for Nonorthogonal Problems," *Technometrics*, 12, 55–67.

Hoerl, A. and R. Kennard (1970b), "Ridge Regression: Applications to Nonorthogonal Problems," *Technometrics*, 12, 69–82.

James, W. and C. Stein (1961), "Estimation with Quadratic Loss," in *Proceedings of the Fourth Berkeley Symposium on Mathematical Statistics and Probability*, Berkeley: University of California Press, 316–379.

Judge, G.G. and M.E. Bock (1978), *The Statistical Implications of Pre-Test and Stein Rule Estimators in Econometrics*, Amsterdam: North-Holland.

Judge, G.G., W.E. Griffiths, R.C. Hill, H. Lüttkepohl and T.C. Lee (1985a), *The Theory and Practice of Econometrics*, 2nd ed., New York: John Wiley.

Judge, G.G., G. Yi, T. Yancey and T. Terasvirta (1985b), "The Extended Stein Procedure (ESP) for Simultaneous Model Selection and Parameter Estimation," *Journal of Econometrics*, 35, 375–382.

Judge, G.G., R.C. Hill and M.E. Bock (1990), "Estimation of the Multivariate Normal Mean Under Quadratic Loss," *Journal of Econometrics*, 44, 189–213.

Lindley, D.V. (1962), "Discussion of Professor Stein's Paper," *Journal of the Royal Statistical Society B*, 24, 285–287.

Mantell, E.H. (1973), "Exact Linear Restrictions on Parameters in the Classical Linear Regression Model," *The American Statistician*, 27, 86–87.

Mittelhammer, R.C. (1985), "Quadratic Risk Domination of Restricted Least Squares Estimators via Stein-Ruled Auxiliary Constraints," *Journal of Econometrics*, 29, 289–304.

Mittelhammer, R.C. and D. Young (1981), "Mitigating the Effects of Multicollinearity Using Exact and Stochastic Restrictions: Reply," *American Journal of Agricultural Economics*, 63, 301–304.

Mundlak, Y. (1981), "On the Concept of Nonsignificant Functions and Its Implications for Regression Analysis," *Journal of Econometrics*, 16, 139–150.

Sclove, S. (1973), "Least Squares Problems with Random Regression Coefficients," Technical Report #87, Institute for Math. Studies in Social Sciences, Stanford University, California.

Stein, C. (1981), "Estimation of the Parameters of a Multivariate Normal Distribution: I. Estimation of the Means," *Annals of Statistics*, 9, 1135–1151.

Zellner, A. (1986), "On Assessing Prior Distributions and Bayesian Regression Analysis with g-prior Distributions," in P. Goel and A. Zellner, eds., *Bayesian Inference and Decision Techniques*, Amsterdam: North-Holland, 237–243.

Zellner, A. and C. Hong (1989), "Forecasting International Growth Rates Using Bayesian Shrinkage and Other Procedures," *Journal of Econometrics*, 40, 183–202.

Readings in Econometric Theory and Practice
W. Griffiths, H. Lütkepohl and M.E. Bock (Editors)

CHAPTER 2

RISK AND POWER FOR INEQUALITY PRE-TEST ESTIMATORS: GENERAL CASE IN TWO DIMENSIONS *

T.A. Yancey [a] and Robert Bohrer [b]

[a] Department of Economics and [b] Department of Statistics, University of Illinois, Champaign, IL 61820, USA

In this paper we investigate the statistical implications for the risk functions of the pre-test estimators for the linear model that follow from two joint, one-sided hypothesis tests. Results are given for a wide range of correlation levels for the variables in the design matrix. We also show that the same values for the risk functions are obtained in either the parameter space associated with orthogonal design matrices or the parameter space associated with nonorthogonal design matrices by a suitable choice of weights in a quadratic loss function.

1. Introduction

In normal linear model specification, investigators frequently use tests of inequality hypotheses to decide whether or not to adjust coefficients of explanatory variables. For instance, the null hypothesis may be that certain explanatory variables with non-negative coefficients do not belong in the model. The outcomes of these hypothesis tests are then used to respecify the model. The resulting estimators of the coefficients in the new model are pre-test estimators whose risk functions are quite different from those of the corresponding estimators which are not based on the same data that were used to test the model.

The consequences for pre-test estimators of testing inequality restrictions on the parameters of the linear statistical model have been explored for special cases in Yancey, Bohrer, and Judge (1989), Judge and Yancey (1986), Judge, Bohrer, and Yancey (1988), Judge, Yancey, and Bock (1983), and Yancey, Bohrer, and Judge (1982). Except for one fixed example, the columns of the design matrices in this series of papers were orthogonal. Inasmuch as

* The authors wish to recognize the contribution of Ivan Chang in plotting the large number of risk functions explored, most of which could not be accommodated in the paper, and Mary Ellen Bock for stimulating suggestions and editorial improvements.

econometric studies usually use passively generated data, often collected for other purposes, the design matrix seldom has orthogonal columns. Hence methods emphasizing design matrices with non-orthogonal columns are of primary interest in economics.

In this paper the one-sided tests of the linear model coefficients involve either a point null and an inequality alternative hypothesis or an inequality null and an unrestrictive alternative hypothesis. The purpose of the paper is to explore the power function of the tests and the risk functions of the pre-test estimators of the coefficients for design matrices of rank two. The product of the design matrix and its transpose is assumed to be a two-dimensional correlation matrix. Our generality comes from the large range of values considered for the correlation coefficient.

The paper is organized as follows. In section 2, the statistical model, estimators and tests are given and the power function characteristics are presented. Section 3 develops the risk functions for the one-sided, pre-test estimators. Section 4 gives the comparisons of pre-test risk functions for two different hypothesis tests and the basis for choosing the associated pre-test estimator. Section 5 discusses unweighted squared-error loss risk functions, and section 6 summarizes the results and presents the conclusions.

2. Statistical Model, Estimators and Test Statistics: the Two-Dimensional Case

Consider the normal linear statistical model

$$y = X\beta + e,$$

where X is a $(T \times K)$ design matrix, β is a $(K \times 1)$ vector of unknown parameters. The $(T \times 1)$ vector of random variables e is distributed normally with zero mean vector and T-dimensional covariance matrix which is the identity matrix multiplied by the scalar σ^2. We consider general linear hypotheses of the form

$$R\beta \geqq r,$$

where the $(J \times K)$ matrix R and the $(J \times 1)$ vector r are assumed to be known.

Following Judge and Yancey (1986), and Yancey, Judge, and Bohrer (1989), the model can be reparameterized to

$$y = Z\theta + e,$$

where $Z'Z$ is the K-dimensional identity matrix and θ is the unknown parameter vector. The linear hypothesis becomes

$$A\theta \geqq r,$$

with A a lower triangular matrix. This is accomplished by finding a matrix P such that $P'X'XP$ is the identity matrix and RP is lower triangular. Then

$$Z = XP, \quad \theta = P^{-1}\beta, \quad A = RP.$$

For expository purposes it is assumed that the scalar σ^2 that multiplies the covariance matrix of e is known and equal to one, that the dimensions J and K are both equal to two, that R is the identity matrix, that r is a vector of zeroes and that $X'X$ is a correlation matrix whose off-diagonal element is the correlation coefficient ρ.

In the beta space the unrestricted maximum likelihood (ML) estimator for β is

$$b = (X'X)^{-1}X'y = \begin{pmatrix} b_1 \\ b_2 \end{pmatrix}.$$

In the θ space the ML estimator for θ is

$$g = P^{-1}b = \begin{pmatrix} g_1 \\ g_2 \end{pmatrix} = \begin{pmatrix} (1-\rho^2)^{1/2}b_1 \\ \rho b_1 + b_2 \end{pmatrix}.$$

In the beta space the restricted ML estimator for β is

$$b^* = \begin{cases} b & \text{if } b_1 \geqq 0 \text{ and } b_2 \geqq 0, \\[2mm] \begin{pmatrix} 0 \\ \hat{b}_2 \end{pmatrix} & \text{if } b_1 < 0 \text{ and } b_2 > -\rho b_1, \\[2mm] \begin{pmatrix} \hat{b}_1 \\ 0 \end{pmatrix} & \text{if } b_2 < 0 \text{ and } b_1 \geqq -\rho b_2, \\[2mm] \begin{pmatrix} 0 \\ 0 \end{pmatrix} & \text{if } b_1 < -\rho b_2 \text{ and } b_2 < -\rho b_1, \end{cases}$$

where

$$\hat{b}_1 = b_1 + \rho b_2 \tag{2.1a}$$

$$\hat{b}_2 = b_2 + \rho b_1. \tag{2.1b}$$

In the theta space the restricted ML estimator for θ is

$$\boldsymbol{g}^* = \begin{cases} \boldsymbol{g} & \text{if } g_1 \geqq 0 \text{ and } g_2 > \left(\rho/\left(1-\rho^2\right)^{1/2}\right)g_1, \\[2mm] \begin{pmatrix} 0 \\ g_2 \end{pmatrix} & \text{if } g_1 < 0 \text{ and } g_2 \geqq 0 \\[2mm] \begin{pmatrix} \hat{g}_1 \\ \hat{g}_2 \end{pmatrix} & \text{if } g_2 < \left(\rho/(1-\rho)^{1/2}\right)g_1 \text{ and } g_2 \geqq -\left(\left(1-\rho^2\right)^{1/2}/\rho\right)g_1, \\[2mm] \begin{pmatrix} 0 \\ 0 \end{pmatrix} & \text{if } g_1 < -\left(\rho/\left(1-\rho^2\right)^{1/2}\right)g_2 \text{ and } g_2 < 0, \end{cases}$$

where

$$\hat{g}_1 = \left(1-\rho^2\right)g_1 + \rho\left(1-\rho^2\right)^{1/2}g_2 = \left(1-\rho^2\right)^{1/2}\hat{b}_1 \tag{2.2a}$$

and

$$\hat{g}_2 = \rho\left(1-\rho^2\right)^{1/2}g_1 + \rho^2 g_2 = \rho\hat{b}_1 + \hat{b}_2. \tag{2.2b}$$

One can obtain the unrestricted ML and restricted ML estimators for either parameter space and find the estimators in the other parameter space since

$$\boldsymbol{g} = \boldsymbol{P}^{-1}\boldsymbol{b}$$

and

$$\boldsymbol{g}^* = \boldsymbol{P}^{-1}\boldsymbol{b}^*.$$

The pre-test estimators will depend on the outcome of testing hypotheses about β or θ in their respective spaces. In the multivariate one-sided hypothesis testing literature, there are two formulations for testing linear hypotheses about β or θ equals $\boldsymbol{P}^{-1}\beta$. The work of Bartholomew (1959), Kudo (1963), Osterhoff (1969), Gourieroux, Holly, and Monfort (1982),

Hillier (1986), Shapiro (1988), and Yancey, Judge, and Bohrer (1989) explores the validity of the linear constraints hypotheses as

$$H_0 : A\theta = 0 \quad \text{and} \quad H_a : A\theta \geq 0.$$

The work of Perlman (1969), Yancey, Judge, and Bohrer (1981), Judge and Yancey (1986), Wolak (1987) and Yancey, Judge and Bohrer (1989) uses

$$H_0 : A\theta \geq 0$$

and

$$H_a : \theta \in R_2$$

where H_a implies θ is unrestricted under the alternative hypothesis.

With either form of null hypothesis, the pre-test estimator depends on the outcome of the hypothesis test. For the point-null hypothesis,

$$A\theta = 0,$$

the restricted estimator g^* is used if the hypothesis is rejected and zero is used if the hypothesis is accepted. With the inequality null hypothesis

$$A\theta \geq 0,$$

the pre-test estimator is the restricted estimator g^*, if the hypothesis is accepted and it is the unrestricted estimator g, if the hypothesis is rejected.

The likelihood ratio (LR) test is used in each formulation to determine the acceptance and rejection regions for the test statistic for given null and alternative hypotheses. With the point null, the LR test statistic in g-space is

$$u_1 = I(g_1 < 0) I(g_2 \geq 0) g_2^2$$

$$+ I(g_1 \geq 0) I\left(g_2 \geq \left(\rho/(1-\rho^2)^{1/2}\right)g_1\right)\left(g_1^2 + g_2^2\right)$$

$$+ I\left(g_1 \geq -\left(\rho/(1-\rho^2)^{1/2}\right)g_2\right) I\left(g_2 < \left(\rho/(1-\rho^2)^{1/2}\right)g_1\right)$$

$$\times \left(\hat{g}_1^2 + \hat{g}_2^2\right)$$

where $\hat{g}_1$ and $\hat{g}_2$ are given by the first equalities in (2.2a) and (2.2b), respectively. $I(x < by)$ is an indicator function which is one when $x < by$ and zero otherwise. The test statistic u_1 is a weighted sum of chi-square random variables. We reject

$$H_0 : A\theta = 0$$

if

$$u_1 \geq c_1^2$$

where c_1^2 is the critical value for the test for a given α level; see Judge and Yancey (1986).

In the b-space, the LR test statistic is

$$u_1^* = I(b_1 < 0)I(b_2 \geq -\rho b_1)(b_2 + \rho b_1)^2$$

$$+ I(b_1 \geq 0)I(b_2 \geq 0)(b_1^2 + 2\rho b_1 b_2 + b_2^2)$$

$$+ I(b_1 \geq -\rho b_2)I(b_2 < 0)\left[\hat{b}_1^2 + 2\rho \hat{b}_1 \hat{b}_2 + \hat{b}_2^2\right]$$

where $\hat{b}_1$ and $\hat{b}_2$ are given by (2.1a) and (2.1b). $I(x < by)$ is again the appropriate indicator function. Using the test statistic u_1^*, we reject

$$H_0 : \beta = 0$$

if

$$u_1^* \geq c_1^{*2}.$$

The critical values c_1^2 and c_1^{*2} are the same in both spaces. This can be seen by noting that the point $(0, c_1)$ in g-space maps into $(0, c_1)$ in b-space, and the point $(c_1(1 - \rho^2)^{1/2}, c_1\rho)$ in g-space maps into $(c_1, 0)$ in b-space. Furthermore, the line $\{g_2 = c_1\}$ maps into the b-space line $\{b_2 = c_1 - \rho b_1\}$, the circle $\{g_1^2 + g_2^2 = c_1^2\}$ becomes the ellipse $\{b_1^2 + 2\rho b_1 b_2 + b_2^2 = c_1^2\}$, and the line $\{g_2 = (c_1/\rho) - ((1 - \rho^2)^{1/2}/\rho)g_1\}$ becomes the line $\{b_2 = c_1/\rho - (1/\rho)b_1\}$ in b-space. Thus, the rejection region in g-space maps exactly into the rejection region in the b-space for the same critical value c_1^2 which equals c_1^{*2}, and the bivariate normal distribution in g-space with zero means and covariance matrix I_2 becomes bivariate normal with zero means, variances $1/(1 - \rho^2)$, and covariance $-\rho/(1-\rho^2)$ in b-space. Thus for a given α-level for the test we have c_1^2 equals c_1^{*2}.

For the inequality null hypothesis

$$H_0: \beta_1 \geq 0, \quad \beta_2 \geq 0$$

in β-space or

$$H_0: \theta_1 \geq 0, \quad \theta_2 \geq \left(\rho/(1-\rho^2)^{1/2}\right)\theta_1$$

in θ-space, the test statistic for the LR test in g-space is

$$u_2 = I(g_1 < 0)I(g_2 \geq 0)g_1^2$$

$$+ I(g_2 < 0)I\left(g_1 < \left(-\rho/(1-\rho^2)^{1/2}\right)g_2\right)\left(g_1^2 + g_2^2\right)$$

$$+ I\left(g_1 \geq -\left(\rho/(1-\rho^2)^{1/2}\right)g_2\right)I\left(g_2 < \left(\rho/(1-\rho^2)^{1/2}\right)g_1\right)$$

$$\times \left[(g_1 - \hat{g}_1)^2 + (g_2 - \hat{g}_2)^2\right]$$

where the restricted estimators $\hat{g}_1$ and $\hat{g}_2$ are given by (2.2a) and (2.2b). Using the test statistic u_2, we reject

$$H_0: A\theta \geq 0$$

if

$$u_2 \geq c_2^2$$

where u_2 is the weighted sum of chi-square random variables.

In b-space, the LR test statistic for

$$H_0: \beta \geq 0$$

is

$$u_2^* = I(b_1 \leq 0)I(b_2 \geq -\rho b_1)b_1^2(1-\rho^2)$$

$$+ I(b_2 < -\rho b_1)I(b_1 < -\rho b_2)\left(b_1^2 + 2\rho b_1 b_2 + b_2^2\right)$$

$$+ I(b_1 \geq -\rho b_2)I(b_2 < 0)b_2^2(1-\rho^2).$$

Using the test statistic u_2^*, we reject

$$H_0 : \beta \geq 0$$

if

$$u_2^* \geq c_2^{*2},$$

the critical value for a given α-level test.
Again using the transformation

$$b = Pg$$

or

$$b_1 = \left(1 / \left(1 - \rho^2\right)^{1/2}\right) g_1$$

and

$$b_2 = -\left(\rho / \left(1 - \rho^2\right)^{1/2}\right) g_1 + g_2,$$

the point $(-c_2, 0)$ in g-space maps into the point $(-c_2/(1-\rho^2)^{1/2}, c_2\rho/(1-\rho^2)^{1/2})$ in b-space. The g-space point $(c_2\rho, -c_2/(1-\rho^2)^{1/2})$ maps into $(c_2\rho/(1-\rho^2)^{1/2}, -c_2/(1-\rho^2)^{1/2})$ in b-space. The circle $\{g_1^2 + g_2^2 = c_2^2\}$ maps into the ellipse $\{b_1^2 + 2\rho b_1 b_2 + b_2^2 = c_2^2\}$, the line $\{g_1 = -c_2\}$ becomes $\{b_1 = -c_2/(1-\rho^2)^{1/2}\}$, and the line $\{g_2 = -c_2/(1-\rho^2)^{1/2} + (\rho/(1-\rho^2)^{1/2}) g_1\}$ becomes the line $\{b_2 = -c_2/(1-\rho^2)^{1/2}\}$.

The density under the null hypothesis in the g-space which is normal with zero means, variances of one and covariance zero, becomes normal with zero means, variances $1/(1-\rho^2)$ and covariance $-\rho/(1-\rho^2)$ in b-space. It follows that c_2 equals c_2^*.

As shown in Yancey, Bohrer and Judge (1982) for ρ equals zero so that the b and g-spaces coincide, the power functions of the two tests for the point null and inequality null hypotheses differ in that the rejection region for the point null is in the positive orthant, and the power function for the inequality null has rejection region in second, third, and fourth quadrants. However, the critical values for the two tests are the same for given α-level as shown in Table 1, and the power at the point (g_1, g_2) for one of the tests will be the same as the power at $(-g_1, -g_2)$ for the other test. As Table 1 shows,

Table 1

Critical Values Classified by ρ, α-Level, and Hypothesis Tested

Null hypo-thesis	α-Level	ρ										
		-0.90	-0.75	-0.50	-0.25	-0.10	0	0.10	0.25	0.50	0.75	0.90
$A\theta = 0$	0.10	1.90	1.86	1.81	1.76	1.74	1.72	1.44	1.52	1.61	1.67	1.44
	0.05	2.22	2.18	2.14	2.10	2.07	2.06	1.80	1.88	1.95	2.01	1.80
	0.01	2.84	2.81	2.77	2.74	2.71	2.70	2.48	2.54	2.61	2.66	2.48
$A\theta \geq 0$	0.10	1.90	1.52	1.61	1.67	1.70	1.72	1.74	1.76	1.81	1.86	1.90
	0.05	1.80	1.88	1.95	2.01	2.04	2.06	2.07	2.10	2.14	2.18	2.22
	0.01	2.48	2.54	2.61	2.66	2.69	2.70	2.71	2.74	2.77	2.81	2.84

when ρ differs from zero, the critical values, c_i^2, which are the same for a given hypothesis, e.g.,

$$\beta \geq 0$$

or

$$A\theta \geq 0,$$

in either the θ or β-spaces, will differ for the point null and inequality null hypothesis for a given α-level and a given ρ value. However for a given level for a test, the critical value for ρ for the point null hypthesis is the same as the critical value for minus ρ for the inequality null hypothesis.

Table 2

Null Hypothesis Power Function Values

Distance from origin	45 Degree line				-45 Degree line			
	$\rho = 0.90$		$\rho = -0.90$		$\rho = 0.90$		$\rho = -0.90$	
	$P(\beta \geq 0)$	$P(\beta = 0)$	$P(\beta \geq 0)$	$P(\beta = 0)$	$P(\beta \geq 0)$	$P(\beta = 0)$	$P(\beta \geq 0)$	$P(\beta = 0)$
0.50	0.127	0.168	0.068	0.064	0.050	0.050	0.068	0.088
1.00	0.292	0.391	0.092	0.076	0.056	0.051	0.092	0.217
2.00	0.771	0.862	0.155	0.118	0.081	0.054	0.155	0.692
4.00	1.000	1.000	0.348	0.259	0.189	0.066	0.348	0.999
8.00	1.000	1.000	0.806	0.801	0.613	0.109	0.806	1.000
12.00	1.000	1.000	0.983	0.960	0.933	0.171	0.983	1.000
16.00	1.000	1.000	1.000	0.999	0.997	0.252	1.000	1.000

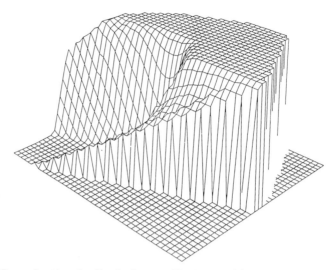

Figure 1. Power functions for $H_0 : \beta \geq 0$ versus $H_a : \beta \in R_2$ with $\alpha = 0.05$ and $\rho = 0.50$ cut along the line $\{\beta_2 = \beta_1\}$ through the first and third quadrants around which the function is symmetric.

When $\rho = 0.90$, Table 2 shows power functions for the point null, $P(\beta = 0)$, and inequality null hypothesis, $P(\beta \geq 0)$, along a 45-degree line in the β-space for five percent level tests, $P(\beta = 0)$ is higher or equal to $P(\beta \geq 0)$ for every point (β_{01}, β_{02}) in the rejection region than at the point $(-\beta_{01}, -\beta_{02})$ for $P(\beta = 0)$. Indeed, $P(\beta = 0)$ is from 15 to 30 percent higher than $P(\beta \geq 0)$ for $P(\beta = 0)$ values ranging from 0.10 to 0.86. When we look at powers for these two hypotheses, only changing ρ to -0.90, exactly the reverse is true, and $P(\beta \geq 0)$ exceeds $P(\beta = 0)$ by from 15 to 30 percent for $P(\beta \geq 0)$ values ranging from 0.08 to 0.81. If we use $\rho = -0.90$ but switch to a -45-degree line, which falls outside the space considered by the equality null hypothesis, we observe $P(\beta = 0)$ exceeds $P(\beta \geq 0)$ by multiples of 2 to 6.5. When $P(\beta = 0)$ becomes 1.00, $P(\beta \geq 0)$ is only 0.37. Changing ρ to 0.90 again reverses the rankings with respect to power and $P(\beta = 0)$ is only 0.252 when $P(\beta \geq 0)$ is 0.997. Patterns for $P(\beta \geq 0)$ and $P(\beta = 0)$ along other lines between 45 degrees and -45 degrees and for ρ values from 0.10 and -0.10 to 0.75 and -0.75 give similar but less dramatic patterns. At $\rho = 0$, the two power function comparisons coincide.

Figures 1 and 2 show three dimensional plots of the power functions for $\rho = 0.5$ with $\alpha = 0.05$. In each case, the view is of half the function where it is sliced along the 45 degree line in β-space. Irregularities in some places in the plots are due to straight line interpolation where missing output values occur.

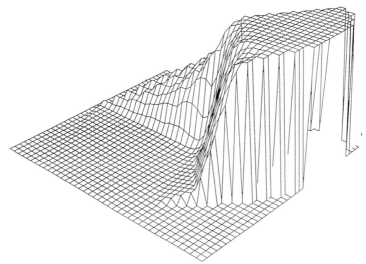

Figure 2. Power functions for $H_0 : \beta = 0$ versus $H_a : \beta \geq 0$ with $\alpha = 0.05$ and $\rho = 0.50$ cut along the line $\{\beta_2 = \beta_1\}$ through the first and third quadrants around which the function is symmetric.

3. Pre-Test Estimator Risk Functions

The direct use of power functions did not give conclusive results on the choice of a test to use with pre-test estimators. We now turn to pre-test estimator risk functions based on squared-error loss, and appropriately weighted risk functions are also considered for β-space, θ-space comparisons. A pre-test estimator is defined by using the estimator implied by the null hypothesis if we accept that hypothesis and using the estimator implied by the alternative hypothesis if we reject the null hypothesis. Thus for the pre-test estimator, $\delta_1(g)$, based on

$$H_0 : \beta = 0 \quad \text{or} \quad A\theta = 0$$

and

$$H_a : \beta \geq 0 \quad \text{or} \quad A\theta \geq 0,$$

we use the restricted ML estimator, g^*, when H_0 is rejected and zero when it is accepted. This pre-test estimator can be expressed by using indicator functions as

$$\delta_1(g) = I\left(u_1 \geq c_1^2\right)g^* + I\left(u_1 < c_1^2\right)0 = I\left(u_1 \geq c_1^2\right)g^*,$$

where u_1 is the test statistic described for testing the point null hypothesis and c_1^2 is the critical value for the test.

For the pre-test estimator based on

$$H_0 : \beta \geq 0 \quad \text{or} \quad A\theta \geq 0$$

and

$$H_a : \beta \in R_2 \quad \text{or} \quad \theta \in R_2,$$

we use the unrestricted ML estimator when H_0 is rejected and use the restricted ML estimator when it is accepted. Hence this pre-test estimator is

$$\delta_2(g) = I\left(u_2 \geq c_2^2\right)g + I\left(u_2 < c_2^2\right)g^*.$$

Again, we can work in either β-space or θ-space, but unlike the power function case, which can be viewed in both spaces as a risk function with weights of zero over the acceptance region and one over the rejection region, a squared-error loss function in β-space becomes a weighted loss function in θ-space. Specifically, if we use the transformation $\gamma_i(b) = P\delta_i(g)$, the loss function

$$L\left(\gamma_i(b), \beta\right) = \left(\gamma_{i1}(b) - \beta_1\right)^2 + \left(\gamma_{i2}(b) - \beta_2\right)^2$$

in β-space becomes

$$L\left(\delta_i(g), \theta\right) = \left(1 + \rho^2\right)\left(\delta_{i1}(g) - \theta_1\right)^2 / \left(1 - \rho^2\right)$$

$$- 2\rho\left(\delta_{i1}(g) - \theta_1\right)\left(\delta_{i2}(g) - \theta_2\right) / \left(1 - \rho^2\right)^{1/2}$$

$$+ \left(\delta_{i2}(g) - \theta_2\right)^2$$

loss in θ-space, or

$$L\left(\gamma_i(b), \beta\right) = \left(\gamma_i(b) - \beta\right)'\left(\gamma_i(b) - \beta\right)$$

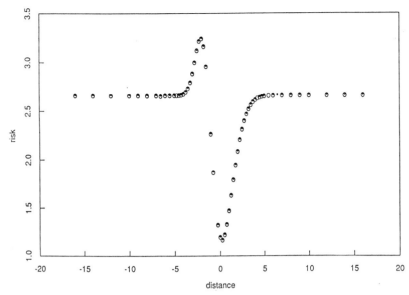

distance

Figure 3. Risk functions for $H_0 : \beta \geq 0$ or $A\theta \geq 0$ versus $H_a : \beta$ or $\theta \in R_2$ for $\alpha = 0.05$ and $\rho = 0.50$ along the line $\{\beta_2 = \beta_1\}$ or $\{\theta_2 = 2.646\theta_1\}$. Circles are β-space values, dots are θ-space values.

is

$$L\big(\delta_i(g), \theta\big) = \big(\delta_i(g) - \theta\big)' P'P\big(\delta_i(g) - \theta\big)$$

where the first row of P is $(1/(1 - \rho^2)^{1/2}, 0)$, and its second row is $(-\rho/(1 - \rho^2)^{1/2}, 1)$.

Using the weighted loss functions in θ-space, the risk function under squared-error loss has values that for any point β_0 in β-space are the same as values for the weighted risk function at θ_0 equals $P^{-1}\beta_0$ in θ-space. Risk functions were computed using numerical integration procedures based on Milton (1972) or on integration by parts where feasible. Figure 3 shows the risk functions $E(\gamma_2(b) - \beta)'(\gamma_2(b) - \beta)$ and $E(\delta_2(g) - \theta)'P'P(\delta_2(g) - \theta)$ for null hypotheses $\beta \geq 0$ and $A\theta \geq 0$, respectively, where ρ is 0.50, α is 0.05 along a 45-degree line with a slope of one in β-space or a line with a slope of 2.646 in θ-space for the inequality null hypothesis case. The dots represent the risks in θ-space and the circles represent the risks in β-space. Figure 4 shows the risk functions for the point null hypothesis with $\rho = -0.75$ and along a 30-degree line with a slope of 0.577 in β-space or -0.655 in θ-space

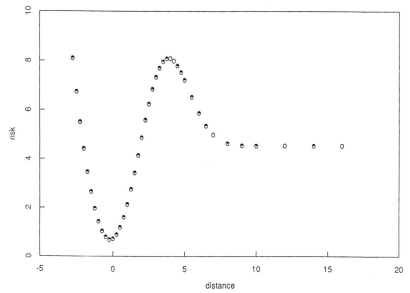

Figure 4. Risk functions for $H_0 : \beta = 0$ or $A\theta = 0$ versus $H_a : \beta \geq 0$ or $A\theta \geq 0$ along a 30-degree line in β-space $\{\beta_2 = 0.577\beta_1\}$ or $\{\theta_2 = -0.655\theta_1\}$ for $\alpha = 0.05$ and $\rho = -0.75$. Circles are β-space values, dots are θ-space values.

and $\alpha = 0.05$. As both figures show, the risk functions from the two spaces agree as they should. The point null risk functions were truncated at the value 10, but they increase in proportion to the square of the distance from β_0 to zero for negative directional distance values.

Other plots of pairs of β and θ-space risk functions for other ρ values and α values along lines with slopes ranging from -1 to 1 in the β-space produce the same agreement in risk functions in the two spaces. Points in the figures with either a dot or a circle but not both reflect a failure of the numerical integration program to get an answer within our 0.0001 error limit. We find integration by parts, which can be used in θ-space for rectangular regions of the domain of the function, give more accurate results than numerical integration giving no cases when results are not obtained for the rectangular regions and fewer cases when risk values are not obtained by numerical integration than in comparable regions in β-space.

4. Risk Evaluations for the Pre-test Estimators

Although comparisons of risk functions for the point and inequality null hypotheses can be made in either space, we have chosen the θ-space results

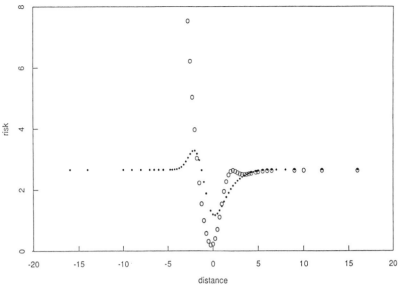

Figure 5. Risk functions for null hypotheses $\beta = 0$ and $\beta \geq 0$ along the line $\{\beta_2 = \beta_1\}$ or $\{\theta_2 = 1.732\theta_1\}$ for $\alpha = 0.05$ and $\rho = 0.50$. Circles are $R(\delta_1(g), \theta)$ values, dots are $R(\delta_2(g), \theta)$ values.

for presentation. The weighted risk functions

$$R\big(\delta_i(g), \theta\big) = E\big(\delta_i(g) - \theta\big)' P'P\big(\delta_i(g) - \theta\big)$$

with pre-test estimators $\delta_1(g)$ and $\delta_2(g)$ for the point null and inequality null hypotheses were computed for three α-levels, 0.10, 0.05, and 0.01; ten ρ values, -0.90, -0.75, -0.50, -0.25, -0.10, 0.10, 0.25, 0.50, 0.75, and 0.90 at 61 points up to sixteen standard deviations from the origin along each of six lines with slopes of 0, 30, 45, 60, 90, and -45 degrees in β-space and the transformation of those points into the θ-space. Figure 5 shows risk comparisons of the inequality null and point null pre-test estimates for $\rho = 0.50$, $\alpha = 0.05$ on line $\{\theta_2 = 1.732\theta_1\}$, which is the line $\{\beta_2 = \beta_1\}$ in β-space. Of the many lines on which the pre-test risk functions for the point null and inequality null hypotheses could be compared, we have chosen to emphasize three: $\{\beta_2 = 0\}$, $\{\beta_2 = \beta_1\}$, and $\{\beta_2 = -\beta_1\}$. The line $\{\beta_2 = 0\}$ gives the same risk values as $\{\beta_1 = 0\}$ and these lines bound the region $\{\beta \geq 0\}$. The line $\{\beta_2 = \beta_1\}$ bisects the region $\{\beta \geq 0\}$ and the line $\{\beta_2 = -\beta_1\}$ is orthogonal to the line $\{\beta_2 = \beta_1\}$. For any given ρ value these lines reflect the range of possibilities for risk function comparisons.

For positive ρ values, the region $\{A\theta \geq 0\}$ is bounded by the lines $\{\theta_1 = 0\}$ and $\{\theta_2 = (\rho/(1 - \rho^2)^{1/2})\theta_1\}$, and the results in general show that as the positive ρ decreases from 0.75 to 0.25, the pre-test risk for the point null hypothesis $R(\delta_1(g), \theta)$ is below that for the inequality null hypothesis at θ equals 0. As θ departs from zero in any direction, both risk functions increase, but $R(\delta_1(g), \theta)$ increases faster than $R(\delta_2(g), \theta)$ so the risk functions always cross within 2.75 standard deviations of $\theta = 0$ in our work. Our scale units are the standard deviations of the unrestricted ML estimators, g, which are one. As ρ decreases toward zero, the level of both risk functions decreases. Along the line $\{\beta_2 = \beta_1\}$, which corresponds to the line $\{\theta_2 = (1 + \rho^2)/(1 - \rho^2)^{1/2}\theta_1\}$, and the line $\{\beta_2 = -\beta_1\}$, which corresponds to the line $\{\theta_2 = -(1 - \rho)/(1 - \rho^2)^{1/2}\theta_1\}$, as θ_1 goes to infinity, $R(\delta_2(g), \theta)$ converges to the risk of the unrestricted ML estimator. That risk is the trace of $P'P$ which is equal to the trace of the inverse of the correlation matrix $X'X$. For ρ values of 0.75, 0.50, and 0.25, the traces of the $(X'X)^{-1}$ matrices are 4.571, 2.667, and 2.133, respectively. Along the boundaries of the region $\{A\theta \geq 0\}$, both risk functions are below the unrestricted ML estimator risk. Along the line $\{\beta_2 = 0\}$ with β_1 positive, $R(\delta_1(g), \theta)$ increases without bound as β_1 or θ_1 goes to infinity. For θ_1 positive, the risk functions cross within 2.2 standard deviations of θ equals 0 for ρ equals 0.75, and that distance decreases to less than 1.0 standard deviation as ρ decreases to 0.25. A similar shift toward zero of the risk functions intersection point occurs for θ negative. At $\rho = 0.75$, with θ_2 negative, the risk intersection is within 2.75 standard deviations of θ equals 0 and this decreases to less than 1.75 standard deviations from θ equals 0 for ρ equals 0.25. The results discussed here are shown in Table 3 for ρ positive. At θ equals 0, as ρ decreases $R(\delta_1(g), \theta)$ decreases and $R(\delta_2(g), \theta)$ increases. For all ρ values with β_1 or θ_1 less than zero, $R(\delta_1(g), \theta)$ increases without bound as β_1 goes to minus infinity while $R(\delta_2(g), \theta)$ increases to a maximum at distances from 1.75 to 4 standard deviations from θ equals 0, and $R(\delta_2(g), \theta)$ decreases to the risk of the unrestricted ML estimator thereafter.

The maximum attained by $R(\delta_2(g), \theta)$ on a given line with β_1 negative decreases with the decrease of ρ toward 0 and is roughly twice the risk of the unrestricted ML estimator for that line. As expected, along the line $\{\beta_2 = -\beta_1\}$, which falls outside the region considered in the alternative for the point null hypothesis, $R(\delta_1(g), \theta)$ compares poorly with $R(\delta_2(g), \theta)$ for all but a small region near θ equals 0 and that region shrinks as ρ decreases.

When ρ is negative, the region $\{A\theta \geq 0\}$ covers all of the first quadrant

Comparisons of Pre-test Risk Functions with $P^{T}P$ Weights with $\alpha = 0.05$

Line	Null hypothesis	ρ value	Risk value at −16	Maximum and (location)	$R(\delta_2(g),\theta)$ and (intersection)	Risk value at 0	$R(\delta_1(g),\theta)$ and (intersection)	Maximum and (location)	$R(\delta_1(g),\theta)$ and (intersection)	Risk value at 16
$\beta_2 = 0$	$\beta \geq 0$	0.75	2.00	3.30 (−2.25)	2.84 (−1.59)	1.067	1.10 (0.81)	2.49 (2.55)	1.59 (4.00)	1.595
	$\beta = 0$	0.75	256			0.267				1.500
	$\beta \geq 0$	0.50	2.00	3.30 (−2.25)	3.08 (−1.75)	1.158	1.31 (1.14)	2.64 (2.25)	1.60 (4.00)	1.603
	$\beta = 0$	0.50	256	–		0.286				1.500
	$\beta \geq 0$	0.25	2.133	3.89 (−2.75)	2.93 (−1.66)	1.203	1.38 (0.98)	–	1.69 (4.20)	2.133
	$\beta = 0$	0.25	205	–		2.75		–		1.567
$\beta_2 = \beta_1$	$\beta \geq 0$	0.75	4.571	4.81 (−2.5)	4.71 (−1.88)	1.511	1.88 (1.09)	–	–	4.571
	$\beta = 0$	0.75	256			0.236				4.571
	$\beta \geq 0$	0.50	2.667	3.25 (−2.00)	3.18 (−1.78)	1.204	1.43 (0.91)	–	–	2.667
	$\beta = 0$	0.50	250			0.255				2.667
	$\beta \geq 0$	0.25	2.133	2.98 (−2.00)	2.83 (−1.67)	1.202	1.25 (0.58)	–	–	2.133
	$\beta = 0$	0.25	205			0.275				2.133
$\beta_2 = -\beta_1$	$\beta \geq 0$	0.75	4.571	10.85 (−5.0)	5.77 (−1.72)	1.511	5.77 (1.72)	10.85 (5.0)		4.571
	$\beta = 0$	0.75	205			0.236				205
	$\beta \geq 0$	0.50	2.667	5.57 (−3.75)	3.01 (−1.72)	1.204	3.01 (1.72)	5.57 (3.75)		2.667
	$\beta = 0$	0.50	161			0.255				161
	$\beta \geq 0$	0.25	2.133	4.07 (−3.25)	2.40 (−1.49)	1.203	2.40 (1.49)	4.07 (3.25)		2.133
	$\beta = 0$	0.25	1.37			2.74		–		137

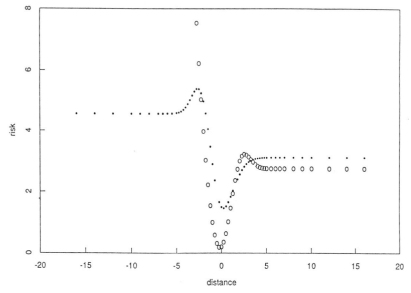

Figure 6. Risk functions for $H_0: \beta = 0$ and $\beta \geq 0$ along the line $\{\beta_2 = \beta_1\}$ or $\{\theta_2 = 0.37817\theta_1\}$ for $\alpha = 0.05$ and $\rho = -0.75$. Circles are $R(\delta_1(g), \theta)$ values, dots are $R(\delta_2(g), \theta)$ values.

and part of the fourth quadrant. At ρ equals -0.90 the boundaries of the region $\{A\theta \geq 0\}$ are the lines $\{\theta_1 = 0\}$ and $\{\theta_2 = -2.0650\theta_1\}$. In these cases the results are qualitatively like those when ρ is positive. The risk functions are higher by a multiple of 1.5 to 2, but as θ_1 goes to infinity or negative infinity the risk functions converge to the same values as they did for $\rho > 0$. Figure 6 gives the risk functions $R(\delta_1(g), \theta)$ and $R(\delta_2(g), \theta)$ for α equals 0.05 and ρ equals -0.75 along the line $\{\beta_2 = \beta_1\}$ or $\{\theta_2 = 0.3780\theta_1\}$. For positive distances the risks converge to 4.571, the unrestricted ML estimator risk. Figure 7 gives the risk functions for ρ equals 0.5 and α equals 0.05 along the line $\{\beta_2 = -\beta_1\}$ or $\{\theta_2 = -0.5774\theta_1\}$ in θ-space.

The patterns shown in Figures 5, 6, and 7 are qualitatively similar to those for other ρ values. Lines of 30 and 60 degrees in β-space yield risk functions similar in shape to those for the lines $\{\beta_2 = 0\}$ and $\{\beta_2 = \beta_1\}$. If the α-level of the test is changed, the patterns in the risk functions are dampened for α equals 0.10 relative to α equals 0.05 and are amplified for α equals 0.01 when compared to the α equals 0.05 risk functions.

Figure 8 shows this pattern for $R(\delta_2(g), \theta)$ along the line $\{\beta_2 = -\beta_1\}$ for α-levels of 0.10, 0.05, and 0.01 and is typical of the effects of α-level changes on risk functions.

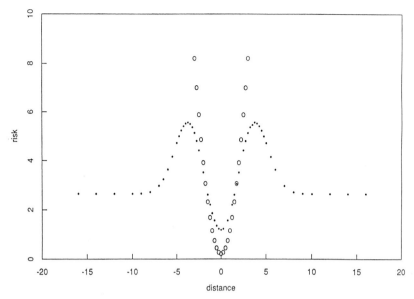

Figure 7. Risk functions for $H_0: \beta = 0$ and $\beta \geq 0$ along the line $\{\beta_2 = -\beta_1\}$ or $\{\theta_2 = -0.577\theta_1\}$ for $\alpha = 0.05$ and $\rho = 0.5$. Circles are $R(\delta_1(g), \theta)$ values, dots are $R(\delta_2(g), \theta)$ values.

5. Unweighted Risk Functions in Theta Space

In our previous papers reporting on pre-test risks, Judge and Yancey (1986), Judge, Yancey, and Bock (1983), Judge, Bohrer and Yancey (1988), Yancey, Judge, and Bohrer (1989), only risk functions based on squared-error loss were used. For the squared error loss case, we have examined the squared-error loss risk functions $R^*(\delta_i(g, \theta)) = E(\delta_i(g) - \theta)'(\delta_i(g) - \theta)$, for $\alpha = 0.05$, the six ρ values 0.75, 0.50, 0.25, -0.25, -0.50, and -0.75, along the lines $\{\theta_2 = ((1+\rho)/(1-\rho^2)^{1/2})\theta_1\}$, $\{\theta_2 = (\rho/(1-\rho^2))^{1/2}\theta_1\}$, and $\{\theta_2 = -((1-\rho)/(1-\rho^2))^{1/2}\theta_1\}$ reflecting β-space lines $\{\beta_2 = 0\}$, $\{\beta_2 = \beta_1\}$, and $\{\beta_2 = -\beta_1\}$ as used in section four.

For ρ positive, the same qualitative patterns are apparent as those for the weighted risk functions for each ρ value and each line. The inequality restricted estimator risk is monotone increasing from θ equals 0 as θ_1 increases and converges to the squared-error risk of the unrestricted ML estimator which is 2.00 for all θ. As θ_1 decreases below zero, the inequality pre-test risk rises to a maximum and declines to the value of the unrestricted ML estimator risk of 2.00. In θ-space, the level of the unweighted squared-error loss risk functions have smaller values than the weighted risk functions.

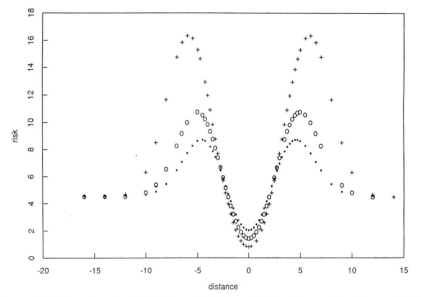

Figure 8. Risk functions for $H_0 : \beta \geq 0$ or $A\theta \geq 0$ along the line $\{\beta_2 = -\beta_1\}$ or $\{\theta_2 = -0.378\theta_1\}$ for α levels of 0.01, crosses; 0.05, circles; and 0.10, dots; and $\rho = 0.75$.

Table 4 shows the pre-test risks for our two hypotheses based on unweighted squared-error loss. The similarity of qualitative patterns in Tables 3 and 4 is quite apparent.

6. Summary and Conclusions

Within the context of the general linear inequality hypothesis for the linear statistical model in two dimensions, we have evaluated numerically the pre-test risk functions for design matrices with different correlation coefficients.

We demonstrated that the risk functions may be evaluated in the β-space using a bivariate normal distribution with a non-zero covariance and a squared-error loss function. The same results can be obtained in the θ-space using independent normal distributions and loss functions weighted by $P'P$.

In addition we presented the pre-test risk functions using squared-error loss functions in the θ-space. In all cases, we found that when the direction of the inequality null hypothesis is correct, the inequality-null pre-test risk is

Comparisons of Pre-test Risk Functions with Squared Error Loss with $\alpha = 0.05$

Line in β-space	Null hypothesis	ρ value	Risk value at -16	Maximum and (location)	$R^*(\delta_2(g),\theta)$ and (intersection)	Risk value	$R^*(\delta_1(g),\theta)$ and (intersection)	Maximum and (location)	$R^*(\delta_1(g),\theta)$ and (intersection)	Risk value at 16
$\beta_2 = 0$	$\beta \geq 0$	0.75	2.00	3.30 (-2.25)	2.84 (-1.59)	1.067	1.10 (0.81)	2.49	1.59 (4.00)	1.595
	$\beta = 0$	0.75	256			0.267				1.500
	$\beta \geq 0$	0.50	2.00	3.30 (-2.25)	3.08 (-1.75)	1.158	1.31 (1.14)	2.64	1.60 (4.00)	1.603
	$\beta = 0$	0.50	256			0.286				1.500
	$\beta \geq 0$	0.25	2.00	3.32 (-2.25)	3.13 (-1.75)	1.240	1.27 (0.79)	2.75	1.61 (4.25)	1.610
	$\beta = 0$	0.25	256			2.97				1.500
$\beta_2 = \beta_1$	$\beta \geq 0$	0.75	2.00	3.28 (-1.75)	3.21 (-1.58)	1.607	1.05 (0.58)	2.41 (1.75)	—	2.000
	$\beta = 0$	0.75	256			0.267				2.000
	$\beta \geq 0$	0.50	2.00	3.23 (-1.75)	2.42 (-1.02)	1.158	1.14 (0.65)	2.66 (1.75)	—	2.000
	$\beta = 0$	0.50	256			0.286				2.000
	$\beta \geq 0$	0.25	2.00	3.19 (-2.00)	3.00 (-1.79)	1.240	1.29 (0.88)	2.85 (2.00)	—	2.000
	$\beta = 0$	0.25	256			0.297				2.000
$\beta_2 = -\beta_1$	$\beta \geq 0$	0.75	2.00	3.77 (-5.00)	3.24 (-3.56)	1.067	3.24 (3.56)	3.77 (5.00)	—	2.000
	$\beta = 0$	0.75	58			0.267				58
	$\beta \geq 0$	0.50	2.00	3.76 (-3.75)	3.06 (-2.47)	1.158	3.06 (2.47)	3.76 (3.75)	—	2.000
	$\beta = 0$	0.50	97			0.286				97
	$\beta \geq 0$	0.25	2.00	3.71 (-3.25)	2.55 (-1.73)	1.240	2.55 (1.73)	3.71 (3.25)	—	2.000
	$\beta = 0$	0.25	121			0.297				121

always less than or equal to the risk for the unrestricted ML estimator. The inequality-null pre-test risk is less than that of the equality null pre-test risk except for a small region around $\theta = 0$.

Even when the direction of the inequality null hypothesis is incorrect, the inequality-null pre-test risk is self-correcting and converges to the unrestricted ML risk as the amount by which the inequality hypothesis is wrong increases. The point-null inequality pre-test estimator risk follows the restricted estimator risk and grows without limit when the direction of the inequality alternative hypothesis is incorrect.

An investigator, choosing to modify a model by testing hypotheses about the parameters, and re-estimating the model by using the same data used in the test, can see the consequences of such tests on the risk functions generated by different pre-test estimators, but the general pattern of the risk functions for either of our pre-test estimators is not altered appreciably by the weights we assigned to the loss function.

Although the effect of changes in the level of the test on the pre-test risk functions has been demonstrated, questions concerning optimum α-levels for a test are unanswered.

Extensions of the analysis to higher dimensions is straightforward but may be hampered by computer hardware capabilities. The θ-space analysis is much faster and more accurate than using β-space, and while minimizing brute force numerical integration procedures, it gives the same results. The insights provided by the weighted squared-error loss risk in the θ-space are highly instructive as to the gain and loss comparisons likely in β-space analysis. The variance unknown case leads to weighted F distributions rather than chi-square distributions for the tests, but adds nothing qualitatively to the results.

References

Bartholomew, D.J. (1959) "Test of homogeneity of ordered alternatives II," *Biometrika*, 46, 328–335.

Gourieroux, C., A. Holly, and A. Monfort (1982), "Likelihood ratio test, Wald test, and Kuhn-Tucker test in linear models with inequality constraints on the regression parameters," *Econometrica*, 50, 63–80.

Hillier, G.H. (1986), "Joint tests for zero restrictions on non-negative regression coefficients," *Biometrika*, 73, 657–669.

Judge, G.G., and M.E. Bock (1978), *The Statistical Implications of Pre-test and Stein-Rule Estimators in Econometrics*, North-Holland, Amsterdam.

Judge, G.G., T.A. Yancey and M.E. Bock (1983), "Pre-test estimations under squared error loss," *Economics Letters* 11, 347–352.

Judge, G.G., and T.A. Yancey (1986), *Improved Methods of Inference in Econometrics*, North-Holland, Amsterdam.

Judge, George, Robert Bohrer and Thomas Yancey (1988), "Some statistical implications of multivariate inequality constrained testing," University of Illinois, Mimeograph.

Kudo, A. (1963), "A multivariate analogue of the one-sided test," *Biometrika* 50, 403–418.

Milton, Roy C. (1972), "Computer evaluation of the multivariate normal integrals," *Technometrics*, 14, 881–889.

Osterhoff, J. (1969), *Combination of One-Sided Statistical Tests*, Amsterdam: Mathematical Centre Tracts, Mathematics Centrum.

Perlman, M.D. (1969), "One-sided problems in multivariate analysis," *Annals of Mathematical Statistics*, 40, 549–567.

Shapiro, A. (1988) "Towards a unified theory of inequality constrained testing in multivariate analysis," *International Statistical Review*, 56, 49–62.

Wolak, F.A. (1987), "Testing inequality constraints in linear econometric models," *Journal of the American Statistical Association*, 82, 782–793.

Yancey, T.A., G.G. Judge, and M.E. Bock (1981), "Testing multiple equality and inequality hypotheses in economics," *Economics Letters*, 7, 249–255.

Yancey, Thomas A., Robert Bohrer, and George G. Judge (1982), "Power function comparisons in inequality hypothesis testing," *Economics Letters*, 9, 161–167.

Yancey, T.A., G.G. Judge and Robert Bohrer (1989), "Sampling performance of some joint one-sided preliminary test estimators under squared error loss," *Econometrica*, 57, 1221–1228.

Readings in Econometric Theory and Practice
W. Griffiths, H. Lütkepohl and M.E. Bock (Editors)
© 1992 Elsevier Science Publishers B.V. All rights reserved

CHAPTER 3

THE EXACT DISTRIBUTION OF A SIMPLE PRE-TEST ESTIMATOR *

David E.A. Giles

Department of Economics, University of Canterbury, Christchurch, New Zealand

We consider the simple preliminary-test estimator that arises when two normal samples may be pooled in order to estimate the population variance. Depending on the outcome of a conventional F-test for variance homogeneity, the data are pooled or not. We derive and numerically evaluate the exact finite-sample distribution of this estimator. The exact p.d.f. is also evaluated, and the implications that pre-testing has for confidence interval construction are explored.

1. Motivation

There is a considerable body of literature relating to the statistical consequences of "preliminary-test estimation", or "inference based on conditional specification". Much of this literature is referenced by Bancroft and Han (1977), and (with special reference to econometric models) discussed by Judge and Bock (1978; 1983), among others.

This literature emphasises the consequences of two-step inference for the first two finite-sample moments of various point estimators. Little is known about the corresponding consequences for interval estimation or hypothesis testing, [1] and multi-stage pre-test estimation is virtually unexplored. [2] In the case of interval estimation, the available results relating to the implications of pre-test strategies are generally based on Monte Carlo experiments. Exact

---

* An earlier version of this paper was presented to the 1988 Australasian Meeting of the Econometric Society. I am grateful to Robert Davies for supplying FORTRAN code for his algorithm AS155 and to Judith Giles for several valuable discussions, and for preparing the figures. I would also like to thank Chien-Pai Han, Mary Ellen Bock, Chris Skeels, Murray Smith and participants in seminars at McMaster University, the University of Guelph and the University of Western Ontario for their helpful comments.
[1] However, see Bennett (1956), King and Giles (1984), Ohtani (1987a,b), Ohtani and Toyoda (1985), and Toyoda and Ohtani (1986).
[2] A recent exception is Ozcam and Judge (1988).

analytic results require knowledge of the full distribution function of the pre-test estimator of interest, and the literature is virtually silent on this matter. Bennett (1952) and Kitagawa (1963) discuss the distribution of a pre-test estimator of the mean under Normal sampling. Bennett (1956) considers the construction of confidence intervals for the mean and variance in a two-sample Normal problem, but does not derive the exact distribution of the pre-test variance estimator in this case. This distribution is discussed in this paper, and a simple derivation is offered which enables straightforward computations to be made. This pre-test estimator was the first to be discussed formally, by Bancroft (1944), and our analysis reveals some interesting features of the way in which pre-testing may affect interval, rather than point, estimation.

2. The Pre-test Problem

We consider the estimation of the scale parameter in a normal population with unknown mean, after a preliminary test of homogeneity of the variances of two independent samples drawn from such populations. This simple inference problem has wide application, such as in the context of linear regression.

Consider two simple random samples,

$$\{x_{ij}\}_{i=1}^{N_j} \sim N(\mu_j, \sigma_j^2); \quad j = 1, 2.$$

The usual unbiased estimator of σ_j^2 is

$$s_j^2 = \frac{1}{n_j} \sum_{i=1}^{N_j} (x_{ij} - \bar{x}_j)^2,$$

where

$$\bar{x}_j = \frac{1}{N_j} \sum_{i=1}^{N_j} x_{ij},$$

$$n_j = N_j - 1; \quad j = 1, 2.$$

Under our assumptions, $(n_j s_j^2)/\sigma_j^2 \sim \chi_{n_j}^2$, and these statistics are independent; $j = 1, 2$.

Now we wish to test the hypothesis

$$H_0 : \sigma_1^2 = \sigma_2^2 \text{ vs. } H_A : \sigma_1^2 > \sigma_1^2.$$

As is well known, the statistic (s_1^2/s_2^2) is F_{n_1, n_2} if H_0 is true. If H_0 is accepted there is an incentive to pool the samples and estimate σ_1^2 by

$$s^2 = \left(n_1 s_1^2 + n_2 s_2^2 \right) / \left(n_1 + n_2 \right).$$

This leads to the "sometimes-pool", or pre-test, estimator of σ_1^2, as suggested first by Bancroft (1944):

$$\hat{\sigma}_1^2 = \begin{cases} s_1^2; & \text{if } \left(s_1^2/s_2^2 \right) > \lambda \\ s^2; & \text{if } \left(s_1^2/s_2^2 \right) \leq \lambda \end{cases}$$

where $\lambda = \lambda(\alpha)$ is the critical F-value for a significance level of α. Bancroft determined the mean and variance of $\hat{\sigma}_1^2$; Giles (1991, 1992) extends these results to the case of more general distributional assumptions; and Toyoda and Wallace (1975), Ohtani and Toyoda (1978), and Bancroft and Han (1983) discuss the optimal choice of α under various criteria. [3]

The sampling properties of $\hat{\sigma}_1^2$ differ from those of the "never pool" estimator, s_1^2, and of the "always pool" estimator, s^2. In particular, $\hat{\sigma}_1^2$ is *biased* in finite samples. Confidence limits for $\hat{\sigma}_1^2$ are considered by Bennett (1956). Clearly, misleading inferences may be drawn if one constructs confidence intervals centred on $\hat{\sigma}_1^2$, but with limits chosen as if no pre-testing had occurred – a common enough situation. To examine the consequences of this the full distribution function of $\hat{\sigma}_1^2$ is required, a task to which we now turn.

3. The Exact Distribution Function

We require an expression for $\text{Pr.}(\hat{\sigma}_1^2 < a)$, for any real $a > 0$. Now,

$$\text{Pr.}\left(\hat{\sigma}_1^2 < a \right) = \text{Pr.}\left(s_2 < a \,|\, \left(s_1^2/s_2^2 \right) \leq \lambda \right) \text{Pr.}\left(\left(s_1^2/s_2^2 \right) \leq \lambda \right)$$

$$+ \text{Pr.}\left(s_1^2 < a \,|\, \left(s_1^2/s_2^2 \right) > \lambda \right) \text{Pr.}\left(\left(s_1^2/s_2^2 \right) > \lambda \right). \quad (1)$$

---

[3] Toyoda and Wallace formulate the problem with $H_A : \sigma_1^2 < \sigma_2^2$, as do Ohtani and Toyoda.

To simplify the notation, let $v_j = s_j^2$; $j = 1, 2$. By independence, the joint density of v_1 and v_2 is

$$f(v_1, v_2) = c v_1^{(n_1/2)-1} v_2^{(n_2/2)-1} \exp\left[-\frac{1}{2}\left(\frac{n_1 v_1}{\sigma_1^2} + \frac{n_2 v_2}{\sigma_2^2} \right) \right]$$

where

$$c = 2^{-(n_1+n_2)/2} \left[\Gamma\left(\frac{n_1}{2}\right) \Gamma\left(\frac{n_2}{2}\right) \right]^{-1} \left(\frac{n_1}{\sigma_1^2} \right)^{n_1/2} \left(\frac{n_2}{\sigma_2^2} \right)^{n_2/2}.$$

First, consider $\Pr.(s^2 < a \mid (s_1^2/s_2^2) \leq \lambda)$:

$$P_a = \Pr.\left[(n_1 v_1 + n_2 v_2)/(n_1 + n_2) < a \mid (v_1/v_2) \leq \lambda \right]$$

$$= \Pr.\left[(n_1 v_1 + n_2 v_2) < a^* \mid (v_1/v_2) \leq \lambda \right],$$

where $a^* = a(n_1 + n_2)$.

Now, change variables:

$$u_1 = (n_1 v_1 + n_2 v_2)$$

$$u_2 = (v_1/v_2).$$

So,

$$P_a = \Pr.(u_1 < a^* \text{ and } u_2 \leq \lambda)/\Pr. (u_2 \leq \lambda)$$

$$= \frac{c}{\Pr.(u_2 \leq \lambda)} \int_0^{a^*} \int_0^{\lambda} u_1^{(n_1+n_2)/2-1} u_2^{1/2 n_1 - 1} (n_1 u_2 + n_2)^{-(n_1+n_2)/2}$$

$$\times \exp\left[-\frac{1}{2}\left(\frac{u_1}{n_1 u_2 + n_2} \right)\left(\frac{n_1 u_2}{\sigma_1^2} + \frac{n_2}{\sigma_2^2} \right) \right] \, du_2 \, du_1. \tag{2}$$

Secondly, consider $\Pr.(s_1^2 < a \mid (s_1^2/s_2^2) > \lambda)$:

$$P_b = \Pr.(v_1 < a \mid (v_1/v_2) > \lambda).$$

Now, change variables:

$$v_1 = v_1'$$

$$y = (v_2/v_1).$$

So,

$$P_b = \Pr.\left(v_1 < a \quad \text{and} \quad y \le \frac{1}{\lambda}\right) \Big/ \Pr.\left(y \le \frac{1}{\lambda}\right)$$

$$= \frac{c}{\Pr.\left(y \le \dfrac{1}{\lambda}\right)} \int_0^a \int_0^{1/\lambda} y^{n_2/2-1} v_1^{(n_1+n_2)/2-1}$$

$$\times \exp\left[-\frac{v_1}{2}\left(\frac{n_1}{\sigma_1^2} + \frac{n_2 y}{\sigma_2^2}\right)\right] \, dy \, dv_1. \tag{3}$$

Equations (2) and (3) are reached by the approach used by Bancroft (1944) in his evaluation [4] of $E(\hat{\sigma}_1^2)$. The next task is to evaluate (2) and (3). This is achieved by using a Mellin Transform (e.g. Oberhettinger (1970)) to integrate analytically with respect to u in (2), and v_1 in (3). Details are given in the Appendix. Applying Appendix equation (A7), the expression in (2) simplifies to:

$$P_a = \frac{c_1^*}{\Pr.(u_2 \le \lambda)} \int_0^\lambda u_2^{n_1/2-1} (n_1 u_2 + n_2)^{-(n_1+n_2)/2}$$

$$\times {}_1F_1\left[\left(\frac{n_1+n_2}{2}\right), \left(\frac{n_1+n_2+2}{2}\right); \frac{-a^*}{2(n_1 u_2+n_2)}\left(\frac{n_1 u_2}{\sigma_1^2} + \frac{n_2}{\sigma_2^2}\right)\right] du_2 \tag{4}$$

[4] Of course, in Bancroft's case improper integrals replace those with respect to u_1 in (2) and v_1 in (3).

and that in (3) simplifies to:

$$P_b = \frac{c_1}{\mathrm{Pr.}\left(y \le \dfrac{1}{\lambda}\right)} \int_0^{1/\lambda} y^{(n_2/2)-1}$$

$$\times {}_1F_1\left[\left(\frac{n_1+n_2}{2}\right), \left(\frac{n_1+n_2+2}{2}\right); -\frac{a}{2}\left(\frac{n_1}{\sigma_1^2} + \frac{n_2 y}{\sigma_2^2}\right)\right] dy \qquad (5)$$

where:

$$c_1^* = 2c(a^*)^{(n_1+n_2)/2}/(n_1+n_2)$$

$$c_1 = 2ca^{(n_1+n_2)/2}/(n_1+n_2).$$

Substituting (4) and (5) in (1) we obtain the following expression for the c.d.f. of $\hat{\sigma}_1^2$

$$\mathrm{Pr.}\left(\hat{\sigma}_1^2 < a\right) = c_1 \int_0^{1/\lambda} y^{(n_2/2)-1}$$

$$\times {}_1F_1\left[\left(\frac{n_1+n_2}{2}\right), \left(\frac{n_1+n_2+2}{2}\right); -\frac{a}{2}\left(\frac{n_1}{\sigma_1^2} + \frac{n_2 y}{\sigma_2^2}\right)\right] dy$$

$$+ c_1^* \int_0^\lambda u^{(n_1/2)-1}(n_1 u + n_2)^{-(n_1+n_2)/2}$$

$$\times {}_1F_1\left[\left(\frac{n_1+n_2}{2}\right), \left(\frac{n_1+n_2+2}{2}\right);\right.$$

$$\left. -\frac{a^*}{2(n_1 u + n_2)} \cdot \left(\frac{n_1 u}{\sigma_1^2} + \frac{n_2}{\sigma_2^2}\right)\right] du. \qquad (6)$$

As expected, this expression is a function of n_1, n_2, σ_1^2, and $\lambda(\alpha)$, *but it does not depend on the sample values.* It is also a function of the nuisance parameter, σ_2^2.

4. Numerical Results

One might consider simplifying (6) further, to eliminate the integrals involved. One possibility is to use the Kummer relationship, which enables each of the two terms in (6) to be expressed as double infinite weighted sums of chi-square probabilities. When $n_1 + n_2$ is even, another possibility is to exploit the simpler form of the confluent hypergeometric function given by Bock et al. (1984). [5] However, in each case it is unclear that anything is gained by such manipulations. The resulting expressions are complicated and require numerical evaluation if they are to be interpreted. The important thing is to have an expression which is computationally easy to evaluate accurately.

The form of the c.d.f. in (6) meets this requirement already, as the univariate definite integrals are easily handled numerically. For our evaluations of (6) we used the algorithms for Simpson's rule and the gamma function given by Press et al. (1986). Note that as the Kummer functions in (6) depend on the variables of integration, repeated evaluation of these functions is necessary within the integration algorithm.

The algorithm used to evaluate the Kummer functions is a generalization of that suggested for the incomplete gamma function by Press et al. In particular, the series representation, (A6), is used if $\lambda < \frac{1}{2}(n_1 + n_2)$ in (4) or if [6] $\lambda > 2/(n_1 + n_2)$ in (5). Otherwise the continued fraction representation, (A8), is used to ensure rapid convergence.

To illustrate the c.d.f. of $\hat{\sigma}_1^2$, (6) has been evaluated in this way for $\alpha = 0.01, 0.05$ and for all combinations of degrees of freedom over the range n_i [4(4)20]; $i = 1, 2$. In each case $\phi = (\sigma_2^2/\sigma_1^2)$ was varied over the range (0.0, 1.0] with $\sigma_1^2 = 1$. A selection of these results is shown in Figures 1–3. In each case the exact distributions of both s_1^2 and s^2 are also plotted for comparison. These two distributions were evaluated using the algorithm for the distribution of linear combinations of chi-square random variables, developed by Davies (1980). The applicability of this algorithm is seen by noting that [7]

$$\text{Pr.}\left(s_1^2 < a\right) = \text{Pr.}\left(\chi_{(n_1)} < n_1 a \sigma_1^2\right)$$

[5] These possibilities were suggested to me by Murray Smith and Mary Ellen Bock respectively. Chris Skeels offered some similar suggestions.
[6] These ranges correspond to $t < (a + 1)$ in the notation of the Appendix, and are chosen in accordance with the suggestion by Press et al. (1986; p. 161).
[7] Clearly, the distribution of s_1^2 is independent of σ_2^2 and holds under H_0 and H_A; while that of s^2 depends on ϕ, and hence on the extent to which the null hypothesis is false.

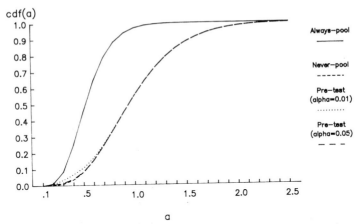

Figure 1. Cumulative Distribution Functions ($n_1 = 12$, $n_2 = 12$, $\phi = 0.1$).

and,

$$\Pr.(s^2 < a) = \Pr.\left(\sigma_1^2\chi_{(n_1)}^2 + \sigma_2^2\chi_{(n_2)}^2 < a(n_1 + n_2)\right).$$

The corresponding density functions appear in Figures 4–6. These were obtained by numerically differentiating the c.d.f.'s by the method of central

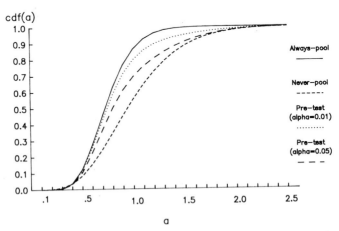

Figure 2. Cumulative Distribution Functions ($n_1 = 12$, $n_2 = 12$, $\phi = 0.5$).

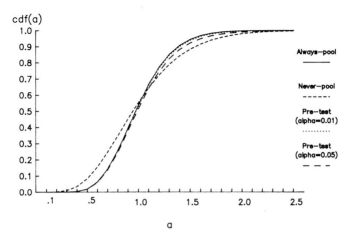

Figure 3. Cumulative Distribution Functions ($n_1 = 12$, $n_2 = 12$, $\phi = 1.0$).

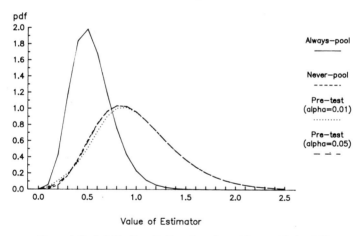

Figure 4. Probability Density Functions ($n_1 = 12$, $n_2 = 12$, $\phi = 0.1$).

differences. The first two moments of each estimator, in each case, are reported in Table 1. In the case of $\hat{\sigma}_1^2$, the relevant formulae are given by [8] Bancroft (1944); those for s_1^2 and s^2 follow immediately from the properties of the chi-square distribution.

---

[8] Bancroft's formula for the variance of $\hat{\sigma}_1^2$, and that given by Bancroft and Han (1983), each contain different typographical errors.

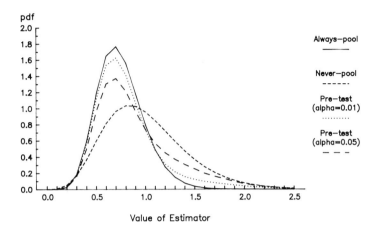

Figure 5. Probability Density Functions ($n_1 = 12$, $n_2 = 12$, $\phi = 0.5$).

The results illustrate the following characteristics of this problem. First, the pre-test estimator has a uni-modal density which reflects the underlying mixture of chi-square variates. The never-pool estimator is, of course, independent of ϕ while the always-pool estimator is a function of the hypothesis error. As $\phi \to 1$ (H_0 is true), the negative bias in s^2 vanishes and its precision exceeds that of s_1^2. In this same situation, the distribution of the pre-test estimator moves close to that of s^2. The extent to which it differs

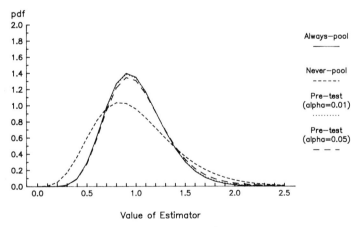

Figure 6. Probability Density Functions ($n_1 = 12$, $n_2 = 12$, $\phi = 1.0$).

Table 1

Moments of Alternative Estimators
$(\sigma_1^2 = 1.0, n_1 = 12, n_2 = 12)$

ϕ	$E(s^2)$	$E(s_1^2)$	$E(\hat{\sigma}_1^2)$	
			$(\alpha = 0.01)$	$(\alpha = 0.05)$
0.1	0.550	1.000	0.988	0.999
0.5	0.750	1.000	0.816	0.901
1.0	1.000	1.000	1.007	1.028
ϕ	$\text{var}(s^2)$	$\text{var}(s_1^2)$	$\text{var}(\hat{\sigma}_1^2)$	
			$(\alpha = 0.01)$	$(\alpha = 0.05)$
0.1	0.042	0.167	0.183	0.169
0.5	0.052	0.167	0.117	0.130
1.0	0.083	0.167	0.089	0.104

depends, of course, on the size of the pre-test, and therefore on the extent to which the never-pool estimator is (inefficiently) incorporated. On the other hand, as $\phi \to 0$, $\hat{\sigma}_1^2 \to s_1^2$ (regardless of the value of α), and this is reflected in the distributions.

In summary, the results shown here in terms of the full distribution of the pre-test estimator provide useful support for the well known results relating to the risk functions of this estimator and its two component parts.

5. Implications for Confidence Intervals

The value in determining the full distribution of $\hat{\sigma}_1^2$ goes further than the results of the previous section. Given this information, we can now directly determine the extent to which pre-testing affects the true confidence level associated with any confidence intervals which may be constructed for σ_1^2. A somewhat related discussion of such confidence intervals is given by Bennett (1956), but no evaluations of the type given below are made.

Recall that $\hat{\sigma}_1^2$ amounts to the use of either s_1^2 or s^2 as the point estimator of $\hat{\sigma}_1^2$, depending on whether H_0 is rejected or accepted. In the former case, a 95% (say) confidence interval for σ_1^2 would be constructed using limits based on the (wrong) assumption that the distribution of the estimator is just that of s_1^2:

$$\frac{n_1\hat{\sigma}_1^2}{\chi_u^2(n_1)} < \sigma_1^2 < \frac{n_1\hat{\sigma}_1^2}{\chi_L^2(n_1)}, \tag{7}$$

where:

$$\text{Pr.}\left(\chi^2(n_1) < \chi_u^2(n_1)\right) = 0.975$$

$$\text{Pr.}\left(\chi^2(n_1) < \chi_L^2(n_1)\right) = 0.025.$$

In the latter case, the corresponding confidence interval for σ_1^2 would be constructed using limits based on the (wrong) assumption that the distribution of the estimator is just that of s^2:

$$\frac{(n_1 + n_2)\hat{\sigma}_1^2}{\chi_u^2(n_1 + n_2)} < \sigma_1^2 < \frac{(n_1 + n_2)\hat{\sigma}_1^2}{\chi_L^2(n_1 + n_2)}, \tag{8}$$

where:

$$\text{Pr.}\left(\chi^2(n_1 + n_2) < \chi_u^2(n_1 + n_2)\right) = 0.975$$

$$\text{Pr.}\left(\chi^2(n_1 + n_2) < \chi_L^2(n_1 + n_2)\right) = 0.025.$$

Clearly, given that the distribution of $\hat{\sigma}_1^2$ differs from those of either s_1^2 or s^2, the probability contents of the intervals (7) and (8) will differ from the nominal 95% which has been set. It appears that this point has not been previously discussed and there are no related quantitative results. Also, it is clear that when assessing the extent to which the true confidence level departs from the nominal level, two comparisons are necessary (unless $\phi = 1$) because the distribution of s^2 departs from the assumed $\chi^2(n_1 + n_2)$ if H_0 is false. [9] So, in Figures 7–9, a comparison is first made between s_1^2 and $\hat{\sigma}_1^2$, where the interval for the latter is determined by (7); and then between s^2 and $\hat{\sigma}_1^2$, where the interval for the pre-test estimator is now determined by (8).

In Figure 7, the size of the pre-test is 5%; in Figure 8, $\lambda = 1$ ($\alpha = 0.4726$), the "optimal" choice suggested by Toyoda and Wallace (1975); and in Figure 9 $\alpha = 0.37$, the "optimal" choice suggested by Bancroft and Han (1983) for this choice of degrees of freedom. (The degrees of freedom used in Figures 7 and 8 match those in Toyoda and Wallace's illustration.)

[9] This means, of course, that the nominal confidence level for any interval based on s^2 is valid only if H_0 is true.

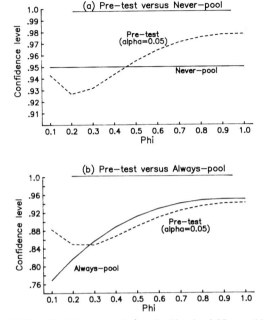

Figure 7. True Confidence Levels (nominal level = 0.95; $n_1 = 16$, $n_2 = 8$).

All three figures show that as $\phi \to 0$ the probability content of interval (7) converges to the nominal confidence level. Of course, as $\phi \to 1$ the probability content of interval (8) differs from this nominal level increasingly, the larger is α. In all three figures we see that as long as the null hypothesis is not "too false", confidence intervals based on pre-testing have *higher* probability content than that based on the never-pool estimator. In this same situation, confidence intervals based on pre-testing have *lower* probability content than that based on the always-pool estimator. Depending on the size of the pre-test, quite substantial discrepancies can arise.

Conversely, if the null hypothesis is "very false", although confidence intervals based on pre-testing have probability content below the nominally stated level, their true confidence level is markedly *greater* than the *true* confidence level of the always-pool estimator. These results are all intuitively plausible.

Three additional interesting results deserve mention. First, in Figure 7 with $\alpha = 0.05$, there is no situation in which the pre-test confidence interval has higher probability content than those of *both* the never-pool and always-

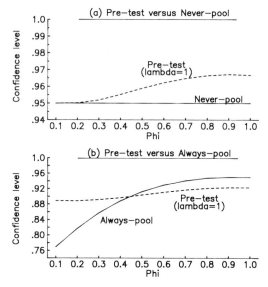

Figure 8. True Confidence Levels (nominal level = 0.95; $n_1 = 16$, $n_2 = 8$).

pool intervals. Secondly, in Figures 8 and 9 the confidence level for the interval based on pre-testing is never less than that for the never-pool confidence interval. Thirdly, there is a range of ϕ values in both Figures 8 and 9 where the confidence level of intervals based on pre-testing exceeds the confidence levels of intervals based on *both* the never-pool and always-pool estimators.

The special interest of these last three results is that they are analogous to the results of Toyoda and Wallace (1975), Ohtani and Toyoda (1978), and Bancroft and Han (1983), where their discussion is in terms of the point estimation of σ_1^2, and the associated risk functions. In short, their suggestions regarding the optimal choice of the size of the pre-test appear to be equally relevant in the context of *interval estimation as well as point estimation*.

6. Conclusions

In this paper the exact distribution function of a simple pre-test estimator has been determined and evaluated, and from this the corresponding density function has been obtained. A limited number of situations has been considered, so the numerical results given here should be interpreted as being

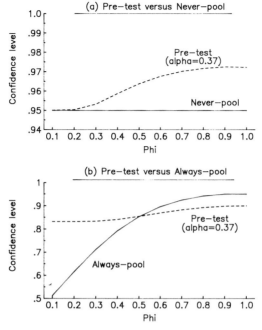

Figure 9. True Confidence Levels (nominal level = 0.95; $n_1 = 12$, $n_2 = 12$).

merely illustrative. Work in progress evaluates these distributions in a wider range of situations.

The distributional results enable us to examine the extent to which pre-testing affects the properties of interval estimates, rather than just point estimates. Again, the numerical results reported are purely illustrative.

One especially interesting aspect of the results is, however, that their qualitative features are precisely analogous to those of the existing results for pre-test point estimation, even as far as the matter of optimal pre-test size is concerned. This point is currently being explored further by the author, both in the context of the problem discussed here, and in relation to other simple pre-test estimators.

Appendix

The Incomplete Gamma Function, defined as

$$\gamma(a; t) = \int_0^t x^{a-1} e^{-x} \, dx,$$

has several equivalent representations:

$$\gamma(a;t) = t^a \sum_{j=0}^{\infty} \frac{(-t)^j}{j!(a+j)} \tag{A1}$$

$$= t^a e^{-t} \sum_{j=0}^{\infty} \frac{\Gamma(a)t^j}{\Gamma(a+j+1)} \tag{A2}$$

$$= (t^a/a)_1F_1(a, a+1; -t); \quad \mathrm{Re}(a) > 0 \tag{A3}$$

where:

$$_1F_1(d, c; z) = \frac{\Gamma(c)}{\Gamma(d)} \sum_{n=0}^{\infty} \frac{\Gamma(d+n)}{\Gamma(c+n)} \left(\frac{z^n}{n!} \right)$$

which is a Kummer-type Confluent Hypergeometric Function. (See Oberhettinger (1970; pp. 265–268).) In addition, $\gamma(a; t)$ can be expressed in terms of Whittaker Functions, or in terms of continued fractions:

$$\gamma(a;t) = \Gamma(a) - e^{-t}t^a \left(\frac{1}{t+} \frac{1-a}{1+} \frac{1}{t+} \frac{2-a}{1+} \frac{2}{t+} \cdots \right) \tag{A4}$$

for $t > 0$.

Computationally, the advantages of these different representations depend on the relative magnitudes of the arguments of γ. (See Press et al. 1986; pp. 160–163).)

Now, the relevant Mellin Transform used to simplify (2) and (3) is a generalisation of $\gamma(a; t)$. Define

$$I(a, b; t) = \int_0^t x^{a-1} e^{-bx} \, dx,$$

which may be written as:

$$I(a, b; t) = t^a \sum_{j=0}^{\infty} \frac{(-bt)^j}{j!(a+j)} \tag{A5}$$

$$= t^a e^{-bt} \sum_{j=0}^{\infty} \frac{\Gamma(a)(bt)^j}{\Gamma(a+j+1)} \tag{A6}$$

$$= (t^a/a)_1F_1(a, a + 1; -bt) \tag{A7}$$

$$= \Gamma(a) - e^{-bt}t^a\left(\frac{1}{bt+} \frac{1-a}{1+} \frac{1}{bt+} \frac{2-a}{1+} \frac{2}{bt+} \cdots \right) \tag{A8}$$

The expressions in (A5–A8) are easily derived from (A1) to (A4) by an appropriate change of variable. Again, the computational merits of the different forms of $I(a, b; t)$ depend on the relative magnitudes of the arguments.

References

Bancroft, T.A. (1944), "On Biases in Estimation Due to the Use of Preliminary Tests of Significance", *Annals of Mathematical Statistics*, 15, 190–204.

Bancroft, T.A. and C-P. Han (1977), "Inference Based on Conditional Specification: A Note and Bibliography", *International Statistical Review*, 45, 117–127.

Bancroft, T.A. and C-P. Han (1983), "A Note on Pooling Variances", *Journal of the American Statistical Association*, 78, 981–983.

Bennett, B.M. (1952), "Estimation of Means on the Basis of Preliminary Tests of Significance", *Annals of the Institute of Statistical Mathematics*, 4, 31–43.

Bennett, B.M. (1956), "On the Use of Preliminary Tests in Certain Statistical Procedures", *Annals of the Institute of Statistical Mathematics*, 8, 45–52.

Davies, R.B. (1980), "The Distribution of a Linear Combination of χ^2 Random Variables (Algorithm AS 155)", *Applied Statistics*, 29, 323–333.

Giles, J.A. (1991), "Estimation of the Scale Parameter after a Pre-Test for Homogeneity in a Mis-specified Regression Model", Discussion Paper No. 9116, Department of Economics, University of Canterbury.

Giles, J.A. (1992), "Estimation of the Error Variance after a Preliminary Test of Homogeneity in a Regression Model with Spherically Symmetric Disturbances", *Journal of Econometrics*, forthcoming.

Judge, G.G. and M.E. Bock (1978), *The Statistical Implications of Pre-Test and Stein-Rule Estimators in Econometrics*, Amsterdam: North-Holland.

Judge, G.G. and M.E. Bock (1983), "Biased Estimation", in Z. Griliches and M.D. Intriligator (eds.), *Handbook of Econometrics*, Amsterdam: North Holland, 599–649.

King, M.L. and D.E.A. Giles (1984), "Autocorrelation Pre-Testing in the Linear Model: Estimation, Testing and Prediction", *Journal of Econometrics*, 25, 35–48.

Kitagawa, T. (1963), "Estimation After Preliminary Test of Significance", *University of California Publications in Statistics*, 3, 147–186.

Oberhettinger, F. (1970), *Tables of Mellin Transforms*, Berlin: Springer-Verlag.

Ohtani, K. (1987a), "On Pooling Disturbance Variances When the Goal is Testing Restrictions on Regression Coefficients", *Journal of Econometrics*, 35, 219–231.

Ohtani, K. (1987b), "Some Sampling Properties of the Two-Stage Test in a Linear Regression With a Proxy Variable", *Communications in Statistics (A)*, 16, 717–729.

Ohtani, K. and T. Toyoda (1978), "Minimax Regret Critical Values for a Preliminary Test in Pooling Variances", *Journal of the Japan Statistical Society*, 8, 15–20.

Ohtani, K. and T. Toyoda (1985), "Testing Linear Hypothesis on Regression Coefficients After a Pre-Test for Disturbance Variance", *Economics Letters*, 17, 111–114.

Ozcam, A. and G.G. Judge (1988), "The Analytical Risk of a Two Stage Pretest Estimator in the Case of Possible Heteroscedasticity", mimeo.

Press, W.H., B.P. Flannery, S.A. Teukolsky and W.T. Vetterling (1986), *Numerical Recipes*, Cambridge: Cambridge University Press.

Toyoda, T. and K. Ohtani (1986), "Testing Equality Between Sets of Coefficients After a Preliminary Test for Equality of Disturbance Variances in Two Linear Regressions", *Journal of Econometrics*, 31, 67–80.

Toyoda, T. and T.D. Wallace (1975), "Estimation of Variance After a Preliminary Test of Homogeneity and Optimal Levels of Significance for the Pre-Test", *Journal of Econometrics*, 3, 395–404.

II. BAYESIAN ECONOMETRICS

Readings in Econometric Theory and Practice
W. Griffiths, H. Lütkepohl and M.E. Bock (Editors)

CHAPTER 4

BAYESIAN ANALYSIS IN ECONOMETRICS *

Arnold Zellner

Graduate School of Business, University of Chicago, Chicago, IL 60637, USA

After briefly reviewing some aspects of the history of Bayesian Analysis in Econometrics, five basic propositions regarding econometrics are put forward and discussed. Challenges relating to these propositions are issued. Then Bayesian estimation, prediction, control and decision procedures are discussed and a number of canonical econometric problems are described and analyzed to illustrate the power of the Bayesian approach in econometrics and other areas of science.

1. Introduction

Since the early 1960s there has been a considerable growth in the volume of Bayesian econometric research. This research has been focussed on the development and application of Bayesian methods to solve econometric problems. These include general problems of science, namely, describing, understanding and modeling economic phenomena, testing hypotheses suggested by economic theory, using econometric models and methods for prediction and policy analysis, and solving a variety of practical economic and business decision problems. Before the early 1960s, almost all econometricians employed non-Bayesian methods in their work in spite of the fact that Edgeworth, an eminent economist and statistician, and Jeffreys, a leading natural scientist, had produced many useful and important Bayesian methods by building on the earlier work of Laplace and others see, e.g., Bowley (1928), Stigler (1978), Jeffreys (1967/1st ed. 1939 and 1973/1st ed. 1931), Geisser (1980), Good (1980), and Lindley (1980). It appears that the works of

* Research financed in part by the National Science Foundation and in part by the H.G.B. Alexander Endowment Fund, Graduate School of Business, University of Chicago. This paper was originally presented at the Conference on Foundations of Statistical Inference: Applications in Medicine, Social Sciences and Engineering, held in Tel Aviv, Israel in 1985, and was subsequently published in *Journal of Econometrics*, Vol. 37, 1988, pp. 27–50. Reproduced with permission.

Savage (1954), Friedman and Savage (1948, 1952), Raiffa and Schlaifer (1961) and a rediscovery of Jeffreys's work stimulated several econometricians, including Albert Ando, Jacques Drècze, Walter Fisher, Tom Rothenberg, Arnold Zellner, and several others to commence research on Bayesian econometrics in the early 1960s. In Zellner (1984) further information is provided about these Bayesian researchers and their publications.

During the 1960s, Bayesian econometric research progressed rapidly and in 1970 the first meeting of the NBER-NSF Seminar on Bayesian Economet-rics was held at the University of Chicago that brought together leading Bayesian econometricians and statisticians. Since 1970, semi-annual meetings of the Seminar have been important in fostering much research in Bayesian econometric and statistics, some of which has been published in Fienberg and Zellner (1975), Zellner (1980) and Goel and Zellner (1986). Also, since the mid-1960s a number of other Bayesian works have been published including Lindley (1965, 1971), DeGroot (1970), Lempers (1971), Morales (1971), Zellner (1971a), Press (1972), Box and Tiao (1973), Aykac and Brumat (1977), Leamer (1978), Bernardo et al. (1980, 1985), Berger (1980), Drèze and Richard (1983), Bauwens (1984), Kadane (1984), Boyer and Kihlstrom (1984), and Broemeling (1985). In addition, current and recent general econometrics textbooks include varying amounts of Bayesian material – see, e.g., Judge et al. (1985), Malinvaud (1980), Maddala (1978), Intriligator (1978), and Theil (1971). These works attest to the remarkable progress that has been made in Bayesian statistics and econometrics. It is accurate to state that the Bayesian approach to inference has had a significant impact on econometrics and that its influence is growing rapidly. Zellner (1984, 1985a) provides additional references to theoretical and applied Bayesian econometric studies.

Since this Conference is concerned with issues in the foundations of statistical inference and their impact on applied statistical work in economet-rics and other fields, I shall review some elements of the foundations of Bayesian inference that I have found to be particularly important in econo-metric applications. Further, some comparisons of particular Bayesian and non-Bayesian solutions to specific estimation, prediction, control and other problems will be provided, in part an extension of the considerations pre-sented in Rothenberg (1975) and Zellner (1975). Finally, I shall state some general propositions that I believe are of key importance for applied work in econometrics and other sciences and issue some challenges relating to them.

2. Foundational Issues and Applied Econometrics

In considering alternative systems of inference for use in econometrics and other sciences, researchers have devoted considerable attention to issues in the philosophy of science. While I shall not attempt to review this vast literature, I shall present some general propositions that I believe have great relevance for applied econometric work. Many references will be made to Jeffreys's work because as Good (1980, p. 32) has written:

"In summary, Jeffreys's pioneering work on neo-Bayesian methods, at a time when such methods were very unpopular, was stimulated by his interest in philosophy, mathematics, and physics, and has had a large permanent influence on statistical logic and techniques. In my review (Good (1962b)) I said that Jeffreys's book on probability "is of greater importance for the philosophy of science, and obviously of greater immediate practical importance, than nearly all the books on probability written by professional philosophers *lumped together.*"

Thus, I and many others believe that there is much to be learned about foundational matters in Jeffreys's work that Jaynes (1983, 1984) regards as a direct continuation and extension of Laplace's work on Bayesian philosophy, inference and applications. Note that Laplace, Jeffreys and Jaynes have their roots in the physical sciences which have been on the whole very successful. It is quite probable that foundational propositions that these Bayesian regard as central are worth considering seriously by econometricians, other social scientists and statisticians. Some of these propositions will be stated and briefly discussed below. To sharpen the discussion and to provoke further considerations, the propositions will be followed by specific challenges.

Proposition 1. The Unity of Science Principle (USP) is valid.

Karl Pearson (1938), Jeffreys (1967) and many others subscribe to the USP that Pearson (1938, p. 16) states as follows: "The unity of science consists alone in its method, not in its material... It is not the facts themselves which form science, but the methods by which they are dealt with." Also, Jeffreys (1967, p. 7) remarks: "No matter what the subject-matter, the fundamental principles of the method must be the same. There must be a uniform standard of validity for all hypotheses, irrespective of the subject. Different laws may hold in different subjects, but they must be tested by the same criteria: otherwise we have no guarantee that our decisions will be those warranted by the data and not merely the result of inadequate analysis or of believing what we want to believe."

Thus the USP implies that the same inductive methods are to be employed in making inferences in the natural, biological, and social sciences and in experimental and non-experimental sciences. That is, the principles of estimation, testing, prediction, etc. that are employed in learning from data in different areas of science should be the same according to the USP.

Challenge I. Demonstrate that fundamentally different inference principles for learning from data, that is fundamentally different principles of testing, estimation, prediction, etc. are required and are fruitful in different areas of science, say in the social sciences as contrasted with the physical and biological sciences.

A second proposition to which many physical scientists, statisticians and some econometricians subscribe is the belief that sophisticatedly simple hypotheses or models will probably work well in explaining facts and in prediction. This belief in the efficacy of sophisticatedly simple hypotheses and models is sometimes supported by an appeal to Ockham's Razor, the Principle of Parsimony or the Jeffreys-Wrinch Simplicity Postulate. Jeffreys (1967, p. 47) explains the Simplicity Postulate as follows:

> "Precise statement of the prior probabilities of the laws in accordance with the condition of convergence requires that they should actually be put in an order of decreasing prior probability. But this corresponds to actual scientific procedure. A physicist would test first whether the whole variation is random as against the existence of a linear trend; then a linear law against a quadratic one, then proceeding in order of increasing complexity. All we have to say is that the simpler laws have the greater prior probabilities. This is what Wrinch and I called the simplicity postulate."

As Jeffreys (1973, pp. 38–39) further explains, scientists cannot consider all possible models at once because they are all not known. What is done is to adopt a simple model that fits the data within a range of error. As new observations are obtained, the model is modified, usually implying greater complexity. However, sometimes this is not the case because a new simple conceptualization is put forward that explains the past data and makes good predictions. Einstein's general theory and quantum theory are cited as examples. With respect to these new theories or laws, Jeffreys (1973, p. 39) writes: "...the very fact that the new laws were simpler than the old ones was widely and influentially claimed to be a reason for accepting them. This amounts to saying that in the absence of observational evidence, the simpler law is the more probable...."

In view of the above considerations, the following proposition is put forward.

Proposition 2. The Jeffreys-Wrinch Simplicity Postulate (SP) is a very useful working principle in econometrics and other sciences.

Many natural scientists and statisticians will probably regard Proposition 2 to be "obvious". For example, Jaynes (1985, p. 334) writes: "We keep our model as simple as possible so as not to obscure the point to be made; and also to heed Arnold Zellner's wise advice about 'sophisticatedly simple' models." Also, some leading quantitative economists, including the Nobel Prize winners Jan Tinbergen, Ragnar Frisch, Milton Friedman, Kenneth Arrow, George Stigler, James Tobin, and Theodore Schultz all appear to appreciate the value of sophisticated simplicity in their work. The same can be said for many leading statisticians including George Box, Morris DeGroot, Seymour Geisser, Bruce Hill, George Tiao, and others. However, there are a number of econometricians and economists who believe strongly that complicated models and methods are required and will work better in explaining and predicting economic phenomena than sophisticatedly simple models. Since I have not found this to be the case in my own econometric work on methods and applications, I have issued the following challenge on many occasions:

Challenge II. Demonstrate that a very complicated model in any area of science has performed well in promoting understanding of past data and in predicting as yet unobserved data.

With respect to very complicated macroeconometric models containing hundreds of non-linear stochastic difference equations and thousands of parameters, the eminent econometrician Christ (1975, p. 59) has written: "...they [the models] disagree so strongly about the effects of important monetary and fiscal policies that they cannot be considered reliable guides to such policy effects, until it can be determined which of them are wrong in this respect and which (if any) are right." Also Litterman (1980, 1985) and McNees (1985) have compared the forecasting performance of several of these large, complicated macroeconometric models and concluded that it is not superior to that of a relatively simple Bayesian vector autoregressive model developed by Litterman (1980, 1985). It is the author's view that a prior preference for complicated methods and models, not only in macroeconomics but also in other areas, has significantly impeded the progress of econometrics and possibly of other social sciences.

A third proposition which most scientists support is the Prediction Principle (PP), namely that prediction is central in science. Indeed, in a review of

philosophical concepts of causality Feigl (1953, p. 408) summarizes philosophers' views by defining causality as predictability according to a law or set of
laws. In Zellner (1984), this concept of causality is compared with others and
it is concluded that there is no need for a special definition of causality in
econometrics in accord with the USP. Further Jeffreys (1967, p. 8) defines
induction as follows: "...part [of our knowledge] consists of making inferences from past experience to predict future experience. This part may be
called generalization or induction." Thus prediction is central in science as
explained above and leads to the following proposition:

*Proposition 3. The Prediction Principle (PP) that predictive performance is
central in evaluating hypotheses and models is of key importance in econometrics and other sciences.*

While the content of Proposition 3 has been emphasized by many, particularly by Friedman (1953) in economics and by Geisser (1980) in statistics, it is
a fact that many econometricians and other social scientists apparently are
not aware of its importance or are openly opposed to it. As Geisser might put
it, they are overly concerned with unobservables, e.g., estimating parameters,
and thus neglect and/or fail to appreciate the all important role of prediction. Further, some of those who work with very complicated models find it
difficult or perhaps unwise to implement predictive testing of their models.
For these and others who do not stress the importance of prediction, the
following challenge is put forward:

*Challenge III. Demonstrate that a principle other than the Prediction Principle
has been effective in producing sound results in econometrics and other sciences.*

Above in the statement of the Jeffreys-Wrinch Simplicity Postulate, probabilities were associated with hypotheses and models and such probabilities
are not "objective" or "frequency-based". Bayesian interpret such probabilities as measures of degrees of belief. Jeffreys (1967, p. 15) views a numerical
probability as measuring "the degree of confidence that we may reasonably
have in a proposition, even though we may not be able to give either a
deductive proof or disproof of it." Savage (1962, p. 163) writes: "Personal
probability is a certain kind of numerical measure of the opinions of some-
body about something." These are subjective concepts of probability that
Bayesians find most useful in applied work. On the other hand, many
econometricians and other workers claim that they use "objective" or
"frequency" concepts of probability in their work, a claim that Jeffreys (1967,

p. 369) disputes in the following words: "In practice no statistician ever uses a frequency definition, but... all use the notion of degree of reasonable belief, usually without even noticing that they are using it and that by using it they are contradicting the principles they have laid down at the outset."

With respect to the classical or axiomatic, the Venn limiting frequency and the Fisher hypothetical infinite population definitions of probability, Jeffreys (1967, ch. 7) provides devastating critiques of these definitions that have been unanswered, perhaps because as some have remarked, they are unanswerable.

In view of the above consideration, I put forward the following proposition:

Proposition 4. A subjective concept of probability is more useful in research and applied work in econometrics and other sciences than are other concepts of probability.

Challenges related to Proposition 4 are:

Challenge IV.a. Demonstrate that Jeffreys's criticisms of axiomatic, limiting frequency, and hypothetical infinite population concepts of probability are invalid.

Challenge IV.b. Demonstrate that subjective probability concepts are not widely used in econometric and other applied areas of research by non-Bayesians.

In connection with Challenge IV.b, the following remarks of several leading non-Bayesians are illuminating. Tukey (1978, p. 52) writes:

> "It is my impression that rather generally, not just in econometrics, it is considered decent to use judgment in choosing a functional form, but indecent to use judgment in choosing a coefficient. If judgment about important things is quite all right, why should it not be used for less important ones as well? Perhaps the real purpose of Bayesian techniques is to let us do the indecent thing while modestly concealed behind a formal apparatus. If so, this would not be a precedent. When Fisher introduced the formalities of the analysis of variance in the early 1920's, its most important function was to conceal the fact that the data was being adjusted for block means, an important step forward which if openly visible would have been considered by too many wiseacres of the

time to be 'cooking the data'. If so, let us hope that day will soon come when the role of decent concealment can be freely admitted. ...The coefficient may be better estimated from one source or another, or, even best, estimated by economic judgment...

It seems to me a breach of the statistician's trust not to use judgment when that appears to be enough better than using data."

Freedman (1986, p. 127) expresses his views as follows:

"When drawing inferences from data, even the most hardbitten objectivist usually has to introduce assumptions and use prior information. The serious question is how to integrate that information into the inferential process and how to test the assumptions underlying the analysis."

Also, Lehmann (1959, p. 62) writes:

"Another consideration that frequently enters into the specification of a significance level is the attitude toward the hypothesis before the experiment is performed. If one firmly believes the hypothesis to be true, extremely convincing evidence will be required before one is willing to give up this belief, and the significance level will accordingly be set very low."

These quotations reveal that leading non-Bayesians use non-frequency, subjective, judgmental information in making inferences in so-called "objective" or "frequency-based" approaches.

Finally, Bayesians who use Bayes's Theorem as a learning model in their work find it extremely useful. Cox (1961), Jaynes (1974, 1983, 1984) and others have provided fundamental analysis rationalizing Bayes's Theorem as a coherent model of inductive reasoning. In Boyer and Kihlstrom (1984), many uses of Bayes's Theorem as a learning model in mathematical economics are described. In estimation, testing, prediction, control, design, and other applied problems, the Bayesian learning model has been found to be very useful. This range of considerations leads to the following proposition:

Proposition 5. The learning model embedded in Bayes's Theorem is very useful in econometrics and other sciences.

Associated with Proposition 5 is the following challenge:

Challenge V. Demonstrate that some other learning model is more general and useful than the Bayesian learning model in econometrics and other areas of science.

These then are some basic propositions and challenges that I put forward to relate to foundational issues that appear to me to be of fundamental importance in applied econometrics. In my own applied econometric work, I have found it fruitful to abide by the USP. In the applied projects on which I have worked, I have found that the best solutions have involved simple formulations in accord with the SP. "Reality" may appear to be complex, but this seems to me to be no more than saying that understanding is lacking. Appropriate, sophisticatedly simple concepts and formulations have been found valuable in accord with the SP. Similarly, the PP has played a vital role in appraising alternative formulations and models. Finally, in many applied studies, use of subjective probabilities and Bayes's Theorem has been very useful. Since it would take too long to describe these specific studies in great detail, in the next section I shall just describe selected "canonical" statistical problems that arise in applied econometrics, provide Bayesian solutions and challenge non-Bayesians to provide better solutions.

3. Specific Problems and Bayesian Solutions

In this section, Bayesian solutions to some statistical problems that arise in applied econometrics will be reviewed. Before presenting these problems and solutions, it is relevant to point out that most non-Bayesian inference results in econometrics can be produced by Bayesian methods under special assumptions. For example, with a large sample assumption, posterior means that are optimal point estimates relative to a quadratic loss function in general are approximately equal to maximum likelihood estimates that are widely used by econometricians and others. Also, many non-Bayesian estimates such as seemingly unrelated regression coefficient estimates, two- and three-stage least squares coefficient estimates for linear structural econometric models, Cochrane-Orcutt regression coefficient estimates that take account of auto-correlated errors, etc., have been shown to be means of conditional posterior pdfs based on diffuse prior pdfs, that is conditional posterior pdfs in which "nuisance" parameters are set equal to sample estimates [see Zellner (1971a) for analyses illustrating these points]. Also sampling theory likelihood ratio test statistics have been related to posterior odds calculated using particular prior distributions – see, e.g., Jeffreys (1967), Leamer (1978), Schwarz (1978), Bernardo (1980), Zellner and Siow (1980), Klein and Brown (1984), and Zellner (1984). Also, many non-Bayesian point predictions can be produced by Bayesian methods. Thus, it is accurate to state that the Bayesian approach encompasses non-Bayesian approaches in the sense that it can produce many important non-Bayesian results as well as other useful results that are difficult to obtain by non-Bayesian methods. The problems and Bayesian solutions to them, presented below, will illustrate this latter point. This situation appears to parallel that in statistics which Jaynes (1984, p. 44) described as follows:

"Indeed, the variety of [Bayesian] applications demonstrated by Jeffreys [1967] included all those for which 'Student', Fisher, Neyman and Pearson had developed 'orthodox' methods."

3.1. Selected point estimation problems
Here we shall present Bayesian solutions to some point estimation problems that arise in applied econometrics. For all of these problems, complete posterior distributions are available. However, since point estimation is emphasized, probably over-emphasized, in the econometric literature, Bayesian solutions to various central point estimation problems will be presented.
It is well known that when quadratic loss functions are appropriate, means of posterior pdfs are optimal, when zero-one loss functions are appropriate, posterior modal values are optimal and when absolute error loss functions are appropriate, posterior medians are optimal. These are very general useful results that relate to a wide range of point estimation problems encountered in applied econometrics. In what follows, general results like these for other types of loss functions and basic point estimation problems are presented.

Problem 1: Estimation of reciprocals of parameters

Let the parameter of interest be $\theta = 1/\beta$ and assume that a posterior pdf for β is available that possesses a finite second moment. This posterior distribution may be based on a diffuse or informative prior distribution for β. Further, assume that a relative squared error loss function is appropriate, that is

$$L = (\theta - d)^2/\theta^2 = (1 - d\beta)^2, \tag{1}$$

where d is an estimate of θ. Using the posterior pdf for β, posterior expected loss is $EL = 1 - 2dE\beta + d^2E\beta^2$ and the optimal point estimate, d^*, is given by

$$d^* = \frac{E\beta}{E\beta^2} = \frac{1}{E\beta} \cdot \frac{1}{1 + \mathrm{var}(\beta)/(E\beta)^2}, \tag{2}$$

where $E\beta$ and var (β) are the posterior mean and variance of β, respectively. The simple result in (2) can be applied to all kinds of "reciprocal estimation" problems, including estimation of reciprocals of population means, regression coefficients, variances, standard deviations, population proportions, etc. To illustrate in the case of the reciprocal of a population mean, assume that the posterior pdf for β is Student-t with mean $\bar{y}$, a sample mean and variance, $\bar{s}^2/n$, where

$$\bar{s}^2 = \sum_{i=1}^{n} (y_i - \bar{y})^2/(n - 3),$$

as would be the case for a normal problem with n iid observations analyzed with a diffuse prior, $p(\beta, \sigma) \propto 1/\sigma$. Then the optimal point estimate is $d^* = (1/\bar{y})[1/(1 + \bar{s}^2/n\bar{y}^2)]$. See Zellner (1978), where it is proved that this estimator is admissible and where other prior assumptions are considered as is also done in Zaman (1981a). Note that the maximum likelihood estimator for θ, $\hat{\theta} = 1/\bar{y}$, does not possess any moments and thus has unbounded risk relative to the loss function in (1). The simplicity, generality and flexibility of the result, d^*, in (2) are noteworthy and it appears difficult, if not impossible, to produce as useful a result in any other system of inference.

Problem 2: Estimation of ratios of parameters

Suppose that the parameter of interest is $\theta = \beta_1/\beta_2$ and that a posterior pdf for β_1 and β_2 is available that possesses finite second moments. Let the loss function be a generalized quadratic loss function.

$$L = \beta_2^2(\theta - d)^2 = (\beta_1 - d\beta_2)^2, \tag{3}$$

where d is an estimate of θ. From the second line of (3), posterior expected loss is $EL = E\beta_1^2 - 2dE\beta_1\beta_2 + d^2E\beta_2^2$ and thus the optimal value of d, d^*, is

$$d^* = \frac{E\beta_1\beta_2}{E\beta_2^2} = \frac{E\beta_1}{E\beta_2}\left(\frac{1 + \mathrm{cov}(\beta_1, \beta_2)/E\beta_1E\beta_2}{1 + \mathrm{var}(\beta_2)/(E\beta_2)^2}\right), \tag{4}$$

where $\text{cov}(\beta_1, \beta_2)$ and $\text{var}(\beta_2)$ denote the posterior covariance of β_1 and β_2 and variance of β_2, respectively. See Zellner (1978), Zellner and Park (1979) and Zellner and Rossi (1984) for applications of (4) to problems of estimating ratios of population means, ratios of regression coefficients, ratios of variances, and lethal dosage rates in bioassay models (or qualitative dichotomous response models as they are called in the econometric literature). Also, (4) is relevant for point estimation in the calibration problem. Maximum likelihood estimators for many of these problems, e.g., $\hat{\theta} = \bar{y}_1/\bar{y}_2$ for the ratio of two normal populations' means, where $\bar{y}_1$ and $\bar{y}_2$ are sample means, do not possess finite moments and hence are inadmissible, whereas it has been established that Bayesian estimators for this problem have finite risk relative to the loss function in (3) and a number of others. Further, it should be appreciated that informative prior pdfs for β_1 and β_2, for example a prior pdf limiting the range of β_2 to 0 to ∞, can be utilized in computing d^* in (4). Thus a wide range of ratio estimation problems relative to the loss function in (3), or generalizations of it, e.g., $L = g(\beta_2^2)(\theta - d)^2$, where $g(\beta_2^2) \propto \beta_2^{2m}$, $m \geq 1$, can be readily solved by Bayesian methods. In addition, the complete posterior pdf of $\theta = \beta_1/\beta_2$ is available.

Problem 3: Estimation of Stein's n-means

Let y be an $n \times 1$ vector of observations assumed generated by $y = \xi + \epsilon$, where ξ is an $n \times 1$ vector of means and ϵ is an $n \times 1$ vector of errors drawn from a population with a zero mean. Assume that a posterior pdf for ξ is available and that the appropriate loss function is

$$L = (\xi - d)'(\xi - d)/(\xi'\xi)^m, \tag{5}$$

where d is an estimate of ξ and $m \geq 1$. Then posterior expected loss is given by $EL = E(\xi'\xi)^{1-m} - 2d'E\xi(\xi'\xi)^{-m} + d'dE(\xi'\xi)^{-m}$ and the optimal point estimate, d^*, is

$$d^* = E\xi(\xi'\xi)^{-m}/E(\xi'\xi)^{-m}, \tag{6}$$

provided, of course, that the relevant moments exist. This is a very general solution to the Stein problem since many different models for the error vector ϵ and many different prior pdfs for ξ can be employed – see Zellner and Vandaele (1975) for such results for a simple case. If the integrals in (6) cannot be evaluated analytically, it will be possible in many cases to evaluate them numerically. A Monte Carlo simulation approach would involve making independent draws from the posterior pdf for ξ and using them to evaluate averages of the quantities in the numerator and denominator of (6). In the context of Friedman's (1957) economic theory, for individual i, y_i is the measured income, ξ_i is "permanent income", ϵ_i is "transitory income", and (6) provides estimates of individuals' permanent incomes.

Problem 4: Estimation of structural parameters

The first problem considered is the estimation of a structural coefficient in an errors in the variables problem. Let y and x be two $n \times 1$ vectors of measurements generated by $y = \eta + u$ and $x = \xi + v$, where η and ξ are mean vectors and u and v are zero mean error vectors. Assume that posterior distributions for η and ξ are available, that interest centers on the structural coefficient β in $\eta = \xi\beta$, and that the appropriate loss function is the following generalized quadratic loss function:

$$L = (\beta - d)^2 \xi'\xi = (\eta - \xi d)'(\eta - \xi d), \tag{7}$$

where d is an estimate of β. Taking the posterior expectation of the loss function yields $EL = E\eta'\eta - 2dE\xi'\eta + d^2E\xi'\xi$ and thus the optimal value of d, d^* is

$$d^* = \frac{E\xi'\eta}{E\xi'\xi} = \frac{\bar{\xi}'\bar{\eta}}{\bar{\xi}'\bar{\xi}}\left[\frac{1 + E(\xi - \bar{\xi})'(\eta - \bar{\eta})/\bar{\xi}'\bar{\eta}}{1 + E(\xi - \bar{\xi})'(\xi - \bar{\xi})/\bar{\xi}'\bar{\xi}}\right], \tag{8}$$

where $\bar{\xi}$ and $\bar{\eta}$ are the posterior means of ξ and η, respectively. Thus given the generalized quadratic loss function in (7) and a posterior pdf for η and ξ, d^* in (8) can be readily computed as can also the posterior pdf for $\beta = \xi'\eta/\xi'\xi$, either analytically or by a Monte Carlo simulation approach. Note that this analysis applies to many possible likelihood functions, including those based on normality and a variety of possible prior distributions.

The second problem involving structural parameters is a structural econometric modeling problem in which we have a reduced form system (or multivariate regression model),

$$\left(\underset{n \times 1}{y} : \underset{n \times m}{Y}\right) = \underset{n \times k}{X}\left(\underset{k \times 1}{\pi} : \underset{k \times m}{\Pi}\right) + \left(\underset{n \times 1}{v} : \underset{n \times m}{V}\right), \tag{9}$$

subject to the restrictions

$$X\pi = X\Pi\gamma + X_1\beta = Z\delta, \tag{10}$$

where $\delta' = (\gamma' \vdots \beta')$ is a vector of structural coefficients, X_1 is an $n \times k_1$ submatrix of X, that is $X = (X_1 \vdots X_0)$, and $Z = (X\Pi \vdots X_1)$. In (10), we assume that the matrix Z is of full column rank. The problem is to estimate δ given the data $(y_1 \vdots Y_1)$, X and a posterior distribution for $(\pi \vdots \Pi)$ that possesses finite second moments. Assume that the following generalized quadratic loss function is appropriate:

$$L = (\delta - d)'Z'Z(\delta - d) = (X\pi - Zd)'(X\pi - Zd), \qquad (11)$$

where d is an estimate of δ and in going from the first right-hand side to the second $Z\delta = X\pi$ has been employed. From the second right-hand side of (11), posterior expected loss is $EL = E\pi'X'X\pi - 2d'EZ'X\pi + d'EZ'Zd$ and thus the optimal value of d is

$$d^* = (EZ'Z)^{-1}EZ'X\pi. \qquad (12)$$

The point estimate d^* in (12) is in a simple form depending on just second posterior moments of $(\pi \vdots \Pi)$. If, for example, the rows of $(v \vdots V)$ in (9) have been independently drawn from a zero mean multivariate normal distribution with positive definite symmetric covariance matrix Ω and if the standard diffuse prior pdf for $(\pi \vdots \Pi)$ and Ω is employed, then it is well known that the marginal posterior pdf for the regression coefficients is a matrix Student-t posterior pdf. Using the second-order moments for this pdf, d^* was evaluated in Zellner (1978) and found to be in the form of a "K-class estimate", with a value of K less than one in finite samples. Thus a form of a particular ad hoc non-Bayesian estimate is a special case of (12) – see Zellner and Park (1979) for computed examples involving the use of d^* in (12) and computation of its approximate risk. In Park (1982), Monte Carlo experiments were performed to evaluate this estimator that has been shown analytically to possess at least finite second-order sampling moments under general conditions in contrast to several other estimators, including the ML estimator that do not possess finite moments either in general or in important specific cases and are thus inadmissible relative to many loss functions, including that shown in (11). Also note that the optimal estimate in (12) can be computed using normal and non-normal likelihood functions, diffuse and informative prior pdfs and for "undersized" samples – see Swamy (1980) and Swamy and Mehta (1983).

Third, the loss function in (11) can be elaborated to take account of goodness-of-fit considerations as follows:

$$L = (X\pi - Zd)'(X\pi - Zd) + g(y - Zd)'(y - Zd), \qquad (13)$$

where g is a non-negative, given constant. The first term on the right-hand side of (13) reflects how well the restrictions in (10) are satisfied, while the second term reflects how well the model fits. On taking the posterior expectation of the loss function in (13) and minimizing it with respect to d, the resulting optimal value for d is

$$d^+ = (d^* + gd_1^*)/(1 + g), \tag{14}$$

where d^* is given in (12) and $d_1^* = (EZ'Z)^{-1}EZ'y$ is the quantity minimizing the posterior expectation of $(y - Zd)'(y - Zd)$. Thus the optimal estimate in (14) is an average of d^* in (12) and d_1^*. When d^+ was evaluated using the matrix Student-t posterior distribution for $(\pi : \Pi)$, mentioned above, it was found that d^+ assumed the form of a "double-K-class estimate", another ad hoc non-Bayesian estimate – see Zellner (1985d) for details. Also, in this last reference, d^+ was explicitly derived employing an informative natural conjugate prior distribution. Van Dijk and Kloek (1980) compute complete posterior distributions for structural coefficients using Monte Carlo numerical integration techniques.

Problem 5: Estimation using an asymmetric loss function

Let θ be a parameter to be estimated and d an estimate and assume that the following asymmetric LINEX loss function, due to Varian (1975), is appropriate:

$$L = b\left[e^{a(d-\theta)} - a(d - \theta) - 1\right], \quad b > 0, \quad a \neq 0. \tag{15}$$

Given that we have a posterior pdf for θ, posterior expected loss is $EL = b[e^{ad}Ee^{-a\theta} - a(d - E\theta) - 1]$ and the value of d that minimizes EL is, from Zellner (1985b),

$$d^* = (-1/a) \log(Ee^{-a\theta}). \tag{16}$$

In (16), note that $Ee^{-a\theta}$ is the moment generating function for the posterior pdf for θ. In the special case in which θ has a normal posterior pdf with mean $\bar{y}$, a sample mean, and variance σ^2/n with σ^2 assumed known,

$$d^* = \bar{y} - a\sigma^2/2n. \tag{17}$$

With $\bar{y}$ normally distributed with mean θ and variance σ^2/n, the risk of d^*

in (17) relative to the loss function in (15) is uniformly lower than the risk of $\bar{y}$, as shown in Zellner (1985b), and thus the sample mean $\bar{y}$ is inadmissible relative to a LINEX loss function. The general solution in (16) can be applied to a number of problems. Also, an extended form of the LINEX loss function involving a vector of parameters has been formulated and used in Zellner (1985b). The ability to analyze problems conveniently with asymmetric loss functions is important since symmetric loss functions are not always appropriate – see Varian (1975) for an applied study using the asymmetric LINEX loss function.

3.2. Some prediction problems

As mentioned above, prediction is central in science and thus it is fortunate that operational Bayesian prediction procedures are available. These utilize predictive pdfs that are defined as follows:

$$p(y \mid D) = \int_{\Theta} f(y \mid \theta) \pi(\theta \mid D) \, d\theta, \tag{18}$$

where $f(y \mid \theta)$ is the pdf for the as yet unobserved vector of observations, y, θ is a vector of parameters contained in the parameter space Θ and $\pi(\theta \mid D)$ is the posterior pdf with D denoting past sample and prior information. Thus (18) yields the complete pdf for the as yet unobserved observations, y. If a point prediction is desired relative to a specific convex predictive loss function, $L(y, \hat{y})$, where $\hat{y}$ is a point prediction, an optimal value for $\hat{y}$ can be obtained, as is well known, by solving the following minimization problem:

$$\min_{\hat{y}} \int L(y, \hat{y}) p(y \mid D) \, dy. \tag{19}$$

The solution to this minimization problem, say $\hat{y}^*$, is the optimal Bayesian point prediction. If $L(y, \hat{y}) = (y - \hat{y})'Q(y - \hat{y})$ with Q a given positive definite symmetric matrix, the optimal value of $\hat{y}$ is the mean of the predictive pdf. For absolute loss functions, $L = |y - \hat{y}|$, the median of the predictive pdf for y is optimal while for zero-one loss functions the modal value is optimal. With diffuse prior pdfs for parameters, some Bayesian point predictions are the same as certain non-Bayesian point predictions. However, this will not be true when informative prior pdfs are employed and in other circumstances. See Litterman (1980, 1985) for use of predictive pdfs in forecasting macroeconomic variables and Monahan (1983) for their use in connection with Box-Jenkins ARMA time series models. Monahan's computed predictive pdfs are noteworthy in that they reflect restrictions on the parameter space associated with stationarity and invertibility assumptions as well as other information regarding parameters' probable values. Aitchison and Dunsmore (1975) also present a number of valuable Bayesian prediction procedures. In what follows several point prediction problems will be solved using Bayesian methods that appear difficult to solve using non-Bayesian techniques.

Problem 6: Prediction using asymmetric loss functions

Let y be a future value of a variable with a given predictive pdf and assume that the following class of asymmetric LINEX loss functions is appropriate:

$$L = b\left[e^{a(\hat{y}-y)} - a(\hat{y}-y) - 1\right], \quad b > 0, \quad a \neq 0, \tag{20}$$

where $\hat{y}$ is some point prediction. Using the predictive pdf for y to compute expected loss and minimizing it with respect to $\hat{y}$ yields the following optimal point prediction – see Zellner (1985b):

$$\hat{y}^* = (-1/a) \log Ee^{-ay}, \tag{21}$$

a general solution applicable to a range of different problems. For example, if y has a normal predictive pdf with mean m and variance v, $\hat{y}^* = m - av/2$, a result used by Varian (1975) in a regression study with informative prior pdfs to predict house prices from observed house characteristics for purposes of tax assessment. Over-assessment is often more costly than under-assessment and thus the asymmetric loss function in (20) with particular values of $a > 0$ and $b > 0$ was deemed more appropriate than a symmetric loss function. It appears difficult to obtain a result like (21) in a non-Bayesian approach.

Problem 7: Prediction using relative squared error loss

This prediction problem involves predicting y when $z = \log y$ has a normal predictive pdf with mean m and variance v and the following relative squared error loss function is employed:

$$L = (y - \hat{y})^2/y^2 = (1 - \hat{y}/y)^2, \tag{22}$$

where $\hat{y}$ is a point prediction. The expectation of this loss function is $EL = 1 - 2\hat{y}E(1/y) + \hat{y}^2 E(1/y^2)$ and the optimal value of $\hat{y}$ is

$$\hat{y}^* = E(1/y)/E(1/y^2) = e^{m - 3v/2}, \tag{23}$$

since $E(1/y) = Ee^{-z} = e^{-m+v/2}$ and $E(1/y^2) = Ee^{-2z} = e^{-2m+2v}$. The simple result in (23) can be computed readily for predictive pdfs based on diffuse or informative prior pdfs and is very useful when logarithmic transformations and relative squared error loss functions are employed. Note that $\hat{y}^*$ differs from the mean of the log-normal predictive pdf for y, namely $Ey = Ee^z = e^{m+v/2}$ that is optimal for a squared error loss function and the posterior median of y, e^m, that is optimal for an absolute error loss function, results that are well known and very useful when these loss functions are appropriate. See Zellner (1971b, 1985c) for further consideration of these problems.

3.3. Control and decision problems

Bayesian methods are particularly useful in solving many control and decision problems that arise in econometrics because they permit incorporation of both sample and judgmental prior information and yield good solutions that are difficult to obtain by non-Bayesian methods – see, e.g., Bawa, Brown and Klein (1979), Fisher (1962), Bowman and Laporte (1975), Harkema (1975), Wright (1983), Zellner and Geisel (1968), and Zellner (1971a, ch. 11; 1973). Below a few problems are analyzed that illustrate the power of the Bayesian approach in this area.

Problem 8: Controlling regression processes

Let $y = x\beta + u$ be a simple regression model for the as yet unobserved dependent variable y with x a variable under control, β a regression coefficient with unknown value and u an unobserved random error with zero mean and variance σ^2. Assume that a posterior pdf for β and σ^2 is available based on past data and prior information. Of course if no past data are available, as is the case in some important control and decision problems, the pdf for β and σ^2 would be a prior pdf. Assume further that the problem is to choose a value for x so as to keep y close to a given target value, denoted by a, and that the following squared error loss function is appropriate:

$$L = (y - a)^2 = (x\beta - a + u)^2. \tag{24}$$

With β and u assumed independent, expected loss is given by $EL = E[x(\beta - b) + xb - a + u]^2$, or

$$EL = x^2 E(\beta - b)^2 + (xb - a)^2 + \sigma_p^2, \tag{25}$$

where b and σ_p^2 are the posterior means of β and σ^2, respectively. On minimizing EL with respect to x, the optimal setting for x, x^*, is

$$x^* = \frac{a}{b}\left[\frac{1}{1 + \mathrm{var}(\beta)/b^2}\right], \tag{26}$$

with $\mathrm{var}(\beta) = E(\beta - b)^2$, the posterior variance of β. Note that uncertainty about the value of β, as measured by $\mathrm{var}(\beta)$, has an impact on the value of x^* in contrast to the sub-optimal certainty-equivalence solution, $x^{ce} = a/b$ in which no such dependence is present. x^{ce} minimizes just the second term on the right-hand side of (25) but fails to take account of the first term that involves x and hence is sub-optimal – see Zellner (1971a, ch. 11), Harkema (1975) and Prescott (1975) for further analysis of the sub-optimality of the certainty-equivalence "solution" that was widely used in econometrics. Further, it is direct to solve the above one-period control problem with the loss function elaborated to take account of costs of changing the control variable, that is $L = (y - a)^2 + c(x - x_0)^2$ with $c > 0$ and x_0 the given initial value of x. See Zellner (1973) for the effects of using mistaken values for a and c in solving this problem, an aspect of robustness with respect to errors in formulating loss functions.

Above only one control variable was considered. If $y = x'\beta + u$ is the regression model generating y, where x is a $k \times 1$ vector of control variables, β is a $k \times 1$ vector of regression coefficients with unknown values and u is a zero mean error term with variance σ^2, then, with a given posterior distribution for β and σ^2 and the quadratic loss function in (24), an optimal value of the vector x can be obtained by minimizing

$$EL = E\left[x'(\beta - b) + x'b - a + u\right]^2 = x'Vx + (x'b - a)^2 + \sigma_p^2, \tag{27}$$

where b and $V = E(\beta - b)(\beta - b)'$ are the posterior mean and covariance matrix for β, respectively. The value of x that minimizes EL in (27) is

$$x^* = (V + bb')^{-1}ba = \left[\frac{1}{1 + b'V^{-1}b}\right]V^{-1}ba, \tag{28}$$

using $(V + bb')^{-1} = V^{-1} - V^{-1}bb'V^{-1}/(1 + b'V^{-1}b)$. x^* can be readily computed for a variety of regression assumptions and prior pdfs. Further, when x^* is substituted in (27), the result is

$$E(L \mid x = x^*) = a^2/(1 + b'V^{-1}b) + \sigma_p^2, \tag{29}$$

a rather simple expression that can be employed to compute average or Bayes risk. If Bayes risk is finite, as it usually is when proper prior pdfs are employed, then the decision $x = x^*$ minimizes Bayes risk and is admissible. See Stein and Zaman (1980) and Zaman (1981b) for admissibility considerations when a diffuse, improper prior, $p(\beta) \propto$ const. is employed with σ^2 known and a normal regression likelihood function. For this problem they find x^* is admissible when it contains four or fewer elements but not for five or more. However, they do not consider at all the use of proper prior pdfs that most practitioners would use and that lead to admissible solutions. Also, with a compact sample space, it is possible that "diffuse prior" solutions may be conditionally admissible in the sense of Villegas (1980, p. 54).

Problem 9: Portfolio selections

Portfolio selection problems are central in both theoretical and applied economics and econometrics. Earlier attempts to solve portfolio selection problems were plagued by the appearance of parameters with unknown values in "solutions". In Zellner and Chetty (1965), it was indicated how Bayesian methods can be employed to overcome this problem and since then Bayesian methods have been used in the work of Brown (1976, 1978), Bawa, Brown and Klein (1979), Jorion (1983, 1985), and others.

In a simple one-period portfolio problem the investor allocates his initial wealth, W_0, among n assets, the ith of which has a random, unknown return per dollar invested, y_i. The amount to be invested in the ith asset is w_i with $\sum_{i=1}^{n} w_i = W_0$. Subject to this constraint, the investor must choose the w_i's values so as to maximize expected utility. Let the $n \times 1$ vector of future returns, y, be generated by

$$y = \theta + u, \tag{30}$$

where θ is an $n \times 1$ mean vector with unknown value and u is a zero mean error vector with an $n \times n$ positive definite symmetric covariance matrix Σ. Assume that a posterior pdf for θ and Σ is available. Further, for any selection of the w_i's, the return on the portfolio is $R = w'y$, where $w' = (w_1,$

$w_2, \ldots, w_n$). The utility of R, the random return is given by a utility function, $U(R)$. The problem then is to maximize $EU(R)$ with respect to w subject to $i'w = W_0$, where the $1 \times n$ vector $i' = (1, 1, \ldots, 1)$ has all elements equal to one. If we use a quadratic utility function

$$U(R) = c_1 R - c_2 R^2, \quad c_1, c_2 > 0, \tag{31}$$

since $R = w'y = w'\theta + w'u$, (31) can be expressed as $U = c_1(w'\theta + w'u) - c_2(w'\theta + w'u)^2$ and expected utility, EU, can be evaluated using the posterior pdf for θ and Σ and minimized with respect to w subject to $w'i = W_0$ to yield the optimal value of w, say w^*, that depends just on the past data and prior information underlying the posterior pdf for θ and Σ. Since the solution is direct, it is left as an exercise for the reader.

In the literature, portfolio problems have been solved using normal and Student-t data processes, diffuse and informative priors and various utility functions. In Brown (1976, 1978) and Jorion (1983, 1985) such Bayesian solutions have been compared with certainty-equivalence solutions with the general finding that Bayesian solutions are better. Also Jorion (1983, 1985) finds that prior assumptions underlying a Bayes-Stein approach to the analysis of the means problem in (30) usually produce better results than use of a diffuse prior pdf for θ and Σ.

Finally, in solving these decision and control problems, we have expressed loss or utility in terms of the parameters of the problems and used parameters' posterior pdfs to compute posterior expectations. As is well known, these problems can also be solved using predictive pdfs for as yet unobserved variables, e.g., the vector y in (30) – see Zellner (1971, ch. 11) for examples.

4. Summary and Concluding Remarks

In section 2 several key propositions were put forward that have important implications for the inductive process in econometrics and for foundational considerations in statistics. The present writer finds them compelling and urges others to consider them carefully. In essence, they lead to emphasis on the fruitfulness of the unity of methods in science, sophisticatedly simple models and methods, the predictive criterion, subjective probability and the Bayesian learning model in making inferences and decisions. Then, in section 3, several problems were described and solved using Bayesian methods rather readily even though most of the problems are difficult to solve satisfactorily using non-Bayesian approaches. In the way of an overall conclusion, it is suggested that more wide-spread adherence to the propositions described in section 2 and further use of Bayesian methods will do much to promote more rapid progress in econometrics and other sciences.

References

Aitchison, J. and I.R. Dunsmore, 1975, Statistical prediction analysis (Cambridge University Press, Cambridge)

Aykac, A. and C. Brumat, eds., 1977, New developments in the applications of Bayesian methods (North-Holland, Amsterdam).

Bauwens, L., 1984, Bayesian full information analysis of simultaneous equation models using integration by Monte Carlo (Springer-Verlag, Berlin).

Bawa, V.S., S.J. Brown and R.W. Klein, 1979, Estimation risk and optimal portfolio choice (North-Holland, Amsterdam).

Berger, J.O., 1980, Statistical decision theory (Springer-Verlag, Berlin); 2nd ed. in 1985.

Bernardo, J.M., 1980, A Bayesian analysis of classical hypothesis testing, in: J.M. Bernardo et al., eds., Bayesian statistics: Proceedings of the first international meeting held in Valencia (Spain), May 28 to June 2, 1979 (University Press, Valencia, Spain) 605–618.

Bernardo, J.M., M.H. DeGroot, D.V. Lindley and A.F.M. Smith, eds., 1980, Bayesian statistics: Proceedings of the first international meeting held in Valencia (Spain), May 28 to June 2, 1979 (University Press, Valencia, Spain).

Bowley, A.L., 1928, F.Y. Edgeworth's contributions to mathematical statistics (Royal Statistical Society, London): reprinted in 1972 (Augustus M. Kelley Publishers, Clifton, NJ).

Bowman, H.W. and A.M. Laporte, 1975, Stochastic optimization in recursive equation systems with random parameters with an application to control of the money supply, in: S.E. Fienberg and A. Zellner, eds., Studies in Bayesian econometrics and statistics in honor of Leonard J. Savage (North-Holland, Amsterdam) 441–462.

Box, G.E.P. and G.C. Tiao, 1973, Bayesian inference in statistical analysis (Addison-Wesley, Reading, MA).

Boyer, M. and R.E. Kihlstrom, eds., 1984, Bayesian models in economic theory (North-Holland, Amsterdam).

Broemeling, L.D., 1985, Bayesian analysis of linear models (Marcel Dekker, New York).

Brown, S.J., 1976, Optimal choice under uncertainty, Unpublished doctoral dissertation (Graduate School of Business, University of Chicago, Chicago, IL).

Brown, S.J., 1978, The portfolio choice problem: Comparison of certainty equivalence and optimal Bayes portfolios, Communications in Statistics B, 321–334.

Christ, C.F., 1975, Judging the performance of econometric models of the U.S. Economy, International Economic Review 16, 54–74.

Cox, R.T., 1961, The algebra of probable inference (Johns Hopkins University Press, Baltimore, MD).

DeGroot, M.H., 1970, Optimal statistical decision (McGraw-Hill, New York).

Drèze, J.H. and J.F. Richard, 1983, Bayesian analysis of simultaneous equation systems, in: Z. Griliches and M.D. Intriligator, eds., Handbook of Econometrics, Vol. 1 (North-Holland, Amsterdam) 517–598.

Feigl, H., 1953, Notes on casuality, in: H. Feigl and M. Brodbeck, eds., Readings in the Philosophy of Science (Appelton-Century-Crofts, New York) 408–418.

Fienberg, S.E. and A. Zellner, eds., 1975, Studies in Bayesian econometrics and statistics in honor of Leonard J. Savage (North Holland-Amsterdam).

Fisher, W.D., 1962, Estimation in the linear decision model, International Economic Review 3, 1–29.

Freedman, D.A., 1986, Reply, Journal of Business and Economic Statistics 4, 126–127.

Friedman, M., 1953, Essays in positive economics (University of Chicago Press, Chicago, IL).

Friedman, M., 1957, A theory of the consumption function (Princeton University Press, Princeton, NJ).

Friedman, M. and L.J. Savage, 1948, The utility analysis of choices involving risk, Journal of Political Economy 56, 279–304.

Friedman, M. and L.J. Savage, 1952, The expected-utility hypothesis and the measurability of utility, Journal of Political Economy 60, 463–474.

Geisser, S., 1980a, The contributions of Sir Harold Jeffreys to Bayesian inference, in: A. Zellner, ed., Bayesian analysis in econometrics and statistics: Essays in honor of Harold Jeffreys (North-Holland, Amsterdam) 13–34.

Geisser, S., 1980b, A predictivistic primer, in: A. Zellner, ed., Bayesian analysis in econometrics and statistics: Essays in honor of Harold Jeffreys (North-Holland, Amsterdam) 363–382.

Goel, P.K. and A. Zellner, 1986, eds., Bayesian inference and decision techniques: Essays in honor of Bruno de Finetti (North-Holland, Amsterdam).

Good, I.J., 1962, Review of Harold Jeffreys' 'Theorem of probability (3rd ed.)', Geophysical Journal of the Royal Astronomical Society 6, 555–558, and Journal of the Royal Statistical Society A 125, 487–489.

Good, I.J., 1980, The contributions of Jeffreys to Bayesian statistics, in: A. Zellner, ed., Bayesian analysis in econometrics and statistics: Essays in honor of Harold Jeffreys (North-Holland, Amsterdam) 21–34.

Harkema, R., 1975, An analytical comparison of certainty equivalence and sequential updating, Journal of the American Statistical Association 70, 348–350.

Intriligator, M.D., 1978, Econometric models, techniques, and applications (Prentice-Hall, Englewood Cliffs, NJ).

Jaynes, E.T., 1974, Probability theory with applications in science and engineering: A series of informal lectures, Manuscript (Department of Physics, Washington University, St. Louis, MO).

Jaynes, E.T., 1983, Papers on probability, statistics and statistical physics, edited by R.D. Rosenkrantz (D. Reidel, Dordrecht, Holland).

Jaynes, E.T., 1984, The intuitive inadequacy of classical statistics, Epistemologia VII (special issue on probability, statistics and inductive logic), 43–74.

Jaynes, E.T., 1985, Highly informative priors, in: J.M. Bernardo et al., eds., Bayesian statistics 2 (North-Holland, Amsterdam) 329–352.

Jeffreys, H., 1967, Theory of probability, 3rd ed. (Oxford University Press, London): 1st ed. in 1939.

Jeffreys, H., 1973, Scientific inference, 3rd ed. (Cambridge University Press, Cambridge): 1st ed. in 1931.

Jorion, P., 1983, Portfolio analysis of international equity investments, Unpublished doctoral dissertation (Graduate School of Business, University of Chicago, Chicago, IL).

Jorion, P., 1985, International portfolio diversification with estimation risk, Journal of Business 58, 259–278.

Judge, G.G., W.E. Griffiths, R.C. Hill, H. Lütkepohl and T.-C. Lee, 1985, The theory and practice of econometrics, 2nd ed. (Wiley, New York).

Kadane, J.B., ed., 1984, Robustness of Bayesian analysis (North-Holland, Amsterdam).

Klein, R.W. and S.J. Brown, 1984, Model selection when there is 'minimal' prior information, Econometrica 52, 1291–1312.

Leamer, E.E., 1978, Specification searches (Wiley, New York).

Lehmann, E., 1959, Testing statistical hypotheses (Wiley, New York).

Lempers, F.B., 1971, Posterior probabilities of alternative linear models (Rotterdam University Press, Rotterdam).

Lindley, D.V., 1965, Introduction to probability and statistics from a Bayesian viewpoint, 2 vols. (Cambridge University Press, Cambridge).

Lindley, D.V., 1971, Bayesian statistics: A review (Society for Industrial and Applied Mathematics, Philadelphia, PA).

Lindley, D.V., 1980, Jeffreys's contribution to modern statistical thought, in: A. Zellner, ed., Bayesian analysis in econometrics and statistics: Essays in honor of Harold Jeffreys (North-Holland, Amsterdam) 35–39.

Litterman, R.B., 1980, A Bayesian procedure for forecasting with Bayesian vector autoregressions (Department of Economics, MIT, Cambridge, MA).

Litterman, R.B., 1985, Forecasting with Bayesian vector autoregressions: Five years of experience, Technical report (Federal Reserve Bank of Minneapolis, Minneapolis, MN); also in: Journal of Business and Economic Statistics 4, 25–38.

Maddala, G.S., 1978, Econometrics (McGraw-Hill, New York).

Malinvaud, E., 1980, Statistical methods of econometrics, 3rd rev. ed. (North-Holland, Amsterdam).

McNees, S.K., 1985, Forecasting accuracy of alternative techniques: A comparison of U.S. macroeconomic forecasts, Invited paper presented at the ASA meetings, Las Vegas, Nevada, August 1985, and with invited discussion in: Journal of Business and Economic Statistics 4, 5–23.

Monahan, J.F., 1983, Fully Bayesian analysis of ARMA time series models, Journal of Econometrics 21, 307–331.

Morales, J.F., 1971, Bayesian full information structural analysis (Springer-Verlag, Berlin).

Park, S.B., 1982, Some sampling properties of minimum expected loss (MELO) estimators of structural coefficients, Journal of Econometrics 18, 295–311.

Pearson, K., 1938, The grammar of science (Everyman Edition, London).

Prescott, E.C., 1975, Adaptive decision rules of macroeconomic planning, in: S.E. Fienberg and A. Zellner, eds., Studies in Bayesian econometrics and statistics in honor of Leonard J. Savage (North-Holland, Amsterdam) 427–440.

Press, S.J., 1972, Applied multivariate analysis including Bayesian techniques (Holt, Rinehart and Winston, New York).

Raiffa, H. and R. Schlaifer, 1961, Applied statistical decision theory (Graduate School of Business Administration, Harvard University, Boston, MA).

Richard, J.F., 1973, Posterior and predictive densities for simultaneous equation models (Springer-Verlag, Berlin).

Rothenberg, T.J., 1975, The Bayesian approach and alternatives in econometrics, in: S.E. Fienberg and A. Zellner, eds., Studies in Bayesian econometrics and statistics in honor of Leonard J. Savage (North-Holland, Amsterdam) 55–68.

Savage, L.J., 1954, The foundation of statistics (Wiley, New York).

Savage, L.J., 1962, Bayesian statistics, in: R.F. Machol and P. Gray, eds., Recent developments in information and decision theory (Macmillan, New York) 161–194: reprinted in 1981 in: The writings of Leonard Jimmie Savage – A memorial selection (American Statistical Association and Institute of Mathematical Statistics, Washington, DC).

Schwarz, G., 1978, Estimating the dimension of a model, Annals of Statistics 6, 461–464.

Stein, C. and A. Zaman, 1980, Admissibility of the Bayes procedure corresponding to the uniform prior distribution for the control problem in four dimensions but not in five, Technical report no. 324 (Department of Statistics, Stanford University, Stanford, CA).

Stigler, S.M., 1978, Francis Ysidro Edgeworth, statistician, Journal of the Royal Statistical Society A 141, 287–313.

Swamy, P.A.V.B., 1980, A comparison of estimators for undersized samples, Journal of Econometrics 14, 161–181.

Swamy, P.A.V.B. and J.S. Mehta, 1983, Further results on Zellner's minimum expected loss and full information maximum likelihood estimators for undersized samples, Journal of Business and Economic Statistics 1, 154–162.

Theil, H., 1971, Principles of econometrics (Wiley, New York).

Tukey, J.W., 1978, Discussion of Granger on seasonality, in: A. Zellner, ed., Seasonal analysis of economic time series (U.S. Government Printing Office, Washington, DC) 50–53.

Van Dijk, H.K. and T. Kloek, 1980, Further experience in Bayesian analysis using Monte Carlo integration, Journal of Econometrics 14, 307–328.

Varian, H.R., 1975, A Bayesian approach to real estate assessment, in: S.E. Fienberg and A. Zellner, eds., Studies in Bayesian econometrics and statistics in honor of Leonard J. Savage (North-Holland, Amsterdam) 195–208.

Villegas, C., 1980, comment on 'On some statistical paradoxes and non-conglomerability' by Bruce M. Hill, in: J.M. Bernardo et al., eds., Bayesian statistics: Proceedings of the first international meeting held in Valencia (Spain), May 28 to June 2, 1979 (University Press, Valencia, Spain) 53–54.

Wright, R., 1983, Measuring the precision of statistical cost allocations, Journal of Business and Economic Statistics 1, 93–100.

Zaman, A., 1981a, Estimators without moments: The case of the reciprocal of a normal mean, Journal of Econometrics 15, 289–298.

Zaman, A., 1981b, A complete class theorem for the control problem and further results on admissibility and inadmissibility, Annals of Statistics 9, 812–821.

Zellner, A., 1971a, An introduction to Bayesian inference in econometrics (Wiley, New York).

Zellner, A., 1971b, Bayesian and non-Bayesian analysis of the log-normal distribution and log-normal regression, Journal of the American Statistical Association 66, 327–330.

Zellner, A., 1973, The quality of quantitative economic policymaking when targets and costs of change are misspecified, in: W. Sellekart, ed., Selected readings in econometrics and economic theory: Essays in honour of Jan Tinbergen, Part II (Macmillan, London) 147–164; reprinted in 1984 in: A. Zellner, Basic issues in econometrics (University of Chicago Press, Chicago, IL) 169–183.

Zellner, A., 1975, The Bayesian approach and alternatives in econometrics, in: S.E. Fienberg and A. Zellner, eds., Studies in Bayesian econometrics and statistics in honor of Leonard J. Savage (North-Holland, Amsterdam) 39–54.

Zellner, A., 1978, Estimation of functions of population means and regression coefficients including structural coefficients: A minimum expected loss (MELO) approach, Journal of Econometrics 8, 125–158.

Zellner, A., 1980, ed., Bayesian analysis in econometrics and statistics: Essays in honor of Harold Jeffreys (North-Holland, Amsterdam).

Zellner, A., 1984, Basic issues in econometrics (University of Chicago Press, Chicago, IL).

Zellner, A., 1985a, Bayesian econometrics, Econometrica 53, 253–270 (a written version of my invited Fisher-Schultz lecture, Econometric society Meeting, Pisa, Italy, 1983).

Zellner, A., 1985b, Bayesian estimation and prediction using asymmetric loss functions, Technical report (H.G.B. Alexander Research Foundation, Graduate School of Business, University
of Chicago, Chicago, IL); also in: Journal of the American Statistical Association 81,
446–451.

Zellner, A., 1985c, A tale of forecasting 1001 series: The Bayesian knight strikes again, Technical
report (H.G.B. Alexander Research Foundation, Graduate School of Business, University of
Chicago, Chicago, IL); also in: Journal of Forecasting 2, 491–494.

Zellner, A., 1985d, Further results on Bayesian minimum expected loss (MELO) estimates and
posterior distributions for structural coefficients, Technical report (H.G.B. Alexander Research Foundation, Graduate School of Business, University of Chicago, Chicago, IL); also
in: Advances in Econometrics 5, 171–182.

Zellner, A. and V.K. Chetty, 1965, Prediction and decision problems in regression models from
the Bayesian point of view, Journal of the American Statistical Association 60, 608–616.

Zellner, A. and M.S. Geisel, 1968, Sensitivity of control to uncertainty and form of the criterion
function, in: D.G. Watts, ed., The future of statistics (Academic Press, New York) 269–289.

Zellner, A. and S.B. Park, 1979, Minimum expected loss (MELO) estimators for functions of
parameters and structural coefficients of econometric models, Journal of the American
Statistical Association 74, 185–193.

Zellner, A. and P.E. Rossi, 1984, Bayesian analysis of dichotomous quantal response models,
Journal of Econometrics 25, 365–393.

Zellner, A. and A. Siow, 1980, Posterior odds ratios for selected regression hypotheses, in J.M.
Bernardo et al., eds., Bayesian statistics: Proceedings of the first international meeting held
in Valencia (Spain), May 28 to June 2, 1979 (University Press, Valencia, Spain) 585–603.

Zellner, A. and W. Vandaele, 1975, Bayes-Stein estimators for k − means, regression and
simultaneous equation models, in: S.E. Fienberg and A. Zellner, eds., Studies in Bayesian
econometrics and statistics in honor of Leonard J. Savage (North-Holland, Amsterdam)
317–343.

Readings in Econometric Theory and Practice
W. Griffiths, H. Lütkepohl and M.E. Bock (Editors)

CHAPTER 5

DATA POOLING AND SELF-SELECTION: A MIXED EFFECTS HIERARCHICAL APPROACH

Khalifa Ghali

Faculté de Droit et des Sciences Economiques et Politiques de Sousse, Cité Erriadh, Sousse 4000, Tunisia

Dennis J. Aigner

Graduate School of Management, University of California, Irvine, CA 92717, USA

This paper presents a mixed effects linear hierarchical model to characterize the possible transferability of data among five residential time-of-use pricing experiments for electricity. The framework allows, for the first time, adequate treatment of the three experiments which use volunteers and the remaining two experiments where mandatory participation of randomly selected households was enforced. The Bayes estimator introduced first by Lindley and Smith (1972) is extended for purposes of model estimation.

The empirical findings suggest that full transferability of results over both the winter and summer seasons is achieved only for the voluntary experiments. Even so, the precision of estimation associated with the parameter of primary interest, the elasticity of substitution, is not so impressive as to exclude the possibility that additional experimentation may be needed in any particular region of subsequent interest.

1. Introduction

After almost a decade of research on time-of-use (TOU) pricing for residential customers in the U.S., the problem of transfering data from the best residential TOU experiments to any other geographical location with its particular socioeconomic and demographic characteristics is an issue for which past research [Christensen Associates (1983), Kohler and Mitchell (1984), Aigner and Leamer (1984), Caves et al. (1984a)] provided no adequate solution, particularly when the critical issues raised in Aigner (1985) and in Aigner and Leamer (1984) are considered. For instance, in the treatment of regional heterogeneity, analysts typically assume that observed data are random outcomes of a controlled experiment. It is well known, however, that if the data are not random outcomes of a homogeneous population, ignoring heterogeneity leads to biased and meaningless estimates [Balestra and Nerlove (1966), Hsiao (1986)]. Second, while experimentation is an innovation in evaluating the effects of proposed government policies compared to inferences based solely on observational survey data, some sampling issues exist and may put a limit on the ultimate usefulness of TOU experimental data. As an example, voluntary participation in some of the experiments is not inconsequential and gives rise to biased and inconsistent estimates of customer response [Manning and Acton (1980), Aigner and Hausman (1980), Aigner and Ghali (1989)].

In this paper we raise the issues of homogeneity and self-selection and focus attention on fostering a unifying framework within which discrepancies among individual experiments can be reconciled and a verdict on the consistency of customer responses from them can be achieved. To characterize data transfer, we develop a mixed effects linear hierarchical model that allows us to capture the dissimilarities among experiments with the advantage of being able to pool the data and investigate the exchangeability hypothesis. To the extent that some of the effects influencing customer response may be regional or utility specific, our model treats weather-related variables as fixed, whereas the effects of prices and interactions with them are considered to vary randomly across experiments. Compared to existing models used to make inferences from panel data, the model we develop herein offers a flexible specification that allows us to control for the effects of both fixed and random factors so that common behavior can be consistently estimated. Within the Bayesian framework this specification can be used to deal with the conceptual problem of incorporating the effects of self-selection into a hierarchical structure.

The paper is organized as follows. In the next section we present the methodology adopted for use in our work. In Section 3 we present the theory of mixed effects linear hierarchical model estimation. Section 4 contains the empirical results and Section 5 concludes.

2. Methodology

Customer responsiveness to TOU pricing is analyzed in this paper based on estimation of the Allen elasticity of substitution between peak and off-peak electricity consumption. The indirect utility function we use to represent customer preferences is given by the constant elasticity of substitution (CES) functional form. For each household i belonging to an experiment j, the CES equation can be written as

$$(\text{LCRATIO})_{ij}$$

$$= \alpha_{0j} + \alpha_{1j}(\text{CDP})_{ij} + \alpha_{2j}(\text{HDP})_{ij} + \alpha_{3j}(\text{CACCDP})_{ij}$$

$$+ \alpha_{4j}(\text{ESHHDP})_{ij} + \beta_{0j}(\text{LPRATIO})_{ij} + \beta_{1j}(\text{CDP} * \text{LPRATIO})_{ij}$$

$$+ \beta_{2j}(\text{HDP} * \text{LPRATIO})_{ij} + \beta_{3j}(\text{CACCDP} * \text{LPRATIO})_{ij}$$

$$+ \beta_{4j}(\text{ESHHDP} * \text{LPRATIO})_{ij} + u_{ij} \qquad (2.1)$$

where

LCRATIO = logarithm of the peak to off-peak consumption ratio,
CDP   = cooling degree days,
HDP   = heating degree days,
CACCDP = interaction between air conditioning dummy variable and cooling degree days,
ESHHDP = interaction between electric space heating dummy variable and heating degree days, and
LPRATIO = logarithm of the peak to off-peak price ratio.

This equation will be estimated in the summer and winter seasons using weekday data collected from the following experiments:
- Los Angeles (LADWP)
- Southern California (SCE)
- Wisconsin
- Connecticut
- North Carolina (CP & L)

The analysis of transferability is primarily a problem relevant to the analysis of panel data. Hence because of the importance of assumptions concerning the stability of structural parameters and because different assumptions have been adopted in the literature dealing with this problem, we herein consider different model specifications and let the data point us to the most suitable representation. In particular we consider the following five model specifications:

Model 1

The coefficients $\theta'_j = (\alpha_{0j}, \ldots, \alpha_{4j}, \beta_{0j}, \ldots, \beta_{4j})$ are fixed and different for different experiments. In this case customer response to prices, weather, and appliance variables are different for different experiments, and therefore each experiment is treated separately. In this case the only advantage of pooling data from the different experiments lies in the possibility of putting the model in the form of Zellner's (1962) seemingly unrelated regression framework to improve the efficiency of the estimates of individual parameters.

Model 2

The coefficients $\theta'_j = \theta' = (\alpha_0, \ldots, \alpha_4, \beta_0, \ldots, \beta_4)$ for all j. In this case all coefficients are restricted to be the same for different experiments, and therefore we have a standard regression problem applied to the cross-section, cross-experiment data. This is the specification adopted by Christensen Associates (1983) for investigating the transferability of data across TOU experiments.

Christensen Associates made use of this assumption to pool data from the same five experiments we consider and computed a common elasticity of substitution. Their method for testing the transferability hypothesis consists of testing the equality of each experiment's elasticity of substitution obtained from the individual experiments (our Model 1) to the elasticity of substitution obtained from the pooled model (our Model 2). In the event there is a significant correspondence between the individual and pooled elasticities of substitution, they conclude that there is no significant departure from the pooled model and the transferability hypothesis is therefore accepted.

Model 3

The parameter vectors θ'_j are randomly distributed with exchangeable distributions having a common mean $\bar{\theta}$ and a common variance-covariance matrix Σ. This is the assumption underlying the linear hierarchical model adopted by Aigner and Leamer (1984). Under this exchangeability hypothesis, data from the five experiments are pooled together in order to estimate a common response vector $\bar{\theta}$ and therefore a common elasticity of substitution. In their work Aigner and Leamer used the Hausman specification test to investigate the exchangeability hypothesis.

Model 4

The intercept term α_{0j} is fixed and different for different experiments and the slope coefficients $(\alpha_1, \ldots, \alpha_4, \beta_0, \ldots, \beta_4)$ are the same. This is the analysis-of-covariance model which, in the event that the overall homogeneity assumption (Model 2) is rejected, corrects for heterogeneity by capturing the effects of three different types of parameters, those associated with variables that are constant within experiments but vary across experiments, variables that are the same across experiments but vary within experiments, and variables that vary within and across experiments. This model corrects for heterogeneity by absorbing the effects of the first type of variables in the intercept term and the effects of the remaining variables through the error component of the model.

The application of this model is insightful in this context because of its ability to indicate the existence of experiment-specific effects through variation of the intercept term across experiments. The existence of such variation in the α_{0j}'s, the coefficients of the experiment dummy variables, would mean that there are factors which are peculiar to a given experiment but stay constant within the experiment.

Model 5

The coefficients $\theta'_{1j} = (\alpha_{0j}, \ldots, \alpha_{4j})$ are fixed and different for different experiments and the coefficients $\theta'_{2j} = \theta'_2 = (\beta_0, \ldots, \beta_4)$ are randomly distributed with common mean $\bar{\theta}'_2$ and common variance-covariance matrix Σ. This model we term the Mixed Effects Linear Hierarchical Model (MELHM), which is developed in the next section. In the event that Model 4 reveals the existence of region (experiment) specific effects, Model 5 allows us to model both the specific effects as well as the random effects.

Our belief is that model specification should be of a primary interest to the analyst and that the degree of success in addressing the transferability issue derives from the degree of success in representing the data. Locking oneself into a predetermined specification may result in misleading inferences especially when the practical relevance of the underlying assumptions is not empirically assessed.

One important aspect of model specification that we emphasize in addition to the heterogeneity issue is that of self-selection. Voluntary participation was analyzed in Aigner and Ghali (1989) and was revealed to bias the individual estimates of customer response. Therefore when estimating the different models we continue analyzing the effects of self-selection, this time on the pooled estimates, by comparing customer responses between equations uncorrected and corrected for selection bias.

Moreover, consideration of the fact that there are two types of experiments, mandatory and voluntary experiments, may raise a critical issue of model specification. Specifically, self-selection requires correcting the dependent variable mean *only* for the voluntary experiments and thus results in two different models for the two types of experiments. Such a distinction, although suggested from a statistical point-of-view, appears to be reasonable in light of the difference in customer incentives and their effects on response during experimentation. In fact, while customers in the mandatory experiments are forced to respond, the response of self-selected customers is influenced by an adverse selection. Therefore suggesting two different models can be justified by the existence of different behavioral relationships for the two types of customers. In particular, the amount of electricity consumed by a self-selected customer is not only determined by the effects of those variables in equation (2.1) but also by those variables influencing his or her decision to participate. Thus the pooling of data from the two types of experiments within the same behavioral model is likely to result in a misrepresentation of either's customer response. The use of the corrected equation for all the experiments may result in incorrect inferences of mandatory customer response, and the use of the uncorrected equation may result in incorrect inferences for the voluntary customers.

In order to cope with this problem we also estimate separate models for the different groups of experiments and investigate the transferability of data within each group. In particular we consider:

- Transferability between all five experiments, i.e., LADWP, SCE, CP & L, Wisconsin, and Connecticut;
- Transferability between voluntary experiments, i.e., LADWP, SCE, and Connecticut; and
- Transferability between mandatory experiments, i.e., CP & L and Wisconsin.

3. A Mixed Effects Linear Hierarchical Model (MELHM)

Within the Bayesian framework, Lindley and Smith (1972) developed the estimation of the linear model under de Finetti's exchangeability hypothesis and proved that this assumption yields substantially improved estimates. Specifically, Lindley and Smith analyzed the linear model

$$Y_j = A_j \theta_j + u_j \quad j = 1, \ldots, p,$$ (3.1)

where A_j is a design matrix and θ_j is a vector of parameters. The second stage of the model is represented by the exchangeability of the distribution of θ_j, namely

$$\theta_j \sim N(\bar{\theta}, \Sigma), \quad \forall_j.$$ (3.2)

This second stage is subject to two interpretations. First, the θ_j's can be regarded as being generated from a multivariate normal distribution in which case the density corresponding to (3.2) is a factor in the likelihood function and the model is therefore a random effects model. Second, the distributional relationship in (3.2) can be thought of as expressing our *prior* belief in the absence of information from the observations Y_j in which case (3.2) represents the prior knowledge about the parameter θ_j. This particular form of prior is based on de Finetti's idea of exchangeability, namely that the distribution of θ_j would be unaltered by any permutation of the suffices, so that, in particular, θ_i and θ_j would have the same distribution for any i and j. The model in (3.1) and (3.2) is a two-stage version of the linear hierarchical model where the prior about $\bar{\theta}$ is flat.

In a general setting, the second stage can represent a non-exchangeable prior,

$$\theta_j \sim N\left(\bar{\theta}_j, \Sigma_j\right), \tag{3.3}$$

and exchangeability can be imposed at the third stage by assuming that the $\bar{\theta}_j$'s have exchangeable prior distributions, or one can proceed to as many stages as he finds convenient. Using the exchangeability of priors, Lindley and Smith proved that although Bayes estimates are biased under fairly general conditions, they have smaller mean squared error than the comparable least squares estimates.

In the case of TOU experimental data, improved estimates for any one utility j can be obtained using the exchangeability of priors by combining the data for all utilities through the Bayes estimator. For a two-stage model as in (3.1) and (3.2), this estimator is seen to be a weighted average of the least squares estimates of θ_j and the grand mean $\bar{\theta}$, with weights proportional to the inverses of the corresponding dispersion matrices of θ_i and u_i,

$$\tilde{\theta}_j = \left(\sigma_j^{-2} A_j' A_j + \Sigma^{-1}\right)^{-1} \left(\sigma_j^{-2} A_j' Y_j + \Sigma^{-1}\hat{\bar{\theta}}\right), \tag{3.4}$$

where $\hat{\sigma}_j^2 I$ is the dispersion matrix of u_i and $\hat{\bar{\theta}}$ is the estimate of the common mean $\bar{\theta}$, namely

$$\hat{\bar{\theta}} = \left[\sum_j \left(\Sigma + \sigma_j^2 (A_j' A_j)^{-1}\right)^{-1}\right]^{-1} \sum_j \left[\Sigma + \sigma_j^2 (A_j' A_j)^{-1}\right]^{-1} \hat{\theta}_j, \tag{3.5}$$

where $\hat{\theta}_j$ is the least squares estimate of θ_j. In other words the Bayes estimates are pulled towards the common mean $\bar{\theta}$. The Bayes estimator downweights the sampling error with the extreme values experiencing the most shift. Comparing the ridge and Bayes estimators, we can interpret the constant in the ridge estimator as being the variance ratio to be estimated from the data and the prior information.

Aigner and Leamer (1984) provide a method of data transfer based on the linear hierarchical model (3.1)–(3.2). Each of the utility companies they considered was assumed to have a separate set of parameters θ_j in the linear function (3.1). In this random coefficients model the degree of similarity in corresponding parameters was taken to be determined by the variance across utilities of each of the various coefficients; if a variance is zero, the corresponding coefficients are treated as identical. If all parameters are identical across utilities, then data from all utilities could be pooled together in order to form a single estimate of the effects of TOU pricing which will apply equally well to each, including a target utility where no experimentation has been performed. At the other extreme, if all the variances are infinite the coefficients are treated as totally dissimilar, and no transferability takes place.

Aigner and Leamer applied this framework to characterize data transfer to the Kansas City Power and Light Company on the basis of data collected from the Los Angeles and Southern California Edison experiments. Although LADWP and SCE relied on customers that self-selected into the experiments, Aigner and Leamer did not account explicitly for this potential source of bias, but suggested dealing with the conceptual problem of incorporating self-selection into the linear hierarchical model.

In what follows we use de Finetti's idea of exchangeability and propose a more flexible specification of the linear model. Specifically, we relax the assumption of exchangeability of all the components of the parameter vector θ_j and consider the exchangeability of only a subset of θ_j. It follows that the Lindley-Smith model is a special case of the MELHM which covers non-randomly distributed effects as well as the random effects analyzed in the linear hierarchical model. We first consider the effects of sample selection on the Lindley-Smith estimator, then derive the estimator of our model.

3.1. The Effects of Self-selection on the Bayes Estimator
The linear model we consider is

$$E(Y) = A_1\theta_1 + A_2\theta_2 \tag{3.6}$$

where Y is a vector of observations, A is a known partitioned design matrix,

θ is a partitioned vector of unknown parameters, with A_2 a vector of Mill's ratios [1] and θ_2 a scalar parameter.

The model written in this way embodies two types of effects, $A_1\theta_1$, considered as random effects, where for θ_1, the parameter of interest, we assume the exchangeability of its distribution, and the self-selection effects, $A_2\theta_2$, considered as fixed effects to the extent that no distributional assumption about θ_2 will be made. We argue that if θ_2 were random, the distribution of θ_2 may fail the exchangeability hypothesis. For instance, in the case of multiple regression equations, different selectivity criteria will lead to significantly different effects, an obvious case being where some equations do not involve self-selection.

In what follows, the notation $Y \sim N(m, D)$ means that the column vector Y has a multivariate normal distribution with mean vector m and dispersion matrix D, a positive semi-definite matrix.

Suppose, given θ_1 a vector of p_1 parameters and θ_2 a scalar parameter, [2]

$$Y \sim N(A_1\theta_1 + A_2\theta_2, C_1) \tag{3.7}$$

and given θ_3 a vector of p_3 hyperparameters,

$$\theta_1 \sim N(A_3\theta_3, C_2) \tag{3.8}$$

then the marginal distribution of Y is $N(A_1 A_3 \theta_3 + A_2 \theta_2, C_1 + A_1 C_2 A_1')$. Applying Bayes' theorem we have

$$P(\theta_1, \theta_2 \mid Y) \propto P(\theta_1, \theta_2) \cdot P(Y \mid \theta_1, \theta_2). \tag{3.9}$$

Assuming that the conditional distribution of θ_2 given θ_1 is diffuse, $P(\theta_2 \mid \theta_1)$ $\propto$ constant, the posterior distribution for θ_1 and θ_2 is

$$P(\theta_1, \theta_2 \mid Y) \propto P(\theta_1) \cdot P(Y \mid \theta_1, \theta_2). \tag{3.10}$$

---

[1] Use of the Mill's ratio $\phi(z)/\Phi(z)$, where $\phi(\cdot)$ and $\Phi(\cdot)$ are, respectively, the standard normal density and distribution functions, as a correction for self-selection in econometric work dates back to the research on labor supply and participation of Heckman (1979).

[2] In this case (3.7) would be an approximation since Y is not necessarily normal when the Mill's ratio is included.

The product on the right hand side is $\exp\{-Q/2\}$ where

$$Q = (Y - A_1\theta_1 - A_2\theta_2)'C_1^{-1}(Y - A_1\theta_1 - A_2\theta_2)$$
$$+ (\theta_1 - A_3\theta_3)'C_2^{-1}(\theta_1 - A_3\theta_3).$$

By simple developments of this quantity, (3.10) can be rewritten as

$$P(\theta_1, \theta_2 | Y) \propto P(\theta_1 | \theta_2, Y) \cdot P(\theta_2 | Y)$$

where

$$P(\theta_1 | \theta_2, Y) \propto \exp\{-Q_1/2\},$$
$$Q_1 = (\theta_1 - Hh)'H^{-1}(\theta_1 - Hh)$$

with

$$H = \left(A_1'C_1^{-1}A_1 + C_2^{-1} \right)^{-1} \tag{3.11}$$

and

$$h = A_1'C_1^{-1}Y + C_2^{-1}A_3\theta_3 - A_1'C_1^{-1}A_2\theta_2 \tag{3.12}$$

Comparing the posterior mean of this conditional distribution to the original Lindley-Smith estimator, we can see the additional term in h, $-A_1'C_1^{-1}A_2\theta_2$, which is a function of A_2. This quantity can be negative, positive, or zero, depending on whether the self-selection bias is upward, downward or non-existent. In addition it can be seen that ignoring the self-selection correction has the same effects as omitted variables in regression. [3]

3.2. Bayes Estimates of the Mixed Effects Linear Hierarchical Model

Returning to the proposed model, we consider estimation of the general form

$$Y = A_1\theta_1 + A_2\theta_2 + u, \tag{3.13}$$

where the elements of θ_1 are random having an exchangeable distribution

---

[3] We owe this point to Arnold Zellner.

and the elements of θ_2 are fixed components. Hence A_2 may include only the vector consisting of the Mill's ratio or a matrix of observations on those variables whose effects on a priori grounds can be specified to be fixed. Hence the second stage of the model can be specified as

$$\theta_1 \sim N(A_3\theta_3, C_2) \tag{3.14}$$

where prior information on θ_3 is supposed to be diffuse so that the model has two stages only. The Appendix provides the posterior distributions of θ_1, θ_2, given Y.

3.3. The Case of Multiple Regression Equations

Considering the particular form of prior information we should stress an important point which Lindley and Smith emphasized about the exchangeability assumption. The estimates that Lindley and Smith suggested can be used only when this assumption is realistic. Exchangeability is an assumption, and its practical relevance *must* be assessed before the estimates based on it are used. To put more emphasis on this point, we should mention the work by Miller and Fortney (1984), who found that a conflict between the data and the prior may result in a bimodality of the posterior distribution, in which case the Lindley-Smith algorithm converges only to a relative mode (i.e., relative maximum) which may not be the absolute maximum. Consequently the estimates we derive herein should be used only if exchangeability of the random effects is in accordance with the data. With this in mind the self-selection problem can be dealt with by simple application of the results of the previous section.

For p regressor variables with inverse Mill's ratio the mathematics goes as follows. Suppose that

$$Y_j \sim N\left(X_j\beta_j + Z_j\lambda_j, \sigma_j^2 I_{n_j}\right), \quad j = 1, \ldots, m \tag{3.15}$$

where β_j is a vector of p parameters and Z_j is the vector of inverse Mill's ratios. That is, we have m linear multiple regressions on $p + 1$ variables. In the notation of the theorem, A_1, expressed in terms of submatrices, is diagonal with X_j as the jth diagonal submatrix. A_2 is a diagonal matrix with Z_j as the jth diagonal element. θ_1' is $(\beta_1', \beta_2', \ldots, \beta_m')$ of mp elements and θ_2' is $(\lambda_1, \lambda_2, \ldots, \lambda_m)$. The exchangeability of the individual β_j added to normality gives us the second stage,

$$\beta_j \sim N(\bar{\beta}, \Sigma) \tag{3.16}$$

Here A_3 is a matrix of order $mp \times p$, all of whose $p \times p$ submatrices are unit matrices and $\theta_3 = \bar{\beta}$. Using vague prior knowledge of $\bar{\beta}$ we can use the special form of Corollary 2 (Appendix).

$(A_2'C_1^{-1}A_2)^{-1}$ is a diagonal matrix with $\sigma_j^2(Z_j'Z_j)^{-1}$ on its jth diagonal and $C_1^{-1}A_2(A_2'C_1^{-1}A_2)^{-1}A_2'C_1^{-1}$ is also diagonal with $\sigma_j^{-2}Z_j(Z_j'Z_j)^{-1}Z_j'$ as its jth diagonal element. Hence the matrix K^{-1} is also diagonal with jth diagonal element $\sigma_j^{-2}I_{n_j} - \sigma_j^{-2}Z_j(Z_j'Z_j)^{-1}Z_j'$.

$$a_0 = A_1'K^{-1}Y$$

$$= \begin{bmatrix} \sigma_1^{-2}X_1'\left(I_{n_1} - Z_1(Z_1'Z_1)^{-1}Z_1'\right)Y_1 \\ \vdots \\ \sigma_m^{-2}X_m'\left(I_{n_m} - Z_m(Z_m'Z_m)^{-1}Z_m'\right)Y_m \end{bmatrix} = \begin{bmatrix} \sigma_1^{-2}X_1'M_1Y_1 \\ \vdots \\ \sigma_m^{-2}X_m'M_mY_m \end{bmatrix}$$

and $A_1'K^{-1}A_1 + C_2^{-1}$ is diagonal with $\sigma_j^{-2}X_j'M_jX_j + \Sigma^{-1}$ as its jth diagonal element.

The equations for the Bayes estimates β_j^* are then found to be

$$\begin{bmatrix} \sigma_1^{-2}X_1'M_1X_1 + \Sigma^{-1} & & & \\ & \ddots & & 0 \\ 0 & & \ddots & \\ & & & \sigma_m^{-2}X_m'M_mX_m + \Sigma^{-1} \end{bmatrix}\begin{bmatrix} \beta_1^* \\ \beta_2^* \\ \vdots \\ \beta_m^* \end{bmatrix} - \Sigma^{-1}\begin{bmatrix} \bar{\beta} \\ \bar{\beta} \\ \vdots \\ \bar{\beta} \end{bmatrix}$$

$$= \begin{bmatrix} \sigma_1^{-2}X_1'M_1Y_1 \\ \vdots \\ \sigma_m^{-2}X_m'M_mY_m \end{bmatrix}$$

where $\bar{\beta} = (1/m)\Sigma\beta_j^*$, $M_j = I - Z_j(Z_j'Z_j)^{-1}Z_j'$. These equations can easily be solved for $\bar{\beta}$ and then, in terms of $\bar{\beta}$, the solution is

$$\beta_j^* = \left(\sigma_j^{-2}X_j'M_jX_j + \Sigma^{-1}\right)^{-1}\left(\sigma_j^{-2}X_j'M_jY_j + \Sigma^{-1}\bar{\beta}\right) \tag{3.17}$$

$$\text{var}\left(\beta_j^* \mid \bar{\beta}\right) = \left(\sigma_j^{-2}X_j'M_jX_j + \Sigma^{-1}\right)^{-1}. \tag{3.18}$$

This estimator is easily seen to be a compromise between the least-squares estimator and an average of various estimates of β. For those equations not involving self-selection, the estimator reduces to Lindley-Smith. However, with self-selection, it is important to notice the significant change in the form of the Bayes estimate in the sense that ignorance of the self-selection correction has the same effects as those for missing variables in the regression context.

Noticing that A_0^{-1} may be written in the form

$$
\begin{bmatrix}
\sigma_1^{-2} X_1' M_1 X_1 + \Sigma^{-1} & & \\
 & \ddots & 0 \\
0 & & \ddots \\
 & & \sigma_m^{-2} X_m' M_m X_m + \Sigma^{-1}
\end{bmatrix}
$$

$$
- m^{-1}
\begin{bmatrix}
\Sigma^{-1} \\
\vdots \\
\Sigma^{-1}
\end{bmatrix}
\begin{bmatrix}
\Sigma & \cdots & 0 \\
\vdots & & \vdots \\
0 & \cdots & \Sigma
\end{bmatrix}
(\Sigma^{-1} \ldots \Sigma^{-1})
$$

and thus can be inverted by the Matrix Lemma (Appendix), we can find an explicit form for β_j^*. After some algebra we obtain the weighted form of (3.17) with $\bar{\beta}$ replaced by $\Sigma w_i \hat{\beta}_i$, where

$$
w_i = \left[\sum_{j=1}^m \left(X_j' M_j X_j \sigma_j^{-2} + \Sigma^{-1} \right)^{-1} X_j' M_j X_j \sigma_j^{-2} \right]^{-1}
$$

$$
\times \left(X_i' M_i X_i \sigma_i^{-2} + \Sigma^{-1} \right)^{-1} X_i' M_i X_i \sigma_i^{-2},
$$

and

$$
\hat{\beta}_i = \left(X_i' M_i X_i \right)^{-1} X_i' M_i Y_i.
$$

To compute the distribution of $\bar{\beta}$ given Y it is necessary to write the distribution of Y given $\bar{\beta}$. Now

$$
Y_j = X_j \beta_j + Z_j \lambda_j + u_j
$$

$$
= X_j \bar{\beta} + Z_j \lambda_j + X_j v_j + u_j,
$$

which is a regression process with mean $X_j\bar{\beta} + Z_j\lambda_j$ and variance $X_j\Sigma X_j' + \sigma_j^2 I_j$. Then with $\bar{\beta}$ a priori diffuse and given all the vectors Y_j, we have straightforwardly

$$\hat{\bar{\beta}} = E(\bar{\beta} \mid Y, X) = \left[\sum_j X_j'M_j\left(X_j\Sigma X_j' + \sigma_j^2 I_j\right)^{-1} M_j X_j \right]^{-1}$$

$$\times \left[\sum_j X_j'M_j\left(X_j\Sigma X_j' + \sigma_j^2 I\right)^{-1} M_j Y_j \right] \qquad (3.19)$$

which is the generalized least squares estimate of $\bar{\beta}$ with

$$\mathrm{var}(\bar{\beta} \mid Y, X) = \left[\sum_j X_j'M_j\left(X_j\Sigma X_j' + \sigma_j^2 I\right)^{-1} M_j X_j \right]^{-1} \qquad (3.20)$$

Thus, the pooling of information across processes where self-selection has been accounted for is summarized for the parameters of interest by two equations. Equation (3.17) describes the posterior location of β_j as a compromise between the least squares estimate and the grand mean β, which itself is a matrix weighted average of each of the least squares estimates.

The equations from which the λ_j^* can be derived are

$$\begin{bmatrix} Z_1'\left(\sigma_1^2 I_1 + X_1\Sigma X_1'\right)^{-1} Z_1 & & \\ & \ddots & 0 \\ 0 & & \ddots \\ & & Z_m'\left(\sigma_m^2 I_m + X_m\Sigma X_m'\right)^{-1} Z_m \end{bmatrix} \begin{bmatrix} \lambda_1^* \\ \vdots \\ \vdots \\ \lambda_m^* \end{bmatrix}$$

$$+ \begin{bmatrix} \sigma_1^{-2} Z_1'X_1\left(\sigma_1^{-2}X_1'X_1 + \Sigma^{-1}\right)^{-1}\Sigma^{-1}\bar{\beta} \\ \vdots \\ \sigma_m^{-2} Z_m'X_m\left(\sigma_m^{-2}X_m'X_m + \Sigma^{-1}\right)^{-1}\Sigma^{-1}\bar{\beta} \end{bmatrix}$$

$$= \begin{bmatrix} Z_1'\left(\sigma_1^2 I_1 + X_1\Sigma X_1'\right)^{-1}Y_1 \\ \vdots \\ Z_m'\left(\sigma_m^2 I_m + X_m\Sigma X_m'\right)^{-1}Y_m \end{bmatrix}$$

Denoting by $S_j = \sigma_j^{-2} I_j + X_j \Sigma X_j'$ and $T_j = \Sigma^{-1} + \sigma_j^{-2} X_j' X_j$, these equations can be solved to find the estimate for λ_j, viz.

$$\lambda_j^* = \left(Z_j' S_j^{-1} Z_j \right)^{-1} \left[Z_j' S_j^{-1} Y_j - \sigma_j^{-2} Z_j' X_j T_j^{-1} \Sigma^{-1} \bar{\beta} \right] \qquad (3.21)$$

and

$$\mathrm{var}\!\left(\lambda_j^* \mid \bar{\beta} \right) = \left[Z_j' \left(\sigma_j^2 I_j + X_j \Sigma X_j' \right)^{-1} Z_j \right]^{-1} \qquad (3.22)$$

3.4. Testing the Exchangeability Hypothesis

The main hypothesis underlying the development of the mixed effects linear hierarchical model is the exchangeability of the random effects, the β_j's in equation (3.15). This null hypothesis restricts the parameters of the prior probability distribution of *each* β_j to be $\bar{\beta}$ and Σ, the same for all j. Under this hypothesis of common mean and variance, the data from all j experiments are pooled together and $\bar{\beta}$ and Σ are estimated by $\hat{\bar{\beta}}$ and $\hat{\Sigma}$ in (3.19) and (3.20) for each experiment. On the other hand, the alternative hypothesis allows each β_j to have its own prior parameters $\bar{\beta}_j$ and Σ_j in which case each experiment j is forced to estimate its own model separately.

In order to test the exchangeability hypothesis we have to determine the degree to which it is in accordance with the data. Whether the data favors the null hypothesis or not can be measured by the posterior odds ratio expressed explicitly for each experiment as

$$\frac{P(H_0 \mid Y)}{P(H_1 \mid Y)} = \frac{P(H_0)}{P(H_1)} \cdot \frac{\int\int P(\theta, \sigma \mid H_0) \cdot P(Y \mid \theta, \sigma, H_0) \, d\sigma \, d\theta}{\int\int P(\theta, \sigma \mid H_1) \cdot P(Y \mid \theta, \sigma, H_1) \, d\sigma \, d\theta}$$

$$(3.23)$$

where $\theta = (\beta, \lambda)'$ and the outer integral is $(p + 1)$ dimensional. The right-hand-side is the prior odds multiplied by the Bayes factor. The Bayes factor is a ratio of averaged likelihoods where the prior densities are the weighting functions.

In our example, where for each experiment j we have

$$Y_j = X_j \beta_j + Z_j \lambda_j + u_j, \quad u_j \sim N\!\left(0, \sigma_j^2 I_{n_j} \right),$$

we should give expression to the ratio in (3.23). Under the null hypothesis, the joint posterior distribution for β_j, λ_j, σ_j and the data Y_j is given by

$$P\left(\beta_j, \lambda_j, \sigma_j, Y_j \mid X_j, Z_j, H_0\right) = P\left(\beta_j, \lambda_j, \sigma_j \mid H_0\right) P\left(Y_j \mid \beta_j, \lambda_j, \sigma_j, H_0\right).$$

The prior distribution for β_j, λ_j and σ_j can be written as

$$P\left(\beta_j, \lambda_j, \sigma_j \mid H_0\right) = P\left(\beta_j, \sigma_j \mid H_0\right) P\left(\lambda_j \mid \beta_j, \sigma_j, H_0\right)$$

where the conditional density $P(\lambda_j \mid \beta_j, \sigma_j, H_0)$ will be assumed to be diffuse and the conditional density $P(\beta_j \mid \sigma_j, H_0)$ we will assume to be multivariate normal with mean $\bar{\beta}$ and covariance matrix $\sigma_j^2 \Sigma$. We will assume in addition that σ_j has the inverted gamma distribution with parameters $\bar{v}_j$ and s_j^2. Hence the posterior distribution for β_j, λ_j, σ_j and Y_j is:

$$P\left(\beta_j, \lambda_j, \sigma_j, Y_j \mid X_j, Z_j, H_0\right)$$

$$= (2\pi)^{-(n+p)/2} \frac{2}{\Gamma\left(\dfrac{\bar{v}_j}{2}\right)}$$

$$\times \left(\frac{\bar{v}_j \bar{s}_j^2}{2}\right)^{\bar{v}_j/2} |\Sigma|^{-1/2} \sigma_j^{-(n+p+\bar{v}_j+1)} \exp\left\{\frac{-1}{2\sigma_j^2}\left(\beta_j - \bar{\beta}\right)' \Sigma^{-1}\left(\beta_j - \bar{\beta}\right)\right\}$$

$$\times \exp\left\{\frac{-1}{2\sigma_j^2}\left[\bar{v}_j \bar{s}_j^2 + \left(Y_j - X_j\beta_j - Z_j\lambda_j\right)'\left(Y_j - X_j\beta_j - Z_j\lambda_j\right)\right]\right\}.$$

$$(3.24)$$

Note that $(Y_j - X_j\beta_j - Z_j\lambda_j)'(Y_j - X_j\beta_j - Z_j\lambda_j)$ can be written as

$$v_j \hat{\sigma}_j^2 + \left(\beta_j - \hat{\beta}_j\right)' X_j' X_j \left(\beta_j - \hat{\beta}_j\right) + \left(\lambda_j - \hat{\lambda}_j\right)' Z_j' Z_j \left(\lambda_j - \hat{\lambda}_j\right)$$

$$+ 2\left(\lambda_j - \hat{\lambda}_j\right)' Z_j' X_j \left(\beta_j - \hat{\beta}_j\right),$$

$$(3.25)$$

where $\hat{\beta}_j$ and $\hat{\lambda}_j$ are the individual OLS estimates, $v_j = n - p - 1$ and

$$v_j\hat{\sigma}_j^2 = \left(Y_j - X_j\hat{\beta}_j - Z_j\hat{\lambda}_j\right)'\left(Y_j - X_j\hat{\beta}_j - Z_j\hat{\lambda}_j\right).$$

Letting

$$M_j = X_j'X_j - X_j'Z_j(Z_j'Z_j)^{-1}Z_j'X_j$$

and

$$\varDelta_j = \hat{\lambda}_j - (Z_j'Z_j)^{-1}Z_j'X_j\left(\beta_j - \hat{\beta}_j\right),$$

(3.25) can be written as

$$v_j\hat{\sigma}_j^2 + \left(\beta_j - \hat{\beta}_j\right)'M_j\left(\beta_j - \hat{\beta}_j\right) + (\lambda_j - \varDelta_j)'Z_j'Z_j(\lambda_j - \varDelta_j)$$

Hence the posterior distribution in (3.24) can now be written as

$$P\left(\beta_j, \lambda_j, \sigma_j, Y_j \mid X_j, Z_j, H_0\right)$$

$$= K_j(2\pi)^{-(n+p)/2}$$

$$\times |\Sigma|^{-1/2}\sigma_j^{-(n+p+\bar{v}_j+1)} \exp\left\{\frac{-1}{2\sigma_j^2}\left(\beta_j - \bar{\beta}\right)'\Sigma^{-1}\left(\beta_j - \bar{\beta}\right)\right\}$$

$$\times \exp\left\{\frac{-1}{2\sigma_j^2}\left[\bar{v}_j\bar{s}_j^2 + v_j\hat{\sigma}_j^2 + \left(\beta_j - \hat{\beta}_j\right)'M_j\left(\beta_j - \hat{\beta}_j\right)\right.\right.$$

$$\left.\left. + (\lambda_j - \varDelta_j)'Z_j'Z_j(\lambda_j - \varDelta_j)\right]\right\}, \quad (3.26)$$

where

$$K_j = \frac{2}{\Gamma\left(\dfrac{\bar{v}_j}{2}\right)}\left(\frac{\bar{v}_j\bar{s}_j^2}{2}\right)^{\bar{v}_j/2}$$

Then

$$P\left(Y_j \mid H_0\right) = K_j(2\pi)^{-(n+p)/2} \mid \Sigma \mid^{-1/2} \int \sigma_j^{-(n+p+\bar{v}_j+1)}$$

$$\times \exp\left\{\frac{-1}{2\sigma_j^2}\left(\beta_j - \bar{\beta}\right)' \Sigma^{-1}\left(\beta_j - \bar{\beta}\right)\right\}$$

$$\times \exp\left\{\frac{-1}{2\sigma_j^2}\left[\bar{v}_j \bar{s}_j^2 + v_j \hat{\sigma}_j^2 + \left(\beta_j - \hat{\beta}_j\right)' M_j\left(\beta_j - \hat{\beta}_j\right)\right.\right.$$

$$\left.\left. + \left(\lambda_j - \Delta_j\right)' Z_j' Z_j(\lambda_j - \Delta_j)\right]\right\} d\lambda_j \, d\beta_j \, d\sigma_j$$

$$(3.27)$$

The integration with respect to λ_j yields

$$K_j(2\pi)^{-(n+p-1)/2} \mid \Sigma \mid^{-1/2} (Z_j' Z_j)^{-1/2} \int \sigma_j^{-(n+p+\bar{v}_j)}$$

$$\times \exp\left\{\frac{-1}{2\sigma_j^2}\left(\bar{v}_j \bar{s}_j^2 + v_j \hat{\sigma}_j^2\right)\right\}$$

$$\times \int \exp\left\{\frac{-1}{2\sigma_j^2}\left[\left(\beta_j - \hat{\beta}_j\right)' M_j\left(\beta_j - \hat{\beta}_j\right)\right.\right.$$

$$\left.\left. + \left(\beta_j - \bar{\beta}\right)' \Sigma^{-1}\left(\beta_j - \bar{\beta}\right)\right]\right\} d\beta_j \, d\sigma_j \qquad (3.28)$$

The inner integral can be written as

$$\int \exp\left\{\frac{-1}{2\sigma_j^2}\left[\left(\beta_j - \bar{\beta}\right)' \Sigma^{-1}\left(\beta_j - \bar{\beta}\right) + \left(\beta_j - \hat{\beta}_j\right)' M_j\left(\beta_j - \hat{\beta}\right)\right]\right\} d\beta_j$$

$$= \exp\left\{\frac{-1}{2\sigma_j^2}\left(\hat{\beta}_j - \bar{\beta}\right)'\left(\Sigma + M_j^{-1}\right)^{-1}\left(\hat{\beta}_j - \bar{\beta}\right)\right\}$$

$$\times \int \exp\left[\frac{-1}{2\sigma_j^2}\left(\beta_j - \bar{\beta}\right)'\left(\Sigma^{-1} + M_j\right)\left(\beta_j - \bar{\beta}\right)\right] d\beta_j,$$

and the integration with respect to the p elements of β_j yields

$$\sigma_j^p (2\pi)^{p/2} \left| \Sigma^{-1} + M_j \right|^{-1/2} \exp\left\{ -\frac{E_{j0}}{2\sigma_j^2} \right\}, \tag{3.29}$$

where $E_{j0} = (\hat{\beta}_j - \bar{\beta})'(\Sigma + M_j^{-1})^{-1}(\hat{\beta}_j - \bar{\beta})$ and the value of the integral is obtained from properties of the multivariate normal distribution. Substituting (3.29) into (3.28) yields

$$P(Y_j \mid H_0) = K_j (2\pi)^{-(n-1)/2} |\Sigma|^{-1/2} \left| \Sigma^{-1} + M_j \right|^{-1/2} (Z_j' Z_j)^{-1/2}$$

$$\times \int \sigma_j^{-(n+\bar{v}_j)} \exp\left\{ \frac{-1}{2_j^2} \left[\bar{v}_j s_j^2 + v_j \hat{\sigma}_j^2 + E_{j0} \right] \right\} d\sigma_j$$

$$= K_j (2\pi)^{-(n-1)/2} \left[|\Sigma^{-1}| / |\Sigma^{-1} + M_j| \right]^{1/2} (Z_j' Z_j)^{-1/2}$$

$$\times \frac{2^{(n+\bar{v}_j-1)/2} \Gamma(n + \bar{v}_j/2)}{\left[v_j \hat{\sigma}_j^2 + \bar{v}_j \bar{s}_j^2 + E_{j0} \right]^{(n+\bar{v}_j-1)/2}}, \tag{3.30}$$

where the last equality is derived from the properties of the gamma function.

Under the alternative hypothesis, H_1, each β_j will have its own prior parameters $\bar{\beta}_j$ and Σ_j. Following the same analysis under H_0, we will have

$$P(\beta_j, \lambda_j, \sigma_j, Y_j \mid X_j, Z_j, H_1)$$

$$= (2\pi)^{-(n+p)/2} \frac{2}{\Gamma(\bar{v}_j/2)} \left(\frac{\bar{v}_j \bar{s}_j^2}{2} \right)^{\bar{v}_j/2}$$

$$\times |\Sigma_j|^{-1/2} \sigma_j^{-(n+p+\bar{v}_j+1)} \exp\left\{ \frac{-1}{2\sigma_j^2} \left(\beta_j - \bar{\beta}_j \right)' \Sigma_j^{-1} \left(\beta_j - \bar{\beta}_j \right) \right\}$$

$$\times \exp\left\{ \frac{-1}{2\sigma_j^2} \left[\bar{v}_j \bar{s}_j^2 + (Y_j - X_j \beta_j - Z_j \lambda_j)' (Y_j - X_j \beta_j - Z_j \lambda_j) \right] \right\},$$

and

$$P(Y_j \mid H_1) = K_j(2\pi)^{-(n-1)/2} \left| \Sigma_j^{-1} \right|^{1/2} \left| \Sigma_j^{-1} + M_j \right|^{-1/2}$$

$$(Z_j'Z_j)^{-1/2} \frac{2^{(n+\bar{v}_j-1)/2}\Gamma\left(n + \bar{v}_j/2\right)}{\left[v_j\hat{\sigma}_j^2 + \bar{v}_j\bar{s}_j^2 + E_{j1} \right]^{(n+\bar{v}_j-1)/2}}$$

where $E_{j1} = (\hat{\beta}_j - \bar{\beta}_j)'(\Sigma_j + M_j^{-1})^{-1}(\hat{\beta}_j - \bar{\beta}_j)$.

Thus the posterior odds ratio for each j will be

$$K_{01}^j = \frac{P(H_0 \mid Y_j)}{P(H_1 \mid Y_j)}$$

$$= \frac{P(H_0)}{P(H_1)} \frac{\left[|\Sigma^{-1}| / |\Sigma^{-1} + M_j| \right]^{1/2} \left[v_j\hat{\sigma}_j^2 + \bar{v}_j\bar{s}_j^2 + E_{j0} \right]^{-(n+\bar{v}_j-1)/2}}{\left[|\Sigma_j^{-1}| / |\Sigma_j^{-1} + M_j| \right]^{1/2} \left[v_j\hat{\sigma}_j^2 + \bar{v}_j\bar{s}_j^2 + E_{j1} \right]^{-(n+\bar{v}_j-1)/2}}$$

$$(3.31)$$

We shall now consider each factor that influences this posterior odds ratio. First, the greater the prior odds $P(H_0)/P(H_1)$ the greater will be the posterior odds. Next, the term $|\Sigma^{-1}| / |\Sigma^{-1} + M_j|$ and its counterpart in the denominator are measures of the precision of prior information. Other things being equal, these terms imply that we will favor the hypothesis with more prior information. And, the quantities E_0 and E_1 are measures of the compatibility of the prior and sample information. The more $\hat{\beta}_j$ deviates from $\bar{\beta}$, the greater will be the posterior odds in favor of H_1.

4. Application

In this section we begin by testing the overall homogeneity between experiments. For this we estimate Model 1 and Model 2 and perform an analysis-of-covariance test. The results of this test will indicate whether Model 2 is a suitable representation of the data. Next we will assume that differences between experiments are due to random factors and estimate Model 3. In this case, and to test the assumption of all random effects, we use the least-squares dummy variable approach and estimate different intercepts for different experiments (Model 4). The spread across these intercepts indicates whether there are effects that are peculiar to the experiment, in which case both random and fixed effects have to be controlled for so that common behavior is consistently estimated. For this we will use the MELHM to pool the data and then proceed by testing the exchangeability hypothesis.

4.1. Testing for Heterogeneity Bias

In this section we test the overall homogeneity assumption, namely that the coefficients θ_j' are the same for different experiments. This test can be viewed as Model 1 subject to the restrictions:

$$H_0 : \theta_j' = \theta' \quad \forall_j, \quad j = 1, \dots, J \tag{4.1}$$

If these restrictions hold then data from different experiments can be pooled using Model 2. Otherwise the parameters are heterogeneous and Model 2 would yield biased estimates of θ'.

To test (4.1) we use an analysis-of-covariance test represented by the F-statistic

$$F = \frac{(s_2 - s_1)/(J-1)K}{s_1/J(n-K)} \sim F[(J-1)K, J(n-K)], \tag{4.2}$$

where s_2 is the sum of squared residuals from Model 2, s_1 is the sum of

Table 1

Estimates of the Uncorrected and Corrected Elasticities of Substitution from Model 1 [a]

Experiment	Summer		Winter	
	Uncorrected	Corrected	Uncorrected	Corrected
LADWP	0.115	0.095	0.028	0.014
	(7.87)	(6.33)	(2.48)	(2.13)
SCE	0.088	0.076	0.047	0.038
	(11.94)	(8.44)	(6.02)	(5.32)
Wisconsin	0.316	0.315	0.143	0.143
	(28.46)	(12.60)	(17.69)	(6.50)
CP&L	0.136	0.136	0.080	0.080
	(11.93)	(8.23)	(3.20)	(2.46)
Connecticut	0.205	0.206	0.165	0.160
	(16.94)	(17.47)	(19.88)	(22.67)

[a] Evaluated at the average values for weather and appliance variables.

Table 2

Estimates of the Uncorrected and Corrected Elasticities of Substitution from Model 2 [a]

Experiment	Summer		Winter	
	Uncorrected	Corrected	Uncorrected	Corrected
Pooled Five	0.146	0.159	0.123	0.126
Experiments	(19.65)	(16.05)	(23.92)	(18.64)
Pooled Mandatory	0.177	0.200	0.046	0.063
Experiments	(21.85)	(12.42)	(6.38)	(8.51)
Pooled Voluntary	0.183	0.177	0.152	0.140
Experiments	(17.59)	(12.04)	(20.54)	(14.54)

[a] Evaluated at the average values of weather and appliance variables.

Table 3

F-values and Degrees of Freedom for Testing Homogeneity Within the Three Groups of Experiments

(homogeneity between the five experiments)

Season	Uncorrected Equation		Corrected Equation	
	F-value	DF [a]	F-value	DF [a]
Summer	365 [b]	(40,20809)	504 [b]	(44,34900)
Winter	621 [b]	(40,20804)	529 [b]	(44,34895)

(homogeneity between the mandatory experiments)

Season	Uncorrected Equation		Corrected Equation	
	F-value	DF [a]	F-value	DF [a]
Summer	40 [b]	(10,6828)	34 [b]	(11,6826)
Winter	57 [b]	(40,20804)	46 [b]	(11,11641)

(homogeneity between the voluntary experiments)

Season	Uncorrected Equation		Corrected Equation	
	F-value	DF [a]	F-value	DF [a]
Summer	387 [b]	(20,13980)	694 [b]	(22,13977)
Winter	638 [b]	(20,23256)	583 [b]	(22,23253)

[a] Degrees of freedom. For such large denominator values, F is well-approximated by χ^2.

[b] Significant at the 1% and 5% levels.

squared residuals from Model 1, J is the number of experiments, K is the number of components in θ'_j and n is the number of observations in each experiment. This statistic is applied to test homogeneity within the three groups of experiments mentioned earlier. Table 1 presents the elasticity of substitution estimates from Model 1 for each experiment. Table 2 presents the elasticity of substitution estimates from Model 2 for each group for experiments. Table 3 presents the values of the F-statistics and their respective degrees of freedom for the three groups of experiments. As indicated in this table, all the F-statistics are significant and therefore the overall homogeneity hypothesis is rejected by the data. Consequently, using Model 2, which assumes identical parameters across experiments, makes no sense because it yields an average of the coefficients which differs greatly across experiments. The pooled least squares estimates obtained from this model are biased and should never be used to infer customer response. Therefore the idea of the "representative experiment" simply does not hold.

4.2. Estimation of a Random Coefficients Model (Model 3)

For the linear hierarchical model we estimated the common mean $\hat{\theta}$ in (3.5) and computed an elasticity of substitution for each group of experiments. These elasticities are presented in Table 4. Model 3 was estimated using the LSHYPER computer program developed by Hirschberg and Aigner (1987).

LSHYPER uses an iterative estimation procedure where Σ in equation (3.16) and σ_j^2 in equation (3.15) are repeatedly updated to estimate $\hat{\theta}$ and θ_j. The convergence criterion we used was to stop iterating once the coefficients

Table 4

Estimates of the Uncorrected and Corrected Elasticities of Substitution from Model 3 [a]

Experiment	Summer		Winter	
	Uncorrected	Corrected	Uncorrected	Corrected
Pooled Five	0.003	0.007	0.042	0.040
Experiments	(0.031)	(0.076)	(0.652)	(0.513)
Pooled Mandatory	0.142	0.151	0.142	0.141
Experiments	(1.61)	(1.81)	(8.82)	(8.75)
Pooled Voluntary	0.121	0.111	0.054	0.050
Experiments	(2.52)	(2.41)	(1.12)	(0.84)

[a] Evaluated at the average values of weather and appliance variables.

Table 5

Estimates of the Uncorrected and Corrected Elasticities of Substitution from Model 4

Pooled Five Experiments (t-ratios in parentheses)

Parameter	Summer		Winter	
	Uncorrected	Corrected	Uncorrected	Corrected
I_1	−1.304	−1.361	−0.927	−0.967
	(−43.63)	(−58.71)	(−30.97)	(−52.14)
I_2	−0.948	−1.214	−1.097	−1.396
	(−61.03)	(−51.27)	(−106.62)	(−88.23)
I_3	0.388	0.186	0.275	0.046
	(19.70)	(8.85)	(16.63)	(3.14)
I_4	0.681	0.206	0.479	−0.088
	(21.74)	(5.35)	(21.74)	(−3.23)
I_5	0.112	0.118	−0.032	−0.307
	(6.86)	(8.19)	(−2.40)	(−25.27)
Elasticity of	0.199	0.185	0.165	0.143
Substitution [a]	(28.30)	(17.38)	(30.09)	(19.52)

[a] Evaluated at the average values of weather and appliance variables.

differed from their previous values by no more than 0.0001%. The particular value of Σ with which we started the estimation uses the maximum entropy covariance matrix proposed by Theil and Fiebig (1984).

Table 6

Estimates of the Uncorrected and Corrected Elasticities of Substitution from Model 4

Pooled Mandatory Experiments (t-ratios in parentheses)

Parameter	Summer		Winter	
	Uncorrected	Corrected	Uncorrected	Corrected
I_1	.0.545	0.554	0.306	0.275
	(16.11)	(9.50)	(12.47)	(8.22)
I_2	−0.051	−0.046	−0.136	−0.152
	(−3.54)	(−3.12)	(−13.05)	(−12.12)
Elasticity of	0.277	0.277	0.128	0.128
Substitution [a]	(29.17)	(13.22)	(19.93)	(11.47)

[a] Evaluated at the average values of weather and appliance variables.

Table 7

Estimates of the Uncorrected and Corrected Elasticities of Substitution from Model 4

Pooled Voluntary Experiments

Parameter	Summer		Winter	
	Uncorrected	Corrected	Uncorrected	Corrected
I_1	−0.852	−0.997	1.858	1.505
	(−20.40)	(−28.93)	(28.13)	(17.88)
I_2	−0.757	−1.101	−0.695	−1.036
	(−38.79)	(−40.93)	(−47.96)	(−53.14)
I_3	0.591	0.323	0.411	0.161
	(25.25)	(12.88)	(21.74)	(9.14)
Elasticity of	0.150	0.123	0.096	0.071
Substitution [a]	(16.60)	(9.81)	(14.34)	(7.80)

[a] Evaluated at the average values of weather and appliance variables.

4.3. Estimation of an Analysis-of-Covariance Model (Model 4)

The linear hierarchical model assumes that all the experiment coefficient vectors are random draws from a common population. However it is possible that some of the factors influencing customer response are utility specific, in which case Model 3 misrepresents the effects of these factors by assuming that they are random. To check the existence of this type of effect we include a dummy variable for each experiment and use the least-squares dummy variable approach to estimate the CES equation.

Tables 5–7 present estimates of the pooled ANCOVA model for the three groups of experiments. As shown in these tables the coefficients of the experiment dummies (I_j) vary widely across experiments and are statistically significant. Therefore the assumption that there is a typical response to changes in prices, weather, and appliances does not hold.

4.4. Estimation of a Mixed Effects Linear Hierarchical Model (Model 5)

In order to control for the effects of both the specific and random factors causing heterogeneity between experiments, we herein specify the effects of weather and appliances along with the experiment intercepts to be fixed and different for different experiments and the effects of prices and interactions with them to be randomly distributed with exchangeable distributions. We also specify the effects of self-selection in the corrected equations to be fixed because of the difference in sample selection procedures across experiments.

Table 8

Estimates of the Uncorrected and Corrected Elasticities of Substitution from Model 5 [a]

(t-ratios in parentheses)

Experiment	Summer		Winter	
	Uncorrected	Corrected	Uncorrected	Corrected
Pooled Five	0.181	0.173	0.126	0.128
Experiments	(5.64)	(4.72)	(3.43)	(3.12)
Pooled Mandatory	0.153	0.159	0.143	0.142
Experiments	(1.71)	(1.89)	(8.93)	(7.47)
Pooled Voluntary	0.119	0.110	0.053	0.048
Experiments	(3.28)	(2.37)	(1.08)	(0.960)

[a] Evaluated at the average values of weather and appliance variables.

Table 8 presents estimates of the elasticities of substitution obtained from Model 5 for the three groups of experiments. Comparing these estimates to their counterparts from Model 3, it is interesting to note the similarities and dissimilarities between results. First, comparing the estimates from pooling the five experiments, Model 5 and Model 3 yield dissimilar elasticities of substitutions. This finding does not seem to contradict the assumption that weather represents an experiment-specific effect that causes the heterogeneity between experiments and biases average customer response when treated the same. However this result does not hold in the case where the mandatory experiments and the voluntary experiments are pooled separately. In this case estimates of the random coefficients are similar between Model 3 and Model 5. The only difference is in the estimates of the fixed effects because Model 3 is pulling these estimates towards their common mean, while Model 5 is yielding different estimates for the different experiments. This could suggest that although there are differences in weather, these differences are not important and do not have a significant effect on the remaining variables when the experiments are pooled together. However, the difference remains in the estimates of the fixed coefficients.

Considering the separation of the voluntary and mandatory experiments, it is important to note the remarkable difference that exists between the elasticities of substitution estimated for both groups. First, when comparing the relative magnitudes of these quantities, a higher elasticity of substitution in the mandatory experiments does not contradict the fact that self-selection leads to an overstatement of customer response because these are two different groups of experiments with different customers. Second, this difference supports the argument that there are two different underlying behavioral models for the two types of experiments, and by grouping all the experiments together we run the risk of misspecification bias. The relevance of this point may be noted by looking at what happens when all experiments are combined. For instance, the elasticity of substitution shrinks towards that of the mandatory experiments in the winter, while it moves out of the range of the separate estimates in the summer.

4.5. Testing the Transferability Hypothesis

The empirical findings of the previous sections suggest the existence of one representation that adequately captures parameter heterogeneity between experiments, that being the mixed effects linear hierarchical model. It improves prediction for any one electric utility by combining information on all the experiments through the Bayes estimator. In particular, any target utility can predict the effects of prices and price interactions θ'_{2j} using the estimator in (3.17), but utility specific-factors are estimated using information on its region only through the estimator in (3.21).

However, the Bayes estimates derived in the previous section are suggested *only* when the priors on θ'_{2j} are exchangeable. Consequently we use this section to empirically assess the relevance of exchangeability and thereby find out if the pooling process can serve as a means for constructing the regional electricity models.

In the following tables we present the estimated elasticities of substitution for the individual experiments and the pooled elasticities estimated from the various models considered above. Although we test for exchangeability within each model, given the revealed heterogeneity results, Model 2 and Model 3 are presented only to contrast the transferability results between models and to see what decision one would take if any one of these models were adopted as a given specification. The following conclusions about transferability are based on the estimation of the mixed effects linear hierarchical model. Tables 9–10 present the results of testing the transferability hypothesis in the case where all five experiments are pooled together, and Tables 11–14 present the results of testing this hypothesis within the mandatory experiments and within the voluntary experiments.

In the case of the five experiments, transferability of data is accepted in the winter but rejected in the summer, when only the Los Angeles and Wisconsin experiments are consistent with this hypothesis. Therefore even after controlling for the effects of the various factors inducing the dissimilarity between experiments a target utility cannot benefit from a full transferability of data in both seasons. Likewise, transferability is accepted in the

Table 9

Measurement of Customer Response (Elasticity of Substitution)

(t-ratios in parentheses)

	Summer		Winter	
	Uncorrected	Corrected	Uncorrected	Corrected
Los Angeles (LADWP)	0.115	0.095	0.028	0.014
	(7.87)	(6.33)	(2.48)	(2.13)
California (SCE)	0.088	0.076	0.047	0.038
	(11.94)	(8.44)	(6.02)	(5.32)
North Carolina (CP & L)	0.136	0.136	0.080	0.080
	(11.93)	(8.23)	(3.20)	(2.46)
Wisconsin	0.316	0.315	0.143	0.143
	(28.46)	(12.60)	(17.69)	(6.50)
Connecticut	0.205	0.206	0.165	0.160
	(16.94)	(17.47)	(19.88)	(22.67)
Pooled (OLS) [a]	0.146	0.159	0.123	0.126
	(19.65)	(16.05)	(23.92)	(18.64)
Pooled (Random Effects) [b]	0.003	0.007	0.042	0.040
	(0.031)	(0.076)	(0.652)	(0.513)
Pooled (ANCOVA) [c]	0.199	0.185	0.165	0.143
	(28.30)	(17.38)	(30.09)	(19.52)
Pooled (Mixed Effects) [d,e]	0.181	0.173	0.126	0.128
	(5.64)	(4.72)	(3.43)	(3.12)

[a] Reject the transferability hypothesis in the summer and the winter at the 1% and 5% levels.

[b] Reject the transferability hypothesis in the summer and the winter at the 1% and 5% levels.

[c] Reject the exchangeability hypothesis.

[d] Accept the exchangeability of the random effects in the winter but not in the summer (prior odds ratio is one).

[e] Weather effects are fixed, price and interactions with price are random.

winter and rejected in the summer in the case of the mandatory experiments. For the voluntary experiments, however, transferability is accepted in the summer as well as in the winter season. The implication of these tests is that full transferability of data in both seasons can be successfully achieved only from the voluntary experiments and would be useful in the context of a voluntary application of TOU rate schedules.

Table 10

Prior and Posterior Probabilities for the Exchangeability Hypothesis Mixed Effects Model for the Five Experiments (H_0: Random effects are exchangeable)

	Summer				Winter			
	Uncorrected		Corrected		Uncorrected		Corrected	
	$P_0(H_0)$	$P_1(H_0)$	$P_0(H_0)$	$P_1(H_0)$	$P_0(H_0)$	$P_1(H_0)$	$P_0(H_0)$	$P_1(H_0)$
Los Angeles (LADWP)	0.5	0.68	0.5	0.64	0.5	0.94	0.5	0.94
California (SCE)	0.5	0.56	0.5	0.39	0.5	0.98	0.5	0.99
North Carolina (CP&L)	0.5	0.62	0.5	0.48	0.5	0.98	0.5	0.98
Wisconsin	0.5	0.66	0.5	0.54	0.5	0.99	0.5	1.00
Connecticut	0.5	0.46	0.5	0.20	0.5	0.79	0.5	0.81

$P_0(H_0)$ is the prior probability in the prior odds ratio.
$P_1(H_0)$ is the posterior probability from the posterior odds ratio.

Table 11

Measurement of Mandatory Customer Response (Elasticity of Substitution)

(t-ratios in parentheses)

	Summer		Winter	
	Uncorrected	Corrected	Uncorrected	Corrected
North Carolina (CP&L)	0.136	0.136	0.080	0.080
	(11.93)	(8.23)	(3.20)	(2.46)
Wisconsin	0.316	0.315	0.143	0.143
	(28.46)	(12.60)	(17.69)	(6.50)
Pooled (OLS) [a]	0.177	0.200	0.046	0.063
	(21.85)	(12.42)	(6.38)	(8.51)
Pooled (ANCOVA) [b]	0.277	0.277	0.128	0.128
	(29.17)	(13.22)	(19.93)	(11.74)
Pooled (Random Effects) [c]	0.142	0.151	0.142	0.141
	(1.61)	(1.81)	(8.82)	(8.75)
Pooled (Mixed Effects) [d,e]	0.153	0.159	0.143	0.142
	(1.71)	(1.89)	(8.93)	(7.47)

[a] Reject the transferability hypothesis at the 1% and 5% levels.

[b] Accept the transferability hypothesis in the winter but not in the summer at the 1% and 5% levels.

[c] Reject the exchangeability hypothesis.

[d] Accept the exchangeability of the random effects in the winter but not in the summer (prior odds ratio is one).

[e] Weather effects are fixed, price and interactions with price are random.

Table 12

Prior and Posterior Probabilities for the Exchangeability Hypothesis Mixed Effects Model for
the Mandatory Experiments (H_0: Random effects are exchangeable)

	Summer				Winter			
	Uncorrected		Corrected		Uncorrected		Corrected	
	$P_0(H_0)$	$P_1(H_0)$	$P_0(H_0)$	$P_1(H_0)$	$P_0(H_0)$	$P_1(H_0)$	$P_0(H_0)$	$P_1(H_0)$
North Carolina (CP&L)	0.5	0.54	0.5	0.54	0.5	0.52	0.5	0.56
Wisconsin	0.5	0.02	0.5	0.02	0.5	0.99	0.5	0.99

$P_0(H_0)$ is the prior probability in the prior odds ratio.
$P_1(H_0)$ is the posterior probability from the posterior odds ratio.

However, consideration of the standard errors associated with the estimated elasticities of substitution raises yet another critical issue, which is the
precision with which a target utility would predict the response of their

Table 13

Measurement of Voluntary Customer Response (Elasticity of Substitution)

(t-ratios in parentheses)

	Summer		Winter	
	Uncorrected	Corrected	Uncorrected	Corrected
Los Angeles (LADWP)	0.115	0.095	0.028	0.014
	(7.87)	(6.33)	(2.48)	(2.13)
California (SCE)	0.088	0.076	0.047	0.038
	(11.94)	(8.44)	(6.02)	(5.32)
Connecticut	0.205	0.206	0.165	0.160
	(16.94)	(17.47)	(19.88)	(22.67)
Pooled (OLS) [a]	0.183	0.177	0.152	0.144
	(17.59)	(12.04)	(20.54)	(14.54)
Pooled (ANCOVA) [b]	0.150	0.123	0.096	0.071
	(16.60)	(9.81)	(14.34)	(7.80)
Pooled (Random Effects) [c]	0.121	0.111	0.054	0.050
	(2.52)	(2.41)	(1.12)	(0.847)
Pooled (Mixed Effects) [d,e]	0.119	0.110	0.053	0.048
	(3.28)	(2.37)	(1.08)	(0.960)

[a] Reject the transferability at the 1% and 5% levels.
[b] Reject the transferability hypothesis in the summer and the winter at the 1% and 5% levels.
[c] Reject the exchangeability hypothesis.
[d] Accept the exchangeability of the random effects both in the summer and the winter (prior
odds ratio is one).
[e] Weather effects are fixed, price and interactions with price are random.

Table 14

Prior and Posterior Probabilities for the Exchangeability Hypothesis Mixed Effects Model for the Voluntary Experiments (H_0: Random effects are exchangeable)

	Summer				Winter			
	Uncorrected		Corrected		Uncorrected		Corrected	
	$P_0(H_0)$	$P_1(H_0)$	$P_0(H_0)$	$P_1(H_0)$	$P_0(H_0)$	$P_1(H_0)$	$P_0(H_0)$	$P_1(H_0)$
Los Angeles (LADWP)	0.5	1.00	0.5	1.00	0.5	0.97	0.5	0.97
California (SCE)	0.5	0.77	0.5	0.78	0.5	0.90	0.5	0.91
Connecticut	0.5	0.67	0.5	0.77	0.5	0.92	0.5	0.92

$P_0(H_0)$ is the prior probability in the prior odds ratio.
$P_1(H_0)$ is the posterior probability from the posterior odds ratio.

customers, particularly when it has no observations to contribute in the transferability process. This result supports a pertinent methodological problem that was raised by Áigner (1985) when he stressed that the transferability should in principle be approached by allowing for a fresh sample to be taken by a target utility in order to achieve a given level of precision for parameter estimates. Hence, given these considerations, the transferability problem should be addressed in a wider context where, given the prior information from the existing experiments, the issue would be the determination of the size of the sample a recipient utility should provide subject to the achievement of a desired level of precision.

5. Conclusion

This paper has developed a mixed effects linear hierarchical model that is useful to the analysis of panel data. The model represents a flexible specification that allows control for the effects of both fixed and random factors affecting common behavior. We developed the estimation procedure for this model within the Bayesian framework and used de Finetti's idea of exchangeability for the random coefficients involved. We also derived the Bayes posterior odds ratio to test the exchangeability hypothesis in the context of a symmetric loss function.

We applied this model to the residential electricity time-of-use experiments to model regional heterogeneity by controlling for the effects of both random and fixed region-specific factors. We specified the effects of weather to be fixed and different for different experiments and the effects of prices to vary randomly with exchangeable distributions. After testing exchangeability for the random components of the model we realized that full transferability of data in both seasons can be achieved successfully only from the voluntary experiments. However, considering the standard errors with which the elasticities of substitution are estimated, we raised the issue of the precision with which a target utility could predict the response of their customers, particularly when they have no observations to contribute in the transferability process.

Given these considerations, we conclude that the transferability problem should be addressed in a wider context where, given prior information from the existing experiments, the issue would be the determination of the number of observations a recipient utility should collect in order to achieve a given level of precision. In principle there is no particular difficulty in addressing this issue.

6. Appendix

LEMMA: *Suppose, given θ_1 a vector of p_1 parameters and θ_2 a vector of p_2 parameters,*

$$Y \sim N(A_1\theta_1 + A_2\theta_2, C_1),$$

and, given θ_3 a vector of p_3 hyperparameters,

$$\theta_1 \sim N(A_3\theta_3, C_2)$$

and suppose that θ_2 given θ_1 is uniformly distributed. Then
   (a) the marginal distribution of Y given θ_2 is $N(A_1A_3\theta_3 + A_2\theta_2, C_1 + A_1C_2A_1')$;
   (b) the distribution of θ_1 given Y is $N(Bb, B)$ with

$$B^{-1} = A_1'K^{-1}A_1 + C_2^{-1}$$

$$b = A_1'K^{-1}Y + C_2^{-1}A_3\theta_3$$

where

$$K^{-1} = C_1^{-1} - C_1^{-1}A_2\left(A_2'C_1^{-1}A_2\right)^{-1}A_2'C_1^{-1};$$

(*c*) *the distribution of* θ_2 *given Y is N(Gg, G) with*

$$G^{-1} = A_2'RA_2$$

$$g = A_2'RY - A_2'C_1^{-1}A_1HC_2^{-1}A_3\theta_3$$

where

$$R = (C_1 + A_1C_2A_1')^{-1} \quad \text{and} \quad H = (C_2^{-1} + A_1'C_1^{-1}A_1)^{-1}.$$

PROOF:
(a) We can write $Y = A_1\theta_1 + A_2\theta_2 + u$ with $\theta_1 = A_3\theta_3 + v$ where $u \sim N(0, C_1)$ and $v \sim N(0, C_2)$. Hence putting the two quantities together we have $Y = A_1A_3\theta_3 + A_2\theta_2 + u + A_1v$. But by the standard properties of normal distributions, $Y \sim N(A_1A_3\theta_3 + A_2\theta_2, C_1 + A_1C_2A_1')$.
(b) In order to prove part (b) of the Lemma, we return to our starting point which is Bayes' theorem, namely

$$P(\theta_1, \theta_2 | Y) \propto P(\theta_1)P(Y | \theta_1, \theta_2),$$

and this after assuming a diffuse prior on $(\theta_2 | \theta_1)$. To get the distribution of $\theta_1 | Y$ we integrate out θ_2. $P(\theta_1, \theta_2 | Y) \propto \exp\{-Q/2\}$, where

$$Q = (Y - A_1\theta_1 - A_2\theta_2)'C_1^{-1}(Y - A_1\theta_1 - A_2\theta_2)$$

$$+ (\theta_1 - A_3\theta_3)'C_2^{-1}(\theta_1 - A_3\theta_3).$$

Q may be written as

$$(Y - A_1\theta_1)'C_1^{-1}(Y - A_1\theta_1) + (\theta_1 - A_3\theta_3)'C_2^{-1}(\theta_1 - A_3\theta_3)$$

$$+ \theta_2'A_2'C_1^{-1}A_2\theta_2 - 2\theta_2'A_2'C_1^{-1}(Y - A_1\theta_1).$$

Completing the square on θ_2, we have

$$Q = (Y - A_1\theta_1)'C_1^{-1}(Y - A_1\theta_1) + (\theta_1 - A_3\theta_3)'C_2^{-1}(\theta_1 - A_3\theta_3)$$

$$+ (\theta_2 - \tilde{\theta}_2)'A_2'C_1^{-1}A_2(\theta_2 - \tilde{\theta}_2)$$

$$- (Y - A_1\theta_1)'C_1^{-1}A_2(A_2'C_1^{-1}A_2)^{-1}A_2'C_1^{-1}(Y - A_1\theta_1),$$

where

$$\tilde{\theta}_2 = (A_2'C_1^{-1}A_2)^{-1}A_2'C_1^{-1}(Y - A_1\theta_1).$$

Integrating with respect to θ_2 yields

$$P(\theta_1 | Y) \propto \exp\left\{ \frac{-1}{2}\left[(Y - A_1\theta_1)'C_1^{-1}(Y - A_1\theta_1) \right. \right.$$

$$+ (\theta_1 - A_3\theta_3)'C_2^{-1}(\theta_1 - A_3\theta_3)$$

$$\left. \left. - (Y - A_1\theta_1)'C_1^{-1}A_2(A_2'C_1^{-1}A_2)^{-1}A_2'C_1^{-1}(Y - A_1\theta_1) \right] \right\}.$$

With $K^{-1} = C_1^{-1} - C_1^{-1}A_2(A_2'C_1^{-1}A_2)^{-1}A_2'C_1^{-1}$, the expression between brackets becomes

$$(Y - A_1\theta_1)'K^{-1}(Y - A_1\theta_1) + (\theta_1 - A_3\theta_3)'C_2^{-1}(\theta_1 - A_3\theta_3)$$

$$= (\theta_1 - Bb)'B^{-1}(\theta_1 - Bb) + \{Y'K^{-1}Y + \theta_3'A_3'C_2^{-1}A_3\theta_3 - b'Bb\}$$

The term in braces is constant as far as the distribution of θ_1 is concerned, and the remainder of the expression demonstrates the truth of (b).

(c) To prove part (c) we can carry out the same calculations but this time we integrate out θ_1. Returning to Q,

$$Q = (Y - A_2\theta_2)'C_1^{-1}(Y - A_2\theta_2) - 2\theta_1'A_1'C_1^{-1}(Y - A_2\theta_2)$$

$$+ \theta_1'A_1'C_1^{-1}A_1\theta_1 + (\theta_1 - A_3\theta_3)'C_2^{-1}(\theta_1 - A_3\theta_3)$$

$$= (Y - A_2\theta_2)'C_1^{-1}(Y - A_2\theta_2) - 2\theta_1'A_1'C_1^{-1}(Y - A_2\theta_2)$$

$$+ \theta_1'A_1'C_1^{-1}A_1\theta_1 + \theta_1'C_2^{-1}\theta_1 - 2\theta_1'C_2^{-1}A_3\theta_3 + \theta_3'A_3'C_2^{-1}A_3\theta_3$$

$$= \theta_1'\left(C_2^{-1} + A_1'C_1^{-1}A_1\right)\theta_1 - 2\theta_1'\left(C_2^{-1}A_3\theta_3 + A_1'C_1^{-1}(Y - A_2\theta_2)\right)$$

$$+ (Y - A_2\theta_2)'C_1^{-1}(Y - A_2\theta_2) + \theta_3'A_3'C_2^{-1}A_3\theta_3$$

Completing the square on θ_1 and integrating it out yields

$$(Y - A_2\theta_2)'C_1^{-1}(Y - A_2\theta_2) + \theta_3'A_3'C_2^{-1}A_3\theta_3$$

$$- \left(\theta_3'A_3'C_2^{-1} + (Y - A_2\theta_2)'C_1^{-1}A_1\right)\left(C_2^{-1} + A_1'C_1^{-1}A_1\right)^{-1}$$

$$\times \left(C_2^{-1}A_3\theta_3 + A_1'C_1^{-1}(Y - A_2\theta_2)\right)$$

$$= (Y - A_2\theta_2)'\left[C_1^{-1} - C_1^{-1}A_1\left(C_2^{-1} + A_1'C_1^{-1}A_1\right)^{-1}A_1'C_1^{-1}\right](Y - A_2\theta_2)$$

$$- 2(Y - A_2\theta_2)'C_1^{-1}A_1HC_2^{-1}A_3\theta_3 + \theta_3'A_3'C_2^{-1}A_3\theta_3$$

$$- \theta_3'A_3'C_2^{-1}\left(C_2^{-1} + A_1'C_1^{-1}A_1\right)^{-1}C_2^{-1}A_3\theta_3.$$

Note that $[C_1^{-1} - C_1^{-1}A_1(C_2^{-1} + A_1'C_1^{-1}A_1)^{-1}A_1'C_1^{-1}] = (C_1 + A_1C_2A_1')^{-1} = R$ given in Rao (1965) and as the matrix lemma in Lindley-Smith (1972) given below. Hence the quantity above is

$$Y'RY - 2\theta_2'A_2'RY + \theta_2'A_2'RA_2\theta_2 - 2Y'C_1^{-1}A_1HC_2^{-1}A_3\theta_3$$

$$+ 2\theta_2'A_2'C_1^{-1}A_1HC_2^{-1}A_3\theta_3 + \theta_3'A_3'C_2^{-1}A_3\theta_3$$

$$- \theta_3'A_3'C_2^{-1}\left(C_2^{-1} + A_1'C_1^{-1}A_1\right)^{-1}C_2^{-1}A_3\theta_3$$

$$= (\theta_2 - Gg)'G^{-1}(\theta_2 - Gg)$$

$$+ \left\{Y'RY - 2Y'C_1^{-1}A_1\left(C_2^{-1} + A_1'C_1^{-1}A_1\right)^{-1}A_1HC_2^{-1}A_3\theta_3\right.$$

$$\left. + \theta_3'A_3'C_2^{-1}A_3\theta_3 - \theta_3'A_3'C_2^{-1}\left(C_2^{-1} + A_1'C_1^{-1}A_1\right)^{-1}C_2^{-1}A_3\theta_3\right\},$$

where

$$G^{-1} = A_2'RA_2$$

$$g = A_2'RY - A_2'C_1^{-1}A_1HC_2^{-1}A_3\theta_3$$

with

$$R = (C_1 + A_1 C_2 A_1')^{-1}$$

$$H = (C_2^{-1} + A_1' C_1^{-1} A_1)^{-1}$$

The term in braces is constant as far as the distribution of θ_2 is concerned and the remainder of the expression proves part (c).

We next proceed to the main result. As explained in Section 3.2, we are dealing with the linear model which is now written in the form $E(Y) = A_1 \theta_1 + A_2 \theta_2$ in the first stage, where θ_1 is expressed in terms of hyperparameters θ_3 as another linear model, $E(\theta_1) = A_3 \theta_3$ with dispersion matrix C_2 and where θ_2 appears only in the first stage of the model by restricting it to be fixed. One can proceed for many stages, but it is enough for the moment to go to three stages, supposing the mean as well as the dispersion is known at the final stage. The following result provides the posterior distribution of θ_1 and the posterior distribution of θ_2:

THEOREM: *Suppose that given θ_1 and θ_2*

$$Y \sim N(A_1 \theta_1 + A_2 \theta_2, C_1). \tag{A.1}$$

Given θ_3,

$$\theta_1 \sim N(A_3 \theta_3, C_2), \tag{A.2}$$

and, given θ_4,

$$\theta_3 \sim N(A_4 \theta_4, C_3). \tag{A.3}$$

Then the posterior distribution of θ_1, given $\{A_i\}$, $\{C_i\}$, θ_4 and Y is $N(Aa, A)$ where

$$A^{-1} = A_1' K^{-1} A_1 + \{C_2 + A_3 C_3 A_3'\}^{-1} \tag{A.4}$$

$$a = A_1' K^{-1} Y + \{C_2 + A_3 C_3 A_3'\}^{-1} A_3 A_4 \theta_4 \tag{A.5}$$

and the posterior distribution of θ_2, given $\{A_i\}$, $\{C_i\}$ and Y is $N(Gg, G)$, where

$$G^{-1} = A_2' R A_2$$

and

$$g = A_2' RY - A_2' C_1^{-1} A_1 H C_2^{-1} A_3 \theta_3.$$

The joint distribution of θ_1 and θ_3 is described in (A.2) and (A.3). Then the use of part (a) of the Lemma enables the marginal distribution of θ_1 to be written as

$$\theta_1 \sim N(A_3 A_4 \theta_4, C_2 + A_3 C_3 A_3')$$

then with (A.1) as the likelihood, part (b) of the Lemma shows that the posterior distribution of θ_1 is as stated.

MATRIX LEMMA: *The following Lemma was used in Lindley-Smith* (1972) *and is very important to the extent that it allows us to obtain several alternative forms for the posterior mean and variance of θ_1.*
For any matrices A_3, C_2 and C_3 for which the inverses exist, we have

$$(C_2 + A_3 C_3 A_3')^{-1} = C_2^{-1} - C_2^{-1} A_3 (A_3' C_2^{-1} A_3 + C_3^{-1})^{-1} A_3' C_2^{-1}. \quad (A.6)$$

With this lemma we have:

COROLLARY 1: *An alternative expression for A^{-1} is*

$$A^{-1} = A_1' K^{-1} A_1 + C_2^{-1} - C_2^{-1} A_3 (A_3' C_2^{-1} A_3 + C_3^{-1})^{-1} A_3 C_2^{-1}. \quad (A.7)$$

With this corollary we can see what happens when $C_3^{-1} = 0$.

COROLLARY 2: *If $C_3^{-1} = 0$, the posterior distribution of θ_1 is*

$$N(A_0 a_0, A_0),$$

with

$$A_0^{-1} = A_1' K^{-1} A_1 + C_2^{-1} - C_2^{-1} A_3 (A_3' C_2^{-1} A_3)^{-1} A_3' C_2^{-1},$$

$$a_0 = A_1' K^{-1} Y,$$

and K^{-1} as before.

References

Acton, J.P., W.G. Manning, Jr. and M. Mitchell, 1978, Lessons to be Learned from the Los Angeles Rate Experiment in Electricity, Rand Report 4–2113-DWP. July (Rand Corporation, Santa Monica, California).

Aigner, D.J., 1979a, Bayesian Analysis of Optimal Sample Size and a Best Decision Rule for Experiments in Direct Load Control, *Journal of Econometrics* 9, 209–221.

Aigner, D.J., 1979b, A Brief Introduction to the Methodology of Optimal Experimental Design, *Journal of Econometrics* 11, 7–26.

Aigner, D.J., 1979c, Sample Design for Electricity Pricing Experiments, *Journal of Econometrics* 11, 195–205.

Aigner, D.J., 1985, The Residential Electricity Time-of-Use Pricing Experiments: What Have We Learned? Chapter 1 in *Social Experimentation*, edited by J.A. Hausman and D. Wise, Chicago: University of Chicago Press, 11–48.

Aigner, D.J. and J.A. Hausman, 1980, Correcting for Truncation Bias in the Analysis of Experiments in Time-of-Day Pricing of Electricity, *Bell Journal of Economics* 11, 131–142.

Aigner, D.J. and K. Ghali, 1989, Self-Selection in the Residential Electricity Time-of-Use Pricing Experiments, *Journal of Applied Econometrics* 4, S131–S144.

Aigner, D.J. and E.E. Leamer, 1984, Estimation of Time-of-Use Pricing Response in the Absence of Experimental Data, *Journal of Econometrics* 26, 205–228.

Balestra, P. and M. Nerlove, 1966, Pooling Cross-Section and Time Series Data in the Estimation of a Dynamic Model: The Demand for Natural Gas, *Econometrica* 34, 585–612.

Box, G.E.P. and G.C. Tiao, 1973, *Bayesian Inference in Statistical Analysis*, Reading, MA: Addison-Wesley.

Caves, D.W. and L.R. Christensen, 1980, Econometric Analysis of Residential Time-of-Use Pricing Experiments, *Journal of Econometrics* 14, 287–306.

Caves, D.W., L.R. Christensen and J.A. Herriges, 1984a, Consistency of Residential Customer Response in Time-of-Use Electricity Pricing Experiments, *Journal of Econometrics* 26, 179–203.

Caves, D.W., L.R. Christensen and J.A. Herriges, 1984b, Modelling Alternative Residential Peak-Load Electricity Rate Structures, *Journal of Econometrics* 24, 249–268.

Christensen Associates, Inc., 1983, Residential Response to Time-of-Use Rates: Development and Demonstration of a Transferability Model, Report RP1956–1, Electric Power Research Institute, Palo Alto, CA.

Dickey, J.M., 1971, The Weighted Likelihood Ratio, Linear Hypotheses on Normal Location Parameters, *The Annals of Mathematical Statistics* 42, 204–223.

Dyer, A.R., 1974, Hypothesis Testing Procedures for Separate Families of Hypotheses, *Journal of the American Statistical Association* 69, 140–145.

Fienberg, S.E. and A. Zellner, eds., 1975, *Studies in Bayesian Econometrics and Statistics*, Amsterdam: North-Holland.

Hausman, J.A., 1977, Social Experimentation, Truncated Distributions, and Efficient Estimation, *Econometrica* 45, 919–938.

Hausman, J.A., and W.E. Taylor, 1981, Panel Data and Unobservable Individual Effects, *Econometrica* 49, 1377–1398.

Heckman, J., 1979, Selection Bias as a Specification Error, *Econometrica* 47, 153–162.

Hirschberg, J.G. and D.J. Aigner, 1987, The Bayesian Estimation of Linear Models: An Application of the Lindley-Smith Hyperparameter Model, Working Paper #8702, Southern Methodist University, Dallas, TX.

Hsiao, C., 1986, *Analysis of Panel Data*, New York: Cambridge University Press.

Kohler, D., and B. Mitchell, 1984, Response to Residential Time-of-Use Electricity Rates: How Transferable are the Findings?, *Journal of Econometrics* 26, 141–178.

Leamer, E.E., 1978, *Specification Searches: Ad Hoc Inference with Non-Experimental Data*, New York: John Wiley and Sons.

Lindley, D.V. and A.F.M. Smith, 1972, Bayes Estimates for the Linear Model, *Journal of the Royal Statistical Society* 34, 1–41.

Manning, W.G. Jr., and J.P. Acton, 1980, Residential Electricity Demand Under Time-of-Day Pricing: Exploratory Data Analysis from the Los Angeles Rate Study, Report R-2426-DWP/HF. December (Rand Corporation, Santa Monica, California).

Miller, R.B., and W.G. Fortney, 1984, Industry Wide Expense Standards Using Random Coefficient Regression, *Mathematics and Economics* 3, 19–33.

Rao, C.R., 1965, *Linear Statistical Inference and Its Applications*, New York: John Wiley and Sons.

Rossi, P.E., 1980, Testing Hypothesis in Multivariate Regression: Bayes vs. Non-Bayes Procedures, Preliminary Draft, H.G.B. Alexander Research Foundation, Graduate School of Business, University of Chicago.

Taylor, L.D., 1975, The Demand for Electricity: A Survey, *Bell Journal of Economics and Management Science* 6, 74–110.

Theil, H., and D.G. Fiebig, 1984, *Exploiting Continuity*, Cambridge, MA: Ballinger Publishing Company.

Zellner, A., 1971, *An Introduction to Bayesian Analysis in Econometrics*, New York: John Wiley and Sons.

Zellner, A., 1978, Estimation of Functions of Population Means and Regression Coefficients Including Structural Coefficients: A Minimum Expected Loss (MELO) Approach, *Journal of Econometrics* 8, 127–158.

Zellner, A., 1979, Posterior Odds Ratios for Regression Hypotheses: General Considerations and Some Specific Results, Paper Presented at the Econometric Society Meeting, Atlanta, Georgia.

Zellner, A., 1986, Further Results on Bayesian Minimum Expected Loss (MELO) Estimates and Posterior Distributions for Structural Coefficients, *Advances in Econometrics* 5, 171–182.

Zellner, A. and A. Siow, 1980, Posterior Odds Ratios for Selected Regression Hypotheses, in J.M. Bernardo et al., eds., *Bayesian Statistics*, University of Valencia Press, Valencia, Spain.

Zellner, A., 1962, An Efficient Method of Estimating Seemingly Unrelated Regressions and Tests for Aggregation Bias, *Journal of the American Statistical Association* 57, 348–368.

Readings in Econometric Theory and Practice
W. Griffiths, H. Lütkepohl and M.E. Bock (Editors)

CHAPTER 6

ESTIMATION OF SYSTEMATIC RISK USING BAYESIAN ANALYSIS WITH HIERARCHICAL AND NON-NORMAL PRIORS *

Anil K. Bera

Department of Economics, University of Illinois, Champaign, IL 61820, USA and Department of Economics, Indiana University, Bloomington, IN 47405, USA

José A.F. Machado

Faculdade de Economia, Universidade Nova de Lisboa, Lisbon, Portugal and Department of Economics, University of Illinois, Champaign, IL 61820, USA

Estimation of systematic risk is one of the most important aspects of investment analysis, and has attracted the attention of many researchers. In spite of substantial contributions in the recent past, there still remains room for improvement in the methodologies currently available for forecasting systematic risk. This paper is concerned with some improved methods of estimating systematic risk for individual securities. We use Bayesian analysis with hierarchical and non-normal priors.

1. Introduction

The central model in most of the research pertaining to systematic risk has been the single index model

$$R_{it} = \alpha_i + \beta_i R_{mt} + \epsilon_{it}, \quad i = 1, 2, \ldots, N, \quad t = 1, 2, \ldots, T \tag{1}$$

* We would like to thank Bill Griffiths for numerous suggestions which improved the paper. Thanks are also due to an anonymous referee, Paul Newbold, Sidhartha Chib and Kim Sawyer for helpful comments and Pin Ng for drawing the figures. Earlier versions of this paper were presented at a Bayesian Conference in Econometrics and the Sixth World Congress of the Econometric Society. Responsibility for any errors and omissions is naturally solely ours. Financial support from the Bureau of Economic and Business Research and the Research Board of the University of Illinois is gratefully acknowledged.

where R_{it} and R_{mt} are, respectively, the random return on security i and the corresponding random market return in period t, α_i and β_i are the regression parameters appropriate to security i and ϵ_{it} is the random disturbance term which is distributed as normal with mean zero and variance σ_i^2. The parameter β_i, called beta, measures the systematic risk of the security i and is defined as $\text{Cov}(R_i, R_m)/\text{Var}(R_m)$.

Estimation of this systematic risk is one of the most important aspects of investment analysis and has attracted the attention of many researchers. Betas are used by the investors to evaluate the relative risk of different portfolios. In the future market context, betas of different stock portfolios are needed to calculate the number of contracts to be bought or sold. In spite of substantial contribution in the recent past, there still remains room for improvement in the methodologies currently available to forecast betas.

Blume (1971) observed that over time betas appear to take less extreme values and exhibit a tendency towards the market risk. This would mean that the historical betas based on ordinary least squares (OLS) estimation would be poor estimators of the future betas. Therefore, it is necessary to adjust the OLS estimators of β_i. Ohlson and Rosenberg (1982) tried to take account for the variation of beta over time by treating it as a stochastic parameter, and provided confidence regions using a mixture of classical and Bayesian perspective. Vasicek (1973) suggested a Bayesian adjustment technique using a normal prior for β_i. As it will be clear from the subsequent discussion, Vasicek's procedure has some drawbacks. It utilizes the information from the other stocks only through the cross-sectional mean and variance. In the New York Stock Exchange more than 2,000 stocks are traded; improved estimates of one stock might be obtained by combining the data from the other stocks as far as possible. We propose to do this utilizing Lindley and Smith's (1972) hyperparameter model and the concept of exchangeable priors. Under this framework, parameters of our linear model (1) themselves will have a general linear structure in terms of other quantities which are called hyperparameters. And exchangeability means that the joint distribution of β_i's is unaltered by any permutation of the suffixes. This assumption is weaker than the traditional independent and identically distributed (IID) set up. Lindley and Smith's linear hierarchical model has been used in many econometric applications, see e.g., Trivedi (1980), Haitovsky (1986), Ilmakunnas (1986), and Kadiyala and Oberhelman (1986). In Section 2, we set up the model in a convenient form and carry out the Bayesian analysis using the hierarchical model.

Recently, Bera and Kannan (1986) studied extensively the empirical distribution of betas. They considered the time period from July 1948 through

June 1983, and divided that period into seven non-overlapping estimation periods of 60 months each. They found that the empirical distributions of betas were highly positively skewed and often platykurtic. However, with a square-root transformation the values of skewness and kurtosis changed in such a way that using the Jarque and Bera (1987) test statistic the normality hypothesis could be accepted in four out of seven periods. Also the values of the test statistic in the remaining three periods were not very high. There-fore, it appears that beta has a root-normal distribution, i.e., the square-root of the variable is normal. The finding casts some doubts on the validity of Vasicek's selection of normal priors. Therefore, our second aim is to do a Bayesian analysis assuming that $\sqrt{\beta_i}$ is normally distributed or, in other words, β_i has a noncentral χ^2 distribution with one degree of freedom. In Section 3, we generalize our results of Section 2 by considering a hierarchical model with non-normal priors; while in Section 4, we present an empirical Bayesian analysis, similar to Vasicek's and based on our non-central chi-square prior distribution. In the last section of the paper, some concluding remarks are offered.

After the publication of Vasicek's paper in 1973, to our knowledge, there is no work along Bayesian lines which attempts to improve upon it. Also in the statistics literature, most Bayesian regression analyses are based on normal priors primarily because of their simplicity. Since here we have some empirical evidence on the distribution of betas, it is appropriate that we utilize that information in the analysis. We hope this will lead to improved estimation of betas.

2. Analysis with Hierarchical Priors

Under the classical framework, the maximum likelihood or the OLS estimator of β_i in model (1) is given by

$$\hat{\beta_i} = \frac{\sum_{t=1}^{T} x_t y_{it}}{\sum_{t=1}^{T} x_t^2} \quad i = 1, 2, \ldots, N$$

with $V(\hat{\beta_i}) = \sigma_i^2 / \sum_{t=1}^{T} x_t^2 \equiv S_i^2$, $y_{it} = R_{it} - \overline{R}_i$ and $x_t = R_{mt} - \overline{R}_m$. Vasicek (1973, pp. 1235–1236) suggested a Bayesian approach with normal prior for β_i

$$\beta_i \sim N(\overline{\beta}, \phi^2) \tag{2}$$

and showed that for large T, the posterior distribution of β_i conditional on $\bar{\beta}$ and ϕ^2 is approximately normal with mean

$$\frac{(\bar{\beta}/\phi^2) + (\hat{\beta}_i/S_i^2)}{(1/\phi^2) + (1/S_i^2)} \tag{3}$$

and variance $((1/\phi^2) + (1/S_i^2))^{-1}$. Vasicek suggested using the mean and variance of the cross-sectional betas in place of $\bar{\beta}$ and ϕ^2 respectively and $\hat{\sigma}_i^2 = \sum_{t=1}^{T}(y_{it} - \hat{\beta}_i x_t)^2/(T-2)$ in place of σ_i^2. As we should expect, had Vasicek assumed complete ignorance about $\bar{\beta}$ instead of $\bar{\beta}$ being known, that is $\phi^2 = \infty$, the posterior mean would be the OLS estimator. Empirical results in Bera and Kannan (1986, Tables VII and VIII) show that forecasts based on the Vasicek's adjusted betas (posterior mean) are superior to the OLS (unadjusted) betas. This indicates that we can improve prediction performance for a security by pooling information from other securities.

Let us now cast the model in Lindley and Smith's hierarchical framework. The sample information conveyed by (1) can be compactly written as

$$R \,|\, \theta_1 \sim N(A_1 \theta_1, C_1) \tag{4}$$

where $R = (R_1', \ldots, R_N')'$, $R_i = (R_{i1}, \ldots, R_{iT})'$, $\theta_1 = (\alpha_1, \ldots, \alpha_N, \beta_1, \ldots, \beta_N)'$, $A_1 = [I_N \otimes j_T \; I_N \otimes R_m]$, $R_m = (R_{m1}, \ldots, R_{mT})'$, $j_T = (1, \ldots, 1)'$ and $C_1 = \Sigma \otimes I_T$ with $\Sigma = \text{diag}\{\sigma_1^2, \ldots, \sigma_N^2\}$.

Next we assume exchangeability among the β_i, specifically

$$\beta_i \,|\, \xi \sim N(\xi, \tau^2) \tag{5}$$

with a second stage non-informative prior for ξ. Due to the randomness of ξ, this is a weaker assumption than the IID assumption in (3). To see it clearly, note that the joint prior distribution of $\beta_1, \beta_2, \ldots, \beta_N$ is given by

$$\pi(\beta_1, \beta_2, \ldots, \beta_N) = \int \left(\prod_{i=1}^{N} \pi(\beta_i \,|\, \xi) \right) f(\xi) \, d\xi$$

where $f(\xi)$ is the probability density function of ξ. Therefore, $\pi(\beta_1, \beta_2, \ldots, \beta_N)$ is a mixture of IID distributions conditional on ξ, but unconditionally the joint distribution does not satisfy the IID assumption. The above specification is a simple special case of Lindley and Smith's (1972, p. 6) general hierarchical model. Using a noninformative prior for $(\alpha_1, \ldots, \alpha_N)$ and ξ, our model can be written as

$$R \mid \theta_1 \sim N(A_1 \theta_1, C_1)$$

$$\theta_1 \mid \theta_2 \sim N(A_2 \theta_2, C_2)$$

with $\theta_2 = (0 \ \xi)'$, $A_2 = I_2 \otimes j_N$, and

$$C_2^{-1} = \begin{bmatrix} 0 & 0 \\ 0 & \dfrac{1}{\tau^2} I_N \end{bmatrix}.$$

For Lindley and Smith's model Bayesian inference can be drawn from the posterior for θ_1 given $\{A_i\}$, $\{C_i\}$, and R which is given by $N(Dd, D)$ where

$$D^{-1} = A_1' C_1^{-1} A_1 + C_2^{-1} - C_2^{-1} A_2 \left(A_2' C_2^{-1} A_2 \right)^{-1} A_2' C_2^{-1}$$

and

$$d = A_1' C_1^{-1} R.$$

Since we are interested only in the β_i parameters it is convenient to isolate their distribution. Partitioning D and d as

$$D = \begin{pmatrix} D_{11} & D_{12} \\ D_{21} & D_{22} \end{pmatrix} \quad \text{and} \quad d = \begin{pmatrix} d_1 \\ d_2 \end{pmatrix}$$

one can write the joint posterior distribution of $\beta_1, \beta_2, \ldots, \beta_N$ as

$$(\beta_1, \ldots, \beta_N)' \sim N(D_{21} d_1 + D_{22} d_2, D_{22})$$

with,

$$d_2 = \left(\frac{1}{\sigma_1^2} R_m' R_1, \ldots, \frac{1}{\sigma_N^2} R_m' R_N \right)'$$

$$d_1 = T \left(\overline{R}_1, \ldots, \overline{R}_N \right)'$$

$$D_{22} = \left[\text{diag}\left(\frac{x'x}{\sigma_1^2} + \frac{1}{\tau^2}, \ldots, \frac{x'x}{\sigma_N^2} + \frac{1}{\tau^2} \right) - \frac{1}{N\tau^2} j_N j_N' \right]^{-1}$$ (6)

$$D_{21} = -\bar{R}_m D_{22}$$

and where $x' = (x_1, \ldots, x_T)$. Using the above expression for the i-th security, the estimate of the systematic risk under a quadratic loss function can be expressed as

$$\beta_i^* = \left(\frac{x'x}{\sigma_i^2} + \frac{1}{\tau^2} \right)^{-1} \frac{x'x}{\sigma_i^2} \hat{\beta}_i + \left(\frac{x'x}{\sigma_i^2} + \frac{1}{\tau^2} \right)^{-1} \frac{1}{\tau^2} \left(\sum_{j=1}^{N} w_j \hat{\beta}_j \right)$$

where

$$w_j = \left[\sum_{i=1}^{N} \frac{x'x}{\tau^2 x'x + \sigma_i^2} \right]^{-1} \frac{x'x}{\tau^2 x'x + \sigma_j^2}.$$

A quick comparison of (3) and (7) reveals that both estimates are linear combinations of the OLS estimator and the mean of the cross-section betas, but for the hierarchical estimate a weighted average of the cross-section betas is used instead of a simple average as in the Vasicek case. β_i^* can also be expressed as

$$\beta_i^* = \frac{\sigma_i^2 \tau^2}{\tau^2(x'x) + \sigma^2} \left(\frac{\hat{\beta}_i}{\sigma^2 / x'x} + \frac{\bar{\beta}^*}{\tau^2} \right)$$

where $\beta^* = \sum_{j=1}^{N} \beta_j^* / N$. This formula, which is directly comparable with (3), reveals how the information from other securities is used in estimating the systematic risk for i-th security. Unlike in (3), the information conveyed by other stocks which is reflected in $\bar{\beta}^*$ is incorporated in a self-fulfilling way, since the cross-sectional average beta is consistent with the estimates for individual securities. This has a rational expectations interpretation in the sense that the market information embodied in $\bar{\beta}^*$ is compatible with all individual β_i^*.

To compare the above estimate with Vasicek's one, let us put his specification in Lindley and Smith's framework. The likelihood function is (4) and the (first stage) prior is

$$\beta_i | \bar{\beta} \sim N(\bar{\beta}, \phi^2).$$ (8)

which is "completely specified" by the cross-section data. The counterparts of (6) and (7) are respectively,

$$
D_{22V} = \left[\text{diag} \left(\frac{x'x}{\sigma_1^2} + \frac{1}{\phi^2}, \ldots, \frac{x'x}{\sigma_N^2} + \frac{1}{\phi^2} \right) \right]^{-1}
\tag{9}
$$

and

$$
\beta_{iV}^* = \left(\frac{x'x}{\sigma_i^2} + \frac{1}{\phi^2} \right)^{-1} \frac{x'x}{\sigma_i^2} \hat{\beta}_i + \left(\frac{x'x}{\sigma_i^2} + \frac{1}{\phi^2} \right)^{-1} \frac{1}{\phi^2} \left(\sum_{j=1}^{N} \frac{\hat{\beta}_j}{N} \right).
\tag{10}
$$

Comparing (7) and (10), we note that to find the average systematic risk in (10), a simple average is used whereas under the Lindley and Smith framework, we use a weighted average. The latter is more reasonable since the precisions in estimating the systematic risks of different securities are different from each other.

It is also interesting to note that

$$
D_{22V}^{-1} - D_{22}^{-1} = \text{diag} \left(\frac{1}{\phi^2} - \frac{1}{\tau^2}, \ldots, \frac{1}{\phi^2} - \frac{1}{\tau^2} \right) + \frac{1}{N\tau^2} j_N j_N'
$$

and as such we cannot say much about this matrix. However, when we put $\phi^2 = \tau^2$, i.e., the first stage prior variances are the same then $D_{22V}^{-1} - D_{22}^{-1}$ is positive semi-definite. In other words, the Vasicek's estimator has higher precision. This result is not at all surprising if we compare the prior distributions. Under the Vasicek prior at the second stage $V(\bar{\beta}) = 0$ whereas for the hyperparameter model we assume a second stage non-informative prior, i.e., $V(\xi)^{-1} = 0$. Therefore, the basic difference between the two approaches are two alternative ways of handling the unknown prior mean $\bar{\beta}$. In Vasicek's approach, the Bayes' estimator is derived assuming $\bar{\beta}$ is known and at the end it is replaced by the simple average. On the other hand, the Lindley and Smith method is more fully Bayesian in the sense that it uses non-informative prior for ξ (or $\bar{\beta}$).

Finally, we should note that the estimator in (7) depends on σ_i^2 and τ^2. In practice these parameters will have to be estimated. Assuming noninformative scale invariant priors, that is $\pi(\sigma_i) \propto \sigma_i^{-1}$ and $\pi(\tau) \propto \tau^{-1}$, the modal values from the joint posterior distribution of $(\beta_1, \beta_2, \ldots, \beta_N, \sigma_1, \sigma_2, \ldots, \sigma_N, \tau)$ are

$$\sigma_i^{*2} = \frac{1}{T} \sum_{t=1}^{T} (y_{it} - x_t \beta_i^*)^2$$

and

$$\tau^{*2} = \frac{1}{N} \sum_{i=1}^{N} (\beta_i^* - \bar{\beta}^*)^2$$

where β_i^* and $\bar{\beta}^*$ are as defined earlier. These equations, together with (7), can be solved iteratively. Other priors for σ_i^2 and τ^2, such as inverse χ^2, could also be handled easily [see Lindley and Smith (1972, p. 13)].

3. Analysis of Hierarchical Model with Non-normal Prior

Vasicek used a normal prior for the cross-sectional distribution of the beta coefficients. As mentioned earlier, the cross-sectional betas are not normally distributed, and recent work by Bera and Kannan (1986) indicates that their distribution tends to normal after a square-root transformation. It is therefore natural to explore the consequences of assuming a root-normal prior for beta, i.e.,

$$\sqrt{\beta_i} \sim N(\xi, \tau^2).$$

Then β_i/τ^2 will be distributed as a noncentral χ^2 with one degree of freedom and noncentrality parameter $(\xi/\tau)^2$, denoted by $\chi_1^2(\xi^2/\tau^2)$. The p.d.f. of β_i can be written as

$$\pi(\beta_i | \xi, \tau^2) = (2\pi)^{-1/2} (\beta_i \tau^2)^{-1/2} \exp\left\{ -\frac{1}{2\tau^2} (\beta_i + \xi)^2 \right\} \cosh\left(\frac{\xi \sqrt{\beta_i}}{\tau^2} \right)$$

$$\times I_{(0,\infty)}(\beta_i) \tag{11}$$

where $\cosh(z) = (e^z + e^{-z})/2$ and $I_{(0,\infty)}$ is an indicator function.

We shall develop a hierarchical framework by assuming non-informative priors for the α_i's and for the hyperparameters ξ and τ. The likelihood function is (4) and we consider the following prior structure

$$\pi(\theta_1) \propto \pi(\beta_1, \ldots, \beta_N)$$

$$\pi(\beta_i \mid \xi, \tau) = \tau^2 \chi^2_{(1)}(\xi^2/\tau^2), \quad i = 1, \ldots, N$$

$$\pi(\sigma_1, \ldots, \sigma_N) \propto \left(\prod_{i=1}^{N} \sigma_i \right)^{-1}$$

and

$$\pi(\xi, \tau) \propto \tau^{-1}.$$

Using (11), later we will find the exact form of the prior distribution $\pi(\beta_1, \ldots, \beta_N)$.

Combining (4) and the above prior structure, the posterior distribution is easily derived. Then integrating $(\alpha_1, \ldots, \alpha_N)$ out of the posterior distribution of θ_1 one gets the conditional posterior,

$$\pi(\beta_1, \ldots, \beta_N \mid R, \Sigma) \propto \pi(\beta_1, \ldots, \beta_N) \times \left(\prod_{i=1}^{N} \sigma_i^2 \right)^{-(T-1)/2}$$

$$\times \exp\left\{ -\sum_{i=1}^{N} \sum_{t=1}^{T} \frac{1}{2\sigma_i^2} (y_{it} - \beta_i x_t)^2 \right\}. \tag{12}$$

Using the noninformative prior for the σ_i's and integrating σ_i's out, one can obtain a general form for the posterior distribution of the β_i's,

$$\pi(\beta_1, \ldots, \beta_N \mid R) \propto \pi(\beta_1, \ldots, \beta_N)$$

$$\times \prod_{i=1}^{N} \left\{ (T-2) + \left(\frac{\beta_i - \hat{\beta}_i}{s_{\hat{\beta}_i}} \right)^2 \right\}^{-(T-1)/2}. \tag{13}$$

To obtain a workable form for the posterior, we next derive the prior $\pi(\beta_1, \ldots, \beta_N)$ from (11), which will then be substituted in the above expression.

The joint prior distribution for $\beta_1, \beta_2, \ldots, \beta_N$, ξ and τ can be written as

$$\pi(\beta_1, \beta_2, \ldots, \beta_N, \xi, \tau) \propto \tau^{-(N+1)} \left(\prod_{i=1}^{N} \beta_i^{-1/2} \right)$$

$$\times \exp\left\{ -\frac{1}{2\tau^2} \sum_{i=1}^{N} (\beta_i + \xi)^2 \right\}$$

$$\times \prod_{i=1}^{N} \left(\cosh\left(\frac{\xi\sqrt{\beta_i}}{\tau^2} \right) \right).$$

Integrating ξ out of the above expression and after some simplification, we obtain

$$\pi(\beta_1, \beta_2, \ldots, \beta_N, \tau) \propto \tau^{-N} \left(\prod_{i=1}^{N} \beta_i^{-1/2} \right)$$

$$\times \exp\left\{ -\frac{1}{2\tau^2} \sum_{i=1}^{N} \left[\beta_i^2 - (\overline{\beta} - \overline{A})^2 \right] \right\} \qquad (14)$$

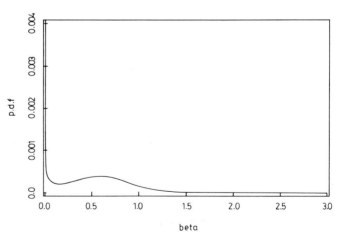

Figure 1. Posterior p.d.f of β for the hierarchical model.

where

$$\bar{\beta} = \frac{1}{N} \sum_{i=1}^{N} \beta_i \quad \text{and} \quad \bar{A} = \frac{1}{N} \sum_{i=1}^{N} \log\left\{\cosh\left(\sqrt{\beta_i}\right)\right\}.$$

From (14), integration with respect to τ gives us the joint prior for $(\beta_1, \beta_2, \ldots, \beta_N)$ as

$$\pi(\beta_1, \beta_2, \ldots, \beta_N) \propto \left(\prod_{i=1}^{N} \beta_i^{-1/2}\right)\left[\sum_{i=1}^{N}\left\{\beta_i^2 - \left(\bar{\beta} - \bar{A}\right)^2\right\}\right]^{-(N-1)/2}$$

$$(15)$$

Substituting (15) in (13), we have the posterior distribution

$$\pi(\beta_1, \beta_2, \ldots, \beta_N \mid R) \propto \left[\sum_{i=1}^{N}\left\{\beta_i^2 - \left(\bar{\beta} - \bar{A}\right)^2\right\}\right]^{-(N-1)/2}$$

$$\times \prod_{i=1}^{N}\left[\beta_i^{-1/2}\left\{(T-2) + \left(\frac{\beta_i - \hat{\beta}_i}{s_{\hat{\beta}_i}}\right)^2\right\}^{-(T-1)/2}\right]$$

$$= \bar{H} \times \prod_{i=1}^{N} H(\beta_i) \quad \text{(say)}. \tag{16}$$

The second part of this posterior is the p.d.f. that would result if no pooling of time series and cross section information occurs. In Figure 1, we plot this part of the posterior density (though still it is called posterior p.d.f.) for $\hat{\beta}_i = 1$, $s_{\hat{\beta}_i} = 0.5$ and $T = 21$. As we observe from the figure, the factor $(\beta^{-1/2})$ moves the "mode" towards zero, as follows easily from the fact that

$$\frac{dH(\beta_i)}{d\beta_i} < 0.$$

Cross-sectional information is truely reflected in the first part of the posterior

$$\bar{H} = \left[\sum_{i=1}^{N}\left\{\beta_i^2 - \left(\bar{\beta} - \bar{A}\right)^2\right\}\right]^{-(N-1)/2}$$

where $\bar{A}$, logarithm of the geometric mean of $\cosh(\sqrt{\beta_i})$, incorporates the information from the other securities. Bayes estimator implied by the posterior (16), is comparable to β_i^* in (7) where the pooling takes place through a weighted average of the cross-section betas. Unfortunately, the expression (16) cannot be integrated further to obtain the posterior p.d.f. of individual security betas.

4. Non-hierarchical Approach with Non-normal Prior

Instead of a hierarchical model, we now adopt a single stage root-normal prior for β. As in Vasicek, the hyperparameters $\bar{\beta}$ and ϕ are assumed to be known, although in applications these will have to be estimated. The prior structure of the model can now be written as,

$$\pi(\beta_i \mid \phi, \beta) = \phi^2 \cdot \chi_1^2(\bar{\beta}^2/\phi^2), \quad i = 1, \ldots, N$$

$$\pi(\sigma_1, \sigma_2, \ldots, \sigma_N) \propto \left(\prod_{i=1}^{N} \sigma_i \right)^{-1}.$$

The joint posterior distribution of $(\beta_1, \ldots, \beta_N)$ conditional on $\bar{\beta}$ and ϕ can be derived along the lines similar to the previous section. However, applied work with that posterior will be slightly messy. Simpler results can be obtained by using a central χ^2 approximation to the priors for β_i's. A central χ^2 approximation to our prior p.d.f. is [see Johnson and Kotz (1970, p. 139)],

$$\frac{\beta_i}{c\phi^2} \sim \chi_f^2$$

where $c = (1 + \delta)^{-1}(1 + 2\delta)$, $f = 1 + \delta^2(1 + 2\delta)^{-1}$ and $\delta = (\bar{\beta}/\phi)^2$. Therefore, the prior for β_i is a gamma density whose kernel is,

$$\beta_i^{f/2-1} \exp\left\{ -\frac{\beta_i}{h} \right\} \beta_i > 0$$

where $h = 2c\phi^2$. It is worth noting that, even though $2c\phi^2$ is, for fixed f, a scale parameter, f is not a location parameter. It is therefore difficult to develop a hierarchical model with non-informative second stage priors based upon this central χ^2 approximation.

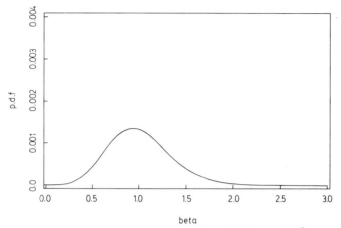

Figure 2. Posterior p.d.f. of β for the nonhierarchical model with central χ^2 approximation.

As the β_i's are (conditional on $\bar{\beta}$ and ϕ) IID, the joint prior is the product of the marginal priors. Substituting this prior specification in the general form (13) one gets,

$$\pi\left(\beta_i \mid R, f, h\right) \propto \beta_i^{f/2-1} \exp\left\{-\frac{\beta_i}{h}\right\}\left\{(T-2) + \left(\frac{\beta_i - \hat{\beta}_i}{s_{\hat{\beta}_i}}\right)^2\right\}^{-(T-1)/2},$$

$$\beta_i > 0.$$

The plot in Figure 2 illustrates the shape of this density. The values of f and h are those implied by $\bar{\beta} = 1.03$ and $\phi = 0.22$. These values were selected from the findings in Bera and Kannan (1986). As in Figure 1, we set $\hat{\beta}_i = 1$, $s_{\hat{\beta}_i} = 0.5$ and $T = 21$.

It can easily be shown that the posterior mean exists. Indeed for $T \geq 3$,

$$\int_0^\infty \beta_i \pi\left(\beta_i \mid R, f, h\right) d\beta_i \leq \int_0^\infty \beta_i^{f/2} \exp\left\{-\frac{\beta_i}{h}\right\} d\beta_i$$

$$= \Gamma(f/2 + 1)h^{(f/2+1)}$$

where the last equality follows from the gamma p.d.f.

It is apparent that, at least for the parameter values used, the posterior p.d.f. is unimodal and almost symmetric though slightly skewed to the right. The least squares estimator can be larger or smaller than the modal value. In fact, straightforward algebra yields

$$\text{sign}\left\{\frac{\mathrm{d}\pi(\beta_i \mid y)}{\mathrm{d}\beta_i}\right\} \equiv \text{sign}\left\{h\left(\frac{f}{2} - 1\right) - \hat{\beta}_i\right\}.$$

Therefore, if $\hat{\beta}_i \lessgtr h(f/2 - 1)$ it follows from the shape of the p.d.f. that the Bayes estimator β_i^* under a quadratic loss will satisfy $\beta_i^* \gtrless \hat{\beta}_i$. Under 0–1 loss function, the Bayes estimators can be obtained from the modal values of $\pi(\beta_i \mid y,\ x,\ f,\ h)$, $i = 1,\ 2, \ldots, N$. For example, with $\bar{\beta} = 1.03$, $\phi = 0.22$ (implying $f = 11.72$ and $h = 0.19$) one has the Bayes' estimator $\beta_i^* = 0.957$, when we set $\hat{\beta}_i = 1$, $s_{\hat{\beta}_i} = 0.5$ and $T = 21$. If we take Bayes estimates as an improved predictor for beta, then the above observation agrees with the findings of earlier researchers that relatively high and low OLS beta estimates tend to overpredict and underpredict, respectively, the corresponding betas for the subsequent time period [see, e.g., Blume (1971) and Klemkosky and Martin (1975)].

5. Concluding Remarks

We have presented only some theoretical results. It would be interesting to apply our procedures to real data, and see whether that leads to improved forecasts for systematic risk. On the theoretical side, some other prior distribution can be used instead of a non-central χ^2 distribution. One possibility is to use a mixture of two (or a few) normal distributions. A second possibility is to take a normal prior for β with mean modeled in terms of a regression function of some firm specific variables. The prior variance could also be defined from a regression model. Lastly, a number of other approximations for non-central χ^2 distribution are available. For example, $\chi_1^2(\delta)$ can be approximated by a central χ^2 with $1 + \nu$ degrees of freedom where ν is a Poisson random variable with mean $\delta/2$.

References

Bera, A.K., and Kannan, S. (1986), "An Adjustment Procedure for Predicting Systematic Risk," *Journal of Applied Econometrics*, 1, 317–332.
Blume, M.E. (1971), "On the Assessment of Risk," *Journal of Finance*, 26, 1–10.

Haitovsky, Y. (1986), "The Linear Hierarchical Model and Its Applications in Econometric Analysis," in *Bayesian Inference and Decision Techniques*, eds., P. Goel and A. Zellner, Amsterdam: Elsevier Science Publishers, pp. 119–138.

Ilmakunnas, P. (1986), "Stochastic Constraints on Cost Function Parameters: Mixed and Hierarchical Approaches," *Empirical Economics*, 11, 69–80.

Jarque, C.M., and Bera, A.K. (1987), "Test for Normality of Observations and Regression Residuals," *International Statistical Review*, 55, 163–172.

Johnson, N.L. and S. Kotz (1970), *Continuous Univariate Distributions,Vol. 2*, New York: Wiley.

Kadiyala, K.R., and Oberhelman, D. (1986), "Estimation of Actual Realizations in Stochastic Parameter Models," in *Bayesian Inference and Decision Techniques*, eds., P. Goel and A. Zellner, Amsterdam: Elsevier Science Publishers, pp. 363–373.

Klemkosky, R.C., and Martin, J.D. (1975), "The Adjustment of Beta Forecasts," *Journal of Finance*, 30, 1123–1128.

Lindley, D.V., and Smith, A.F. M. (1972), "Bayes Estimates for the Linear Model," *Journal of the Royal Statistical Society*, Series B, 34, 1–41.

Ohlson, J., and Rosenberg, B. (1982), "Systematic Risk of the CRSP Equal-weighted Common Stock Index: A History Estimated by Stochastic-Parameter Regression," *Journal of Business*, 55, 121–145.

Trivedi, P.K. (1980), "Small Samples and Collateral Information: An Application of the Hyperparameter Model," *Journal of Econometrics*, 12, 301–318.

Vasicek, O.A. (1973), "A Note on Using Cross-Sectional Information in Bayesian Estimation of Security Betas," *Journal of Finance*, 28, 1233–1239.

Readings in Econometric Theory and Practice
W. Griffiths, H. Lütkepohl and M.E. Bock (Editors)

CHAPTER 7

BAYESIAN ANALYSIS AND REGULARITY CONDITIONS ON FLEXIBLE FUNCTIONAL FORMS: APPLICATION TO THE U.S. MOTOR CARRIER INDUSTRY

James A. Chalfant

Department of Agricultural Economics, University of California, Davis, CA 95616, USA

Nancy E. Wallace *

Haas School of Business, University of California, Berkeley, CA 94720, USA

Flexible functional forms often do not satisfy underlying restrictions from microeconomic theory. These restrictions can be viewed as prior information, taking the form of constraints on the parameters of the flexible form. Equality restrictions can easily be incorporated into such models, but inequality restrictions such as concavity and monotonicity are more difficult to handle. This paper illustrates the imposition of these restrictions in a generalized Leontief cost function, using a Bayesian approach and Monte Carlo integration via importance sampling. The application to the U.S. motor carrier industry shows that concavity is much more consistent with the data than is monotonicity.

1. Introduction

Most empirical production studies of transportation industries rely on flexible functional forms for estimation. Flexible functional forms are used because they do not impose *a priori* restrictions on the input substitution and own-price elasticities. Econometric estimates of cost functions can therefore be used to reveal the underlying structure of production technology. One problem with the most commonly used flexible functional forms, such as the translog or generalized Leontief, is that violations of underlying theoretical restrictions are frequently encountered. The most difficult restrictions to

* We owe thanks to a number of individuals, especially David Giles, Richard Gray, William Griffiths, and Kenneth White. A large debt is owed also to George Judge, for encouraging us to think about prior beliefs and the Bayesian approach and for generosity and enthusiasm more than two standard deviations above the mean.

impose on a cost function are concavity and monotonicity, since they require inequality restrictions on parameters. These restrictions cannot be handled easily with conventional estimation methods. The existing strategy to impose curvature restrictions (e.g. Jorgensen and Fraumeni, 1981) is known to bias parameter estimates in the case of the translog and omits the possibility of complementarity between pairs of inputs in the case of the generalized Leontief (Diewert and Wales, 1987).

One purpose of this paper is to demonstrate how the Bayesian approach to inference can accommodate inequality restrictions in transportation production studies. Based on Geweke (1986, 1988, 1989) and Chalfant and White (1988), curvature and monotonicity restrictions are imposed on the generalized Leontief cost function, estimated for a sample of Class I and II general freight motor carriers in the United States. The firms in the sample are those that did not purchase supplemental transportation services from other firms in the pre- and post-deregulation environments (1979 and 1981). [1]

These carriers are selected because most recent empirical studies of highway motor carriers focus either exclusively on firms that purchase transportation or do not distinguish between firms that do and do not purchase transportation services (Daughety et al. (1986), Daughety and Nelson (1987), Rose (1986)). There is, therefore, little information available on the production technology of firms that solve the linehaul deployment problem internally, rather than purchase linehaul transportation either through brokers or on long term contracts from other firms.

The generalized Leontief specification is chosen for estimation because existing techniques to impose concavity on this cost function always impose the additional restriction that all input pairs are substitutes. This is not implied by the theory but by the sufficient restrictions used for concavity. For this reason, the Bayesian technique we use offers the only convenient method to impose the necessary conditions for concavity. The generalized Leontief can also be shown to be a special case of other flexible functional forms, such as the generalized McFadden or the generalized Barnett (Diewert and Wales (1987)), so the techniques presented in this paper are applicable to a broad class of models. Finally, it is a convenient flexible form that has not been

---

[1] The Motor Carrier Act of 1980 substantially changed motor carrier regulation in the United States by easing the regulatory control of market entry and restricting the use of collective rate making. As a result, the industry has been under considerable pressure to change from a market structure largely determined by regulatory policies to one determined by the structure of cost and technology in motor carrier service provision.

applied as often in this literature, so its compatibility with these data is of some intrinsic interest.

The paper is organized as follows. The cost function and input demand equations for the highway motor carrier industry are introduced in Section 2. The problems with concavity restrictions in this context are discussed. Section 3 presents the Bayesian approach to estimation with concavity and monotonicity restrictions. The data are presented in Section 4 and the results are discussed. Conclusions follow in Section 5.

2. The Model

Following standard notation for the representation of the dual cost function, assume that the restricted production possibility set for the highway motor carrier firm can be denoted by $Y(t)$, composed of all feasible input/output bundles consistent with the network technology t used by the firm. If the input vector is $x \in R^N$ and the output vector is $y \in R^1$, the transformation function can be written as $T(y, x, t)$ with feasibility written as $T(y, x, t) \le 0$.

Letting $p \in R^N$ be the vector of input prices and assuming that the firm takes input prices as exogenous and minimizes the cost of producing a chosen level of output, the cost function can be represented by

$$C = C(y, p, t). \tag{1}$$

Our specification of the motor carrier cost function is similar to an adaptation of the generalized Leontief used by Lopez (1980):

$$C(y, p, t) = y \sum_{i=1}^{N} \sum_{j=1}^{N} b_{ij} p_i^{1/2} p_j^{1/2} + y^2 \sum_{i=1}^{N} \alpha_i p_i + y \sum_{k=1}^{T} \sum_{j=1}^{N} \gamma_{jk} p_j t_k \tag{2}$$

where y is output, defined in millions of ton-miles, the t_k's are the T attributes of the firm's network, the p_i's are the input prices, and N is the number of inputs. Typically, the only theoretical restrictions that are imposed *a priori* are continuity, linear homogeneity in the input prices, and symmetry ($b_{ij} = b_{ji}$ for $i, j = 1, 2, \ldots, N$). All other conditions required for a well defined cost function, such as nonnegativity, monotonicity, and concavity, depend on the estimated parameters b_{ij}, α_i, and γ_{jk}.

Checks for global concavity are usually carried out by checking whether the matrix of second derivatives of the cost function is negative semi-definite for each observation in the sample. Monotonicity requires that the predicted budget shares are positive and that costs are nondecreasing in output. It is common to observe violations of both concavity and monotonicity for some subset of firms in most samples. Alternatively, concavity can be imposed globally on the generalized Leontief by constraining each b_{ij} in (2) for $i \neq j$ to be nonnegative (Diewert and Wales (1987)). Imposition of these restrictions, however, rules out complementarity between all pairs of inputs and therefore destroys the second order flexibility of this functional form. The constraints are also difficult to interpret statistically, since the usual likelihood ratio test does not apply.

Using Shepard's Lemma, the cost minimizing input demand equations can be obtained from (2):

$$x_i = \frac{\partial C}{\partial p_i} = \sum_{j=1}^{N} b_{ij} \left(\frac{p_j}{p_i}\right)^{1/2} \cdot y + \alpha_i \cdot y^2 + \sum_{k=1}^{T} \gamma_{ik} t_k y \tag{3}$$

where, as defined above, x_i is the quantity demanded of the ith factor input. Assuming that the observed firm's input demands are distributed stochastically around the efficient cost minimizing input bundle for the industry, a disturbance term, e_{im}, for the ith input of firm m, is appended to (3). It is assumed that $E(e_{im}) = 0$. However, from preliminary tests and following Diewert and Wales (1987), we assume that the variance of the disturbance term for the ith input is proportional to the square of the level of output ($V(e_{im}) = y_m^2 \sigma_i^2$). The advantage of this admittedly arbitrary assumption is that the factor demand equations above can be estimated in terms of input/output ratios by dividing through by output for the mth observation, y_m. Equation (3) above becomes

$$\frac{x_i}{y_m} = \sum_{j=1}^{N} b_{ij} \left(\frac{p_j}{p_i}\right)^{1/2} + \alpha_i \cdot y_m + \sum_{k=1}^{T} \gamma_{ik} t_k + \mu_{im} \tag{4}$$

where $\mu_{im} = e_{im}/y_m$, which has a homoscedastic variance.

Two estimation strategies could be used to estimate the parameters in the generalized Leontief system of equations. The system defined by (4) could be estimated using the N input-output equations and Zellner's (1962) iterated seemingly unrelated regression technique, to impose across-equation restrictions. Alternatively, the cost function could be appended to that system of equations, and the $N + 1$ equation system could be estimated using the same method. The advantage of including the cost function is that the intercept of the cost function, unrecoverable by the first method, can be explicitly estimated. It also seems reasonable to expect additional efficiency in estimation, when the model is correctly specified, by not throwing away the information contained in the equation for the cost function.

3. The Bayesian Approach to Inequality Restrictions

The Bayesian approach offers an alternative to the more common strategies of imposing inequality restrictions on cost and input demand systems in conventional approaches to estimation. Following Geweke (1986) and Chalfant and White (1988), inequality restrictions can be treated as prior beliefs about parameters and easily accommodated within the framework of Bayesian inference.

As is well known, the Bayesian approach begins with the specification of a prior density function defined over the parameter vector θ, call it $p(\theta)$ (e.g. Zellner (1971); Judge et al. (1985)). The prior density summarizes all of the available information about θ prior to estimation. A simple example would be the case in which all parameter values that satisfy the inequality constraint were considered equally likely. A prior density proportional to a constant, $p(\theta) \propto c$ for $\theta \in D$, where D denotes the region of the parameter space that is consistent with the inequality constraints, could then be used to summarize prior information. Presumably, D is a region specified by the particular economic theory, such as concavity of the cost function in the present example.

From Bayes' Theorem, the prior density and sample information can be combined to obtain the posterior distribution for the parameters of the θ vector, given some data set z:

$$f(\theta \mid z) \propto p(\theta) \cdot L(\theta \mid z)$$

where $L(\ )$ denotes the sample likelihood function. The Bayesian approach differs from sampling-theoretic approaches in that posterior beliefs are conditional only on prior beliefs and on the observed data set, instead of emphasizing the performance of an estimator in repeated samples. If the prior density has a positive mass only within D, the posterior density is truncated, unlike the sample likelihood. The posterior density is thus defined only over the restricted parameter space and summarizes the available information about the parameters in the model given the restrictions. It can be used to calculate various confidence intervals and probabilities related to hypotheses about θ, to obtain a point estimate of θ, or to derive related estimates such as a set of substitution elasticities.

The Bayesian approach to estimation selects the point estimator that minimizes the expected value of the researcher's loss function. A plausible and convenient choice for the loss function is the quadratic loss function, in which case the mean of the posterior distribution for θ minimizes expected loss (e.g. Judge et al., 1985). [2] Bayesian point estimates of the parameters of the input demand system can be obtained once prior beliefs in the form of inequality restrictions using $p(\theta)$ have been set, the posterior density has been derived, and the mean of the posterior density has been calculated.

An advantage of taking the Bayesian approach to concavity restrictions in the case of the Leontief cost function turns out to be that the inequality restrictions on the parameters can be described solely in terms of elasticities of substitution. The concavity restriction implies that the matrix of substitution elasticities must be negative semi-definite; there is no need to express the inequality restrictions in terms of the parameters of the model. As with most flexible forms, these are not of any particular interest, and elasticities are the preferred means of presenting results.

In the case of the generalized Leontief cost function, the own price elasticities, E_{ii}, are obtained from

$$E_{ii} = -\frac{y}{2x_i} \sum_{j=1}^{N} b_{ij} \left(\frac{p_j}{p_i}\right)^{1/2} \tag{5}$$

where all terms are as previously defined. Similarly,

$$E_{ij} = -\frac{y}{2x_j} \left(\frac{p_j}{p_i}\right)^{1/2} \tag{6}$$

where $i \neq j$. The Hicks-Allen partial elasticities of substitution can then be calculated as follows

$$\sigma_{ij} = \frac{E_{ij}}{S_j} \tag{7}$$

where $\sigma_{ij} = \sigma_{ji}$ is the partial elasticity of substitution between input i and input j and S_j is the cost share of input j.

The validity of inequality restrictions for concavity can be checked by examination of the substitution elasticities everywhere in the parameter space where the restrictions hold. Monotonicity can be checked using pre-

---

[2] Zellner (1988) notes that the posterior mode (i.e. the inequality constrained maximum-likelihood estimate) corresponds to a zero-one loss function, which seems implausible for most applications.

dicted budget shares. The posterior mean, call it $\bar{\theta}$, the Bayesian point estimate corresponding to a quadratic loss function, can be obtained by finding the mean of the truncated posterior distribution for the parameter vector. In principle, this is a straightforward calculation; in practice, there may be numerical problems to overcome, to which we turn after describing the details of the estimation process.

Given the generalized Leontief specification of the data generating mechanism, the cost function and the input/output ratio equations are assumed to form a seemingly unrelated regression with normally distributed errors and a contemporaneous covariance matrix Σ. Unconstrained maximum likelihood (via iterated seemingly unrelated regressions) can be used to obtain an estimate of θ and an associated variance-covariance matrix Ω. The vector of G dependent variables for this system is

$$z = \left(C, \frac{x_1}{y}, \frac{x_2}{y}, \ldots, \frac{x_N}{y} \right)'$$

where $G = N + 1$ is the number of equations. Following Zellner (1971) and Judge et al. (1985), a suitable diffuse prior density for Σ is

$$p(\Sigma) \propto |\Sigma|^{-((G+1)/2)} \tag{8}$$

For the case of an uninformative prior on θ, and *a priori* independence of θ and Σ, the kernel of the marginal posterior density function for θ is given by

$$f(\theta \mid z) = |A|^{-M/2} \tag{9}$$

where M is the sample size. The G by G matrix A has typical elements a_{ij} given by

$$a_{ij} = \left[e_i(\theta)' e_j(\theta) \right], \tag{10}$$

where $e_i(\theta)$ is the M-dimensional vector of residuals for the ith equation, evaluated using any value of θ for which the posterior is defined. With a completely uninformative prior, one would use the density in (9) to express posterior beliefs. When prior beliefs take the form of inequality restrictions, one obtains a truncated version of (9). For example, D may represent the region over which concavity holds. The truncated posterior density, $\tau \cdot f^R(\theta \mid z)$, is obtained by truncating the posterior density so that θ is within the region of the parameter space consistent with the inequality restrictions (concavity or monotonicity). τ is a constant of proportionality and $f^R(\theta \mid z) = I(\theta) \cdot f(\theta \mid z)$, where $I(\theta) = 1$ if $\theta \in D$ and 0 otherwise.

Given the specification of the quadratic loss function and the restrictions, the posterior mean of interest is the solution to

$$E(\theta \mid z) = \int_\theta \theta \tau \cdot f^R(\theta \mid z) \ \mathrm{d}\theta, \tag{11}$$

which is guaranteed to be consistent with the inequality restrictions. It is also possible to calculate what would be the posterior probability that the restrictions hold, given completely uninformative priors:

$$p = \int_\theta I(\theta) \kappa \cdot f(\theta \mid z) \ \mathrm{d}\theta, \tag{12}$$

where κ normalizes $f(\theta \mid z)$ to be a proper density function. This value is of interest even if the restrictions are satisfied by the sample maximum likelihood estimate; a well-behaved maximum likelihood estimate does not imply that the posterior probability that the restrictions hold is one.

The integrals above would be intractable, even if it were possible to specify the region D. Also, numerical integration over so many dimensions is impractical, so random sampling is necessary to estimate the expectations of interest. Following Geweke (1986) and others, Chalfant and White (1988) made use of the method of importance sampling to examine concavity and monotonicity, estimating the expectations defined above without a random sample from the unknown density. Importance sampling replaces the unknown posterior density with a convenient density for θ and adjusts for the fact that the sampling is not from the correct density. This method of obtaining the posterior mean can be motivated by observing that (11) is equivalent to

$$E(\theta \mid z) = \int_\theta \theta \frac{\tau \cdot f^R(\theta \mid z)}{g^R(\theta \mid z)} g^R(\theta \mid z) \ \mathrm{d}\theta, \tag{13}$$

where $g(\theta \mid z)$ is a more convenient probability density function for θ (for instance, the multivariate normal or multivariate t). Replications from the truncated density $g^R(\theta \mid z)$ can be obtained by sampling from $g(\theta \mid z)$ and then deleting those replications not contained in D. Given a random sample of sufficient size from $g^R(\theta \mid z)$, it would be possible to estimate the expected value of interest by averaging the observed values of

$$\theta \frac{\tau \cdot f^R(\theta \mid z)}{g^R(\theta \mid z)}.$$

For this method to work, the density $g^R(\theta \mid z)$ must cover the same range as the posterior density function. The truncated multivariate t density function is used for the calculations below. [3]

The steps involved are:

(1) Estimate the parameters of the generalized Leontief cost function, as discussed in Section 2, and obtain the maximum likelihood estimate $\hat{\theta}$ and its estimated variance-covariance matrix $\hat{\Omega}$.

(2) Generate replications of θ from the multivariate t distribution. Since fairly thick tails are desired, to ensure sampling over the entire range of the posterior density, we do so for the case of 4 degrees of freedom. The steps involved are those in van Dijk and Kloek (1980), using the estimates from step 1 for location and scale parameters. We also used the antithetic replications to improve convergence, as discussed by Geweke (1988).

(3) Examine each replication to see whether, using elasticities and predicted input-output ratios calculated using each θ and the sample mean values for prices and any other independent variables, the concavity and monotonicity restrictions are violated. [4] Concavity is evaluated by calculating the substitution elasticities at each replication, to see if the matrix of elasticities is negative semi-definite, and monotonicity by calculating the predicted input-output ratios using each new θ and the independent variables from every observation in the original sample. Each of these calculations is repeated for every replication of θ.

(4) Estimate the mean of the posterior distribution using the n replications that satisfy the restrictions:

$$\bar{\theta} = \frac{\sum\limits_{k=1}^{n} \theta_k \dfrac{f^R(\theta_k \mid z)}{g^R(\theta_k \mid z)}}{\sum\limits_{k=1}^{n} \dfrac{f^R(\theta_k \mid z)}{g^R(\theta_k \mid z)}}. \tag{15}$$

The denominator in (15) serves as a normalizing constant to correct for the use of the kernels of the proper densities.

---

[3] Geweke (1989) gives an excellent discussion of the evaluation of a suitable density to use for importance sampling. In particular, it should have tails with at least as much probability as those of the posterior density. See Geweke (1989) or Chalfant and White (1988) for further discussion.
[4] Any other price vector or vectors could be used for this check, depending on where one would like the restrictions to be satisfied. Similarly, either restriction could be examined alone, without imposing the other.

(5) Estimate the posterior probability (appropriate for the case of completely uninformative priors) that the restrictions hold by using all the replications and letting the first n be consistent with the restrictions. The probability is then estimated as

$$
\hat{p} = \frac{\displaystyle\sum_{k=1}^{N} I(\theta_k) \frac{f(\theta_k \mid z)}{g(\theta_k \mid z)}}{\displaystyle\sum_{k=1}^{N} \frac{f(\theta_k \mid z)}{g(\theta_k \mid z)}} = \frac{\displaystyle\sum_{k=1}^{n} \frac{f^R(\theta_k \mid z)}{g^R(\theta_k \mid z)}}{\displaystyle\sum_{k=1}^{N} \frac{f(\theta_k \mid z)}{g(\theta_k \mid z)}} . \tag{16}
$$

The second equality holds because the two numerators match for the last $(N - n)$ replications, where $I(\theta) = 0$.

4. Application to the Motor Carrier Industry

An accurate assessment of the results of the Highway Motor Carrier Act of 1980 requires an unbiased portrayal of the nature of the production technology—i.e. the own price and substitution elasticities—both prior to and after deregulation. Little evidence exists about the nature of the post-deregulation technology, so we examine a sample of 60 firms from 1981. Estimated elasticities are important because they reveal the basic properties of the underlying production technology and can be used to assess structural shifts arising from policy changes.

The segment of the Class I and II Motor Carrier Industry that does not purchase transportation services is of interest because it provides an opportunity to evaluate the production tradeoffs facing firms who are solving the linehaul deployment problem within a single network. These tradeoffs would be much less clear for firms purchasing transportation, because data for the itinerant and contract truckers from whom linehaul services are usually purchased are not available.

Data for the analysis were obtained from the TRINC's *Bluebook of the Trucking Industry* and the *American Motor Carrier Directory*. On average, the Class I and II carriers that did not purchase transportation in 1981 operated smaller terminal operations than carriers that purchased transportation in the same period. Average length of haul and average vehicle loads for these firms were also smaller than for their counterparts that purchased transportation.

The variables used to estimate the parameters of the generalized Leontief cost function are as defined in Chalfant and Wallace (1991). There are four factor inputs: fuel, labor, vehicular capital, and terminal capital. Output is measured as millions of ton-miles. The attributes of each firm's network vector t are defined as average vehicle load and average length of haul. This results in a system of equations for the cost function and input-output ratios with 23 parameters. The cost function offers no additional parameters except an intercept, but, it is hoped, improves the precision of parameter estimates by adding information to the system.

Previous studies (Daughety et al. (1985); Daughety and Nelson (1988)) of Class I and II highway motor carriers, using both purchasers and nonpurchasers of transportation, have found that elasticities of substitution appear to suggest that trucking technology is best characterized by two production processes; one external and one internal to the firm. The internal process takes fuel, labor and terminal capital in fixed proportions to produce output. The external process packages fuel, labor and vehicle capital either to produce transportation for other firms to purchase or to produce output by purchasing transportation. Firms then substitute across these processes to produce total linehaul activity. Evidence of these distinct processes is usually attributed to the empirical finding that purchased transportation is extremely sensitive to price changes in other factor inputs. In contrast, the labor factor is usually found to be less sensitive to changes in prices of other factor inputs. This result suggests that firms can readily substitute vehicles and terminals because purchased transportation is always an alternative in the event of short-run capital constraints. Fuel is also a strong substitute for the capital factors, again through the purchase of transportation.

Parameter estimates from iterated seemingly unrelated regression without inequality restrictions were first used to calculate elasticities of substitution. Eight firms violated monotonicity (predicted costs or levels of inputs were negative, though concavity always was satisfied). Table 1 gives the mean values of elasticities of substitution calculated for the 52 firms consistent with monotonicity. As expected, highway motor carriers not purchasing transportation exhibit an internal production process in which fuel, labor, and terminal capital are used in relatively fixed proportions to produce output; most of the substitution elasticities are small. The own-price elasticities are all negative and fuel is found to be the most price elastic, as well as a relatively good substitute for vehicle capital.

To examine the posterior distribution of the parameters of the constrained generalized Leontief, as well as of these elasticities, we followed the procedure outlined in section 3. A total of 10,000 draws (5,000 observations plus the antithetic replications) were made from the multivariate t distribution, using the in-sample maximum likelihood estimates of θ and Ω to specify the

Table 1
Unconstrained Estimates of Substitution Elasticities

Elasticity	Estimate
Partial Elasticities of Substitution	
Fuel/Labor	0.83
Fuel/Vehicle Capital	1.97
Fuel/Terminal Capital	0.55
Labor/Vehicle Capital	0.85
Labor/Terminal Capital	0.69
Vehicle Cap./Terminal Cap.	0.16
Own-Elasticities	
Fuel	-12.32
Labor	-0.45
Vehicle Capital	-8.46
Terminal Capital	-3.13
Own-Price Elasticities	
Fuel	-0.79
Labor	-0.27
Vehicle Capital	-0.67
Terminal Capital	-0.49

parameters of that distribution. The posterior mean values for elasticities of substitution, after imposing the concavity restriction, are reported in Table 2. For each replication, these elasticities were calculated at the in-sample mean

Table 2
Concavity-Constrained Estimates of Substitution Elasticities

Elasticity	Posterior Mean	Numerical Standard Error
Partial Elasticities of Substitution		
Fuel/Labor	0.77	0.004
Fuel/Vehicle Capital	1.46	0.001
Fuel/Terminal Capital	0.30	0.003
Labor/Vehicle Capital	0.65	0.003
Labor/Terminal Capital	0.42	0.001
Vehicle Cap./Terminal Cap.	0.06	0.002
Own-Elasticities		
Fuel	-11.30	0.050
Labor	-0.43	0.001
Vehicle Capital	-4.50	0.016
Terminal Capital	-0.89	0.002

of the independent variables, using the parameter values obtained in the particular replication. [5]

To reiterate, concavity was checked for each matrix of elasticities over the 10,000 replications by checking substitution matrices for positive eigenvalues. Of these, 9,850 were found to be consistent with concavity; this represents, under completely diffuse prior beliefs, a posterior probability that concavity holds of over 0.99, using the formula in step 5 above. The results certainly suggest that these systems of equations are well behaved with respect to the concavity criterion, at least at the sample mean of the data set.

The monotonicity restriction fared much more poorly, however. Of these 9,850 replications, only 9 were consistent with monotonicity holding for every firm. A preliminary analysis with the translog cost function suggests that a few firms are simply not well represented by the generalized Leontief cost function, since predicted budget shares from the translog were positive for all 60 firms. Of the 9,850 replications, monotonicity is violated more than 10% of the time for only 13 firms. [6] Thus, we present only the results for concavity, and note that the restriction can be imposed on any subset of firms when data from some firms suggest a region where monotonicity does not hold.

The results continue to show the fuel/vehicle substitution elasticity to be large. Overall, the results remain much the same, since the restriction turns out to be a mild one. The technology is characterized by rather limited substitution possibilities, is sensitive to fuel price changes but insensitive to the changes in the wage rate of the labor input. This result may suggest why labor has been found to have garnered the largest share of the economic rents arising from entry and operating ratio regulation (Rose (1986)).

Another finding that is of interest in some applications is whether or not complementarity between inputs exists. [7] Since the procedure yields empirical posterior distributions for elasticities of substitution, this can be examined simultaneously for all combinations of inputs. We estimated the posterior probability that all inputs are substitutes by finding the expected value of an indicator function, analogous to the one in step 5 above, that takes the value one if the parameter vector is consistent with all partial elasticities of

---

[5] In most cases, interest will be in concavity at all data points, or for some other region in price space. The method we use extends trivially to other price vectors – use of the mean of sample data is chosen mainly for convenience in illustration.

[6] We also examined the same firms using 1979 data, prior to deregulation, finding that 4 firms violate monotonicity. Three of these are in the group of eight 1981 violations.

[7] See Chalfant, Gray, and White (1991) for the same restriction in the context of consumer demand analysis.

substitution being positive and zero otherwise. By finding the expectation of that indicator function, as in step 5, we estimated the probability that all these elasticities are positive to be 0.63. Interestingly, there is very little effect on the posterior mean values of the elasticities of substitution when this restriction is imposed. This is apparently due to the combination of the restriction being a relatively mild one and the fact that truncating the distribution of each elasticity from below, at zero, might be balanced by losing some replications from the high end of each posterior distribution.

A final note concerns the evaluation of these results. Expressions given in Geweke (1989) and Barnett, Geweke, and Yue (1991) for the numerical standard errors of our estimates were used to examine the accuracy of our results. These values, given in Table 2, are clearly of a small enough magnitude to have confidence in the results.

Two further checks on the method are worth noting. First, the calculations can be performed for subsets of replications to check the rate of convergence. Second, as Geweke (1989) emphasizes, the density $g^R(\theta \mid z)$ used to generate replications in importance sampling must include all of D, the region over which the posterior density is defined. Plots of the ratio of the posterior to the importance density against each element of θ in our replications showed that the largest and smallest values of each θ_i were associated with very small values for the ratio of density functions, suggesting that coverage of the tails of the posterior density $f^R(\theta \mid z)$ was adequate. [8]

5. Conclusions

We have shown how to impose curvature or other inequality restrictions on a cost function of the generalized Leontief form. The method applies to other cost functions as well; for the generalized Leontief form it has the additional advantage of retaining the flexibility of the form in a way that a more conventional approach to imposing concavity would not. The application to trucking data permits the analysis of productivity, substitution possibilities, etc., to be performed in a model which retains contact with the underlying theory, rather than with a cost function that does not satisfy the underlying inequality restrictions.

The Bayesian procedures appear to perform well in cases where it is important to be able to impose or make inferences about inequality restrictions. As was shown, it is possible to produce constrained parameter esti-

---

[8] Geweke (1989) discusses tailoring the importance density g^R to more closely fit the posterior density for each particular element in the parameter vector.

mates as well as an estimate of the probability that the restrictions are true using the necessary conditions for concavity rather than the sufficient conditions required in conventional approaches. There appears to be considerable support for the concavity of the cost function for motor carriers not purchasing externally generated transportation services in the pre- and post-deregulation market environments. This is a very desirable finding, given the theoretical importance of concavity assumptions in the economic theory of the firm. The very high level of probability that we find that the restriction holds in the posterior distribution suggests that the same might hold for other firms, such as those that purchased transportation during this period. Unfortunately, monotonicity proves to be much less consistent with the data, but this seems to be due to observations from a few firms.

Because the necessary integrals over the exact posterior density are not computationally feasible, Monte Carlo integration was used to estimate parameter values. The method of importance sampling was used to overcome the difficulty of sampling from the known but not recognizable probability density function corresponding to the exact posterior distribution. The substitution elasticities derived from these results were consistent with results from other empirical studies of motor carrier production technology which identified two production processes; one internal and one external.

Since the firms in this sample do not purchase transportation, the internal fixed factor production technology appears to dominate and suggests that firms are not able to easily adjust inputs in response to price changes. This finding is particularly interesting in light of the growing importance of brokered and short term contract linehaul traffic in the aftermath of deregulation, both in the U.S. and in Australia. Apparently, it is the purchased transportation factor which provides important flexibility in input decisions for motor carrier producers.

Finally, it is important to note that these findings are conditional not only on the observed data in this sample but also on the specification of the Generalized Leontief motor carrier cost function. Given these caveats, the findings in this study suggest that motor carrier cost functions for the firms not purchasing externally generated transportation services are consistent with concavity assumptions and that this segment of the industry operates with a production technology in which substitution possibilities are rather limited.

References

Barnett, W.A., Geweke, J., and Yue, P. (1991), "Semiparametric Bayesian Estimation of the Asymptotically Ideal Model: The AIM Demand System," In *Nonparametric and Semipara-*

metric Methods in Econometrics and Statistics, edited by W.A. Barnett, J. Powell and G. Tauchen, Cambridge University Press, Cambridge.

Chalfant, J. and Wallace, N. (1991), "Testing the Translog Specification with the Fourier Cost Function" Department of Agricultural and Resource Economics, University of California, Berkeley.

Chalfant, J. and White, K. (1988) "Estimation of Demand Systems with Concavity and Monotonicity Constraints," Working Paper No. 454, Department of Agricultural and Resource Economics, University of California, Berkeley.

Chalfant, J., Gray, R., and White, K. (1991) "Evaluating Prior Beliefs in a Demand System: The Case of Meat Demand in Canada," *American Journal of Agricultural Economics* 73, 476–490.

Daughety, A., and Nelson, F.D., (1988) "An Econometric Analysis of Changes in the Cost and Production Structure of the Trucking Industry, 1953–1982," *The Review of Economics and Statistics*, 55, 67–75.

Daughety, A., Nelson, F.D., and Vigdon, W., (1986), "An Econometric Analysis of the Cost and Production Structure of the Trucking Industry," In *Analytical Studies in Transportation*, edited by A. Daughety, Cambridge University Press, Cambridge.

Diewert, W.E., and Wales, T.J. (1987), "Flexible Functional Forms and Global Curvature Conditions," *Econometrica*, 55, 43–68.

Geweke, J. (1986), "Exact Inference in the Inequality Constrained Normal Linear Regression Model," *Journal of Applied Econometrics*, 1, 127–141.

Geweke, J. (1988), "Antithetic Acceleration of Monte Carlo Integration in Bayesian Inference," *Journal of Econometrics*, 38, 73–89.

Geweke, J. (1989), "Bayesian Inference in Econometric Models Using Monte Carlo Integration" *Econometrica*, 57, 1317–1339.

Jorgensen, D.W., and Fraumeni, B. (1981), "Relative Prices and Technical Change," In *Modeling and Measuring Natural Resource Substitution*, edited by E. Berndt and B. Field, MIT Press, Cambridge, MA.

Judge, G.G., Griffiths, W.E., Hill, R.C., Lütkepohl, H., and Lee, T-C. (1985), *The Theory and Practice of Econometrics, 2nd Ed.*, John Wiley and Sons, New York.

Lopez, R. (1980) "The Structure of Production and the Derived Demand for Inputs in Canadian Agriculture," *American Journal of Agricultural Economics*, 62, 38–45.

Rose, N.L. (1987), "Labor Rent Sharing and Regulation: Evidence from the Trucking Industry," *Journal of Political Economy*, 95, 1146–78.

Van Dijk, H.K., and Kloek, T. (1980), "Further Experience in Bayesian Analysis Using Monte Carlo Integration," *Journal of Econometrics*, 14, 307–328.

Zellner, A. (1962), "An Efficient Method of Estimating Seemingly Unrelated Regressions and Tests for Aggregation Bias," *Journal of the American Statistical Association*, 57, 348–368.

Zellner, A. (1971), *An Introduction to Bayesian Inference in Econometrics*, John Wiley and Sons, New York.

Zellner, A. (1988), "Bayesian Analysis in Econometrics," *Journal of Econometrics*, 37, 27–50.

Readings in Econometric Theory and Practice
W. Griffiths, H. Lütkepohl and M.E. Bock (Editors)
© 1992 Elsevier Science Publishers B.V. All rights reserved

CHAPTER 8

FURTHER RESULTS ON INTERVAL ESTIMATION
IN AN AR(1) ERROR MODEL

H.E. Doran, W.E. Griffiths and P.A. Beesley

Department of Econometrics, University of New England, Armidale, NSW 2351, Australia

The poor finite sample performance of confidence interval estimates for the slope coefficient of a trended explanatory variable in a linear model with AR(1) error has been well documented. Both 1-pass Cochrane-Orcutt and maximum-likelihood estimation have not performed well in this regard; attempts to provide more accurate confidence intervals have met with limited success. Some further attempts are made in this paper. In particular, we examine the generalized least squares confidence intervals which result when the first-order correlation coefficient ρ is estimated by (a) residuals from the model estimated in first differences, (b) a bias corrected Cochrane-Orcutt estimate, and (c) the mean of the Bayesian posterior p.d.f. All three methods lead to a dramatic improvement in finite sample accuracy, although there is still room for improvement when ρ is close to one. A frequency domain rationale for the observed results from this and other studies is provided.

1. Introduction

The poor finite sample performance of asymptotic confidence intervals in AR(1) error models has been reported by many authors. For a model with a single explanatory variable that is trended, it is well-known that least squares is asymptotically the best linear unbiased estimator regardless of the error process [Grenander and Rosenblatt (1957)]. However, the overwhelming evidence, in both this and other studies, is that in finite samples, least squares confidence intervals perform poorly. Also, when the error is positively correlated AR(1), the conventional asymptotic confidence interval for the slope coefficient, based on estimated generalized least squares, is typically too narrow. In other words, for hypothesis tests concerning the slope coefficient, the finite sample size of such tests is greater than the nominal size provided by asymptotic theory. Furthermore, the difference between the finite sample and asymptotic results can be substantial in sample sizes of 50 or less. For example, using the Cochrane-Orcutt iterative procedure for estimating the AR(1) parameter ρ, Nakamura and Nakamura (1978) found that a nominal significance level of 5% led to a correct null hypothesis being rejected 20% of the time, given $\rho = 0.7$ and a sample size of 30. The situation improves as sample size increases, but deteriorates for larger ρ. For $\rho = 0.9$ and a sample size of 50, the percentage of rejections was 28. Equally disturbing and similar results have been found by authors using other estimation techniques for ρ, such as two-step Cochrane-Orcutt, the "Durbin estimator", or maximum-likelihood estimation [Park and Mitchell (1980), Beesley and Griffiths (1982), Griffiths and Beesley (1984), King and Giles (1984)].

The major cause of the problem seems to be a negative small sample bias in the estimation of ρ, a characteristic which is common to all of the estimators we have mentioned. For certain types of explanatory variables, underestimation of ρ leads to underestimation of the generalized least squares standard errors; these relatively small standard errors lead in turn to confidence intervals which are too narrow or, when testing, to an excessive number of type I errors. To obtain improved finite sample standard errors, and hence more accurate finite sample confidence intervals, it seems necessary to find a better estimator for ρ. When the true value of ρ is used, the finite sample performance of the asymptotic standard errors is reasonable [Nakamura and Nakamura (1978), Miyazaki and Griffiths (1984)]. Furthermore, a second-order approximation to the finite sample standard errors leads to no appreciable improvement in the results [Ullah et al. (1983), Miyazaki and Griffiths (1984)].

The problem of underestimating ρ in finite samples has been recognized for a long time. Cochrane and Orcutt (1949) suggested that the least squares residuals would not exhibit as much autocorrelation as the disturbance terms for which they are estimates. Others, for example, Lomnicki and Zaremba (1957), Hildreth and Dent (1974), Malinvaud (1980, p. 504) and Pantula and Fuller (1985), have derived explicit approximations for the bias; such approximations lead to the possibility of using "bias-corrected" estimates for ρ. Although adjusted estimators of this type have been suggested in the literature, they do not seem to have had much acceptance in empirical work, possibly because there have been no clear demonstrations of how an adjusted estimator for ρ can improve the finite sample accuracy of asymptotic confidence intervals. Kwok and Veall (1986) have made some efforts in this direction. They show that a "jackknife estimator" for ρ produces more acceptable finite sample confidence intervals, but that there is still room for improvement for large ρ.

In this paper three further estimators for ρ and their consequences for the finite sample accuracy of confidence intervals are considered. The first is an estimator based on the residuals from a first-differenced regression rather than those from ordinary least squares. The second is an adjusted estimator which is based on the bias approximation derived by Lomnicki and Zaremba (1957); and the third is the mean of a Bayesian marginal posterior density function for ρ. Our results indicate that all three estimators for ρ produce confidence intervals which are substantially more accurate than those produced by more conventional estimators. However, like Kwok and Veall (1986), we find that there is still some scope for improving finite sample accuracy when ρ is close to one. Other results, such as the means and mean-squared errors of the estimators, are also presented. Whether there is a large discrepancy between the finite sample and asymptotic results, or not, depends heavily on the nature of the explanatory variables. King and Giles (1984) made this observation. Griffiths and Beesley (1984) found that, if a single explanatory variable is stationary rather than trended, a downward bias in the estimation of ρ still exists; however, the bias is less pronounced, and there are no adverse effects on the finite sample performance of standard errors and confidence intervals. A simple explanation for these observed results can be made in terms of a frequency domain expression for the variance of the generalized least squares estimator. In this paper we provide such an explanation, in addition to the results of the Monte Carlo experiment.

In Section 2 the model and estimators used in the Monte Carlo study are outlined. The results of the Monte Carlo experiments are presented in Section 3, and a frequency domain explanation for these and other results is given in Section 4. Some concluding remarks are made in Section 5.

2. The Model, Experiments and Estimators

Following previous studies [see Beach and MacKinnon (1978), Harvey (1980), Miyazaki and Griffiths (1984), Griffiths and Beesley (1984)], our experiments are based on the model

$$y_t = \beta_0 + \beta_1 X_t + u_t, \tag{1}$$

where

$$u_t = \rho u_{t-1} + v_t, \tag{2}$$

and

$$v_t \sim \text{NID}(0, 0.0036). \tag{3}$$

The trended explanatory variable was generated by the process

$$x_t = \exp(0.04t) + w_t, \tag{4}$$

where

$$w_t \sim \text{NID}(0, 0.0009). \tag{5}$$

Two sample sizes, $T = 20$ and $T = 50$, were used, and once the x's were drawn initially from (4) and (5), they were held fixed in repeated samples. It is, of course, rather restrictive to consider a model with only one explanatory variable. However, in line with many earlier studies [e.g., Engle (1974), Nicholls and Pagan (1977), Fomby and Guilkey (1978)], we have made this restriction to keep the study within manageable limits. The true values for β_0 and β_1 were set at one, and a wide range of values for ρ between -0.98 and $+0.98$ were chosen. In each case 5000 samples were generated.

We are concerned with the finite sample properties of five alternative estimators for ρ, and the finite sample performance of corresponding confidence interval estimators for β_1. All the confidence interval estimators are of the estimated generalized least squares type, differing only in the method used to estimate the AR(1) parameter ρ. The five estimators for ρ which are compared are
1. One-pass Cochrane-Orcutt (CO);
2. Maximum likelihood (ML);
3. Estimator from first-differenced data;
4. Bayesian;
5. Bias corrected Cochrane-Orcutt.
The first two are conventional estimators; most applied studies would use one of these two estimators. The remaining three are alternatives which we hope will yield confidence interval estimators with an improved finite sample performance. These estimators are outlined below.

2.1. One-pass Cochrane-Orcutt

This estimator is very common and needs little explanation; it is given by

$$\hat{\rho} = \frac{\sum \hat{u}_t \hat{u}_{t-1}}{\sum \hat{u}_{t-1}^2} \tag{6}$$

where the $\hat{u}_t$ are the ordinary least squares residuals.

2.2. Maximum-likelihood Estimator

Apart from a constant, the log-likelihood function of the sample is given by [see, for example, Judge et al. (1985, 289–290)]

$$L(\beta, \sigma^2, \rho \mid y) = -\frac{T}{2}\ln \sigma_v^2 + \tfrac{1}{2}\ln(1 - \rho^2)$$

$$- \tfrac{1}{2}\sigma_v^2 (y - X\beta)' \Psi^{-1}(y - X\beta) \tag{7}$$

where y, X and β are the matrix representations necessary to specify (1) in matrix notation, σ_v^2 is the variance of v_t, and $\sigma_v^2\Psi$ is the covariance matrix of the error vector $u = (u_1, u_2, \ldots, u_T)'$. Following Hildreth and Dent (1974), ρ is estimated by concentrating σ_v^2 and β out of the likelihood function, and searching over the range $(-1, 1)$ for the ρ which maximizes the concentrated function.

2.3. Estimator from First-differenced Data

As mentioned earlier, past experience [Nakamura and Nakamura (1978), Park and Mitchell (1980), King and Giles (1984), Griffiths and Beesley (1984) and Miyazaki and Griffiths (1984)] has shown that most problems arise when the serial correlation is large and the explanatory variable is trended. This suggests that if the trend is removed by differencing, it may be possible to obtain an improved estimator of ρ and consequently improved confidence interval performance. Also, since a regression on first differences is appropriate when $\rho = 1$, it is possible that, when ρ is close to one, the residuals from such a regression may show more promise for estimation of ρ than the residuals from ordinary least squares applied to the original model.

Applying first differences to model (1) yields

$$\Delta y_t = \beta_1 \Delta x_t + \epsilon_t \tag{8}$$

where $\Delta y_t = y_t - y_{t-1}$, $\Delta x_t = x_t - x_{t-1}$ and $\epsilon_t = u_t - u_{t-1}$. Given the error structure in (2) it can be shown that

$$E[\epsilon_t^2] = \frac{2\sigma_v^2}{1 + \rho} \tag{9}$$

and

$$E[\epsilon_t \epsilon_{t-\tau}] = -\frac{\sigma_v^2(1 - \rho)\rho^{\tau-1}}{1 + \rho}, \quad \tau = 1, 2, 3, \ldots \tag{10}$$

Thus, the autocorrelation function for ϵ_t is

$$
\begin{aligned}
r_\tau &= 1, & \tau &= 0 \\
&= -\tfrac{1}{2}(1-\rho)\rho^{\tau-1}, & \tau &= 1, 2, 3, \ldots
\end{aligned}
\tag{11}
$$

The first order autocorrelation is

$$
r_1 = -\tfrac{1}{2}(1-\rho),
$$

leading to an estimator of ρ of the form

$$
\tilde{\rho} = 1 + 2\hat{r}_1,
\tag{12}
$$

where

$$
\hat{r}_1 = \frac{\sum \hat{\epsilon}_t \hat{\epsilon}_{t-1}}{\sum \hat{\epsilon}_{t-1}^2}
\tag{13}
$$

is the sample first-order autocorrelation computed from the least squares residuals ($\hat{\epsilon}_t$'s) from the regression in (8). Clearly, a feasible $\tilde{\rho}$ implies that $\hat{r}_1$ must lie in the range $-1 < \hat{r}_1 < 0$. In the Monte Carlo experiments, whenever $\hat{r}_1$ lay outside the permissible range, $\tilde{\rho}$ was set at ± 0.999, as appropriate.

2.4. Bayesian Estimator

To obtain the Bayesian estimator we consider the noninformative prior

$$
g(\beta, \rho, \sigma_v) \propto \left(1 - \rho^2\right)^{-1/2} \sigma_v^{-1}
\tag{14}
$$

which was used by Fomby and Guilkey (1978), and which is outlined again in Judge et al. (1985, p. 292). The marginal posterior density for ρ derived from (14) is given by $g(\rho \mid y) \propto f(\rho \mid y)$ where

$$
f(\rho \mid y) = |X'\Psi^{-1}X|^{-1/2} \left[\left(y - X\hat{\beta}\right)' \Psi^{-1}\left(y - X\hat{\beta}\right)\right]^{-(T-2)/2},
\tag{15}
$$

and $\hat{\beta} = (X'\Psi^{-1}X)^{-1}X'\Psi^{-1}y$. The Bayesian estimator for ρ was taken as the posterior mean of $g(\rho \mid y)$, which was obtained by numerically evaluating

$$
\hat{\rho}_B = \frac{\displaystyle\int_{-1}^{1} \rho f(\rho \mid y)\, d\rho}{\displaystyle\int_{-1}^{1} f(\rho \mid y)\, d\rho}.
\tag{16}
$$

Although the function in (15) is, apart from a constant, a proper density function, it approaches ∞ as ρ approaches 1. This characteristic leads to a posterior mean which is typically greater than conventional sampling theory estimates for ρ, and which, therefore, is a good candidate for overcoming the ' negative-bias problem.

2.5. Bias Corrected Cochrane-Orcutt

It has been shown by Lomnicki and Zaremba (1957), that when ρ is estimated by ordinary least squares residuals, and the explanatory variable is a polynomial of degree m, then to $0(T^{-1})$,

$$\lim_{T \to \infty} \text{TE}(\hat{\rho} - \rho) = -(m+1)(1-\rho) \sum_{\tau=-\infty}^{\infty} \rho_\tau + 2 \sum_{\tau=-\infty}^{\infty} \left(\rho \rho_\tau^2 - \rho \rho_{\tau+1} \right),$$

(17)

where ρ_τ is the τth autocorrelation coefficient of the disturbance. For our case, in which the disturbance is an AR(1) process, this result specializes to

$$\lim_{T \to \infty} \text{TE}(\hat{\rho} - \rho) = -[(m+1)(1+\rho) + 2\rho].$$

(18)

This suggests a correction to the Cochrane-Orcutt estimator $\hat{\rho}$, leading to a new estimator $\hat{\hat{\rho}}$, given by

$$\hat{\hat{\rho}} = \hat{\rho} + T^{-1}[(m+1)(1+\hat{\rho}) + 2\hat{\rho}].$$

(19)

When $T = 20$, the regressor $x_t = \exp(0.04t)$ can be approximated by a quadratic trend ($m = 2$), leading to

$$\hat{\hat{\rho}} = \hat{\rho} + (5\hat{\rho} + 3)/20.$$

(20)

Likewise, when $T = 50$, $m = 4$, and

$$\hat{\hat{\rho}} = \hat{\rho} + (7\hat{\rho} + 5)/50.$$

(21)

3. Monte Carlo Results

We will first report on the bias and relative efficiency of each of the five estimators of ρ, and then examine confidence interval performance.

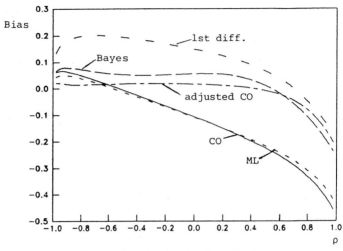

Figure 1. Bias in estimators for ρ, $T = 20$.

3.1. Bias

The bias of the five estimators is illustrated in Figures 1 and 2 for $T = 20$ and 50, respectively. As can be seen from these figures, the five estimators fall into two groups. Firstly, CO and ML virtually have identical properties,

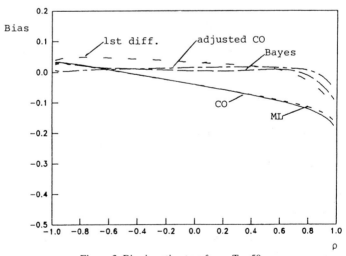

Figure 2. Bias in estimators for ρ, $T = 50$.

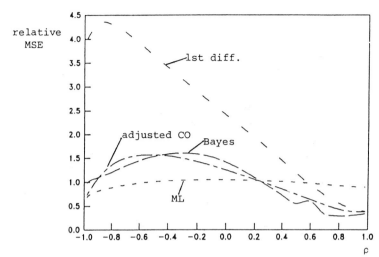

Figure 3. Relative MSE of estimators for ρ, relative to CO, $T = 20$.

showing the usual severe underestimation of ρ near $\rho = 1$. As far as CO is concerned, this is completely in accord with the result (18) from Lomnicki and Zaremba (1957). Secondly, the differenced, Bayesian and corrected CO estimators perform considerably better than CO and ML for positive values of ρ. Within this second group, the differenced estimator is slightly superior when $T = 20$ for values of ρ beyond about $\rho = 0.7$; for values of ρ less than 0.4 it is decidedly inferior. As will be seen subsequently from both Monte Carlo results and frequency domain analysis, the markedly inferior results for $\rho < 0.4$ have little influence on confidence interval performance.

3.2. Relative Efficiency

The mean squared errors of the various estimators for ρ, relative to the mean-squared error of the CO estimator, are illustrated in Figures 3 and 4. Not only are CO and ML similar in terms of their bias; there is no discernible difference between these two estimators in terms of mean-squared error, except perhaps for ρ close to -1. Also, Bayesian and corrected CO have virtually the same relative efficiency having higher mean-squared errors than CO for ρ less than about 0.2, but exhibiting a gain in efficiency for higher values of ρ. The differenced estimator appears to be very inefficient for all values of ρ when $T = 50$, and for values of $\rho < 0.5$ when $T = 20$. For both

H.E. Doran, W.E. Griffiths and P.A. Beesley

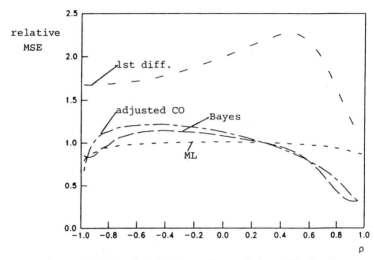

Figure 4. Relative MSE of estimators for ρ, relative to CO, $T = 50$.

$T = 20$ and $T = 50$ it is always less efficient than the Bayesian and corrected CO estimators.

3.3. Confidence Interval Performance

As would be expected from the above discussion, the CO and ML estimators for ρ lead to confidence interval estimators for β_1 with almost identical properties. See Figures 5 and 6. For negative values of ρ, the actual proportion of intervals containing the true value of β_1 is quite close to the nominal value of 0.95, irrespective of which estimator for ρ is used. As ρ increases the proportions corresponding to the CO and ML estimators decrease rapidly, as has been observed in the previous studies already cited.

The other three estimators, viz, the differenced, Bayesian and corrected CO, have considerably better properties. Even for $T = 20$, the actual proportion is close to 0.95 for ρ up to about 0.5. For example, when $\rho = 0.5$, the proportion is approximately 0.92 for each of these estimators. For $\rho > 0.5$ the proportion decreases but at a slower rate than the first two estimators. For large ρ, e.g., $\rho = 0.98$, the proportion is still unacceptably low, being between 0.7 and 0.8. See Figure 5. It does appear, at least for positive ρ, that reducing the bias in the estimation of ρ translates into confidence intervals with finite sample properties which are more in line with nominal asymptotic properties.

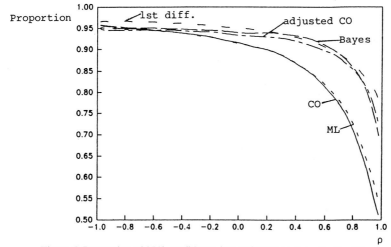

Figure 5. Proportion of 95% confidence intervals that contain β_1, $T = 20$.

When the sample size is increased to $T = 50$, the same general features remain, but the properties improve as can be seen from Figure 6. One difference is that the confidence interval performance of the differenced

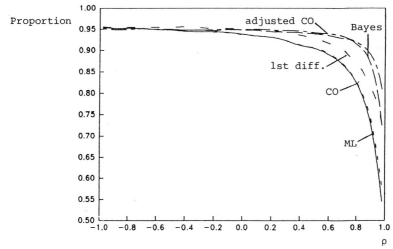

Figure 6. Proportion of 95% confidence intervals that contain β_1, $T = 50$.

estimator is now not as good as that for the Bayesian and corrected CO estimators for $\rho > 0.5$. It is interesting to note that the relatively poor estimation performance of the differenced estimator when ρ is less than about 0.4 is not reflected in confidence interval performance. We return to this point in the next section.

4. Frequency Domain Interpretation

It has been observed that poor estimates of ρ sometimes result in correspondingly poor confidence interval performance and at other times produce satisfactory results. For example, for $\rho < 0$, confidence interval performance is satisfactory even when ρ is estimated poorly. In the introduction we reported that, for $\rho > 0$, an underestimate of ρ has adverse effects on the confidence intervals if the explanatory variable is trended, but not if it is stationary. Given the Lomnicki and Zaremba (1957) result in equation (18), and a visual appreciation of some basic frequency domain concepts, it is possible to predict these and other results.

For the purpose of exposition, we will confine our attention to the ordinary least squares and one-pass CO techniques applied to the two cases of a trended and a stationary regressor. Ordinary least squares may be regarded as being the same as CO with $\hat{\rho}$ always set at zero. If the estimated variance for an estimator $\hat{\beta}_1$ is biased downwards, confidence intervals which are too narrow will result, and the empirical confidence interval proportions will be less than 0.95. The converse occurs if the estimated variance is biased upwards. Thus, our frequency domain discussion will be in terms of the effect of a biased estimate of ρ on the estimated variance of $\hat{\beta}_1$.

The model (1) is expressed in the frequency domain form by applying a linear transformation of the type

$$w_z(\lambda_j) = T^{-1/2} \sum_{t=1}^{T} z_t e^{i\lambda_j t}, \quad j = 1, 2, \ldots, T \tag{22}$$

to each of the variables z_t of the model. The term "variable" includes the column of ones associated with the intercept. Assuming for convenience that T is even, the λ_j are the so-called "harmonic frequencies", given by

$$\lambda_j = \frac{2\pi}{T} \left(j - \frac{T}{2} \right). \tag{23}$$

It is well known [see, for example, Fishman (1969, p. 153)] that when the model is transformed in this way, the covariance matrix of the disturbance u_t becomes approximately diagonal with the jth diagonal being $2\pi f_u(\lambda_j)$, where $f_u(\lambda)$ is the spectrum of the disturbance process u_t at frequency λ.

It is now possible [see Fishman (1969), Harvey (1981)] to write the variance of $\hat{\beta}_1$ in the form

$$\text{var}(\hat{\beta}_1) = 2\pi \left[\sum_{\lambda_j \neq 0} I_x(\lambda_j) f_u^{-1}(\lambda_j) \right]^{-1}. \tag{24}$$

The frequency $\lambda_j = 0$ is omitted from the summation because an intercept is included in the model. In both the Fishman and Harvey treatments there is

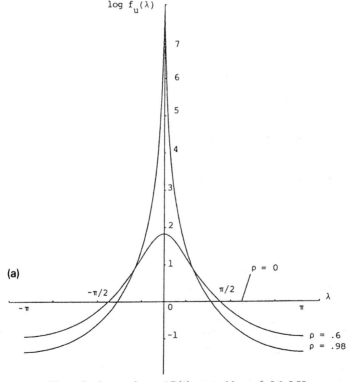

Figure 7a. Spectra for an AR(1) error with $\rho = 0, 0.6, 0.98$.

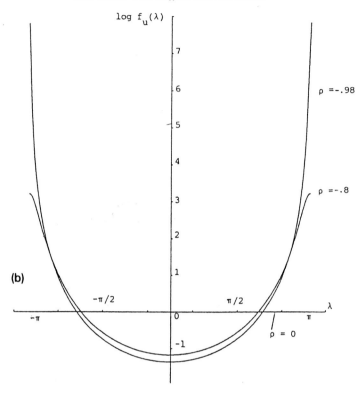

Figure 7b. Spectra for an AR(1) error with $\rho = 0$, -0.8, -0.98.

no intercept. The term $I_x(\lambda_j)$ is the periodogram of the regressor x_t at the frequency λ_j, and is defined by

$$I_x(\lambda_j) = |w_x(\lambda_j)|^2. \tag{25}$$

Note that $I_x(\lambda_j)$ is always observable. The spectrum $f_u(\lambda_j)$ is not observable, but any estimate $\hat{\rho}$ implies a corresponding estimate $\hat{f}_u(\lambda_j)$. It is clear from (24) that any bias in the estimator of $\mathrm{var}(\hat{\beta}_1)$ arises because of bias in $\hat{f}_u(\lambda_j)$. The nature of the bias of $\mathrm{v\hat{a}r}(\hat{\beta}_1)$ is determined by the interaction of $I_x(\lambda_j)$ and $\hat{f}_u(\lambda_j)$ at the T discrete frequencies given in (23). The periodogram $I_x(\lambda_j)$ may be regarded as a *weighting function* on the estimators $\hat{f}_u(\lambda_j)$ used to determine $\mathrm{v\hat{a}r}(\hat{\beta}_1)$. The nature of these two functions $I_x(\lambda)$ and $f_u(\lambda)$ for cases of special interest are shown in Figures 7 and 8. In the light of these figures, and the expression (18), we can now discuss the relationship between estimation of ρ and estimation of var($\hat{\beta}_1$).

The basic principle is this: if the frequencies at which $\hat{f}_u(\lambda)$ has large biases correspond to those at which the weighting function $I_x(\lambda)$ also is large, then vâr($\hat{\beta}_1$) will have a large bias. On the other hand, if large biases in $\hat{f}_u(\lambda)$ receive a small weighting, due to small values of $I_x(\lambda)$ at those frequencies, a large bias in $\hat{\rho}$ will not be reflected in vâr($\hat{\beta}_1$).

We will examine six cases, for sample size $T = 20$, in accordance with Table 1. Before discussing these cases in some detail, we set out in Table 2 the results of the analysis, together with corresponding Monte Carlo results from this and earlier studies. In interpreting Table 2, we recall that negative biases in vâr($\hat{\beta}_1$) are associated with confidence interval proportions which are less than the nominal value (here always 0.95) and vice-versa.

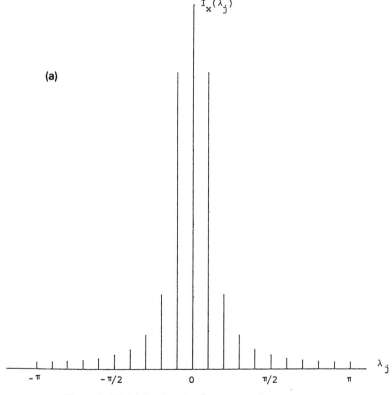

Figure 8a. Weighting function (periodogram) for trended x.

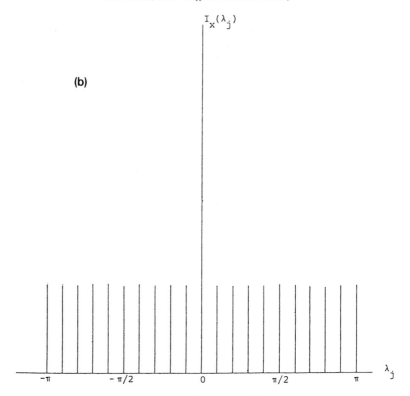

Figure 8b. Weighting function (periodogram) for stationary x.

Case I: x_t Trended

Here, by equation (20), the bias in the CO estimator $\hat{\rho}$ is approximately $-(5\rho + 3)/20$.

(a) $\rho = 0.98$

The mean value of $\hat{\rho}$ would be expected to be near 0.6. From Figure 7a, $\hat{\rho} = 0.6$ corresponds to a $\hat{f}_u(\lambda)$ which seriously underestimates $f_u(\lambda)$ near

Table 1

Case I: x_t trended	Case II: x_t random
(a) ρ large positive	ρ large positive
(b) $\rho = 0$	$\rho = 0$
(c) ρ large negative	ρ large negative

Table 2 [a]

Predicted Biases in vâr($\hat{\beta}_1$) and Empirical Confidence Interval Proportions

	Case I: x_t trended	Case II: x_t random
(a) $\rho = 0.98$	CO large neg bias (0.55 [b], 0.51 [d]) OLS very large neg bias (0.37) [b]	CO slight neg bias (0.94) [c] OLS moderate neg bias (0.92) [c]
(b) $\rho = 0.0$	CO very small neg bias (0.91 [b], 0.92 [d]) OLS unbiased (0.95) [b]	CO almost unbiased (0.94) [c] OLS unbiased (0.96) [c]
(c) $\rho = -0.98$	CO small pos bias (0.94 [b], 0.96 [d]) OLS moderate pos bias (1.00) [b]	CO almost unbiased (0.96) [c] OLS large neg bias (0.51) [c]

[a] Numbers in parentheses are empirical proportions.
[b] Griffiths and Beesley (1984).
[c] Beesley and Griffiths (1982).
[d] Current paper.

$\lambda = 0$ and slightly overestimates when $|\lambda| > \pi/5$. (We draw attention to the fact that $f_u(\lambda)$ is for convenience plotted on a log-scale.) The weighting function $I_x(\lambda)$ for the trended variable (see Figure 8a) magnifies this under-estimation by a factor of about 40 (relative to its magnitude when $|\lambda| > \pi/5$). Thus, from (24), vâr($\hat{\beta}_1$) has a large negative bias.

When OLS is applied, we are implicitly setting $\hat{\rho} = 0$. That is, we are estimating $f_u(\lambda)$ by the flat spectrum corresponding to $\rho = 0$. This will result in vâr($\hat{\beta}_1$) having an even larger negative bias.

(b) $\rho = 0$

Obviously OLS is BLUE in this case and gives unbiased interval estima-tors. The CO estimator $\hat{\rho}$ has a bias of -0.15, approximately. From Figure 7b, we can infer that the estimated spectrum is slightly below the true (flat) spectrum near $\lambda = 0$ and slightly above near $\lambda = \pm\pi$. The weighting function determines that vâr($\hat{\beta}_1$) underestimates var($\hat{\beta}_1$), but only slightly.

(c) $\rho = -0.98$

The bias in CO $\hat{\rho}$ is now approximately $+0.1$, which is only a quarter the magnitude of the bias when $\rho = 0.98$. From Figure 7b, the estimated spectrum slightly overestimates near $\lambda = 0$ and underestimates by a greater amount near $\lambda = \pm\pi$. However, because of the weighting function, only the bias near $\lambda = 0$ is relevant, leading to a slight positive bias in vâr($\hat{\beta}_1$).

Application of OLS again implies estimating the true spectrum $f_u(\lambda)$ by the flat spectrum. This results in a larger positive bias near $\lambda = 0$, and hence a greater positive bias in vâr($\hat{\beta}_1$).

Case II: x_t Random

Here the regressor is not trended ($m = 0$) and so the bias in $\hat{\rho}$ is now approximately $-(3\rho + 1)/20$.

(a) $\rho = 0.98$

The bias is approximately -0.2, so the average value of $\hat{\rho}$ would be about 0.8. From Figure 7a, $\hat{f}_u(\lambda)$ would underestimate $f_u(\lambda)$ near $\lambda = 0$, but overestimate near $\lambda = \pm\pi$. The bias is larger near $\lambda = 0$. The weighting function now weights each frequency equally, so we would expect a slight negative bias in vâr($\hat{\beta}_1$). The much smaller bias than in the corresponding case when x_t is trended occurs because (i) the bias in $\hat{\rho}$ is smaller and (ii) the weighting function does not magnify the negative bias near $\lambda = 0$.

Likewise, OLS will give rise to a negative bias, of larger magnitude.

(b) $\rho = 0$

Once again least squares is BLUE. The bias in $\hat{\rho}$ is here only about -0.05 so vâr($\hat{\beta}_1$) for CO should also be almost unbiased.

(c) $\rho = -0.98$

The mean of the CO $\hat{\rho}$ is about -0.9. The estimated spectrum is virtually unbiased everywhere except near $\lambda = \pm\pi$, where it has a negative bias. However, as the weighting function weights each frequency equally, this bias can be regarded as being spread over the whole range of λ. The overall effect would be negligible.

When the OLS is used, there is a huge negative bias at $\lambda = \pm\pi$, which leads to a serious negative bias in vâr($\hat{\beta}_1$).

Although the above discussion relates only to CO and OLS estimators, the principles carry over to the remaining four estimators examined in this paper. Good estimators of ρ naturally produce good confidence interval estimators. However, the converse is not necessarily true. We have seen (see Figure 1, 2, 5 and 6) that large biases in $\hat{\rho}$ do not always produce inferior interval estimators. When x is trended, poor estimation of ρ will only translate into poor confidence interval performance when there is a large bias in the estimate of the spectrum of u_t near the zero frequency. This only happens when ρ is near 1. It is best illustrated by comparing Figures 1 and 5. Near $\rho = 1$, ordering of the estimators according to bias (Figure 1) corresponds to the ordering of the confidence intervals (Figure 5). Even small reductions in bias lead to appreciate improvements in confidence interval performance. However, as ρ decreases poor performance in estimating ρ becomes less and less significant. For example, for negative ρ, a bias in the differenced estimator which is ten times the bias in the adjusted CO produced no real difference in the confidence interval performance.

One final comment is appropriate. If there were no intercept in the model, then the frequency $\lambda_j = 0$ would be included in the summation in equation (24). This would mean that the effects already noted for ρ large and positive would be even more marked, but for ρ negative the changes would be negligible.

5. Summary and Conclusions

In the past, confidence interval estimation of regression coefficients in AR(1) error models has usually been based on one-pass Cochrane-Orcutt or maximum-likelihood estimation of the autoregressive parameter ρ. Many authors have noted the poor confidence interval performance of these estimators when ρ is large and the regressor is trended.

In this paper, three new estimators of ρ have been used in an attempt to improve this performance. These estimators are
1. an estimator based on first-differenced data;
2. a Bayesian estimator; and
3. an adjusted one-pass Cochrane-Orcutt estimator.
Monte Carlo experiments were conducted using the five estimators, and clear evidence has emerged that the three new estimators give considerably superior confidence interval performance in finite samples. In addition, using frequency domain analysis, a rationale for the observed empirical results of this and other studies has been provided. In particular, an explanation is given as to why poor estimation of ρ sometimes does and sometimes does not affect confidence interval performance.

The prescription for applied researchers is clear. It is important to adjust positive estimates of ρ upwards. Such an adjustment can be achieved by using a Bayesian estimator, or the adjusted CO estimator. Since the adjusted CO estimator is very easy to implement, it seems difficult to justify the continued use of one-pass CO or maximum-likelihood estimation.

References

Beach, C.M. and J.G. MacKinnon, 1978, A maximum likelihood procedure for regression with autocorrelated errors, Econometrica 46, 51–58.

Beesley, P.A.A. and W.E. Griffiths, 1982, A simulation study of the effects of autocorrelation misspecification in a linear statistical model, Proceedings of the Fifth Biennial Conference of the Simulation Society of Australia (Armidale) 120–127.

Cochrane, D. and G.H. Orcutt, 1949, Application of least squares regressions to relationships containing autocorrelated error terms, Journal of the American Statistical Association 44, 32–61.

Engle, R.F., 1974, Specification of the disturbance term for efficient estimation, Econometrica 42, 135–146.

Fishman, G.S., 1969, Spectral methods in econometrics (Harvard University Press, Cambridge).

Fomby, T.B. and D.K. Guilkey, 1978, On choosing the optimal level of significance for the Durbin-Watson test and the Bayesian alternative, Journal of Econometrics 8, 203–213.

Grenander, U. and M. Rosenblatt, 1957, Statistical analysis of stationary time series (Wiley, New York).

Griffiths, W.E. and P.A.A. Beesley, 1984, The small sample properties of some preliminary-test estimators in a linear model with autocorrelated errors, Journal of Econometrics 25, 49–62.

Harvey, A.C., 1980, On comparing regression models in levels and first differences, International Economic Review 21, 707–720.

Harvey, A.C., 1981, Time series models (Philip Allan, Oxford).

Hildreth, C. and W. Dent, 1974, An adjusted maximum likelihood estimator, in W. Sellekaert, ed., Econometrics and economic theory: Essays in honor of Jan Tinbergen (Macmillan, London) 3–25.

Judge, G.G., W.E. Griffiths, R.C. Hill, H. Lutkepohl and T.C. Lee, 1985, The theory and practice of econometrics, 2nd ed. (Wiley, New York).

King, M.L. and D.E.A. Giles, 1984, Autocorrelation pretesting in the linear model: Estimation, testing and prediction, Journal of Econometrics 25, 35–48.

Kwok, B. and M.R. Veall, 1986, The jackknife and regression with AR(1) errors, Working paper (University of Western Ontario, London, Ontario).

Lomnicki, Z.A. and S.K. Zaremba, 1957, On the estimation of autocorrelation in time series, Annals of Mathematical Statistics 28, 140–158.

Malinvaud, E., 1980, Statistical methods of econometrics, 3rd ed. (North-Holland, Amsterdam).

Miyazaki, S. and W.E. Griffiths, 1984, The properties of some covariance matrix estimators in linear models with AR(1) errors, Economics Letters 14, 351–356.

Nakamura, A. and M. Nakamura, 1978, On the impact of the tests for serial correlation upon the test of significance for the regression coefficient, Journal of Econometrics 7, 199–210.

Nicholls, D.F. and A.R. Pagan, 1977, Specification of the disturbance for efficient estimation: An extended analysis, Econometrica 45, 211–217.

Pantula, S.G. and W.A. Fuller, 1985, Mean estimation bias in least squares estimation of autoregressive processes, Journal of Econometrics 27, 99–122.

Park, Rolla Edward and Bridgen M. Mitchell, 1980, Estimating the autocorrelated error model with trended data, Journal of Econometrics 13, 185–201.

Ullah, A., V.K. Srivastava, L. Magee and A. Srivastava, 1983, Estimation of linear regression model with autocorrelated disturbances, Journal of Time Series Analysis 4, 127–135.

III. TOPICS IN ECONOMETRICS AND TIME SERIES

Readings in Econometric Theory and Practice
W. Griffiths, H. Lütkepohl and M.E. Bock (Editors)
© 1992 Elsevier Science Publishers B.V. All rights reserved

CHAPTER 9

SMOOTH IMPROVED ESTIMATORS OF ECONOMETRIC
PARAMETERS *

Aman Ullah

*Graduate School of Management, University of California, Riverside, CA 92521, USA
and Department of Economics, University of Western Ontario, London, Ontario, Canada*

Jeff Racine

Department of Economics, York University, Toronto, Ontario, Canada

In this paper we use nonparametric kernel density estimation techniques to develop a new class
of smooth estimators for the parameters in SURE and simultaneous equations models. The
efficiency property of the proposed estimators is also analysed.

1. Introduction

In the last three decades there has been significant growth in the literature
on improved shrinkage estimation; see for example, Judge and Bock (1978),
Judge et al. (1985) and Vinod and Ullah (1981) for the details. The estimators of the econometric parameters developed in this literature are usually
biased but they have a smaller mean squared error (MSE) compared to the
usual least squares estimator. Most of these improved estimators have been
developed both by frequentist and Bayesian methods.

In this paper we consider an alternative approach towards developing
improved estimators. This approach is based on the smooth kernel density
estimation of Rosenblatt (1956) and Parzen (1962), which has been recently
used in economics in other contexts; see Ullah (1988) for a survey. It has
been shown here that kernel density estimation techniques provide a
"smooth" class of unbiased shrinkage estimators for the parameters of
seemingly unrelated regression equations (SURE) models. Using density

* The authors are thankful to H. Lütkepohl and a referee for useful comments on the earlier
version of this paper.

estimation techniques we also develop a class of smooth estimators for structural models.

The plan of this paper is as follows. In section 2 we consider the estimation of the SURE model and present the smooth class of shrinkage estimators along with their bias and variances. Then in section 3 we further analyze the properties of smooth estimators through a simulation experiment. Section 4 develops the smooth estimators for the structural model. Finally section 5 gives the derivation of results in section 2.

2. The Model and Estimators

Let us consider a system of M seemingly unrelated regression equations (SURE) model as

$$y_i = X_i \beta_i + u_i, \quad i = 1, \ldots, M \tag{2.1}$$

where y_i is a $T \times 1$ vector of observations on the dependent variable y, X_i is a $T \times K_i$ matrix of nonstochastic regressors, β_i is a $K_i \times 1$ vector of the unknown regression coefficients and u_i is a $T \times 1$ vector of unobservable disturbances.

The equations (2.1) can be written as

$$
\begin{pmatrix} y_1 \\ y_2 \\ \vdots \\ y_M \end{pmatrix} =
\begin{pmatrix} X_1 & 0 & \cdots & 0 \\ 0 & X_2 & \cdots & 0 \\ \vdots & \vdots & \ddots & \vdots \\ 0 & 0 & \cdots & X_M \end{pmatrix}
\begin{pmatrix} \beta_1 \\ \beta_2 \\ \vdots \\ \beta_M \end{pmatrix} +
\begin{pmatrix} u_1 \\ u_2 \\ \vdots \\ u_M \end{pmatrix} \tag{2.2}
$$

and more compactly as

$$y = X\beta + u \tag{2.3}$$

where y is an $MT \times 1$ vector, X is an $MT \times K$ matrix, β is a $K \times 1$ vector, and u is an $MT \times 1$ vector of disturbances. Note that $K = \sum_{i=1}^{M} K_i$.

It is assumed that the disturbances are contemporaneously correlated with mean zero and variance-covariance matrix given by

$$
\Omega =
\begin{pmatrix} \sigma_{11}I & \sigma_{12}I & \cdots & \sigma_{1M}I \\ \sigma_{21}I & \sigma_{22}I & \cdots & \sigma_{2M}I \\ \vdots & \vdots & \ddots & \vdots \\ \sigma_{M1}I & \sigma_{M2}I & \cdots & \sigma_{MM}I \end{pmatrix} = \Sigma \otimes I \tag{2.4}
$$

where $\otimes$ is the Kronecker product operator, I is an identity matrix of order $T \times T$ and

$$E(u_i u_j') = \sigma_{ii} I \quad \text{for } i = j$$

$$= \sigma_{ij} I, \quad i \neq j, \quad i, j = 1, \ldots, M \tag{2.5}$$

Applying ordinary least squares separately to each equation in the system will be called systems ordinary least squares (SOLS) estimation. This yields the SOLS estimator of β in (2.3)

$$b = (X'X)^{-1} X'y. \tag{2.6}$$

The exact covariance matrix of the SOLS estimator will be

$$V(b) = (X'X)^{-1} X'\Omega X (X'X)^{-1}. \tag{2.7}$$

For known Ω, the generalized least squares (GLS) estimator is

$$\hat{\beta} = (X'\Omega^{-1}X)^{-1} X'\Omega^{-1}y \tag{2.8}$$

and its exact covariance matrix is

$$V(\hat{\beta}) = (X'\Omega^{-1}X)^{-1}. \tag{2.9}$$

In general Ω will be unknown, and therefore the estimator $\hat{\beta}$ cannot be applied in this form. Zellner (1962) proposed an operational estimator based on an estimator of Ω in which the ijth element of Σ is replaced with the unrestricted estimator

$$s_{ij} = y_i' \frac{\left(I - X^*(X^{*\prime}X^*)^{-1}X^{*\prime}\right)}{T} y_j \tag{2.10}$$

where X^* is the $T \times k$ matrix of k distinct regressors. Results similar to those found in this paper hold for restricted residuals as well. Zellner's SURE estimator is given by

$$\tilde{\beta} = (X'\hat{\Omega}^{-1}X)^{-1} X'\hat{\Omega}^{-1}y \tag{2.11}$$

where $\hat{\Omega} = S \otimes I$ is a consistent estimator of Ω, $S = ((s_{ij}))$. $\tilde{\beta}$ is also known as a two-step GLS (2SGLS) estimator and its asymptotic covariance matrix is the same as (2.9).

Zellner's estimator of the asymptotic covariance matrix of $\tilde{\beta}$ is given by

$$AV(\tilde{\beta}) = (X'\hat{\Omega}^{-1}X)^{-1} \tag{2.12}$$

Kakwani (1967) proved the unbiasedness of $\tilde{\beta}$ and Srivastava (1970) worked out its second order covariance matrix to order $O(T^{-2})$. This latter result, under the assumption of normality of disturbances in (2.1) is

$$V(\tilde{\beta}) = \left[\left(1 + \frac{M}{T}\right)I - \Omega_0 H\right]\Omega_0 \tag{2.13}$$

where $\Omega_0 = (X'\Omega^{-1}X)^{-1}$ and $H = X'(\Sigma^{-1} \otimes W)X - X'PX$; $W = \Sigma_{i=1}^{M}R_{ii}$ where R_{ii} is a $T \times T$ diagonal submatrix of $R = ((R_{ij})) = X\Omega_0 X'\Omega^{-1}$ and $P = ((P_{ij}))$, where P_{ij} is the transpose of the submatrix Q_{ij} in $Q = ((Q_{ij})) = \Omega^{-1} - \Omega^{-1}X\Omega_0 X'\Omega^{-1}$. For further properties of $\tilde{\beta}$, see Kariya (1981), Toyooka and Kariya (1986), and Phillips (1986).

The biased shrinkage estimators of β and their properties have been considered in Srivastava and Giles (1987). Here we consider unbiased improved estimators of β which are based on (biased) improved estimators of Ω.

2.1. A New Class of Unbiased Smooth 2SGLS Estimators

Recall that $\Omega = \Sigma \otimes I$ and that the estimation of Ω requires an estimate of Σ. The main-diagonal elements of Σ are unconditional variances and are given by $E(u_{it}^2) = \sigma_{ii}$ while the off-diagonal elements, the unconditional covariances, are $E(u_{it}u_{jt}) = \sigma_{ij}$.

The smooth estimator of the matrix Σ will be denoted as $\hat{\Sigma}_{sm}$, and can be estimated as follows. Consider first

$$\sigma_{ii} = E(u_{it}^2)$$

$$= \int u_i^2 f(u_i)\, du_i \tag{2.14}$$

where the second equality follows since u_{it} is i.i.d. for $t = 1, \ldots, T$. Notice that Zellner's estimator of $\sigma_{ii} = \int u_i^2 f(u_i)\, du_i = \int u_i^2\, dF(u_i)$ is $s_{ii} = \int u_i^2\, d\hat{F}(u_i)$

where $\hat{F}(u_i)$ is the empirical distribution. A smooth estimator of σ_{ii} can, however, be obtained as follows:

$$\hat{\sigma}_{ii} = \int u_i^2 \hat{f}(u_i) \, du_i \tag{2.15}$$

where, for $Z_t = (u_i - u_{it})/h$

$$\hat{f}(u_i) = \frac{1}{Th} \sum_{t=1}^{T} K\left(\frac{u_i - u_{it}}{h}\right)$$

$$= \frac{1}{Th} \sum_{t=1}^{T} K(Z_t) \tag{2.16}$$

is a Rosenblatt (1956) and Parzen (1962) type consistent nonparametric kernel estimator of the probability density function of the random variable u_i; $h = h_T$ is the window-width which tends to zero as $T \to \infty$, and $K(\cdot)$ is the real valued kernel function. Usually, but not always, $K(\cdot)$ will be a symmetric density function, e.g. the normal density. Also, $K(\cdot)$ is such that for values of u_{it} having further distance from u_i, with any given h, Z_t will be large in absolute value and so $K(\cdot)$ will be small. $\hat{f}(u_i)$ is thus obtained by local averaging or smoothing. The choices of h and $K(\cdot)$ will be discussed in section 3. For the analysis below we consider $K(Z_t)$ to be any kernel function satisfying

(A1) $\int K(Z_t) \, dz_t = 1$

(A2) $\int Z_t K(Z_t) \, dz_t = 0$

(A3) $\int Z_t^2 K(Z_t) \, dz_t = \omega_{22}$

(A4) $\int\int Z_t Z_{t'} K(Z_t, Z_{t'}) \, dz_t \, dz_{t'} = \omega_{12}$

By substituting the kernel estimator of $f(u_i)$ into the expression for the variance of u_i, and noting that u_{it} is i.i.d. for $t = 1, \ldots, T$, we obtain

$$\hat{\sigma}_{ii} = \int u_i^2 \frac{1}{Th} \sum_{t=1}^{T} K\left(\frac{u_i - u_{it}}{h}\right) \, du_i$$

$$= \frac{1}{Th} \sum_{t=1}^{T} \int u_i^2 K\left(\frac{u_i - u_{it}}{h}\right) \, du_i$$

$$= \frac{1}{Th} \sum_{t=1}^{T} \int (u_{it} + hZ_t)^2 K(Z_t) h \, dz_t$$

$$= \frac{1}{T} \sum_{t=1}^{T} \int (u_{it}^2 + h^2 Z_t^2 + 2hZ_t) K(Z_t) \, dz_t$$

$$= \frac{1}{T} \sum_{t=1}^{T} \left(u_{it}^2 \int K(Z_t) \, dz_t + h^2 \int Z_t^2 K(Z_t) \, dz_t + 2hu_{it} \int Z_t K(Z_t) \, dz_t \right)$$

$$= \frac{1}{T} \sum_{t=1}^{T} u_{it}^2 + h^2 \omega_{22} \tag{2.17}$$

Next we need to obtain $\hat{\sigma}_{ij} = E(u_{it} u_{jt})$. Dropping the subscript t for notational simplicity, we write the nonparametric estimator of σ_{ij} as follows:

$$\hat{\sigma}_{ij} = \int \int u_i u_j \hat{f}(u_i, u_j) \, du_i \, du_j$$

$$= \int \int u_i u_j \frac{1}{Th^2} \sum_{t=1}^{T} K\left(\frac{u_i - u_{it}}{h}, \frac{u_j - u_{jt}}{h}\right) \, du_i \, du_j$$

$$= \frac{1}{Th^2} \sum_{t=1}^{T} \int \int (hZ_{it} + u_{it})(hZ_{jt} + u_{jt}) K(Z_{it}, Z_{jt}) h \, dz_{it} h \, dz_{jt}$$

$$= \frac{1}{T} \sum_{t=1}^{T} \int \int (hZ_{it} + u_{it})(hZ_{jt} + u_{jt}) K(Z_{it}, Z_{jt}) \, dz_{it} \, dz_{jt}$$

$$= \frac{1}{T} \sum_{t=1}^{T} \int \int \left(h^2 Z_{it} Z_{jt} + u_{it} hZ_{jt} + u_{jt} hZ_{it} + u_{it} u_{jt} \right)$$

$$\times K(Z_{it}, Z_{jt})\, \mathrm{d}z_{it}\, \mathrm{d}z_{jt}$$

$$= \frac{1}{T} \sum_{t=1}^{T} \left(u_{it} u_{jt} \int \int K(Z_{it}, Z_{jt})\, \mathrm{d}z_{it}\, \mathrm{d}z_{jt} \right)$$

$$+ \frac{1}{T} \sum_{t=1}^{T} \left(h^2 \int \int Z_{it} Z_{jt} K(Z_{it}, Z_{jt})\, \mathrm{d}z_{it}\, \mathrm{d}z_{jt} \right)$$

$$+ \frac{1}{T} \sum_{t=1}^{T} \left(u_{it} h \int \int Z_{it} K(Z_{it}, Z_{jt})\, \mathrm{d}z_{it}\, \mathrm{d}z_{jt} \right)$$

$$+ \frac{1}{T} \sum_{t=1}^{T} \left(u_{jt} h \int \int Z_{jt} K(Z_{it}, Z_{jt})\, \mathrm{d}z_{it}\, \mathrm{d}z_{jt} \right)$$

$$= \frac{1}{T} \sum_{t=1}^{T} u_{it} u_{jt} + h^2 \omega_{12} \tag{2.18}$$

by assumptions (A1–A4). The consistent estimator $\hat{f}(u_i, u_j)$ is the bivariate extension of the kernel estimator in (2.16). For details about it see Silverman (1986) and Ullah (1988). For the product kernel, $\hat{\sigma}_{ij} = T^{-1}\sum_{t=1}^{T} u_{it} u_{jt}$ for $i \neq j$.

These are the nonparametric estimators of σ_{ii} and σ_{ij}, the unconditional nonparametric variance and cross-equation covariance estimators for a system of equations model. For $h = 0$ they collapse to Zellner's estimator.

This gives us a nonparametric estimator of Ω, $\hat{\Omega}_{sm} = \hat{\Sigma}_{sm} \otimes I_T$, where $\hat{\Sigma}_{sm}$ is an $(M \times M)$ matrix with typical main-diagonal element $(1/T)\sum_{t=1}^{T} u_{it}^2 + h^2 \omega_{22}$ and typical off-diagonal element $(1/T)\sum_{t=1}^{T} u_{it} u_{jt} + h^2 \omega_{12}$. This estimator is a consistent estimator of Ω which is demonstrated by noting that ω_{22} and ω_{12} are constant terms which depend on the choice of the kernel, and $h \to 0$ as $T \to \infty$, so asymptotically these are equivalent to Zellner's estimators, which are consistent. Note that the nonparametric estimator of Ω can be written as a linear combination of Zellner's original estimator plus a matrix which is a function of the smoothing parameter h, i.e.

$$\hat{\Omega}_{sm} = \hat{\Sigma}_{sm} \otimes I$$

$$= (S + \Theta(h)) \otimes I \tag{2.19}$$

where $\Theta(h)$ is a matrix with the typical main diagonal element $h^2 \omega_{22}$ and the typical off diagonal element $h^2 \omega_{12}$. The asymptotic properties of $\hat{\beta}$ based on $\hat{\Omega}_{sm}$ will be the same as those of the feasible SURE estimator. This is because $\Theta(h) \to 0$ and $h \to 0$ as $T \to \infty$, thus for large T, $\hat{\Omega}_{sm} = \hat{\Sigma}_{sm} \otimes I \simeq S \otimes I$ (see White (1984) for a proof).

The operational smoothed estimator, denoted by $\hat{\beta}_{sm}$, is obtained by replacing Ω in (2.8) by $\hat{\Omega}_{sm}$. This gives a new estimator

$$\tilde{\beta}_{sm} = \left(X' \hat{\Omega}_{sm}^{-1} X \right)^{-1} X' \hat{\Omega}_{sm}^{-1} y \tag{2.20}$$

whose asymptotic covariance matrix is the same as in (2.9).

Two problems remain which must be addressed before these estimators can be applied, namely, the choices of the kernel and of the window width. Rosenblatt suggested choosing a kernel and window width which minimize the integrated mean square error of the (joint) probability density function. The optimal kernel based on this approach is a parabola. Several authors have compared the relative efficiencies of the optimal kernel versus other kernels. Their results suggest that the relative efficiencies are very close to one for various kernel specifications. Therefore the choice of kernel ought to be based instead on considerations such as tractability and computational simplicity. For a detailed discussion see Silverman (1986). In our numerical analysis in section 3 we have employed a Gaussian kernel.

The choice of the window width, however, can have dramatic effects on estimation results (see Silverman (1986)). Choosing too large a value for h will result in over-smoothing, while values for h which are too small will lead to estimates which may be too noisy. As mentioned, one way in which h can be chosen is to minimize the integrated mean square error of the estimator of the density function with respect to h. The optimal h based on this approach is

$$h_{opt}^* = \left[\frac{\int K^2(W) \, dW}{\omega_{22}^2 \int \left(f''(u_i) \right)^2 \, du_i} \right]^{1/5} T^{-1/5} \tag{2.21}$$

which is $\propto T^{-1/5}$ (see Silverman (1986) and Ullah (1988)). The h_{opt}^* which minimizes the joint density of the disturbances in any two equations is $\propto T^{-1/6}$.

The objective at hand, however, is not the direct estimation of density functions per se but rather the estimation of the covariance matrix Ω. For this reason we choose h for which the estimator of Ω is optimal under a certain loss function.

Theorem 1: *Under the loss function* $\text{tr}(\tilde{\Sigma}_{sm}\Sigma^{-1} - I)^2$,

$$\frac{1}{2}E\left[\text{tr}\left(\tilde{\Sigma}_{sm}\Sigma^{-1} - I\right)^2\right] = \frac{1}{2}E\left[\text{tr}(S\Sigma^{-1} - I)^2\right]$$
$$+ \frac{1}{2}h^2\omega_{22}^2(\text{tr } \Sigma^{-2})\left(h^2 - \frac{2k}{T\omega_{22}}\frac{\text{tr } \Sigma^{-1}}{\text{tr } \Sigma^{-2}}\right)$$

$$(2.22)$$

The proof is given in section 5. It follows from the result in (2.22) that $\tilde{\Sigma}_{sm}$ dominates S so long as

$$0 < h < \left[\frac{2k}{T\omega_{22}}\left(\frac{\text{tr } \Sigma^{-1}}{\text{tr } \Sigma^{-2}}\right)\right]^{1/2} \qquad (2.23)$$

But $1 \leq (\text{tr } \Sigma^{-1})^2(\text{tr } \Sigma^{-2})^{-1} \leq M$. Thus (2.23) is satisfied if $0 < h < [(2kM/T\omega_{22})(\text{tr } \Sigma^{-1})^{-1}]^{1/2}$.
    The optimal h for which (2.22) is minimized is given by

$$h_{\text{opt}} = \left(\frac{k}{T\omega_{22}}\frac{\text{tr } \Sigma^{-1}}{\text{tr } \Sigma^{-2}}\right)^{1/2} \qquad (2.24)$$

which is $\alpha T^{-1/2}$. This optimal h differs with h_{opt}^* in (2.21) in a few important respects. First, they are obtained from different criteria. Second, while the rate of convergence to zero is $T^{-1/2}$ for h_{opt}, it is $T^{-1/5}$ for h_{opt}^*. Third, while h_{opt} depends on the unknown matrix Σ, h_{opt}^* depends on the second derivative of the density. In practice, however, both of these optimal window widths can be operationalized by replacing Σ with S and f'' by $\hat{f}''$. For example, for known ω_{22},

$$\hat{h}_{\text{opt}} = \left(\frac{k}{T\omega_{22}}\frac{\text{tr } S^{-1}}{\text{tr } S^{-2}}\right)^{1/2} \qquad (2.25)$$

    It is interesting to note that $\tilde{\Sigma}_{sm}$, as in the case of S, is an even function of the disturbance vector u. Thus the unbiasedness of $\tilde{\beta}_{sm}$ follows from the result of Kakwani (1967).

Theorem 2: *Under the assumption of normality of the disturbance vector u and $h = \hat{h}_{\text{opt}}$, $V(\tilde{\beta}_{sm})$ up to $O(T^{-2})$ is the same as $V(\tilde{\beta})$ given in (2.12). However, for $h = h_{\text{opt}}^*$, $V(\tilde{\beta}_{sm})$ up to $O(T^{-2})$ is not the same as $V(\tilde{\beta})$.*

The proof is given in section 5. Theorem 2 implies that the second order efficiency of $\tilde{\beta}_{sm}$ is the same as that of $\tilde{\beta}$. Thus an investigation of the higher order efficiency of $\tilde{\beta}_{sm}$ will be useful. This requires the expression for $V(\tilde{\beta}_{sm})$ up to $O(T^{-3})$ which is quite difficult to derive. In view of this, and the result that $V(\tilde{\beta}_{sm}) \neq V(\tilde{\beta})$ for $h = h_{\text{opt}}^*$, we study the higher order efficiency of $\tilde{\beta}_{sm}$ through a simulation experiment in section 3. It has been found that $\tilde{\beta}_{sm}$ performs better than Zellner's estimator $\tilde{\beta}$.

3. Simulation

The data employed for the simulation is based on a widely used data set, Theil's 1971 data. Theil's data was generated data on investment figures for General Electric and Westinghouse as a function of market values and capital stocks. Since Theil's sample contained only 20 observations, larger samples were generated to possess the same two first moments as Theil's data. This approach to obtaining data has been taken since the coefficients from Theil's model have been estimated in numerous studies and such studies will therefore serve as useful benchmarks.

The two equation model underlying the simulation experiment is given by the following two equations.

$$y_1 = -28.0x_{11} + 0.04x_{12} + 0.14x_{13} + e_1$$
$$y_2 = -1.3x_{21} + 0.06x_{22} + 0.06x_{23} + e_2 \tag{3.1}$$

For the evaluation of the estimators under the unconditional covariance scenario, the covariance matrix is $\Omega = \Sigma \otimes I$. The disturbance vector for each equation was generated as bivariate normal where the matrix Σ takes on the value

$$\Sigma = \begin{pmatrix} \sigma_{11} & \sigma_{12} \\ \sigma_{21} & \sigma_{22} \end{pmatrix} = \begin{pmatrix} 660.0 & 174.3 \\ 174.3 & 90.0 \end{pmatrix} \tag{3.2}$$

The data for the regressors was generated using the IMSL double precision subroutine DRNNOR, while the data for the bivariate normal disturbance vector was generated using the subroutine DRNMVN.

For each experiment, four estimation techniques were considered. The techniques and notation used are:

(i) The GLS estimator based on the true covariance matrix, $\hat{\beta}$.
(ii) The Zellner estimator $\tilde{\beta}$ in which step one involves applying OLS to each equation to obtain the residuals, and in step two the matrix Σ is estimated using these OLS residuals.

(iii) The SOLS estimator b obtained by applying OLS to each equation separately.

(iv) The smooth estimator, $\tilde{\beta}_{sm}$. The Gaussian kernel was employed for this experiment, and h was chosen according to (2.21) and (2.24).

The sample sizes that were chosen for the experiment were 25, 50, and 200. These are assumed to represent small, moderate, and large samples respectively.

Each of the estimation techniques mentioned above was applied to the two-equation model. For each of the six regression coefficients in the model, the bias, variance, and mean square error were calculated. The results are · then summarized in the following tables.

The experiment summarized in the tables below presents a comparison of a system of equations model estimated in two general ways. The first group of estimators, $\hat{\beta}$, presented in each table give properties of the estimator which would be obtained if the true covariance matrix of the disturbances was known. The second group of estimators, b, $\tilde{\beta}$, and $\tilde{\beta}_{sm}$, are estimators which are unbiased.

The results found in the tables reveal that the smooth nonparametric estimator $\tilde{\beta}_{sm}$ clearly dominates Zellner's estimator $\tilde{\beta}$, and the SOLS estimator b (in the MSE sense) for the model considered here for the sample sizes of 25 and 50 (see tables 1 and 2). As mentioned above, the sample size of 200 was included to represent a *large* sample, thus we would expect the results found for this large sample to be asymptotic in nature. Recall that, asymptotically, both Zellner's estimator and the smooth nonparametric estimator are equivalent. This is borne out by the simulation results (table 3). In table 3 the MSE of $\tilde{\beta}$ and of β_{sm} are identical to three significant figures.

4. Smooth 2SLS Estimators

Let us consider a single equation

$$y = x\beta + u \tag{4.1}$$

where y is the dependent variable, u is the disturbance, β is a $k \times 1$ coefficient vector and x is an $1 \times k$ vector of stochastic regressors generated by

$$x = z\Pi + v \tag{4.2}$$

where z is an $1 \times L$ matrix of stochastic regressors which is uncorrelated with v, Π is an $L \times 1$ coefficient vector and v is the disturbance term. The equation (4.1) can be considered as a single equation of the M equations

Table 1

Sample Size = 25

	Bias	Variance	Relative MSE
$\hat{\beta}_{11}$	-0.370883	393.786	1.00000
$\hat{\beta}_{12}$	0.169036E$-$03	0.748366E$-$04	1.00000
$\hat{\beta}_{13}$	0.432692E$-$03	0.232470E$-$03	1.00000
$\hat{\beta}_{21}$	-0.612731E$-$01	16.9741	1.00000
$\hat{\beta}_{22}$	0.237626E$-$03	0.357171E$-$04	1.00000
$\hat{\beta}_{23}$	-0.931346E$-$03	0.707766E$-$03	1.00000
b_{11}	-0.935594	753.068	1.91393
b_{12}	0.363613E$-$03	0.147877E$-$03	1.97608
b_{13}	0.896165E$-$03	0.487083E$-$03	2.09393
b_{21}	-0.938936E$-$01	30.2179	1.78036
b_{22}	0.316592E$-$03	0.712529E$-$04	1.99310
b_{23}	-0.116977E$-$02	0.148208E$-$02	2.09229
$\tilde{\beta}_{11}$	-0.478431	426.576	1.08347
$\tilde{\beta}_{12}$	0.184470E$-$03	0.807754E$-$04	1.07889
$\tilde{\beta}_{13}$	0.640936E$-$03	0.254076E$-$03	1.09221
$\tilde{\beta}_{21}$	-0.622394E$-$01	17.8461	1.05136
$\tilde{\beta}_{22}$	0.240553E$-$03	0.384841E$-$04	1.07658
$\tilde{\beta}_{23}$	-0.943504E$-$03	0.754778E$-$03	1.06582
$\tilde{\beta}_{sm,11}$	-0.436495	412.197	1.04687
$\tilde{\beta}_{sm,12}$	0.170583E$-$03	0.777665E$-$04	1.03866
$\tilde{\beta}_{sm,13}$	0.603396E$-$03	0.243390E$-$03	1.04615
$\tilde{\beta}_{sm,21}$	-0.567702E$-$01	17.3281	1.02082
$\tilde{\beta}_{sm,22}$	0.227835E$-$03	0.370970E$-$04	1.03767
$\tilde{\beta}_{sm;23}$	-0.908056E$-$03	0.733260E$-$03	1.03537

structural model with (4.2) as the reduced form for the endogenous regressors x. Alternatively (4.1) and (4.2) is a simple generated regressor model (see Pagan (1984)). When x and u are uncorrelated, the parameter of interest is $\beta = (Ex'x)^{-1}Ex'y$ which minimizes $Eu^2 = E(y - x\beta)^2$. Given the T observations on y and x, $\hat{E}(x'x) = \int x'x \, d\hat{F}(x) = X'X$ where $\hat{F}(x)$ is the empirical distribution function. Similarly $\hat{E}x'y = X'y$. Thus the estimator of β is $b = (X'X)^{-1}X'y$ which is the well known least squares estimator. However, if instead of the unsmooth empirical distribution we use the

Table 2

Sample Size = 50

	Bias	Variance	Relative MSE
$\hat{\beta}_{11}$	0.994149E−01	238.362	1.00000
$\hat{\beta}_{12}$	−0.476667E−04	0.421307E−04	1.00000
$\hat{\beta}_{13}$	−0.348709E−03	0.107187E−03	1.00000
$\hat{\beta}_{21}$	−0.641919E−01	9.79153	1.00000
$\hat{\beta}_{22}$	0.446434E−04	0.174033E−04	1.00000
$\hat{\beta}_{23}$	0.640645E−03	0.331908E−03	1.00000
b_{11}	−0.546463	473.069	1.98583
b_{12}	0.230831E−03	0.866782E−04	2.06012
b_{13}	−0.157442E−03	0.212652E−03	1.98763
b_{21}	−0.976621E−01	17.8821	1.82648
b_{22}	0.239074E−03	0.371131E−04	2.13622
b_{23}	−0.375935E−03	0.691620E−03	2.08361
$\tilde{\beta}_{11}$	0.127169E−01	246.917	1.03585
$\tilde{\beta}_{12}$	−0.150491E−04	0.437367E−04	1.03888
$\tilde{\beta}_{13}$	−0.299839E−03	0.110078E−03	1.02960
$\tilde{\beta}_{21}$	−0.451370E−01	10.0643	1.02763
$\tilde{\beta}_{22}$	0.267682E−04	0.180254E−04	1.03598
$\tilde{\beta}_{23}$	0.558312E−03	0.340156E−03	1.02550
$\tilde{\beta}_{sm,11}$	0.529729E−01	244.401	1.02530
$\tilde{\beta}_{sm,12}$	−0.312107E−04	0.433250E−04	1.02912
$\tilde{\beta}_{sm,13}$	−0.317583E−03	0.109698E−03	1.02615
$\tilde{\beta}_{sm,21}$	−0.432657E−01	9.96641	1.01762
$\tilde{\beta}_{sm,22}$	0.948868E−05	0.177072E−04	1.01766
$\tilde{\beta}_{sm,23}$	0.660798E−03	0.337663E−03	1.01837

nonparametric smooth density estimator described in (2.15), we get the smooth estimator $b_{sm} = (X'X + h^2\omega_{22}I)^{-1}(X'y + h^2\omega_{12}\iota)$ where ω_{22}, ω_{12} are as defined in section (2) and ι is a vector of unity. When $\omega_{12} = 0$, the estimator b_{sm} reduces to a ridge-type smooth estimator $(X'X + h^2\omega_{22}I)^{-1}X'y$. This estimator and its properties are given in Faraldo et al. (1985) and Cristobal et al. (1987). It has been shown by these authors that, while the asymptotic distribution of b_{sm} is the same as that of b, in small samples b_{sm} performs better than b in the MSE sense. When x and u are

Table 3

Sample Size = 200

	Bias	Variance	Relative MSE
$\hat{\beta}_{11}$	$-0.204594\text{E}{-}01$	49.6180	1.00000
$\hat{\beta}_{12}$	$-0.425109\text{E}{-}05$	$0.101972\text{E}{-}04$	1.00000
$\hat{\beta}_{13}$	$0.128951\text{E}{-}03$	$0.231310\text{E}{-}04$	1.00000
$\hat{\beta}_{21}$	$-0.237457\text{E}{-}01$	2.76872	1.00000
$\hat{\beta}_{22}$	$0.907647\text{E}{-}04$	$0.416338\text{E}{-}05$	1.00000
$\hat{\beta}_{23}$	$-0.164040\text{E}{-}03$	$0.545099\text{E}{-}04$	1.00000
b_{11}	$-0.880621\text{E}{-}01$	94.2179	1.89900
b_{12}	$0.424952\text{E}{-}04$	$0.200990\text{E}{-}04$	1.97066
b_{13}	$0.649084\text{E}{-}04$	$0.491100\text{E}{-}04$	2.12615
b_{21}	$0.653702\text{E}{-}01$	5.44475	1.96766
b_{22}	$-0.186818\text{E}{-}04$	$0.908986\text{E}{-}05$	2.17990
b_{23}	$-0.328139\text{E}{-}03$	$0.119549\text{E}{-}03$	2.19554
$\tilde{\beta}_{11}$	$-0.111556\text{E}{-}01$	49.5944	0.99951
$\tilde{\beta}_{12}$	$-0.610612\text{E}{-}05$	$0.101870\text{E}{-}04$	0.99873
$\tilde{\beta}_{13}$	$0.115012\text{E}{-}03$	$0.232000\text{E}{-}04$	1.00490
$\tilde{\beta}_{21}$	$-0.233857\text{E}{-}01$	2.80742	1.01396
$\tilde{\beta}_{22}$	$0.902357\text{E}{-}04$	$0.420467\text{E}{-}05$	1.01026
$\tilde{\beta}_{23}$	$-0.164009\text{E}{-}03$	$0.546522\text{E}{-}04$	1.00328
$\tilde{\beta}_{sm,11}$	$-0.104400\text{E}{-}01$	49.6594	1.00082
$\tilde{\beta}_{sm,12}$	$-0.677480\text{E}{-}05$	$0.101947\text{E}{-}04$	0.99948
$\tilde{\beta}_{sm,13}$	$0.116553\text{E}{-}03$	$0.232198\text{E}{-}04$	1.00577
$\tilde{\beta}_{sm,21}$	$-0.256550\text{E}{-}01$	2.80184	1.01198
$\tilde{\beta}_{sm,22}$	$0.928901\text{E}{-}04$	$0.419316\text{E}{-}05$	1.00762
$\tilde{\beta}_{sm,23}$	$-0.158769\text{E}{-}03$	$0.545519\text{E}{-}04$	1.00141

correlated the parameter of interest is $\beta = (E(\Pi'z'x))^{-1}E(\Pi'z'y)$, where $\Pi = (Ez'z)^{-1}Ez'x$. Substitution of Π gives us

$$\beta = \left[(Ez'x)'(Ez'z)^{-1}(Ez'x) \right]^{-1}(Ez'x)'(Ez'z)^{-1}Ez'y \qquad (4.3)$$

Again, given T observations on y and z, if we use a nonsmooth empirical distribution to estimate expectations in (4.3) we get

$$\hat{\beta} = \left(X'Z(Z'Z)^{-1}Z'X \right)^{-1} X'Z(Z'Z)^{-1}Z'y \qquad (4.4)$$

which is the well known 2SLS estimator. However if we use the nonparametric smooth density estimator then (assuming all $\omega_{12} = 0$) we get a new class of the smooth 2SLS estimators which will be written as

$$\hat{\beta}_{sm} = \left(X'Z(Z'Z + h^2\omega_{22}I)^{-1}Z'X \right)^{-1} X'Z(Z'Z + h^2\omega_{22}I)^{-1} Z'y$$

$$(4.5)$$

When $L = k$, equation (2.2) is just identified, and $\hat{\beta}_{sm} = \hat{\beta} = (Z'X)^{-1}Z'y$. Since $h \to 0$ as $T \to \infty$, it is easy to verify that the asymptotic distribution of $\sqrt{T}(\hat{\beta}_{sm} - \beta)$ is the same as the well known asymptotic distribution of the 2SLS estimator $\sqrt{T}(\hat{\beta} - \beta)$. In the finite sample case $\hat{\beta}_{sm}$ is expected to perform better than $\hat{\beta}$, and a detailed investigation remains the subject of further investigation.

5. Derivation of Results in Section 3

Here we give the proofs of results in Theorems 1 and 2 given in section 3. For the result found in Theorem 1 we note that using $\tilde{\Sigma}_{sm} = S + h^2\omega_{22}$

$$\tfrac{1}{2}E \text{ tr}(\tilde{\Sigma}\Sigma^{-1} - I)^2 - \tfrac{1}{2}E \text{ tr}(S\Sigma^{-1} - I)^2$$

$$= \tfrac{1}{2}h^2\omega_{22}\left[h^2\omega_{22} \text{ tr } \Sigma^{-2} + 2E \text{ tr}(S\Sigma^{-1} - I)\Sigma^{-1} \right]$$

$$= \tfrac{1}{2}h^2\omega_{22}\left[h^2\omega_{22} \text{ tr } \Sigma^{-2} - 2\frac{k}{T}\text{tr } \Sigma^{-1} \right] \qquad (5.1)$$

where we use $ES = T^{-1}(T - k)\Sigma$.

To obtain the result in Theorem 2 we first observe that $S = S - \Sigma + \Sigma = \Delta + \Sigma$ where $\Delta = S - \Sigma = O_p(T^{-1/2})$. Thus

$$\frac{\text{tr } S^{-1}}{\text{tr } S^{-2}} = \frac{\text{tr } \Sigma^{-1}}{\text{tr } \Sigma^{-2}} + O_p(T^{-1/2}) \qquad (5.2)$$

and using this in (2.25) we obtain

$$\hat{h}^2_{\text{opt}} = h^2_{\text{opt}} + O_p(T^{-3/2}) \qquad (5.3)$$

where $h_{opt}^2 \omega_{22} = kT^{-1}(\text{tr } \Sigma^{-1})(\text{tr } \Sigma^{-2})^{-1} = O(T^{-1})$. Using (5.3) we can write, up to $O(T^{-1})$,

$$\tilde{\Sigma}_{sm}^{-1} = \left(S + \hat{h}_{opt}^2 \omega_{22} I\right)^{-1}$$

$$= \left(\Delta + \Sigma + h_{opt}^2 \omega_{22} I + O_p(T^{-3/2})\right)^{-1}$$

$$= \Sigma^{-1} - \Sigma^{-1}\Delta\Sigma^{-1} - h_{opt}^2 \omega_{22}\Sigma^{-2} + \Sigma^{-1}\Delta\Sigma^{-1}\Delta\Sigma^{-1} \qquad (5.4)$$

From this it is easy to verify that

$$\tilde{\beta}_{sm} - \beta = e_{-1/2} + e_{-1} + \left(e_{-3/2} + h_{opt}^2 \omega_{22}\Omega_0 X'\Omega Qu\right) + O_p(T^{-2-g}),$$

$$g \geq 0 \qquad (5.5)$$

where

$$e_{-1/2} = \Omega_0 X'\Omega u$$
$$e_{-1} = -\Omega_0 X'(\Sigma^{-1}\Delta \otimes I)Qu$$
$$e_{-3/2} = \Omega_0 X'(\Sigma^{-1}\Delta \otimes I)Q(\Delta \otimes I)Qu \qquad (5.6)$$
$$Q = \Omega - \Omega X\Omega_0 X'\Omega$$

Thus, using Srivastava (1970)

$$V(\tilde{\beta}_{sm}) = E(e_{-1/2}e'_{-1/2}) + E(e_{-1}e'_{-1/2} + e_{-1/2}e'_{-1})$$

$$+ E(e_{-1}e'_{-1} + e_{-3/2}e'_{-1/2} + e_{-1/2}e'_{-3/2})$$

$$= V(\tilde{\beta}) + h_{opt}^2 \omega_{22}[\Omega_0 X'\Omega Q(Euu')\Omega X\Omega_0 + \text{its transpose}]$$

$$= V(\tilde{\beta}) + h_{opt}^2 \omega_{22}[\Omega_0 X'\Omega QX\Omega_0 + \text{its transpose}]$$

$$= V(\tilde{\beta}) \qquad (5.7)$$

because $QX = 0$. The first part of Theorem 2 is thus complete. For the second part of the proof it is easy to verify that for h_{opt}^*, $\tilde{\beta}_{sm} - \beta$ will contain several terms between $e_{-1/2}$ and $e_{-3/2}$ and so $\tilde{\beta}_{sm} - \beta$ in this case will be quite different compared to (5.5), and so will be the case with $V(\tilde{\beta}_{sm})$ in (5.7). An explicit expression could be obtained but it is complicated and will not be presented here.

References

Cristobal, J.A., and P.F. Roca and W.G. Manteiga (1987), "A class of linear regression parameter estimates constructed by nonparametric estimation", *The Annals of Statistics*, 15, 602–609.

Faraldo, R.P. and G.W. Manteiga (1987), "On efficiency of a new class of linear regression estimates obtained by preliminary nonparametric estimation," in *New Perspectives in Theoretical and Applied Statistics*, (M. Puri et al. eds.), New York: Wiley.

Judge, G.D. and W.E. Bock (1978), *The Statistical Implications of Pretest and Stein Rule Estimators in Econometrics*, New York: North Holland Publishing.

Judge, G.G., W.E. Griffiths, R.C. Hill, H. Lütkepohl, and T.C. Lee (1985), *The Theory and Practice of Econometrics*, 2nd ed. New York: Wiley.

Kakwani, N.C. (1967), "The unbiasedness of Zellner's seemingly unrelated regression equations estimators", *Journal of the American Statistical Association*, 62, 141–142.

Kariya, T. (1981), " Bounds for the covariance matrices of Zellner's estimator in the SUR model and the 2SAE in a heteroskedastic model," *The Annals of Statistics*, 9, 975–979.

Pagan, A.R. (1984), "Econometric Issues in the Analysis of Regressions with Generated Regressors", *International Economic Review*, 25, 221–247.

Parzen, E. (1962), "On estimation of probability function and mode." *Annals of Mathematical Statistics*, 33, 1065–1076.

Phillips, P.C.B. (1986), "The exact distribution of the SUR estimator," *Econometrica*, 53, 745–756.

Rosenblatt, M. (1956), "Remarks on some nonparametric estimates of a density function." *Annals of Mathematical Statistics*, 27, 823–837.

Silverman, B.W. (1986), *Density Estimation for Statistics and Data Analysis*, New York: Chapman and Hall.

Srivastava, V.K. (1970), "The efficiency of estimating seemingly unrelated regression equations," *Annals of the Institute of Statistical Mathematics*, 483–493.

Srivastava,V.K. and D.E.A. Giles (1987), *Seemingly Unrelated Regression Equations Models*, New York: Marcel Dekker Inc.

Toyooka, Y. and T. Kariya (1986), "An approach to upper bound problems for risks of generalized least squares estimators," *The Annals of Statistics*, 14, 679–690.

Ullah, A. (1988), "Non-parametric estimation of econometric functionals," *Canadian Journal of Economics* 3, 625–658.

Vinod, H.D. and A. Ullah (1981), *Recent Advances in Regression Methods*, New York: Marcel Dekker Inc.

White, H. (1984), *Asymptotic theory for econometricians*, Academic Press.

Zellner, A. (1962), "An efficient method of estimating seemingly unrelated regressions and tests of aggregation bias", *Journal of the American Statistical Association*, 57, 348–368.

Readings in Econometric Theory and Practice
W. Griffiths, H. Lütkepohl and M.E. Bock (Editors)

CHAPTER 10

ESTIMATING THE SMOOTHING PARAMETER IN PIECEWISE
CONSTANT REGRESSION *

Ilkka Mellin

Department of Statistics, University of Helsinki, SF-00100 Helsinki, Finland

Timo Teräsvirta

Research Institute of the Finnish Economy, SF-00120 Helsinki, Finland

1. Introduction

Determining the amount of smoothness or estimating the value of a
smoothing parameter is an important problem in nonparametric estimation
of unknown functional forms. It appears in spectral and other density
estimation and also in nonlinear regression like kernel estimation and spline
smoothing. Marron (1988) surveyed this area, whereas Rice (1984) and
Härdle et al. (1988a), among other things, carried out simulation studies
concerning the behaviour of various data-driven smoothers in kernel estimation. Titterington (1985) is a useful survey of smoothing in general. In this
paper we shall consider the determination of the degree of smoothness in
piecewise constant regression. Our starting-point is that the unknown function is approximated by a piecewise constant function. An accompanying
assumption is that the unknown function is smooth and that the degree of
smoothness is in practice controlled by a smoothing parameter λ. For
econometric applications of this technique, see e.g. Engle et al. (1986), and

* We wish to thank Markku Rahiala and Pentti Saikkonen for useful discussions, Juha Puranen
for help in programming and Elina Järvinen for research assistance. The responsibility for any
errors remains ours. Financial support from the Yrjö Jahnsson Foundation is gratefully acknowledged.

Mellin and Teräsvirta (1989). We shall focus on the estimation of the values of the unknown function at the mid-points of the constancy intervals. Various data-driven techniques have been suggested for determining λ: a well-known example is the generalized cross-validation (GCV), see e.g. Golub et al. (1979) and Engle et al. (1986).

Smoothing is most needed when sample information is scarce. We shall investigate the small-sample properties of several data-driven smoothing methods which we call smoothers. A whole family of them may be derived by generalizing well-known model selection criteria in a proper way. Our simulation results show that no single smoother can be recommended in all situations. Techniques that generally oversmooth perform best in small samples when the unknown function is rather smooth. Smoothers that undersmooth rather than oversmooth do best when the function is not smooth and the error variance of the model is relatively large. Of various ad hoc smoothers popular in ridge regression, the few we consider generally behave badly except for some isolated cases. By and large, our results are in accord with those Rice (1984) and Härdle et al. (1988a) have obtained by considering a more limited set of smoothers. Autocorrelated errors tend to increase the smoothness of the estimated function when data-driven smoothers are applied.

The plan of the paper is as follows. Section 2 presents the piecewise constant model and the smoothers we are going to consider. Section 3 discusses the design of the simulation experiment whose results are considered in section 4. Section 5 concludes.

2. Model and Smoothers

2.1. Piecewise Constant Regression Model

Consider the following linear model

$$y_t = x_t \beta + u_t, \quad t = 1, \ldots, n \tag{2.1}$$

where $\beta = (\beta_1, \ldots, \beta_k)'$, and one of the elements of $x_t = (x_{t1}, \ldots, x_{tk})$ equals unity whereas the rest equal zero. In matrix form, and assuming $Eu_t = 0$, $\mathrm{cov}(u_t, u_s) = \delta_{st}\sigma^2$, we have

$$y = X\beta + u, \quad Eu = 0, \quad \mathrm{cov}(u) = \sigma^2 I. \tag{2.2}$$

Matrix X is thus an indicator matrix with exactly one non-zero element for each row so that $X'X$ is a diagonal matrix. If $X'X = I$, we have the spline smoothing model.

In this paper, (2.2) and the estimation of β will be our primary concern. However, (2.2) is often an approximation of a non-linear model

$$y_t = f(z_t) + \epsilon_t, \quad t = 1, \ldots, n \tag{2.3}$$

where z_t is a non-stochastic variable and f is an unknown function to be estimated. This is seen as follows. Suppose we want to approximate f with a piecewise constant function. To define the approximation assume $z_t \in (a, b]$, $t = 1, \ldots, n$ and select $z^{(1)} = a$, $z^{(2)} < \ldots < z^{(k)} < z^{(k+1)} = b$ such that $(a, b]$ is divided into k subintervals $(z^{(j)}, z^{(j+1)}]$, $j = 1, \ldots, k$, of positive length. Set $C^{(j)} = \{z \mid z \in (z^{(j-1)}, z^{(j)}]\}$ and define $x_t = (x_{t1}, \ldots, x_{tk})$ where $x_{tj} = 1$ if $z_t \in C^{(j)}$ and zero otherwise. Approximate f by β_j when $z_t \in C^{(j)}$. This yields (2.1). There are many ways of constructing the subintervals and the choice affects the accuracy of the approximation. We shall ignore this problem and focus on the estimation of β.

The coefficient vector β may be estimated using ordinary least squares if $n > k$. Interpreting (2.2) in the light of (2.3), the elements of β constitute a piecewise constant approximation of f. Assume now that we have prior information telling us that f is smooth in the sense that the mth derivatives of f are small in absolute value. In the framework of (2.2) this requirement translates into the condition that the mth differences of β_j are small. We shall incorporate this in (2.2) as linear prior restrictions on β. Assume for simplicity that all subintervals are of equal length. Let R be an $h \times k$ matrix containing the smoothness information so that our assumption becomes "the components of $R\beta$ are small." Then R is a $(k - m) \times k$ matrix whose jth row

$$[R]_j = \left(0, \ldots, 0, 1, -m, \ldots, (-1)^j \binom{m}{j}, \ldots, (-1)^m, 0, \ldots, 0\right),$$

$$j = 1, \ldots, k - m. \tag{2.4}$$

The number of zeroes in the beginning equals $j - 1$ and at the end $k - j - m$. Setting $m = 2$ is a popular choice in practice, but higher order differences may be used as well if prior information excludes the lower order polynomials. For more discussion, cf. e.g. Shiller (1984).

Taking account of (2.2) and the smoothness assumption leads to the following optimization problem: Find β such that

$$q(\beta) = (y - X\beta)'(y - X\beta) + \lambda \beta' R' R \beta$$

is minimized. The non-negative scalar λ indicates the proportional weight of the sample and prior information, respectively. The resulting estimator

$$b_R(\lambda) = H_R(\lambda)b \tag{2.5}$$

where $b = UX'y$ with $U = (X'X)^{-1}$,

$$H_R(\lambda) = (X'X + \lambda R'R)^{-1} X'X = I - UR'S_\lambda R$$

and

$$S_\lambda = (\lambda^{-1}I + RUR')^{-1}.$$

It can be seen from (2.5) that the smoothed estimator is a linear transformation of the unsmoothed estimator b. If $\lambda \to \infty$, (2.5) approaches a restricted least squares estimator $b_R = (I - UR'(RUR')^{-1}R)b$. $H_R(\lambda)$ as a function of λ defines a continuous path in the parameter space from b to b_R.

2.2. Techniques for Estimating the Smoothing Parameter

Bayesian Smoothers

If λ is known, (2.5) has a Bayesian interpretation. Assume β has a partially improper prior distribution: $s = R\beta \sim N(0, \sigma^2 I/\lambda)$. Then (2.5) is the Bayes linear estimator of β. There is rarely prior information available about λ, but one may apply empirical Bayes techniques for determining λ. Set $\hat{s} = Rb$. The marginal distribution of $\hat{s}$ is $N(0, (\sigma^2/\lambda)T_\lambda^{-1})$ where $T_\lambda = \lambda^{-1}S_\lambda$ so that $(\lambda/\sigma^2)\hat{s}'T_\lambda\hat{s} \sim \chi^2(k - m)$, as rank $(R) = k - m$. This χ^2 variate may be made operational by substituting $\tilde{\sigma}^2 = (n - k)^{-1}(y - Xb)'(y - Xb)$ for σ^2. Furthermore, setting that equal to the mean of the distribution one obtains

$$(\lambda/\tilde{\sigma}^2)\hat{s}'T_\lambda\hat{s} = k - m. \tag{2.6}$$

Solving (2.6) for λ then yields an estimator of λ we shall call Empirical Bayes (EB). Letting $n \to \infty$ in (2.6), the l.h.s. converges to $\lambda\sigma^{-2}s's$, for $s \neq 0$. The asymptotic solution of (2.6) is thus

$$\lambda = \sigma^2(k - m)/s's. \tag{2.7}$$

Mellin (1988) discussed another way of applying Bayesian techniques to the problem of determining λ. It is based on the idea of maximizing the likelihood of a Bayesian model Akaike (1981) considered. The smoother is called ABIC and has the form

$$\text{ABIC}(\lambda) = -m \ln \lambda + \ln\{\det(X'X + \lambda R'R)\}$$

$$+ \{n\hat{\sigma}^2(\lambda) + b_R(\lambda)' R'R b_R(\lambda)\}/\tilde{\sigma}^2 \qquad (2.8)$$

where $\hat{\sigma}^2(\lambda) = n^{-1}(y - Xb_R(\lambda))'(y - Xb_R(\lambda))$, and λ is determined by minimizing (2.8). If $n \to \infty$, the estimated λ approaches (2.7); for technical details see Mellin (1988).

Smoothers Based on Model Selection Criteria

Teräsvirta (1987) suggested that the customary model selection criteria (see, e.g., Judge et al., 1985, chapter 21; Teräsvirta and Mellin, 1986) be generalized to the present problem. Rice (1984) and Härdle et al. (1988a) considered a similar generalization for kernel estimation. This can be done by generalizing the number of parameters in the model in a suitable way. The generalization may be called the equivalent number of regressors as in Engle et al. (1986). We shall call it the generalized dimension (GD) of the model. It is defined as

$$k_n(\lambda) = \text{tr } H_R(\lambda) = k - \text{tr}(RUR'S_\lambda).$$

Note that $k_n(\lambda)$ is a monotonically decreasing function of λ. Furthermore, $k_n(0) = k$, and $k_n(\lambda) \to k - m$, as $\lambda \to \infty$.

The model selection criteria are generalized by substituting $k_n(\lambda)$ for the number of regressors in their definition. We do not consider theoretical underpinnings of this, but at least in some cases the original interpretation remains intact. For instance, if we assume λ non-stochastic minimizing the generalized C_P (Mallows, 1973) amounts to minimizing the unbiased estimator of the mean squared error of prediction (MSEP)

$$q_n(\lambda) = E\{(b_R(\lambda) - \beta)' X'X(b_R(\lambda) - \beta)\} \qquad (2.9)$$

with respect to λ.

The generalized criteria may be divided into three classes in the same way as the model selection criteria in Teräsvirta and Mellin (1986). They are

$$SC1(\lambda) = \ln \hat{\sigma}^2(\lambda) + k_n(\lambda)g(n, 0)/n$$

$$SC2(\lambda) = \hat{\sigma}^2(\lambda) + \tilde{\sigma}^2 k_n(\lambda)g(n, 0)/n$$

$$SC3(\lambda) = \hat{\sigma}^2(\lambda) + \hat{\sigma}^2(\lambda)k_n(\lambda)g(n, k_n(\lambda))/n$$

Table 1

Smoothers Derived from Model Selection Criteria and Compared in this Paper

Smoother	Class	$g(n, \cdot)$	$\lim_{n\to\infty} g(n, \cdot$
AIC (Akaike, 1974)	1	2	2
SBIC (Schwarz, 1978; Rissanen, 1978)	1	$\ln n$	∞
HQ (Hannan and Quinn, 1979) [a]	1	$2 \ln \ln n$	∞
C_P (Mallows, 1973)	¯2	2	2
BEC (Geweke and Meese, 1981)	2	$\ln n$	∞
URV (Unbiased Residual Variance; Theil, 1961)	3	$\{1 - k_n(\lambda)/n\}^{-1}$	1
S (Shibata, 1981)	3	2	2
FPE (Akaike, 1969) or			
PC (Amemiya, 1980)	3	$2\{1 - k_n(\lambda)/n\}^{-1}$	2
GCV (Golub et al., 1979)	3	$\{2 - k_n(\lambda)/n\}\{1 - k_n(\lambda)/n\}^{-2}$	2
T (Rice, 1984)	3	$2\{1 - 2k_n(\lambda)/n\}^{-1}$	2
T2	3	$2\{1 - (\ln n)k_n(\lambda)/n\}^{-1}$	2

[a] The authors define a constant $c > 2$ in place of 2 and leave the choice of c to the (intelligent) user.
make things automatic for simulation, we assume $c = 2$ throughout.

where $g(n, \cdot)/n \to 0$ as $n \to \infty$. Function g identifies the member of the class. The smoothers belonging to the three classes and those included in this study appear in Table 1. Smoother T2 is a modification of T (Rice, 1984) with the property that it smoothes more (yields systematically larger values of λ) than T. It requires $k < n/\ln n$ so that it is not always available in small samples. The corresponding requirement for T is $k < n/2$. In fact, the class 3 smoothers and AIC may be ordered in ascending order of smoothing as follows: URV < S < AIC < PC < GCV < T < T2, where " < " is equivalent to "smooths less than"; see Engle and Brown (1986) and Mellin and Teräsvirta (1989).

The model selection criterion BIC (Sawa, 1978) does not belong to any of the three classes mentioned above. However, it may also be generalized to apply here, see Teräsvirta (1987), and is therefore included in this study.

Teräsvirta (1987) considered the asymptotic optimality of the smoothers in Table 1 in the sense that a smoother asymptotically minimizing (2.9) is optimal. He proved that the criteria for which $\lim_{n\to\infty} g(n, \cdot) = 2$ are optimal. A necessary assumption for this result is $R\beta \neq 0$. However, the result tells little about the behaviour of the smoothers in small samples. One problem is that when n is finite, (2.9) may have several local minima.

When the above smoothers are applied, determining λ calls for numerical optimization. If we wish to avoid that, we may choose $H_R(\lambda) = I - \lambda UR'(RUR')^{-1}R$. This is equivalent to defining

$$b_R^*(\lambda) = \lambda b_R + (1 - \lambda)b, \quad 0 \leq \lambda \leq 1. \tag{2.10}$$

Titterington (1985) called (2.10) a convex smoother because it is a convex combination of the unsmoothed and the completely smoothed extremes. The model selection criteria, those belonging to class 2 in particular, may be generalized to choose λ. The GD of the model becomes

$$k_n(\lambda) = (1 - \lambda)k + \lambda m, \quad 0 \leq \lambda \leq 1$$

i.e., a simple linear function of λ. A convex smoother based on class 2 model selection criteria equals

$$CS(\lambda) = \hat{\sigma}^{*2}(\lambda) + \tilde{\sigma}^2 k_n(\lambda) g_2(n)/n, \quad 0 \leq \lambda \leq 1 \tag{2.11}$$

where $\hat{\sigma}^{*2}(\lambda) = n^{-1}(y - Xb_R^*(\lambda))'(y - Xb_R^*(\lambda))$, and $\lim_{n \to \infty} g_2(n)/n = 0$, see Teräsvirta et al. (1988). The minimizer of (2.11) is an analytic function

$$\hat{\lambda} = (k - m)\tilde{\sigma}^2 g_2(n)/(2\tilde{g}^2)$$

where $\tilde{g}^2 = b'R'(RUR')^{-1}Rb$. In practice, a positive part estimator $\hat{\lambda}^+ = 1 - [1 - \hat{\lambda}]^+$, where $[a]^+ = \max(a, 0)$, is recommended because $\hat{\lambda} > 1$ has a positive probability. In this paper we use a positive part estimator and select $g_2(n) = 1, 2, 2 \ln \ln n, \ln n$, and call the corresponding smoothers CS1, CS2, CSLL and CSL, respectively. If $g_2(n) = 2$, (2.11) is a modification of C_P.

Ad Hoc Smoothers
If $R = I$ in (2.5) that estimator becomes the ordinary ridge regression estimator (see Judge et al., 1985, chapter 22). Thus ideas from ridge regression literature may be applied in constructing techniques for determining the value of the smoothing parameter. Consider first the problem of minimizing the MSEP (2.9); for a similar problem (minimizing the MSE) in ridge regression see Dempster et al. (1977). The minimizer is the solution of

$$\lambda \beta'R'P_\lambda R\beta = \sigma^2 \operatorname{tr} P_\lambda \tag{2.12}$$

where $P_\lambda = T_\lambda^3 RC_n^{-1}R'$ with $C_n = n^{-1}X'X$ and $T_\lambda = \lambda^{-1}S_\lambda$, cf. Teräsvirta (1987). If $s \neq 0$ and $n \to \infty$ in (2.12), the unique minimizer is

$$\lambda_\infty = \sigma^2 \operatorname{tr} RC^{-1}R'/s'RC^{-1}R's \tag{2.13}$$

where $C = \lim_{n \to \infty} C_n$. We may obtain an applicable smoother by operationalizing (2.12) or (2.13). Replacing both sides of (2.12) by their unbiased
estimators yields

$$\lambda \left[\hat{s}' P_\lambda \hat{s} - (\tilde{\sigma}^2/n) \, \mathrm{tr}\left\{ T_\lambda^3 \left(RC_n^{-1}R' \right)^2 \right\} \right] = \tilde{\sigma}^2 \, \mathrm{tr} \, P_\lambda \qquad (2.14)$$

see Teräsvirta (1987). The solution of (2.14) gives the value of λ. To guard
against negative values, we prefer the positive part variant from

$$\lambda \left[\hat{s}' P_\lambda \hat{s} - (\tilde{\sigma}^2/n) \, \mathrm{tr}\left\{ T_\lambda^3 \left(RC_n^{-1}R' \right)^2 \right\} \right]^+ = \tilde{\sigma}^2 \, \mathrm{tr} \, P_\lambda.$$

The corresponding smoother is called the Positive Part Operational Smoother
(PPOS). It resembles the RIDGM smoother Dempster et al. (1977) discussed. Gibbons (1981) conducted an extensive simulation study in which
RIDGM was one of the best ridge estimators. PPOS is asymptotically optimal
because $\hat{\lambda}_{PPOS}^+$ converges to (2.13) as $n \to \infty$. Note that $[\,]^+ = 0$ is taken to
yield $\lambda = \infty$.

The asymptotic minimizer may be made operational in the same way: the
numerator and the denominator are replaced by their unbiased estimators.
The positive part minimizer, called the Operational Asymptotic Smoother
(OAS) is

$$\hat{\lambda}_{OAS} = \frac{\tilde{\sigma}^2 \, \mathrm{tr} \, RUR'}{\left[\hat{s}' RUR' \hat{s} - \tilde{\sigma}^2 \, \mathrm{tr}(RUR')^2 \right]^+} \qquad (2.15)$$

(Teräsvirta, 1987). The prime motivation of (2.15) lies in its computational
simplicity.

Another smoother inspired by ridge regression considerations is due to
Thurman et al. (1984). Let the mean square error matrix $M(b) = E(b - \beta)(b - \beta)'$. The necessary and sufficient condition for $M(b) - M(b_R(\lambda)) \geqq 0$ equals

$$\sigma^{-2} s' (2\lambda^{-1}I + R\dot{U}R')^{-1} s \leqq 1. \qquad (2.16)$$

Replace the inequality (2.16) by an equality and substitute least squares
estimates for the parameters β and σ^2. The solution of

$$\tilde{\sigma}^{-2} \lambda \hat{s}' \left\{ 2I + (\lambda/n) RC_n^{-1}R' \right\}^{-1} \hat{s} = 1$$

is the value of the smoothing parameter. This smoother is called TSM. For more discussion, see Swamy and Mehta (1983).

Finally, in connection with the estimation of a smooth distributed lag Shiller (1973) suggested a rule of thumb (SRT): estimate λ using

$$SRT = 8(\mathbf{1}'\beta)/k^2 \qquad (2.17)$$

where $\mathbf{1} = (1, 1, \ldots, 1)'$. This requires that the elements of β are positive. In practice, b is used in place of the unknown β. Shiller pointed out that in his Bayesian context the investigator must be supposed to have prior knowledge about λ. He just remarked that (2.17) has seemed useful in some instances.

3. Simulation Experiment

In order to assess the performance of the above smoothers in small samples we have conducted an extensive simulation study. An important purpose of the experiment has been to obtain information for making recommendations to practitioners facing the estimation of a piecewise constant regression model. In this section we shall discuss the salient features of the experiment.

3.1. Design of the Experiment

In order to be viable, our Monte Carlo experiment has to contain functions of different degrees of smoothness. Seven types of β are selected and they appear in Figure 1, called Models 1–7. They are standardized in such a way that $\beta'\beta = 1$ for all piecewise constant approximations. The criterion of smoothness is always the same: the second differences of f must be small. The "squared biases" in Figure 1 are a measure of smoothness of the function. The last function f, corresponding to Model 7, may already be termed an outlier, because it is not smooth at all and its squared bias is far outside the range of that of the other models. The number of observations n is varied ($n = 30, 60, 120, 240, 480$) as well as the error variance σ^2 (Table 2); the latter obtains 8 values. This amounts to $7 \times 5 \times 8 = 280$ different designs. In (2.2) it is assumed that ϵ_t is white noise. It is of interest to see what happens if this assumption is violated. To assess the effects of ignored error autocorrelation, (2.2) is augmented by assuming

$$u_t = \rho u_{t-1} + \epsilon_t, \quad \epsilon_t \sim nid(0, \sigma^2), \quad \rho = 0, \pm 0.4, \pm 0.8. \qquad (3.1)$$

For the experiment with autocorrelated errors we only report results for

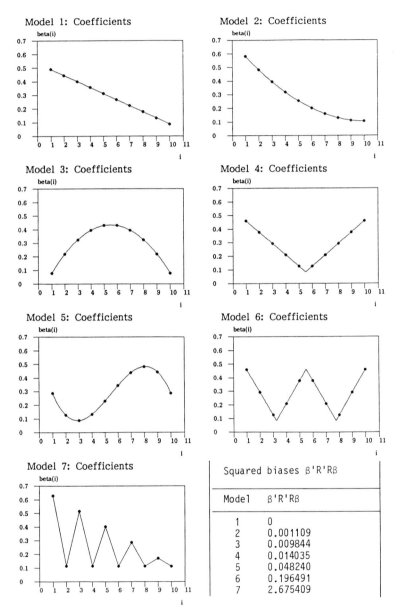

Figure 1. Coefficients β_i, $i = 1,\dots,10$, of Models 1–7 simulated in the Monte Carlo experiment, $\Sigma\beta_i^2 = 1$, and the squared biases $\beta'R'R\beta$.

Table 2

Error Variances, Signal-to-Noise Ratios, and Coefficients of
Determination of Models of the Monte Carlo Experiment

Variance number (see Figure 2)	σ^2	$\beta'\beta/\sigma^2$	R^2
S1	0.0009	1111.11	0.991
S2	0.0016	625.00	0.984
S3	0.0036	277.78	0.965
S4	0.0081	123.46	0.925
S5	0.0169	59.17	0.855
S6	0.0324	30.86	0.755
S7	0.0576	17.36	0.635
S8	0.0961	10.41	0.510

Note: $\beta'\beta = 1$.

$n = 60$ and selected combinations of f and σ^2. The total number of designs ($n = 60$) with autocorrelated errors is $4 \times 7 \times 8 = 224$.

The whole experiment is designed in such a way that $X = [I_{10} \ldots I_{10}]'$ in (2.2). X is thus a $10a \times 10$ indicator matrix where I_{10} is a 10×10 identity matrix and $a = n/10$, so that $X'X = aI_{10}$. The corresponding signal-to-noise ratios and theoretical values of the coefficients of determination R^2 appear in Table 2.

3.2. Other Features of the Experiment

Random Numbers
The (pseudo) random numbers used in the experiments were generated in two steps. First, uniformly $(0, 1)$ distributed random numbers were generated using the mixed congruential generator

$$v_{t+1} \equiv av_t + b(\bmod m)$$

where $a = 100485$, $b = 99991$, $m = 2^{35}$ and the seed $v_0 = 211246$. This generator should have good properties according to Atkinson (1980). Second, these numbers were converted to standard normal random numbers using the polar method of Marsaglia, see Ripley (1983). They were generated in the blocks of 1000. The first 260 random numbers were always discarded, and the next 260 numbers were reserved to allowing the AR(1)-process in (3.1) to stabilize.

Finally, the next n numbers were used to generate the n observations and the last $480 - n$ observations were discarded. The observations used when $n = 30$ were the first 30 observations of the case $n = 60$ and so on up to $n = 480$. The same sets of random numbers were used in all experiments. The number of replications is 500, which is a large number given the amount of computation in the study.

Optimization
There were no less than 18 different functions to be optimized numerically or searched for zeroes, and multiple optima were theoretically possible. Thus, in view of computational costs, a grid search was considered the only realistic optimization alternative. It was performed on a grid of 370 points for all functions simultaneously.

Measures of Performance
The main performance criterion of each smoothing technique considered is the MSEP, estimated from 500 trials. Note that because of the structure of X in the simulations $\text{MSEP} = (n/10) \times \text{MSE}$ (MSE = the mean squared error). We also compute MSEP from the same 500 trials for two "theoretical smoothers", BESTL and BESTC, which for each trial minimize the squared loss of prediction (SLP) of the stochastic restricted estimator (2.5) and the convex combination (2.9), respectively. These smoothers are useful as they provide theoretical lower bounds for the attainable MSEP in the two classes of estimators considered; for a discussion see Gibbons (1981). In addition to the MSEP the corresponding GD are estimated. We have also ordered the SLP of all our smoothers for each trial and computed the number of times each smoother is among the best three (smallest SLP) in the 500 trials performed. Finally, SLP densities are estimated to compare the loss distributions of selected smoothers.

4. Results

4.1. MSEP Comparisons when the Function is Linear
We begin a discussion of results by considering some standardized MSEP (SMSEP) estimates. To facilitate comparisons between designs we have divided the estimated MSEP by $n\sigma^2$. This makes things easier: for instance, when the true function is linear (Model 1), the standardized estimates are equal for all error variances for almost all techniques considered. They are

Table 3

Standardized MSEP values for various smoothers in
Model 1, $n = 30, 60, 240$

Smoother	$n = 30$	$n = 60$	$n = 240$
OLS	0.3332	0.1665	0.0404
RLS	0.0666	0.0318	0.0081
CS1	0.1589	0.0766	0.0178
CS2	0.0977	0.0448	0.0103
CSLL	0.0860	0.0364	0.0083
CSL	0.0738	0.0327	0.0081
SRT	0.3170	0.1622	0.0401
OAS	0.1294	0.0623	0.0137
AIC	0.1350	0.0575	0.0121
HQ	0.1093	0.0409	0.0089
SBIC	0.0808	0.0337	0.0082
C_P	0.1143	0.0526	0.0119
BEC	0.0802	0.0343	0.0082
URV	0.2006	0.0958	0.0222
PC	0.1305	0.0571	0.0120
GCV	0.1097	0.0519	0.0119
S	0.1834	0.0671	0.0126
T	0.0894	0.0474	0.0117
T2		0.0371	0.0106
BIC	0.1161	0.0530	0.0119
PPOS	0.0946	0.0450	0.0108
EB	0.1067	0.0498	0.0113
TSM	0.2479	0.1231	0.0296
ABIC	0.0875	0.0401	0.0099
BESTL	0.0666	0.0318	0.0081
BESTC	0.0666	0.0318	0.0081

Note: The standardized MSEP values are invariant of σ^2 except those for SRT. In that case the values in the table correspond to S1. Other values are smaller. The standard deviations of the estimates are not included, but they vary between 0.002851 and 0.006798 for $n = 30$, 0.001376 and 0.003249 for $n = 60$ and 0.000379 and 0.000757 for $n = 240$, respectively.

also roughly halved when the sample size is doubled. Table 3 contains the SMSEP and the corresponding GD for all estimators when Model 1 is used and $n = 30$, 60 and 240. Note that as $R\beta = 0$ no smoother will overestimate the optimal value for λ which equals infinity. We may expect the criteria that smooth most heavily to perform best.

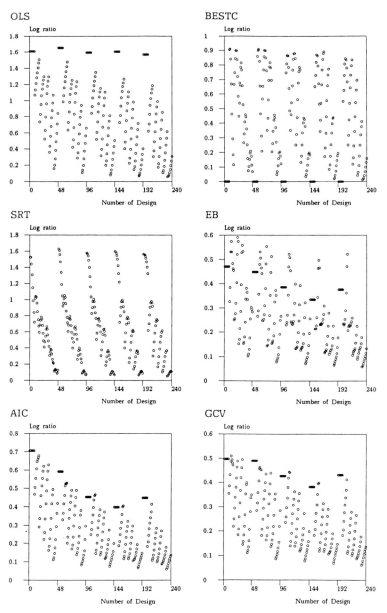

Figure 2. Logarithmic ratios of MSEP and the theoretically lowest MSEP attainable in the simulation study (BESTL) for Models 1–6 (240 designs). Model 7 is excluded as too extreme. Designs 1–48 refer to $n = 30$, Designs 49–96 to $n = 60$, etc. Designs 1–6, 49–54, ... refer to Model 1, Designs 7–12, 55–60, ... to Model 2, etc. Designs 1, 9, 17, ... refer to error variance S1, Designs 2, 10, 18, ... to error variance S2, etc.

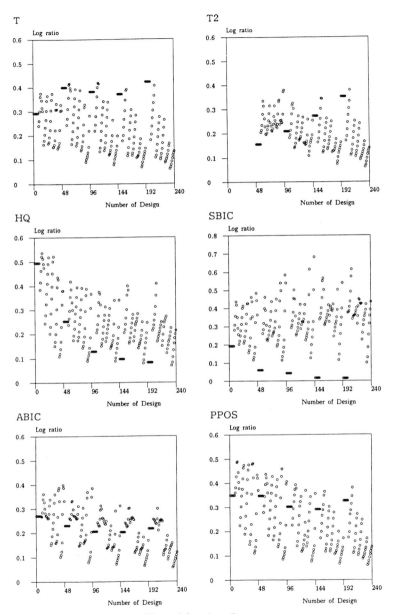

Figure 2 (continued).

From Table 3 it can be seen that the ad hoc estimators TSM and SRT grossly undersmooth when the true function is linear. To a lesser extent this also holds for OAM. Smoothers S, URV and CS1 can be removed from serious consideration for the same reason. The performance of S does improve as it should when the sample size increases, and we shall keep S for demonstration purposes in some comparisons. On the other hand, PPOS seems to perform rather well. As $R\beta = 0$ so that f is perfectly smooth (linear) even globally, the convex smoothers seem quite competitive. CSL is the best because it smooths most, and it comes already very close to BESTL for $n \geq 60$. Class 3 smoothing criteria behave as may be expected from Table 2: the more they smooth, the better they are. The smoothers AIC, C_P, PC and GCV (see Table 1) that are "optimal" for $R\beta \neq 0$ form an intermediate group whereas T when $n = 30, 60$, and T2 when $n = 60$, are closer to the top performers of the table, the smoothers for which $\lim_{n \to \infty} g(n, \cdot) = \infty$. When $n = 240$ (24 observations in each interval) T and T2 join the intermediate group; the asymptotic properties already weigh rather heavily. Finally, measured by SMSEP, ABIC has a very satisfactory performance.

4.2. Relative MSEP Performance

Figure 2 gives a more detailed picture of the whole simulation experiment. It consists of logarithmic ratios of the MSEP of the estimator and the corresponding "best" MSEP, that of BESTL. They are shown principally for estimators we do not want to rule out yet because of their fair to excellent MSEP-performance in connection with Model 1. (We have simulated all techniques for all models: the complete results are available from the authors upon request. The results for Model 7 have been excluded from Figure 2, because even the theoretical risk improvement over OLS is very small in that case.) For comparison, the corresponding ratios for OLS are included. We shall also show the ratio between the MSEP of BESTC and BESTL. It illustrates well the theoretical difference in performance between the convex and local smoothers.

Figure 2 indicates that of the smoothers that perform well when the model is linear, SBIC as well as BEC yield sometimes relatively large MSEP when the function is less smooth. In fact, BEC is always very close to SBIC; in what follows we only discuss SBIC but what is said also holds for BEC. SBIC is not asymptotically optimal, which may explain its mediocre performance for $n \geq 240$. On the other hand, HQ improves when the sample size increases and is better than SBIC for $n \geq 120$. However, it clearly undersmooths for small n. The best optimal criteria seem to be T and T2 when available. The eyeball test indicates that in small samples GCV is inferior to these two. As can be expected, the difference, in particular that between GCV and T, becomes small when n grows large. AIC is inferior to GCV, whereas BIC, PC and C_P not shown in Figure 2 remain somewhere between these two.

After studying Figure 2 we may also rule out EB which yields too many large values of the MSEP as does SRT. On the other hand, PPOS seems a better alternative than, say, GCV when the sample size is small ($n \leq 60$). For large n, it seems to perform very similarly to the optimal criteria. This may not be surprising, because the unbiased estimates needed in making the criterion operational are then rather accurate already. PPOS is in fact the only ad hoc criterion which is not clearly inferior to smoothing criteria. On the other hand, we may also note that the convex smoothers are not sufficiently flexible when the functional form becomes more twisted. In fact, we may expect them to perform better only if we are able to vary R as well, i.e., if there are several functional forms to choose among; see Teräsvirta et al. (1988).

Last but not least, ABIC seems to be quite a reliable criterion. It never performs badly, and in many occasions the ratio seems to vary less with the error variance of the model than is the case for most other techniques.

4.3. SMSEP Comparisons

In order to shed more light on the performance of different smoothers we study their SMSEP for Models 2, 4 and 6 in more detail. The smoothers are OLS (no smoothing), ABIC, GCV, S, SBIC, T and T2. ABIC, T and T2 are selected because they have performed well in previous comparisons. SBIC is included, because it often performs well, but it also represents non-optimal oversmoothers. S undersmooths most of all optimal smoothers. GCV is the optimal smoother most often applied in practice. Figure 3 contains their SMSEP as the function of error variance for $n = 60, 240$. To obtain a better idea of their smoothing characteristics we also depict the corresponding GD in the figure. To illustrate the theoretical lower bound to the SMSEP, Figure 3 also contains the SMSEP of BESTL and BESTC and their GD. [1]

It is easy to see from the figures that SBIC systematically oversmooths. Its GD is consistently below that of BESTL. When the number of observations is

---

[1] The average standard errors for simulated SMSEP values in Figure 3 are 0.002 and 0.0006 when $n = 60$ and 240, respectively. They are helpful in comparing points of the same curve. On the other hand, the standard errors constitute a very conservative basis for comparing two estimated SMSEP functions because of the strong correlation between them.

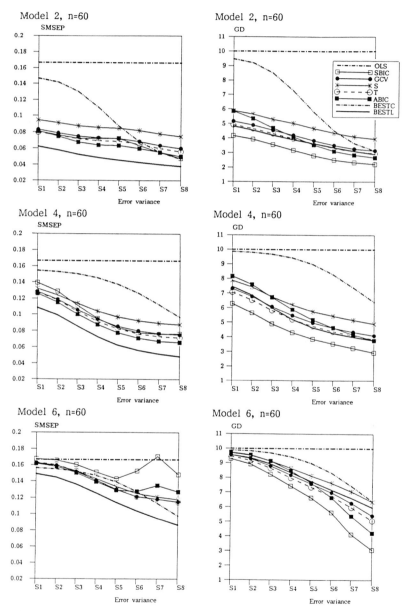

Figure 3. SMSEP and corresponding GD estimates for selected smoothers based on 500 trials in the simulation experiment; Models 2, 4, 6; $n = 60, 240$.

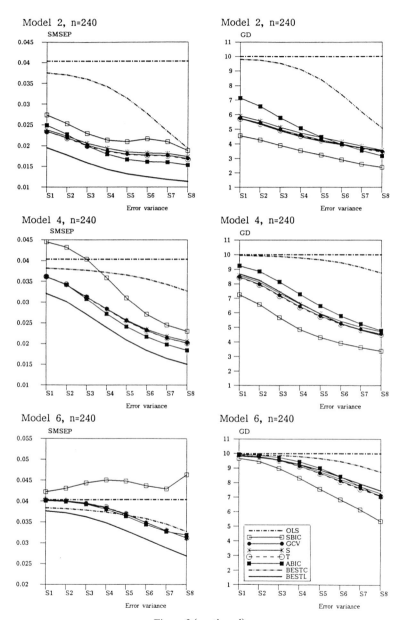

Figure 3 (continued).

not large and the function smooth (Model 2) this seems to be an advantage. However, it turns to a disadvantage when $n = 240$ and the model is less smooth. In the extreme case (Model 6) the use of SBIC leads to a larger MSEP than OLS for all values of σ^2. For large n, the asymptotic non-optimality thus seems to have practical implications. The behaviour of the optimal smoothers is seen to be more desirable in that they are never worse than OLS. It is also interesting to observe the hump in the SMSEP curve of SBIC for Model 6. Quite obviously, the GD of the estimated model decreases too fast with growing error variance, and at a certain stage there is a penalty for that in the form of re-increasing SMSEP.

In general, the smoothers for which the GD remains close to that of BESTL have good MSEP properties. T and ABIC are the best examples. ABIC rather under- than oversmooths; T2 oversmooths somewhat for $n = 60$, but that does not seem a drawback for small n. GCV systematically undersmooths and is inferior to ABIC, T and T2. However, it has consistently smaller SMSEP than S which undersmooths even more. Figure 3 also indicates that the convex smoothers may improve when the model becomes less smooth. In Model 6 the gap between BESTL and BESTC is rather narrow, but then it has to be because the gap between BESTL and OLS is no longer wide either.

Summing up, the asymptotic optimality property of smoothing criteria has at least some practical significance at sample sizes considered here. SBIC, which does not have the property but tends to oversmooth, does not perform well in all experiments whereas some other criteria with this property do. On the other hand, ABIC which performs well in this study is not optimal either, compare (2.7) and (2.13).

The results obtained here might be generalized by using response surfaces; see Hendry (1984) for their use in econometrics. Indeed, we estimated response surfaces for the logarithmic ratio of MSEP of each smoother to that of BESTL. This was the only feasible dependent variable of the many we considered. However, the estimated equations did not reveal any new features in the behaviour of the smoothers or suggest new interpretations over those discussed elsewhere in this report. Consequently, no results from fitting response surfaces are reported here, but they are available from the authors on request.

4.4. Comparing Estimated SLP Densities

The MSEP comparisons may not necessarily reveal all essential information about the behaviour of smoothers, because their squared loss of prediction (SLP) densities may be skewed and even multimodal. Comparing SLP

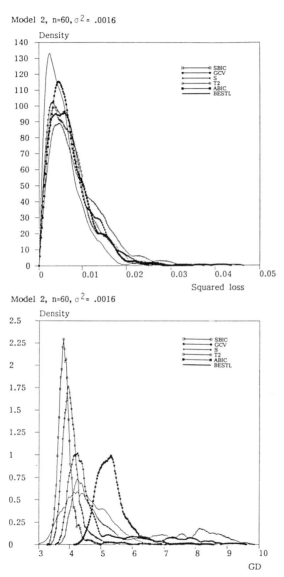

Figure 4. Estimated density of SLP and the corresponding density of GD for selected smoothers in the simulation experiment.

densities of our smoothers could therefore be interesting. Power and Ullah (1987) have recently advocated the use of non-parametric density estimation in connection with Monte Carlo experiments, and we shall take up this

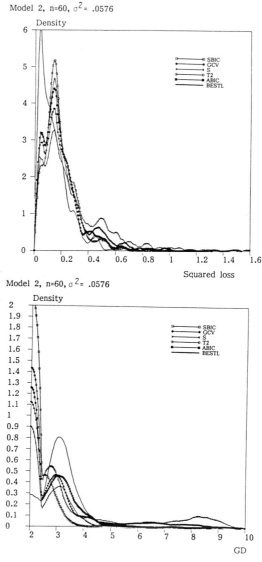

Figure 4 (continued).

recommendation. As a matter of fact, using our 500 replications, we may apply non-parametric estimation and estimate SLP densities for any given design. Because of space constraints, we shall choose only a few illuminating

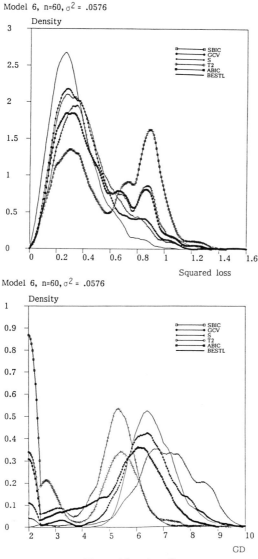

Figure 4 (continued).

designs, estimate the densities of SLP and the corresponding GD based on selected smoothers and compare them with each other.

The densities $g(\cdot)$ are estimated by the kernel method with the Epanechnikov kernel. Note that the problem of bounded domains has to be treated in two different ways when estimating the densities of SLP and GD, respectively. In the former case, SLP is bounded from below to zero. Because zero is not attainable, we apply a technique called negative reflection which forces $g(0 +) = 0$; see Silverman (1986, p. 31). On the other hand, in our experiments GD always lies between 2 and 10, but now at least the lower boundary is attainable. In this case we use (ordinary) reflection which forces $g'(0 +) = 0$. The window width is selected subjectively to produce density estimates that preserve the interesting features of the densities. Note that the modes on the boundaries in the estimated densities of GD are mostly due to discrete components of these densities.

We begin the discussion of the density estimation results with the case where the function is smooth. As an example, take Model 2 with $\sigma^2 = 0.0016$ and $n = 60$. The estimated densities for ABIC, GCV, S, SBIC and T2 appear in Figure 4. The density of BESTL is also included for comparison. It is seen that the undersmoothing S and GCV have densities with a heavy right-hand tail. S in particular has this property, and it is seen that its GD density even has a peak around 8.2. The densities of SBIC and GCV are bimodal but probably for different reasons: as is seen from the GD densities, SBIC oversmooths whereas GCV undersmooths. Although ABIC clearly undersmooths, its density is not very far from that of BESTL; the slight shift to the right can be ascribed to undersmoothing. Note that the GD density of BESTL is flatter than that of the smoothers.

When the error variance of the mode is increased to 0.0576, remarkable changes occur. All densities are now at least trimodal. One maximum is located roughly at the point where the mode of the BESTL density is situated. However, next to it there is a global maximum clearly exceeding the local one. This is due to the tendency of the smoothers to yield a linear function $\hat{\lambda} = \infty$): the GD densities all have a maximum at GD = 2. A third maximum is due to high GD values; the most pronounced example is S which still has a heavy tail and a GD density with a local maximum at around 8.2. The mode of the SLP densities is thus due to oversmoothing, and putting the smoothers in descending order according to oversmoothing yields the following, not surprising, result: SBIC, T2, ABIC, GCV and S.

Consider now the situation where the function is not very smooth (Model 6). If the error variance is small, all densities are unimodal, and their maxima lie to the right of that of BESTL. From the GD densities it appears that in this case, oversmoothing causes a heavy right-hand tail. SBIC and T2 again oversmooth. The situation changes again when the error variance increases. Consider $\sigma^2 = 0.0576$; this case appears in Figure 4(c). Many SLP densities then have three maxima. The density of SBIC has a global maximum around 0.9: it is due to the choice of a linear function. T2 and ABIC have a clear secondary peak there for the same reason. An adjacent maximum of SLP of SBIC is seen to correspond to GD around 3, i.e., an approximation of the unknown W-type function with a second degree polynomial. The leftmost peak finally corresponds to the GD between 5 and 6. All densities have a peak near the mode of the SLP density of BESTL. Using MSEP as a sole criterion of performance in a situation like this is rather misleading. Two smoothers remain: S is seen to undersmooth, and its SLP density therefore lies slightly to the right of that of GCV. Both smoothers are, however, among the best in Figure 4 for this design.

These considerations illustrate the fact that there is not a single smoother which would behave well in all possible situations. If the sample is rather small and the function to be estimated fairly smooth, undersmoothers are at a disadvantage. This changes into an advantage if the function is not very smooth and uncertainty in the form of error variance is large.

4.5. Autocorrelated Errors

The above results concern uncorrelated errors. We repeated a few of previous experiments but introduced first order autocorrelation in the errors. This autocorrelation was subsequently ignored in applying the smoothers. The results indicate that the smoothers are particularly sensitive to negative first order autocorrelation. Oversmoothers like SBIC seem to suffer most. In fact, all criteria tend to smooth more when the absolute value of the autocorrelation coefficient increases. This tendency which is already visible when the function is rather smooth becomes even more conspicuous when the function is less smooth. This being the case, the smoothers that under-smooth when the errors are not autocorrelated are less adversely affected than the others. The general message is that ignored error autocorrelation impairs smoothing as far as the smoothing techniques of this paper are concerned. It tends to make the estimated function smoother than the true function.

5. Conclusions

The simulation study clearly shows that there is not a smoother that would be uniformly best and behave well in all situations. Sometimes many smoothers may even have multimodal MSEP densities. The ad hoc smoothers included in this study do not generally compare favourably with the others; PPOS is the only thinkable exception. If the function to be estimated is fairly smooth and the sample is small so that there are not many observations per class, ABIC, T and T2, if available, emerge as the most attractive alternatives. On the other hand, the widely applied GCV is not among the best smoothers in our study and cannot be recommended for practical work as easily as the previous three. (For a different opinion in kernel estimation, see Härdle et al. (1988b).) However, if the function to be estimated is less smooth the situation changes, and the smoothers that undersmooth improve their relative position in our comparisons. On the other hand, all the convex smoothers fail because they are too inflexible. The error autocorrelation has an adverse effect on the performance of the smoothers considered here.

References

Akaike, H. (1969). Fitting autoregressive models for prediction. *Annals of the Institute of Statistical Mathematics* 21, 243–247.

Akaike, H. (1974). A new look at the statistical model identification. *IEEE Transactions of Automatic Control* AC-19, 716–723.

Akaike, H. (1981). Seasonal adjustment by a Bayesian modeling. *Journal of Time Series Analysis* 1, 1–13.

Amemiya, T. (1980). Selection of regressors. *International Economic Review* 21, 331–354.

Atkinson, A.C. (1980). Tests of pseudo-random numbers. *Applied Statistics* 29, 164–171.

Dempster, A.P., M. Schatzoff and N. Wermuth (1977). A simulation study of alternatives to ordinary least squares. *Journal of the American Statistical Association* 72, 77–91.

Engle, R.F.and S.J. Brown (1986). Model selection for forecasting. *Applied Mathematics and Computation* 20, 313–327.

Engle, R.F., C.W.J. Granger, J. Rice and A. Weiss (1986). Semiparametric estimates of the relation between weather and electricity sales. *Journal of the American Statistical Association* 81, 310–320.

Geweke, J.F. and R. Meese (1981). Estimating regression models of finite but unknown order. *International Economic Review* 22, 55–70.

Gibbons, J.G. (1981). A simulation study of some estimators. *Journal of the American Statistical Association* 76, 131–139.

Golub, G.H., M. Heath and G. Wahba (1979). Generalized cross-validation as a method for choosing a good ridge parameter. *Technometrics* 21, 215–223.

Hannan, E.J. and B.G. Quinn (1979). The determination of the order of an autoregression. *Journal of the Royal Statistical Society* B 41, 190–195.

Härdle, W., P. Hall and J.S. Marron (1988a). How far are automatically chosen regression parameters from their optimum? *Journal of the American Statistical Association* 83, 86–95.

Härdle, W., P. Hall and J.S. Marron (1988b). Rejoinder. *Journal of the American Statistical Association* 83, 100–101.

Hendry, D.F. (1984). Monte Carlo experimentation in econometrics. In: Z. Griliches and M.D. Intriligator, eds. *Handbook of econometrics*, Vol 2, 937–976. Amsterdam: North-Holland.

Judge, G.G., W.E. Griffiths, R.C. Hill, H. Lütkepohl and T.-C. Lee (1985). *The theory and practice of econometrics*, 2nd edition. New York: Wiley.

Mallows, C.L. (1973). Some comments on C_P. *Technometrics* 15, 661–676.

Marron, J.S. (1988). Automatic smoothing parameter selection: A survey. *Empirical Economics* 13, 187–208.

Mellin, I. (1992). Smoothing and Bayes likelihood. Unpublished manuscript.

Mellin, I. and T. Teräsvirta (1989). Smoothing in piecewise constant regression: An application to electric utility industry. Unpublished paper.

Power, S. and A. Ullah (1987). Non-parametric Monte Carlo density estimation of rational expectations estimators and their t-ratios. Paper presented to the Econometric Society European Meeting, Copenhagen.

Rice, J. (1984). Bandwidth choice for nonparametric regression. *Annals of Statistics* 12, 1215–1230.

Ripley, B.D. (1983). Computer generation of random variables: A tutorial. *International Statistical Review* 51, 301–319.

Rissanen, J. (1978). Modeling by shortest data description. *Automatica* 14, 465–471.

Sawa, T. (1978). Information criteria for discriminating among alternative regression models. *Econometrica* 46, 1273–1291.

Schwarz, G. (1978). Estimating the dimension of a model. *Annals of Statistics* 6, 461–464.

Shibata, R. (1981). An optimal selection of regression variables. *Biometrika* 63, 45–54.

Shiller, R. (1973). A distributed lag estimator derived from smoothness priors. *Econometrica* 41, 775–788.

Silverman, B.W. (1986). *Density estimation for statistics and data analysis*. London: Chapman and Hall.

Swamy, P.A.V.B. and J.S. Mehta (1983). Ridge regression estimation of the Rotterdam model. *Journal of Econometrics* 22, 365–390.

Teräsvirta, T. (1987). Smoothness in regression: Asymptotic considerations. In: I.B. MacNeill and G.J. Umphrey, eds.: *Time series and econometric modelling*, 47–64. Dordrecht: Reidel.

Teräsvirta, T. and I. Mellin (1986). Model selection criteria and model selection tests in regression models. *Scandinavian Journal of Statistics* 13, 159–171.

Teräsvirta, T., G. Yi and G. Judge (1988). Model selection, smoothing and parameter estimation in linear models under squared error loss. *Computational Statistics Quarterly* 4, 191–205.

Theil, H. (1961). *Economic forecasts and policy*, 2nd edition. Amsterdam: North-Holland.

Thurman, S.S., P.A.V.B. Swamy, and J.S. Mehta (1984). An examination of distributed lag model coefficients estimated with smoothness priors. Federal Reserve Board, Washington, D.C., Special Studies Paper 185.

Titterington, D.M. (1985). Common structure of smoothing techniques in statistics. *International Statistical Review* 53, 141–170.

Readings in Econometric Theory and Practice
W. Griffiths, H. Lütkepohl and M.E. Bock (Editors)
© 1992 Elsevier Science Publishers B.V. All rights reserved

CHAPTER 11

TESTING FOR TIME VARYING PARAMETERS IN VECTOR
AUTOREGRESSIVE MODELS

Helmut Lütkepohl *

Institut für Statistik und Ökonometrie, Christian-Albrechts-Universität, Kiel, Germany

Stationarity is a fundamental condition of time series models. Violation of this property means that the first and/or second moments of the assumed data generation process are not time invariant. In the context of parametric time series models such as autoregressive (AR) or autoregressive moving average (ARMA) models nonstationarity may be reflected in time varying parameters. A large class of time series models with time varying parameters is considered and tests of the null hypothesis of parameter constancy are discussed.

1. Introduction

Much of the time series literature is preoccupied with the discussion of stationary models such as ARMA processes and series that are stationary after some simple transformation like taking logarithms and differences. The main reason for the preference for these models seems to be that stationarity implies relatively simple inference procedures, a clear advantage for applied work. In practice, however, many time series are not likely to be stationary and stationary or near stationary models are very rough approximations at best. This fact has led some authors to suggest certain nonstationary models. For instance, periodic models have been proposed by Pagano (1978), Cleveland and Tiao (1979), Cipra (1985), Anděl (1987), and Li and Hui (1988) and intervention models were investigated, e.g., by Box and Tiao (1975) and Abraham (1980). In both types of models it is assumed that some parameters

---

* The author thanks Holger Claessen for carrying out the computations for the examples and Christian Durán for preparing the final manuscript.

vary over time, an assumption which is plausible in many practical situations. The ease of working with stationary models makes it desirable, however, to use them if possible. Therefore we will give a systematic account of a wide class of time series models with time varying parameters and discuss testing for parameter constancy.

We consider vector autoregressive (VAR) models for the following reasons:

1. They are the most frequently used *multivariate* time series models in economic analyses.
2. The discussion of the tests in the framework of VAR models avoids the notational complications of more complex models and thereby facilitates the understanding of the main problems.
3. Once the methodology has been clarified in a simple model class it is straightforward to develope extensions for more complex situations and models.

In the next section a general model class is presented that includes periodic and some intervention models as special cases. Maximum likelihood (ML) estimation is discussed under the assumption of normally distributed error terms. Likelihood ratio, Lagrange multiplier, and Wald tests for time varying parameters are presented. These results are applied to periodic and intervention models in Sections 3 and 4 where also practical aspects of the tests are treated and examples are given. Conclusions follow in Section 5.

2. The General Model and Tests

The general model considered in the following is a K-dimensional VAR process of order p (VAR(p) process) with time varying parameters,

$$y_t = \nu_t + A_{1t}y_{t-1} + \cdots + A_{pt}y_{t-p} + u_t$$

$$= \nu_t + A_t Y_{t-1} + u_t,$$ \hfill (1)

where $y_t = (y_{1t}, \cdots, y_{Kt})'$ is of dimension K, $Y_{t-1} = (y'_{t-1}, \cdots, y'_{t-p})'$ is a $(Kp \times 1)$ vector, ν_t is a K-dimensional vector of intercept terms, $A_t = [A_{1t}, \cdots, A_{pt}]$ is a $(K \times Kp)$ matrix of VAR coefficients, and u_t is K-dimensional Gaussian white noise with covariance matrix Σ_t, that is, $u_t \sim N(0, \Sigma_t)$ and u_t and u_s are independent for $s \neq t$. The normality assumption for the white noise process is useful in deriving ML estimators and likelihood ratio tests. It is not essential for much of the asymptotic theory developed later. The "ML estimators" may be regarded as pseudo ML estimators.

The following assumptions are made regarding the coefficients ν_t, A_t, and Σ_t:

$$\nu_t = n_{1t}\nu_1 + \cdots + n_{qt}\nu_q, \quad \text{where } n_{it} = 0 \text{ or } 1 \quad \text{and} \quad \sum_{i=1}^{q} n_{it} = 1, \qquad (2)$$

$$A_t = a_{1t}A_1 + \cdots + a_{rt}A_r, \quad \text{where } a_{it} = 0 \text{ or } 1 \quad \text{and} \quad \sum_{i=1}^{r} a_{it} = 1, \qquad (3)$$

and

$$\Sigma_t = s_{1t}\Sigma_1 + \cdots + s_{mt}\Sigma_m, \quad \text{where } s_{it} = 0 \text{ or } 1 \quad \text{and} \quad \sum_{i=1}^{m} s_{it} = 1. \qquad (4)$$

In other words, the n_{it}, a_{it}, and s_{it} are dummy variables. As we will see in the next sections, these assumptions are general enough to accommodate many models of practical interest.

A specification in mean adjusted form would be an alternative to (1):

$$y_t - \mu_t = A_{1t}(y_{t-1} - \mu_{t-1}) + \cdots + A_{pt}(y_{t-p} - \mu_{t-p}) + u_t, \qquad (5)$$

where μ_t may be specified in a similar fashion as the other parameters. This model form is more difficult to handle for our purposes. It is often just an equivalent representation of (1). An exception is noted in Section 4 where the details are given. Until then we will stick to (1).

Assuming that T observations $y_1, \cdots, y_T$ and p fixed presample values $y_{-p+1}, \cdots, y_0$ are available the Gaussian log-likelihood function of the model (1) is

$$\ln l = -\frac{KT}{2} \ln 2\pi - \tfrac{1}{2} \sum_{t=1}^{T} \ln |\Sigma_t| - \tfrac{1}{2} \sum_{t=1}^{T} u_t' \Sigma_t^{-1} u_t, \qquad (6)$$

where $u_t = y_t - \nu_t - A_t Y_{t-1}$ and $|.|$ denotes the determinant. Defining $\alpha_t =$

vec(A_t) and α_i = vec(A_i), vec being the column vectorizing operator, the first partial derivatives with respect to the parameters are

$$\frac{\partial \ln l}{\partial \nu_i} = \sum_t n_{it} \Sigma_t^{-1}(y_t - \nu_t - A_t Y_{t-1})$$

$$= \sum_t n_{it} \Sigma_t^{-1} y_t - \sum_t n_{it}(Y_{t-1}' \otimes \Sigma_t^{-1})\alpha_t - \left(\sum_t n_{it} \Sigma_t^{-1}\right)\nu_i,$$

$$i = 1, \cdots, q, \tag{7}$$

$$\frac{\partial \ln l}{\partial \alpha_i} = \sum_t a_{it}(Y_{t-1} \otimes I_K) \Sigma_t^{-1}[y_t - \nu_t - (Y_{t-1}' \otimes I_K)\alpha_t]$$

$$= \sum_t a_{it}(Y_{t-1} \otimes \Sigma_t^{-1}) y_t - \sum_t a_{it}(Y_{t-1} \otimes \Sigma_t^{-1})\nu_t$$

$$- \left[\sum_t a_{it}(Y_{t-1} Y_{t-1}' \otimes \Sigma_t^{-1})\right]\alpha_i, \quad i = 1, \cdots, r, \tag{8}$$

$$\frac{\partial \ln l}{\partial \Sigma_i} = -\frac{1}{2}\sum_t s_{it} \Sigma_t^{-1} + \frac{1}{2}\sum_t s_{it} \Sigma_t^{-1} u_t u_t' \Sigma_t^{-1}$$

$$= -\frac{1}{2} T \bar{s}_i \Sigma_i^{-1}$$

$$+ \frac{1}{2}\Sigma_i^{-1}\left[\sum_t s_{it}(y_t - \nu_t - A_t Y_{t-1})(y_t - \nu_t - A_t Y_{t-1})'\right]\Sigma_i^{-1},$$

$$i = 1, \cdots, m, \tag{9}$$

where $\bar{s}_i = \Sigma_t s_{it}/T$. Equating these three systems of equations to zero gives the normal equations:

$$\sum_t \left[n_{it}\left(Y_{t-1}' \otimes \sum_{j=1}^m s_{jt}\bar{\Sigma}_j^{-1}\right) \sum_{k=1}^r a_{kt}\tilde{\alpha}_k\right] + \left[\sum_t n_{it} \sum_{j=1}^m s_{jt}\bar{\Sigma}_j^{-1}\right]\tilde{\nu}_i$$

$$= \sum_t \left[n_{it} \sum_{j=1}^m s_{jt}\bar{\Sigma}_j^{-1} y_t\right], \quad i = 1, \cdots, q, \tag{10}$$

$$\sum_t \left[a_{it} \left(Y'_{t-1} \otimes \sum_{j=1}^{m} s_{jt} \tilde{\Sigma}_j^{-1} \right) \sum_{k=1}^{q} n_{kt} \tilde{\nu}_k \right]$$

$$+ \left[\sum_t a_{it} \left(Y_{t-1} Y'_{t-1} \otimes \sum_{j=1}^{m} s_{jt} \tilde{\Sigma}_j^{-1} \right) \right] \tilde{\alpha}_i$$

$$= \sum_t a_{it} \left[Y_{t-1} \otimes \sum_{j=1}^{m} s_{jt} \tilde{\Sigma}_j^{-1} \right] y_t, \quad i = 1, \cdots, r, \tag{11}$$

and

$$\tilde{\Sigma}_i = \frac{1}{T\bar{s}_i} \sum_t s_{it} \left(y_t - \tilde{\nu}_t - \tilde{A}_t Y_{t-1} \right) \left(y_t - \tilde{\nu}_t - \tilde{A}_t Y_{t-1} \right)' \quad i = 1, \cdots, m. \tag{12}$$

Here

$$\Sigma_t^{-1} = \sum_{j=1}^{m} s_{jt} \Sigma_j^{-1}$$

has been used. Obviously, in general this is a nonlinear system of equations. However, simplifications result for most cases of practical interest as will be seen in the next two sections.

We are interested in testing whether some or all of the parameters are time invariant. In most cases of interest in the following, LR tests will be easy to execute and are therefore considered. The LR statistic is defined to be minus twice the difference between the restricted and the unrestricted maximum of the log-likelihood function (Judge et al., 1985, Section 5.7). From (12) it is obvious that the log-likelihood reaches its maximum at

$$\max \ln l = \text{constant} - \tfrac{1}{2} \sum_t \ln \left| \tilde{\Sigma}_t \right|.$$

Thus, the LR statistic has the form

$$\lambda_{\mathrm{LR}} = \sum_t \ln \left| \tilde{\Sigma}_t^r \right| - \sum_t \ln \left| \tilde{\Sigma}_t^u \right|, \tag{13}$$

where $\tilde{\Sigma}_t^r$ and $\tilde{\Sigma}_t^u$ are the ML estimators of Σ_t in the restricted and unrestricted models, respectively.

In one case of interest it turns out to be more practical to perform a Lagrange multiplier (LM) test. The general form of the LM statistic is

$$\lambda_{LM} = \left[\frac{\partial \ln l}{\partial \gamma'} \bigg| \gamma_r \right] I(\gamma_r)^{-1} \left[\frac{\partial \ln l}{\partial \gamma} \bigg| \gamma_r \right], \tag{14}$$

where γ denotes the vector of all parameters, γ_r is its ML estimator under the null hypothesis, and $I(\gamma)$ is the information matrix evaluated at γ, that is,

$$I(\gamma) = -E\left[\frac{\partial^2 \ln l}{\partial \gamma \partial \gamma'} \bigg| \gamma \right]$$

(e.g., Judge et al., 1985, Section 5.7). Obviously, the LM test is useful when the restricted estimator satisfying the restrictions of the null hypothesis is more easily obtained than the unrestricted ML estimator. In the next section the information matrix and the partial derivatives are evaluated for the special case needed.

On two occasions the Wald principle will be used to construct a test. This test is based on the following idea: Suppose the ML estimator $\tilde{\gamma}$ of the vector of all coefficients γ has an asymptotic normal distribution,

$$\sqrt{T}\,(\tilde{\gamma} - \gamma) \xrightarrow{d} N(0, \Sigma_\gamma)$$

with Σ_γ positive definite and restrictions are given in the form $R\gamma = 0$, where R is a suitable matrix of full row rank J. Then

$$\sqrt{T}\,R\tilde{\gamma} \xrightarrow{d} N(0, R\Sigma_\gamma R')$$

and hence, denoting the Wald statistic by λ_W,

$$\lambda_W = T\tilde{\gamma}'R'\left[R\tilde{\Sigma}_\gamma R' \right]^{-1} R\tilde{\gamma} \xrightarrow{d} \chi^2(J), \tag{15}$$

where $\tilde{\Sigma}_\gamma$ is a consistent estimator of Σ_γ (e.g., Judge et al., 1985, Section 5.7). The details for the cases of interest here are given in the next sections.

3. Periodic Processes

Periodic processes may be useful models for seasonal data. The idea is that a different VAR(p) model is valid in each of q, say, consecutive periods and these q models are repeated every q periods. For instance, in a seasonal context a different process may apply in each season of a year so that, if t belongs to the i-th season,

$$y_t = \nu_i + A_i Y_{t-1} + u_t, \quad E(u_t u_t') = \Sigma_i.$$

Thus, a periodic process can be expressed conveniently in the form (1) with

$$q = r = m \quad \text{and} \quad n_{it} = a_{it} = s_{it}, \quad i = 1, \cdots, q. \tag{16}$$

An important special case is a VAR model with seasonal dummies and time invariant covariance structure, that is, $A_i = A_1$ and $\Sigma_i = \Sigma_1$ for $i = 1, \cdots, q$. In general, hypotheses of interest are that some or all of the parameters are time invariant. If they are all time invariant y_t may be stationary. Some situations of practical interest are considered in the following and simple expressions for the resulting ML estimators are given. For a Bayesian analysis see Anděl (1987).

3.1. All Parameters Time Varying

We begin by considering the hypothesis that all coefficients are time varying, that is,

$$H_1: \nu_t = \sum_{i=1}^{q} n_{it} \nu_i, \quad A_t = \sum_i n_{it} A_i, \quad \Sigma_t = \sum_i n_{it} \Sigma_i. \tag{17}$$

Defining

$$Z_t = \begin{bmatrix} 1 \\ Y_t \end{bmatrix}$$

and $B_i = [\nu_i, A_i]$ and using a little algebra, the ML estimators of B_i and Σ_i can be shown to be

$$\tilde{B}_i^{(1)} = \left[\sum_t n_{it} y_t Z_{t-1}' \right] \left[\sum_t n_{it} Z_{t-1} Z_{t-1}' \right]^{-1} \tag{18}$$

$$\tilde{\Sigma}_i^{(1)} = \sum_t n_{it} \left(y_t - \tilde{B}_i^{(1)} Z_{t-1} \right) \left(y_t - \tilde{B}_i^{(1)} Z_{t-1} \right)' / T \bar{n}_i \tag{19}$$

(see (10)–(12)). Hence,

$$\lambda_1 := \sum_t \ln\left|\tilde{\Sigma}_t^{(1)}\right| = T\left(\bar{n}_1 \ln\left|\tilde{\Sigma}_1^{(1)}\right| + \cdots + \bar{n}_q \ln\left|\tilde{\Sigma}_q^{(1)}\right|\right) \tag{20}$$

3.2. All Parameters Time Invariant

The next case we consider is that of a stationary process where all parameters are time invariant:

$$H_2: \nu_i = \nu_1, \quad A_i = A_1, \quad \Sigma_i = \Sigma_1, \quad i = 1, \cdots, q. \tag{21}$$

Replacing all n_{it} by one in (18) and (19) the ML estimators of B_1 and Σ_1 are seen to be

$$\tilde{B}_1^{(2)} = \left[\sum_t y_t Z_{t-1}'\right]\left[\sum_t Z_{t-1} Z_{t-1}'\right]^{-1}, \tag{22}$$

$$\tilde{\Sigma}_1^{(2)} = \sum_t \left(y_t - \tilde{B}_1^{(2)} Z_{t-1}\right)\left(y_t - \tilde{B}_1^{(2)} Z_{t-1}\right)'/T. \tag{23}$$

Thus,

$$\lambda_2 := \sum_t \ln\left|\tilde{\Sigma}_t^{(2)}\right| = T \ln\left|\tilde{\Sigma}_1^{(2)}\right|. \tag{24}$$

3.3. White Noise Covariance Time Invariant

If just the white noise covariance matrices are time invariant, that is, u_t is stationary, we get

$$H_3: \Sigma_i = \Sigma_1, \quad i = 1, \cdots, q, \quad \nu_t = \sum_{i=1}^q n_{it}\nu_i, \quad A_t = \sum_i n_{it}A_i. \tag{25}$$

For this case the ML estimators follow from (18) and (12), that is, $\tilde{B}_i^{(3)} = \tilde{B}_i^{(1)}$ and

$$\tilde{\Sigma}_1^{(3)} = \sum_{i=1}^q \sum_t n_{it}\left(y_t - \tilde{B}_i^{(1)} Z_{t-1}\right)\left(y_t - \tilde{B}_i^{(1)} Z_{t-1}\right)'/T. \tag{26}$$

Consequently

$$\lambda_3 := \sum_t \ln \left| \tilde{\Sigma}_t^{(3)} \right| = T \ln \left| \tilde{\Sigma}_1^{(3)} \right|. \tag{27}$$

3.4. Time Varying Means

If just the means are time varying we have

$$H_4 : \nu_t = \sum_{i=1}^{q} n_{it} \nu_i, \quad A_i = A_1, \quad \Sigma_i = \Sigma_1, \quad i = 1, \cdots, q. \tag{28}$$

For this case the ML estimators are easily obtained by defining

$$W_t = \begin{bmatrix} n_{1,t+1} \\ \vdots \\ n_{q,t+1} \\ Y_t \end{bmatrix} \quad \text{and} \quad C = \left[\nu_1, \cdots, \nu_q, A_1 \right].$$

The ML estimator of C is

$$\tilde{C} = \left[\sum_t y_t W_{t-1}' \right] \left[\sum_t W_{t-1} W_{t-1}' \right]^{-1}, \tag{29}$$

and that of Σ_1 is

$$\tilde{\Sigma}_1^{(4)} = \sum_t \left(y_t - \tilde{C} W_{t-1} \right) \left(y_t - \tilde{C} W_{t-1} \right)' / T. \tag{30}$$

These estimates imply

$$\lambda_4 := \sum_t \ln \left| \tilde{\Sigma}_t^{(4)} \right| = T \ln \left| \tilde{\Sigma}_1^{(4)} \right|. \tag{31}$$

In Table 1 the LR tests of some hypotheses of interest are listed. The LR statistics, under general conditions, all have asymptotic χ^2 distributions with the given degrees of freedom. For this result to hold it is important that the $\bar{n}_i$ are approximately equal for $i = 1, \cdots, q$ as assumed in periodic models.

Table 1

Degrees of Freedom of Asymptotic χ^2 Distributions of
LR Statistics $\lambda_{LR} = \lambda_i - \lambda_j$ for testing H_i against H_j

H_i	H_j	degrees of freedom
H_2	H_1	$(q-1)K[K(p+\frac{1}{2})+\frac{3}{2}]$
H_3	H_1	$(q-1)K(K+1)/2$
H_4	H_1	$(q-1)K(Kp+(K+1)/2)$
H_2	H_3	$(q-1)K(Kp+1)$
H_2	H_4	$(q-1)K$

3.5. Time Varying White Noise Covariance
In the hypothesis

$$H_5: \nu_i = \nu_1, \quad A_i = A_1, \quad i = 1, \cdots, q \quad \text{and} \quad \Sigma_t = \sum_i n_{it} \Sigma_i, \tag{32}$$

the white noise covariance matrices are allowed to vary only. In this case the
ML estimators are more difficult to obtain because Σ_t^{-1} does not cancel in
(11) and (12) and a system of nonlinear normal equations results. Possible
tests involving H_5 would be

$$H_5 \text{ against } H_1 \tag{33}$$

and

$$H_2 \text{ against } H_5. \tag{34}$$

In the first set of hypotheses the ML estimators are easily obtained under the
alternative while in the second set ML estimation under the null is easy to
handle. Thus, for (33) a Wald test is the obvious choice while a LM test
suggests itself for (34). We consider these two tests in turn.

3.5.1. Testing H_5 against H_1
Since constraints are imposed on the intercept terms and VAR coefficients only, we just consider the $q(K^2p + K)$-dimensional vector of coeffi-
cients $\gamma = \text{vec}[B_1, \cdots, B_q]$ and denote its ML estimator under H_1 by $\tilde{\gamma}$.
Standard asymptotic theory implies that it has an asymptotic normal distribu-
tion,

$$\sqrt{T}(\tilde{\gamma} - \gamma) \xrightarrow{d} N(0, \Sigma_\gamma)$$

where $\Sigma_\gamma = \lim_{T \to \infty} TI(\gamma)^{-1}$ and

$$I(\gamma) = -E\left[\frac{\partial^2 \ln l}{\partial\gamma\partial\gamma'}\right]$$

is the information matrix. From (7) and (8) it is seen to be block diagonal with i-th $((K^2p + K) \times (K^2p + K))$ diagonal block

$$E\left[\sum_t n_{it}Z_{t-1}Z'_{t-1}\right] \otimes \Sigma_i^{-1}.$$

Thus, Σ_γ is also block-diagonal and the i-th block is consistently estimated by

$$\left[\frac{1}{T}\sum_t n_{it}Z_{t-1}Z'_{t-1}\right]^{-1} \otimes \tilde{\Sigma}_i^{(1)}.$$

We denote the resulting estimator of Σ_γ by $\tilde{\Sigma}_\gamma$. Defining

$$R = \begin{bmatrix} 1 & -1 & & 0 \\ \vdots & & \ddots & \\ 1 & 0 & & -1 \end{bmatrix} \otimes I_{K^2p+K} \tag{35}$$
$$((q-1) \times q)$$

the restrictions under H_5 can be expressed as $R\gamma = 0$. Hence, the Wald statistic

$$\lambda_W = T\tilde{\gamma}'R'\left[R\tilde{\Sigma}_\gamma R'\right]^{-1}R\tilde{\gamma} \tag{36}$$

may be used to test H_5 against H_1. If H_5 is true, λ_W has an asymptotic χ^2 distribution with $(q-1)K(Kp+1)$ degrees of freedom. A disadvantage of the test is that the computation of λ_W requires the inversion of a rather large matrix.

3.5.2. Testing H_2 against H_5

In order to test H_2 against H_5 the LM test is convenient because it requires the ML estimator under H_2 only. To develop the LM statistic for this case we observe that $\partial \ln l/\partial\nu_i$ and $\partial \ln l/\partial\alpha_i$ are zero when the unknown parameters are replaced by the ML estimators under H_2 because $\Sigma_i^{(2)}$ cancels in (10) and (11) and what remains are just the normal equations under H_2. Hence, what we need is just the lower right-hand corner block of the inverse information matrix that goes with $\partial \ln l/\partial \sigma$, where $\sigma = [\text{vech}(\Sigma_1)', \cdots, \text{vech}(\Sigma_q)']'$. Here vech denotes the column stacking operator that stacks the elements on and below the diagonal only. Thus, σ contains all the potentially different elements in the covariance matrices.

Next we observe from (9) that the information matrix is block-diagonal with lower right-hand corner block

$$-E\frac{\partial^2 \ln l}{\partial \sigma \partial \sigma'} = \begin{bmatrix} \dfrac{T\bar{n}_1}{2}D_K'(\Sigma_1^{-1} \otimes \Sigma_1^{-1})D_K & & 0 \\ & \ddots & \\ 0 & & \dfrac{T\bar{n}_q}{2}D_K'(\Sigma_q^{-1} \otimes \Sigma_q^{-1})D_K \end{bmatrix},$$

where D_K is the $(K^2 \times K(K+1)/2)$ duplication matrix defined such that $D_K\text{vech}(F) = \text{vec}(F)$ for any symmetric $(K \times K)$ matrix F and it has been used that

$$\frac{\partial^2 \ln l}{\partial\, \text{vech}(\Sigma_i)\partial\, \text{vech}(\Sigma_i)'} = D_K'\frac{\partial^2 \ln l}{\partial\, \text{vec}(\Sigma_i)\partial\, \text{vec}(\Sigma_i)'}D_K.$$

Consequently, using

$$\frac{\partial \ln l}{\partial\, \text{vech}(\Sigma_i)} = D_K'\left[\frac{T\bar{n}_i}{2}\text{vec}(\Sigma_i^{-1}) + \tfrac{1}{2}(\Sigma_i^{-1} \otimes \Sigma_i^{-1})\text{vec}\left(\sum_t n_{it}u_t u_t'\right)\right]$$

(see (9)), the LM statistic is seen to be

$$\begin{aligned}
\lambda_{\text{LM}} &= \left[\frac{\partial \ln l}{\partial \sigma'}\bigg|\sigma_r\right]I(\sigma_r)^{-1}\left[\frac{\partial \ln l}{\partial \sigma}\bigg|\sigma_r\right] \\
&= \sum_{i=1}^{q}\frac{T\bar{n}_i}{2}\text{vec}(\tilde{\Sigma}_i^{(5)})'\left(\tilde{\Sigma}_1^{(2)} \otimes \tilde{\Sigma}_1^{(2)}\right)^{-1}D_K\left[D_K^+\left(\tilde{\Sigma}_1^{(2)} \otimes \tilde{\Sigma}_1^{(2)}\right)D_K^{+\prime}\right] \\
&\quad \times D_K'\left(\tilde{\Sigma}_1^{(2)} \otimes \tilde{\Sigma}_1^{(2)}\right)^{-1}\text{vec}(\tilde{\Sigma}_i^{(5)}) \\
&\quad - \frac{T}{2}\text{vec}\left((\tilde{\Sigma}_1^{(2)})^{-1}\right)'D_K\left[D_K^+\left(\tilde{\Sigma}_1^{(2)} \otimes \tilde{\Sigma}_1^{(2)}\right)D_K^{+\prime}\right]D_K'\,\text{vec}\left((\tilde{\Sigma}_1^{(2)})^{-1}\right),
\end{aligned}$$

$$(37)$$

where $D_K^+ = (D_K' D_K)^{-1} D_K'$,

$$\tilde{\Sigma}_i^{(5)} = \frac{1}{T\bar{n}_i} \sum_t n_{it} \tilde{u}_t \tilde{u}_t'$$

and $\tilde{u}_t = y_t - \tilde{B}_1^{(2)} Z_{t-1}$. The statistic λ_{LM} has an asymptotic χ^2 distribution with $(q-1)K(K+1)/2$ degrees of freedom if under general conditions H_2 is correct.

3.6. Example

As an example we consider quarterly, unadjusted West German consumption and income data for the years 1960–1987. In particular y_1 and y_2 represent rates of change (first differences of logarithms) of real per capita personal consumption expenditures and personal disposable income, respectively, as published by the DIW (Deutsches Institut für Wirtschaftsforschung, Berlin). The two series are plotted in Figure 1. Obviously they have a quite strong seasonal component. There are various problems that may be brought up with respect to this data. For instance, it is possible that the logarithms of the original variables are cointegrated. In this case fitting a finite order VAR process to the rates of change may be inappropriate. We ignore such problems here because we just want to provide an illustrative example for the theoretical results of the previous subsections.

Fitting bivariate constant parameter VAR models to the data different criteria for order selection (FPE, AIC, HQ, SC; see Judge et al., 1985, Section 16.6) indicate an order $p = 5$ when a maximum of 8 is allowed. Of course, this may not mean too much if the parameters are time varying. However, the order 5 seems to be a reasonable choice because it includes lags from a whole year and the corresponding quarter of the previous year. Therefore we will work with $p = 5$ in the following. Of course, $q = 4$ is given naturally by the choice of quarterly data.

The first test is one of H_2 against H_1, that is, a stationary model is tested against one where all the parameters are time varying. The test value $\lambda_{LR} = \lambda_2 - \lambda_1 = 223.79$ is clearly significant at the 1% level. Note that the number of degrees of freedom of the asymptotic χ^2 distribution is 75. Thus, we conclude that at least some parameters are varying. To see whether the white noise series may be regarded as stationary we also tested H_3 against H_1. The resulting test value is $\lambda_{LR} = \lambda_3 - \lambda_1 = 35.95$ which is also significant at the 1% level since we now have 9 degrees of freedom. Next we have used the Wald test described in Section 3.5.1 to see whether any of the VAR coefficients or intercept terms may be assumed constant through time. In

1.diff. of ln income

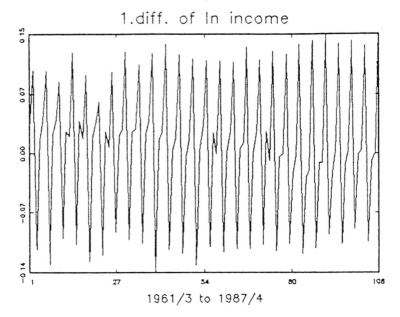

1961/3 to 1987/4

1.diff. of ln consumption

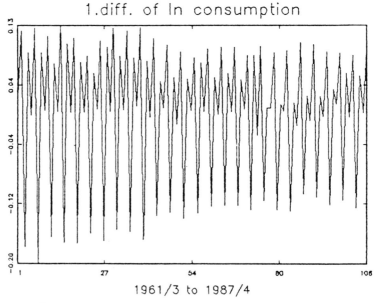

1961/3 to 1987/4

Figure 1. Unadjusted West German income and consumption series.

other words we have tested H_5 against H_1. The test value becomes $\lambda_W = 347$. Comparing this with critical values from the $\chi^2(66)$ distribution we again reject the null hypothesis H_5 at the 1% level.

Further tests on these data are possible. We do not give them here because for illustrative purposes the ones given may be sufficient. In summary the tests performed so far indicate that a simple model with seasonal dummies is hardly appropriate.

4. Intervention Models

Interventions can also be modeled in the framework of Section 2. Roughly the idea is that a particular stationary data generation mechanism is in operation until period T_1, say. Then some outside intervention occurs and another process generates the data after period T_1. For instance,

$$y_t = \nu_1 + A_1 Y_{t-1} + u_t, \quad E(u_t u_t') = \Sigma_1, \quad t \leq T_1 \tag{38}$$

and

$$y_t = \nu_2 + A_2 Y_{t-1} + u_t, \quad E(u_t u_t') = \Sigma_2, \quad t > T_1. \tag{39}$$

Interventions in economic systems may be due to legislative activities, catastrophic weather conditions or wars. Of course there could be more than one intervention in the stretch of a time series.

4.1. Interventions in the Intercept Model

Before we consider more general situations it may be useful to study the consequences of (38) and (39) in a little more detail. For simplicity suppose that $A_2 = A_1$ and $\Sigma_2 = \Sigma_1$ so that there is just a shift in intercept terms. In this case the mean of the y_t is

$$E(y_t) = \begin{cases} \displaystyle\sum_{i=0}^{\infty} \Phi_i \nu_1, & t \leq T_1 \\[2ex] \displaystyle\sum_{i=0}^{t-T_1} \Phi_i \nu_2 + \sum_{i=t-T_1+1}^{\infty} \Phi_i \nu_1, & t > T_1 \end{cases}$$

where the Φ_i are the coefficient matrices of the moving average representation of the process, i.e.,

$$\sum_{i=0}^{\infty} \Phi_i z^i = \left(I_K - A_{11} z - \cdots - A_{p1} z^p \right)^{-1}.$$

Hence, after the intervention the process mean does not reach a fixed new level immediately but only asymptotically,

$$E(y_t) \xrightarrow[t \to \infty]{} \sum_{i=0}^{\infty} \Phi_i \nu_2.$$

In the more general situation in (38)/(39) similar results also hold for the autocovariance structure. Of course, such a behaviour may be quite plausible in practice because a system may react slowly to an intervention. On the other hand it is also conceivable that an abrupt change occurs. For the case of a change in the mean we will discuss this situation shortly.

Before that we note that a model of the form considered in Section 3 may be used for intervention models as well with properly specified n_{it}. All the hypotheses considered in Section 3 are also of interest in the present context. For instance, a test of H_2 against H_3, that is, a test for time varying intercepts and VAR parameters, may be viewed as a generalized Chow test.

The test statistics may be computed with the same formulas as in Section 3. However, the statistics do not necessarily have the indicated asymptotic distributions in the present case. The problem is that the ML estimators given in the previous section may not be consistent anymore. To see this, consider, for instance, H_1 (all parameters time varying) and the model in (38)/(39). If T_1 is some fixed finite point and $T > T_1$,

$$\tilde{B}_1 = \left[\sum_{t=1}^{T_1} y_t Z'_{t-1} \right] \left[\sum_{t=1}^{T_1} Z_{t-1} Z'_{t-1} \right]^{-1} \tag{40}$$

will not be consistent because the sample information regarding A_1 does not increase when T goes to infinity. As a way out of this problem it may be assumed that T_1 increases with T. For instance, T_1 may be a fixed proportion of T. Then

$$\text{plim } \tilde{B}_1 = \left[\frac{1}{T} \sum_{t=1}^{T_1} y_t Z'_{t-1} \right] \left[\frac{1}{T} \sum_{t=1}^{T_1} Z_{t-1} Z'_{t-1} \right]^{-1} = B_1. \tag{41}$$

Also asymptotic normality is easy to obtain in this case and the test statistics have the limiting χ^2 distributions given in the previous section.

A logical problem may arise if more than one intervention is present. In that case it may not be easy to justify the assumption that all subperiods approach infinity with the sample period T. Whether or not this is a problem of practical relevance must be decided on the basis of the as yet unknown small sample properties of the tests. In any event, the large sample χ^2 distribution is just meant to be a guide for the small sample performance of the tests and as such it may be used if the periods between the interventions are reasonably large. Since no small sample results are available it is not clear, however, how large is large enough to obtain a good approximation to the asymptotic χ^2 distributions of the test statistics.

4.2. A Discrete Change in Mean

As mentioned earlier, in an intercept model like (38)/(39) one implication of an intervention is that the mean smoothly approaches a new level. Occasionally it may be more plausible to assume that there is a one time jump in the process mean after time T_1. In such a situation a model in mean adjusted form,

$$y_t - \mu_t = A_1(y_{t-1} - \mu_{t-1}) + \cdots + A_p(y_{t-p} - \mu_{t-p}) + u_t, \qquad (42)$$

is easier to work with. Here $\mu_t = E(y_t)$ and, for simplicity, we assume that all other coefficients are time invariant. Therefore the second subscript is dropped from the VAR coefficient matrices. The resulting model seems to have some practical importance. Let

$$\mu_t = m_{1t}\mu_1 + \cdots + m_{qt}\mu_q, \quad m_{it} = 0 \text{ or } 1, \quad \sum_{i=1}^{q} m_{it} = 1. \qquad (43)$$

In other words, we assume to face q interventions so that for each i, the m_{it}, $t = 1, \cdots, T$, are a sequence of zeros and ones, the latter appearing in consecutive positions.

In general the exact ML estimators for the parameters of this model are not easy to obtain. However, the μ_i may be estimated as

$$\tilde{\mu}_i = \frac{1}{T\overline{m}_i} \sum_{t=1}^{T} m_{it} y_t, \quad i = 1, \cdots, q. \qquad (44)$$

Providing $T\overline{m}_i = \Sigma_t m_{it}$ approaches infinity with T, it can be shown that, under general conditions, $\tilde{\mu}_i$ is consistent and

$$\sqrt{T\overline{m}_i}\,(\tilde{\mu}_i - \mu_i) \xrightarrow{d} N(0, \Sigma_\mu) \qquad (45)$$

where

$$\Sigma_\mu = \left(I_K - A_1 - \cdots - A_p\right)^{-1} \Sigma \left(I_K - A_1 - \cdots - A_p\right)'^{-1}$$

with $\Sigma = E(u_t u_t')$ (e.g., Lütkepohl, 1987, Sec. 2.4.2). Note that the asymptotic covariance matrix does not depend on i. Moreover, the $\tilde{\mu}_i$ are asymptotically independent. Hence, it is quite easy to perform a Wald test of the hypothesis

$$H_6: \mu_i = \mu_1, \quad i = 1, \cdots, q \quad \text{or} \quad R \begin{bmatrix} \mu_1 \\ \vdots \\ \mu_q \end{bmatrix} = 0, \tag{46}$$

where R has a similar structure as in (35). The corresponding Wald statistic is

$$\lambda_W = T \left[\sqrt{m_1}\, \tilde{\mu}_1', \cdots, \sqrt{m_q}\, \tilde{\mu}_q'\right] R' \left[R\left(I_q \otimes \tilde{\Sigma}_\mu\right) R'\right]^{-1} R \begin{bmatrix} \sqrt{m_1}\, \tilde{\mu}_1 \\ \vdots \\ \sqrt{m_q}\, \tilde{\mu}_q \end{bmatrix}, \tag{47}$$

where $[R(I_q \otimes \tilde{\Sigma}_\mu)R']^{-1}$ reduces to

$$\begin{bmatrix} 2 & 1 & \cdots & 1 \\ 1 & 2 & & 1 \\ \vdots & & \ddots & \vdots \\ 1 & 1 & \cdots & 2 \end{bmatrix}^{-1} \otimes \tilde{\Sigma}_\mu^{-1}$$

and $\tilde{\Sigma}_\mu$ is the usual estimator. In other words,

$$\tilde{A}_i^{(2)} = \left[\sum_t \tilde{y}_t \tilde{Y}_{t-1}'\right]\left[\sum_t \tilde{Y}_{t-1}\tilde{Y}_{t-1}'\right]^{-1}, \tag{48}$$

$$\tilde{\Sigma}_u = \sum_t \left(\tilde{y}_t - \tilde{A}\tilde{Y}_{t-1}\right)\left(\tilde{y}_t - \tilde{A}\tilde{Y}_{t-1}\right)' / T, \tag{49}$$

where $\tilde{y}_t = y_t - \tilde{\mu}_t$ and

$$\tilde{Y}_{t-1} = \begin{bmatrix} y_{t-1} - \tilde{\mu}_{t-1} \\ \vdots \\ y_{t-p} - \tilde{\mu}_{t-p} \end{bmatrix}.$$

Under H_6, λ_W has an asymptotic χ^2 distribution with $(q-1)K$ degrees of freedom.

Before we give an example it is perhaps worth noting that in the framework of Section 2 it is also possible to combine periodic and intervention models. Although we have used the label "intervention" for the type of change that occurs in the models considered in this section they could also be regarded as outliers if, for instance, a change in the process mean occurs only for a small number of periods. Tsay (1988) discusses univariate time series models with outliers and structural changes and lists a number of further references.

4.3. Examples

As an example of testing for structural change we consider seasonally adjusted quarterly West German disposable income (y_1) and consumption expenditures (y_2) from 1960–1978 as published by the Deutsche Bundesbank. Again rates of change are used. They are plotted in Figure 2. The oil price crisis in late 1973 is often regarded as event which has caused substantial turbulences in some economic systems. Therefore we test for a structural break in the fourth quarter of 1973. For such an event a smooth adjustment to the new conditions seems more plausible than a discrete change. Therefore the intercept version of the model is chosen with $n_{1t} = 1$, $n_{2t} = 0$ for $t \leq 1973.3$ and $n_{1t} = 0$, $n_{2t} = 1$ for $t \geq 1973.4$ (see Section 3).

Using tests based on predictions Lütkepohl (1989) did not find a structural break in the aftermath of the first oil crisis in a similar system. It is therefore interesting to see whether the tests suggested in the foregoing have more power against the relevant alternatives. Lütkepohl did find a possible structural instability in 1979. Therefore we are just using data up to 1978 in the present example. Allowing for a maximum VAR order of 8 both the AIC and the FPE criterion recommended an order of $p = 3$ for a constant coefficient model. Therefore we use this order in the following tests.

We first test a stationary model (H_2) against one in which all parameters are allowed to vary (H_1). The resulting value of the LR statistic is $\lambda_{LR} = 26.61$ which is slightly smaller than the critical value of the $\chi^2(17)$ distribution for a 5% level test. Thus, we cannot reject the stationarity hypothesis at the 5% level. This test, of course, may have low power if some of the parameters are constant and some are time varying. Therefore we also test the stationary model against a shift in the intercept term (H_2 against H_4). In this case the LR statistic assumes the value $\lambda_{LR} = 1.66$ which is clearly below any reasonable critical value of the relevant $\chi^2(2)$ distribution. In view of the plots of the series in Figure 2 a change in the white noise covariance matrix cannot be

1.diff. of ln income

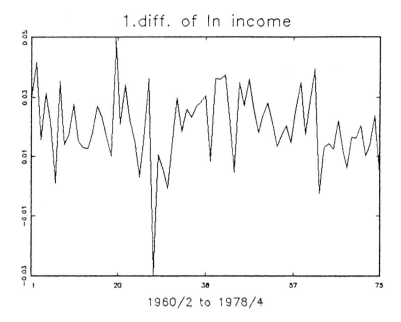

1960/2 to 1978/4

1.diff. of ln consumption

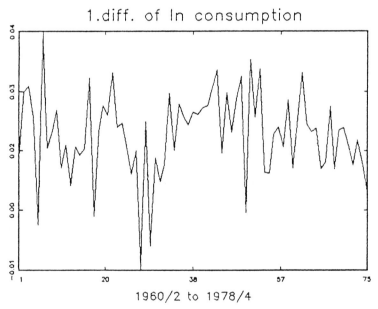

1960/2 to 1978/4

Figure 2. Seasonally adjusted West German income and consumption series.

excluded a priori. Hence we also test the stationary model against one with time varying white noise covariance matrix (H_5). For this situation the LM test described in Section 3.5.2 is suitable. The LM statistic assumes the value $\lambda_{LM} = 13.76$ and we have 3 degrees of freedom for the asymptotic χ^2 distribution. Hence, we reject the null hypothesis at a 1% level of significance. Thus there is some indication of a structural change due to the first oil price shock in the series considered.

5. Conclusions

In practice it is often questionable whether the models we are working with remain constant over time. Therefore we have developed tests for time varying parameters in a class of models that has become quite popular in recent years, namely VAR models. The general framework is broad enough to include periodic VAR processes and certain intervention models. Assuming normally distributed variables we have considered ML estimation and we have given easy expressions of the resulting estimators for a wide range of situations. In most cases considered, LR tests of the null hypothesis of time invariant parameters are relatively easy to execute. For other cases we have developed LM and Wald tests.

In the literature other models with time varying parameters have also been considered. For instance, models with stochastically varying coefficients have been investigated as well as models that permit different types of interventions. The advantage of the models treated in this paper is that they allow for a priori plausible types of nonstationarities as they may, for instance, occur in seasonal data and they are relatively easy to handle. The estimation procedures and tests can in principle be extended to the more general VARMA models. For these models closed form expressions for the ML estimators are not available, though. Therefore the class of models considered here seems to represent an acceptable compromise between theoretical generality and practicability.

References

Abraham, B. (1980), "Intervention Analysis and Multiple Time Series," *Biometrika*, 67, 73–80.

Anděl, J. (1987), "On Multiple Periodic Autoregression," *Aplikace Matematiky*, 32, 63–80.

Box, G.E.P., and Tiao, G.C. (1975), "Intervention Analysis with Applications to Economic and Environmental Problems," *Journal of the American Statistical Association*, 70, 70–79.

Cipra, T. (1985), "Periodic Moving Average Processes," *Aplikace Matematiky*, 30, 218–229.

Cleveland, W.P., and Tiao, G.C. (1979), "Modeling Seasonal Time Series," *Economie Appliquée*, 32, 107–129.

Judge, G.G., Griffiths, W.E., Hill, R.C., Lütkepohl, H., and Lee, T.-C. (1985), *The Theory and Practice of Econometrics (2nd. ed.)*, New York: John Wiley.

Li, W.K., and Hui, Y.V. (1988), "An Algorithm for the Exact Likelihood of Periodic Autoregressive Moving Average Models," *Communications in Statistics — Simulation and Computation*, 17, 1483–1494.

Lütkepohl, H. (1987), *Forecasting Aggregated Vector ARMA Processes*, Berlin: Springer-Verlag.

Lütkepohl, H. (1989), "Prediction Tests for Structural Stability of Multiple Time Series," *Journal of Business & Economic Statistics*, 7, 129–135.

Pagano, M. (1978), "On Periodic and Multiple Autoregressions," *Annals of Statistics*, 6, 1310–1317.

Tsay, R.S. (1988), "Outliers, Level Shifts and Variance Changes in Time Series," *Journal of Forecasting*, 7, 1–20.

Readings in Econometric Theory and Practice
W. Griffiths, H. Lütkepohl and M.E. Bock (Editors)
© 1992 Elsevier Science Publishers B.V. All rights reserved

CHAPTER 12

CHANGES OF EMPLOYMENT AMONG SECTORS OF THE FAST
GROWING ECONOMY IN TAIWAN: A MARKOV CHAIN ANALYSIS *

Tsoung-Chao Lee

*Department of Agricultural and Resource Economics, University of Connecticut, Storrs, CT 06268,
USA*

Agricultural development in Taiwan has been classified into four periods since 1952. A series of
transition probability matrices is estimated by using the employment shares among sectors of the
economy with the methodology described in Appendix A. The estimated transition matrices
show the important role of agriculture in production during 1952–1961 period, the absorbing
nature of industrial sector during 1962–1971 period, the increasing probability of a worker
moving from service to industry during 1972–1978 period, and the probability of a farm worker
staying with farm declining to 0.8 in 1979–1987 from the peak of 0.9626 in the previous period.
In the nonstationary Markov chain framework, per capita income is used to explain the changes
of transition probabilities for 1979–1987. The future employments among sectors of the economy
are forecast, showing the patterns of changes toward equilibrium. The sum of the forecast errors
for the Markov chain models is smaller than those for the Chenery-Taylor model and the Fuchs
model.

1. Introduction

The fast growing economy in Taiwan over the past 30 years has caused
agriculture in Taiwan to undergo structural changes. Significant changes in
the structure of agriculture are labor migration from agriculture to other
sectors of the economy, aging of the farm operators [Lee, 1989], and tendency toward part-time farming, among other changes [Lo, 1989]. It is
important that we understand the dynamic changes of agricultural structure
so that we can cope with the future changes, and the results provide a
reference for policy decision making. The purpose of this study is to estimate
the probabilities of changing employment among sectors of the economy with

* This research was conducted at National Taiwan University while the author was on sabbatic
leave from The University of Connecticut. This research was supported by National Science
Council, Taiwan, NSC78-0301-H002-11.

special attention to the declining nature of agricultural employment. Given the transition probabilities of changing employment, the time-paths of employment shares among sectors of the economy are projected, and the position of economic development are assessed.

2. Economic Background

One of the important literatures in the development economics is the intersectoral flow of funds. The issue of whether increased output and productivity in agriculture contributes to the growth in other sectors in the early stage of economic development has been a major unsolved issue in development economics. The experience of Taiwan certainly proved it to be affirmative. Following the sectoral social accounting framework developed by Ishikawa [1967], Lee [1970] measured the net capital flow between sectors in Taiwan as the balance of intersectoral commodity trade. The results indicate that the net real capital outflow from the agriculture to other sectors did occur during the entire period from 1895 to 1960. His results confirm that traditional peasant agriculture, as in Taiwan, can increase output and productivity at a sufficiently rapid rate so that it can generate surplus or savings to be transferred for investment in the modern industrial sector. How was this remarkable industrialization possible? Lee [1974] attributed the possibility of the industrial development to the increased domestic absorption of manufacturing goods during the 1950's. The significant increase in agricultural production made it possible for Taiwan not only to meet the domestic food requirements of the population but also to leave a surplus for export. The living conditions of farm families improved greatly due to favorable changes in distribution of income through the land reform program. Savings behavior of poor and rich in Taiwan was studied by Krzyzaniak [1972], who found that the rich and the poor share the same saving behavior. Sun [1974] compared the labor productivity in agricultural and industrial sectors in Taiwan and found that from 1952 to 1971, real productivity grew much slowly in agriculture than in industry, yet the ratio between nominal productivities remained approximately the same. Rapid growth with improved income distribution has been documented by Kuo, Ranis, and Fei [1981].

Structural changes of agriculture have been studied by Lee [1958] by using balance sheet approach. Shih [1971] compared the changes from the point of view of farm household real assets. The effects of trade policy on agricultural production and income were studied by Shei [1979]. Long-term projections of supply, demand, and trade for selected agricultural products in Taiwan were conducted by Chang [1982]. Shei [1982] studied the impacts of general economic policy on agricultural development in Taiwan, and implications of Taiwan's economic change on agriculture for the 1980's were also made by Shei [1984].

In order to identify patterns of structural change during the development process, many attempts over the last 30 years concentrate on the relationship between agricultural and industrial sectors using cross-section or time-series data. Among the literature are Kuznets [1957], Chenery [1960], Fuchs [1968], Chenery and Taylor [1968], Bhalla [1970], Turnham [1971], Bhalla [1973], Chenery and Syrquin [1975], Bacon and Eltis [1976], Berry [1978], Blackaby [1978], and Gemmell [1982]. For example, Fuchs [1968] tested the hypothesis that sector shares in employment are linear functions of the reciprocal of per capita income. He found highly significant regression coefficients in all three sectors — agriculture, industry, and service sector. Chenery and Taylor [1968], using cross-section data for 54 countries over the period 1950–1963, found strong evidence for a relationship between per capita income and the shares of industry and agriculture in GNP, but little evidence to support a similar relationship for the service sector. The evidence of Chenery and Taylor [1968], Fuchs [1968], and Chenery and Syrquin [1975] may be summarized as strongly supporting the following hypotheses with respect to per capita income: (1) The employment share for agriculture is declining at an increasing rate. (2) The employment share for industry is increasing at a decreasing rate. (3) The employment share for service sector is increasing but at a decreasing rate. In other words, agricultural employment falls most rapidly in the early stages of development, giving rise to rapid increases in the shares of industry and services in total employment. However, the decline in the share of agricultural employment slows down with increasing development, approaching asymptotically a share of about three percent, while industry and services approach asymptotically, shares of about 57 percent and 40 percent respectively. Gemmell [1982] argued that functional forms used previously were inappropriate and because they would lead to false predictions. New functional forms were proposed for inter-sectoral relationships. In particular, it allows for the industry/service relationship to be both positively and negatively sloping for different ranges of income. His purpose was to provide evidence on patterns of structural change during development and to accommodate the recent evidence on de-industrialization in many developed countries.

In this study, employment shares among sectors of Taiwan economy over the past 36 years will be used to estimate the transition probabilities of changing employment from one sector to another. Then, the transition matrix will be used to generate future time paths of employment shares, and

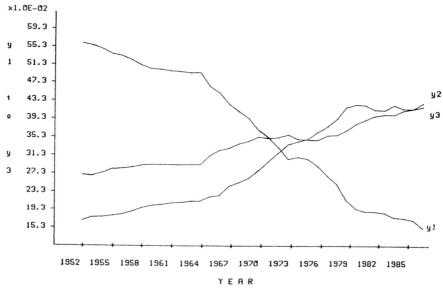

Figure 1. Observed employment shares among sectors, Taiwan, 1952–1987; y1 is primary
industry, y2 is secondary industry, y3 is tertiary industry.

henceforth to assess the position and potential of economic development.
The goodness-of-fit for the Markov chain model will be compared with those
of other models that used different functional forms. Alternative possible
future time paths of sector shares will be forecast.

3. Employment Shares Among Sectors of Taiwan Economy

Based on the data given by Directorate-General of Budget, Accounting
and Statistics, Executive Yuan, the agricultural share of employment has
been steadily declining through out the entire period of this study, from
56.1% in 1952 to 15.3% in 1987. The employment share in the secondary
industry, which includes mining, manufacturing, construction, and utilities is
increasing from 16.9% in 1952 to 42.7% in 1987. The employment share in
the tertiary industry, which includes communication, transportation, and
other services, is also increasing from 27% in 1952 to 42.0% in 1987. The
graphs showing the changes of the three sector shares of employment are
given by Figure 1. The employment by industries is given by Table 1.

Table 1

Employment by Industries, Taiwan, 1952–1987

Year	Industries (1,000 persons)						Total Employment	Per Capita GNP (Index)
	Primary	%	Secondary	%	Tertiary	%		
1952	1642	56.1	495	16.9	792	27.0	2929	100.0
1953	1647	55.6	522	17.6	795	26.8	2964	105.8
1954	1657	54.8	536	17.7	833	27.5	3026	112.0
1955	1667	53.6	560	18.0	881	28.4	3108	116.7
1956	1675	53.2	577	18.3	897	28.5	3149	118.8
1957	1689	52.3	612	19.0	928	28.7	3229	123.5
1958	1707	51.1	659	19.7	974	29.2	3340	127.5
1959	1722	50.3	695	20.3	1005	29.4	3422	133.0
1960	1742	50.2	713	20.5	1018	29.3	3473	137.2
1961	1747	49.8	732	20.9	1026	29.3	3505	142.0
1962	1760	49.7	745	21.0	1036	29.3	3541	148.7
1963	1775	49.4	764	21.3	1053	29.3	3592	157.9
1964	1810	49.5	779	21.3	1070	29.2	3658	172.3
1965	1748	46.5	839	22.3	1176	31.2	3763	185.9
1966	1735	45.0	870	22.6	1250	32.4	3856	197.3
1967	1723	42.5	995	24.6	1332	32.9	4050	212.8
1968	1725	40.8	1072	25.4	1428	33.8	4225	226.6
1969	1726	39.3	1155	26.3	1509	34.4	4390	241.5
1970	1680	36.7	1278	28.0	1617	35.3	4576	263.1
1971	1665	35.1	1417	29.9	1656	35.0	4738	291.1
1972	1632	33.0	1575	31.8	1741	35.2	4948	323.8
1973	1624	30.5	1795	33.7	1908	35.8	5327	358.5
1974	1697	30.9	1882	34.3	1907	34.8	5486	356.0
1975	1681	30.4	1927	34.9	1913	34.7	5521	364.5
1976	1641	29.0	2065	36.4	1964	34.6	5669	405.3
1977	1597	26.7	2250	37.6	2133	35.7	5980	437.2
1978	1553	24.9	2447	39.3	2227	35.8	6228	488.8
1979	1380	21.5	2683	41.8	2360	36.7	6424	519.9
1980	1277	19.5	2774	42.4	2497	38.1	6547	546.4
1981	1257	18.8	2814	42.2	2601	39.0	6672	567.1
1982	1284	18.9	2808	41.2	2718	39.9	6811	575.3
1983	1317	18.6	3090	41.1	2845	40.3	7070	610.7
1984	1286	17.6	3090	42.3	2932	40.1	7308	665.1
1985	1297	17.5	3078	41.4	3054	41.1	7428	689.3
1986	1317	17.0	3207	41.5	3209	41.5	7733	760.7
1987	1226	15.3	3430	42.7	3367	42.0	8022	836.3

Source: Directorate-General of Budget, Accounting and Statistics, Executive Yuan.
Note: Primary industry includes agriculture, forestry, and fishery. Secondary industry includes mining, manufacturing, construction and utilities. Tertiary industry includes communication, transportation, and other services.

The sector employment shares in Taiwan will be studied using three alternative models: Chenery and Taylor model, Fuchs model, and the Markov chain model. Results will be compared in terms of the residual sum of squares. Future changes will then be forecast by the Markov process.

Testing the relationship between sector shares and per capita income has produced consistent results with those results reported by Chenery and Taylor [1968], and Fuchs [1968]. We firstly used a relationship of the form proposed by Chenery and Taylor [1968]. That is, we regressed logarithm of sector share in employment as a function of logarithm of per capita income, its square, and the logarithm of population, in the form

$$\log y = a + b \log x + c (\log x)(\log x) + \log N$$

where y represents the respective sector share in GNP, x is per capita income, and N is population. The regression results show strong evidence for a relationship between per capita income and the shares of industry and agriculture in employment, but little evidence to support a similar relationship for the service sector. The coefficients of determination R^2 are very high, 0.9929, 0.9828, and 0.9639 respectively for primary, secondary and tertiary sector respectively. The regression results are given by Table 2. These results are better than 0.5 obtained by Chenery and Syrquin [1975, pp. 38, 39, and 49].

Following Fuchs, we also tested the hypothesis

$$y = a + b/x$$

where y represents the respective sector shares in employment, and x is per capita income. We found highly significant regression coefficients for all three sectors. The R^2 values are all over 0.9. The results are given by Table 3.

4. Estimation of Employment Transition Probabilities

In order to analyze the changes of employment shares among sectors of the economy, a certain type of data is required. If the micro counts of individual employees's past history of changing employment are available, then the transition probabilities can be estimated based on the micro counts as the ratio of the number of transitions from sector i to sector j and the number of the individuals in sector i at the previous period in the years under study. For the maximum likelihood estimator, see Anderson and

Table 2

Results with the Chenery-Taylor Model

Variable	Primary	Secondary	Tertiary	Mean
Intercept	− 15.3440	− 24.8394	− 1.5424	1.0000
	(− 3.9067) **	(− 7.0264) **	(− 0.6203)	
log x	3.1042	4.9503	− 0.5024	10.7226
	(3.0098) **	(5.3328) **	(− 0.7694)	
$(\log x)^2$	− 0.1761	− 0.1931	0.0275	115.4063
	(− 4.0267) **	(− 4.9050) **	(0.9938)	
log N	0.1369	− 0.7603	0.2790	9.5232
	(0.538)	(− 3.3248) **	(1.7344)	
R^2	0.991112	0.987957	0.964876	
F-statistics	1189.40	875.02	293.02	
Sum of squared forecast errors	0.0039	0.0043	0.0026	

Note: x is per capita income.
  N is population.
  The figures in parentheses are t values and ** indicates significant parameters at 1% critical level.

Table 3

Results with the Fuchs Model

Variable	Primary	Secondary	Tertiary	Mean
Intercept	0.1474	0.4434	0.4092	1.0000
	(11.4974) **	(45.5988) **	(85.5298) **	
RPCI	8262.8	− 5569.9	− 2692.9	26.9000
	(20.1978) **	(− 17.9443) **	(− 17.6322) **	
R^2	0.923068	0.904494	0.901419	
F-statistics	407.95	322.00	310.90	
Sum of squared forecast errors	0.0524	0.0302	0.0073	

Note: RPCI is reciprocal of per capita income. The figures in parentheses are t values and ** indicates significant parameters at 1% critical level.

Goodman [1957]. However, this type of micro data is often not available or incomplete. For example, *Report on The Manpower Utilization Survey in Taiwan Area* provides detailed transitional counts based on industries, townships, sex, and other characteristics, but only started from 1976. On the other hand, the macro or aggregate shares of employment are available. For the estimation of transition probabilities using aggregate or macro type of proportional data in each sector or Markov state, the methodology is given in Appendix A at the end of this paper. The stationary method is primarily based on the Lee, Judge, and Zellner [1968, 1977] procedures reformulated in the form of least squares with additional lower bound restrictions. For estimation of non-stationary transition probabilities, it is also given in Appendix A, and is primarily based on Lee and Judge [1972] except with additional a priori constraint of lower bounds imposed. An alternative formulation is proposed by MacRae [1977] incorporating logistic function, which requires more transition information than Lee, Judge and Zellner [1977] required. However, computational software is not available for MacRae's method. For the comparison of techniques see Kelton [1981].

In the Markov chain analysis, the stationary transition matrices are estimated for different periods based on the belief that the transition matrix cannot be stationary for too long. Since the data available are from 1952 to 1987, the following periods are considered: From 1952 to 1961 is a period of agricultural redevelopment according to Tuan [1983, Chapter 1]. Four-year economic planning started in 1953 with the principle of increasing production efficiency in order to provide stable agricultural products for the need of developing industries. Also according to Tuan [1983], the period 1962 to 1971 is the transition period of Taiwan agriculture. New agricultural products such as mushrooms were successfully commercialized enabling agriculture to continue to grow at the annual rate of 4.2% while industries were growing even at a faster rate of 20%. In this period, the role of agriculture in terms of national income became less important than industries. Migration of rural population to cities and conversion of farm lands to industrial complex resulted in the loss of resources in agriculture, increase in farm wage rate, and resource reallocations in agriculture. After 1972 is another period in which agricultural development depends on the cooperation and support of other sectors. Government programs including support price for rice, abolition of fertilizer and rice barter system, reduction of farm tax rate, and so on were implemented. Based on the classification of the above periods, transition matrices were estimated and the chi-square goodness-of-fit tests are performed. Since the last period from 1972 is rather long and resulted in a relatively poor goodness-of-fit, with chi-square value of 73.51, it is then further decomposed into two periods. Many combinations of decomposition are tried and the best decomposition in terms of the smallest chi-square is chosen to split the period into two subperiods, 1972–1978 and 1979–1987, for which the chi-square values are 18.20 and 21.12 respectively. The results, including the estimated transition matrices, chi-square test statistics, and equilibrium vectors, are given in Table 4.

For the period 1976–1988, *Report on The Manpower Utilization Survey in Taiwan Area* provides transitional counts on changing employments, based on a sample of about one tenth of the population. The transition matrix for 1970–1975 average is as follows:

	Agriculture	Industry	Service
Agriculture	0.1448	0.5697	0.2855
Industry	0.0591	0.6751	0.2658
Service	0.0520	0.2890	0.6590

The figure for the probability of staying in agriculture is.1448 which is, in this researcher's opinion, too low to be consistent with the Markov chain process. For example, in 1975, the percentages of agriculture, industry, and service sectors are 30.5%, 34.9%, and 34.6% respectively. According to the Markov process, the forecast percentages for 1976 are 8.27%, 50.91%, and 40.82% for agriculture, industry, and service sector respectively. These forecast percentages are too far off from the actual observed percentages of 29.2%, 36.4%, and 34.6% respectively for agriculture, industry, and service sector. It appears that the transition matrix based on the micro counts gives too low a probability for a worker staying with agriculture, resulting in erroneous results for the following years. One explanation is that the sample may not truly represent the total population that generated the relative percentages of three sectors. Therefore, in the following section, the forecasts are entirely based on the estimates of the aggregate proportions.

5. Forecast of Employment Shares among Sectors

The Markov chain analysis of sector employment shares is superior to the Chenery-Taylor model and the Fuchs model in terms of forecast. The sum of squared forecast errors for each sector is computed for each of the models involved and the results are given in Table 5. As Table 5 shows, the sum of squared forecast errors for Markov chain is smaller than those of the

Table 4

Transition Probability Matrices

Period	Primary	Secondary	Tertiary	Equilibrium vector			Chi ^{2}
1952–1961	0.9585	0.0000	0.0415				
	0.0492	0.8883	0.0624	0.7673	0.1034	0.1293	
	0.0207	0.0894	0.8899				2.11*
1962–1971	0.9626	0.0000	0.0374				
	0.0000	1.0000	0.0000	0.0000	1.0	0.0000	
	0.0000	0.0317	0.9683				19.40*
1972–1978	0.9541	0.0000	0.0459				
	0.0000	0.9342	0.0658	0.0000	0.6059	0.3941	
	0.0000	0.1012	0.8988				18.28*
1979–1987	0.8000	0.2000	0.0000				
	0.0700	0.6806	0.2494	0.1480	0.4229	0.4291	
	0.0000	0.2458	0.7542				21.12*
1952–1987	0.9672	0.0022	0.0306				
	0.0000	0.9466	0.0534	0.0000	0.5538	0.4462	
	0.0000	0.0662	0.9338				125.11
1952–1966	0.9845	0.0000	0.0155				
	0.0000	0.8806	0.1194	0.0000	0.4471	0.5529	
	0.0000	0.0956	0.9044				13.57*
1967–1987	0.9454	0.0519	0.0027				
	0.0000	0.9852	0.0148	0.0409	0.1779	0.7812	
	0.0029	0.0006	0.9965				73.51
1972–1987	0.9319	0.0681	0.0000				
	0.0000	0.8902	0.1098	0.0725	0.4435	0.4840	
	0.0102	0.0904	0.8994				63.50
1952–1967	0.9819	0.0000	0.0181				
	0.0000	0.9000	0.1000	0.0000	0.4632	0.5368	
	0.0000	0.0863	0.9137				20.33*
1968–1987	0.9410	0.0590	0.0000				
	0.0000	0.9736	0.0264	0.0547	0.3245	0.6208	
	0.0052	0.0086	0.9861				70.44
1952–1968	0.9807	0.0000	0.0193				
	0.0000	0.9000	0.1000	0.0000	0.4661	0.5339	
	0.0000	0.0873	0.9127				21.79*
1969–1987	0.9344	0.0656	0.0000				
	0.0000	0.9532	0.0468	0.0714	0.3961	0.5326	
	0.0088	0.0260	0.9652				67.07
1952–1969	0.9798	0.0000	0.0202				
	0.0000	0.9170	0.0830	0.0000	0.4799	0.5201	
	0.0000	0.0766	0.9234				22.79*
1970–1987	0.9360	0.0640	0.0000				
	0.0000	0.9163	0.0837	0.0632	0.4377	0.4991	
	0.0081	0.0653	0.9266				64.40
1952–1970	0.9776	0.0000	0.0224				
	0.0000	0.9444	0.0556	0.0000	0.5182	0.4818	
	0.0000	0.0598	0.9402				29.07*

Table 4 (continued)

Period	Primary	Secondary	Tertiary	Equilibrium vector			Chi ^{2}
1971–1987	0.9315	0.0685	0.0000				
	0.0000	0.9112	0.0888	0.0739	0.4345	0.4916	
	0.0103	0.0682	0.9216				63.85
1952–1971	0.9765	0.0000	0.0235				
	0.0000	1.0000	0.0000	0.0000	1.0	0.0000	
	0.0000	0.0234	0.9766				32.64*
1972–1987	0.9316	0.0681	0.0000				
	0.0000	0.8902	0.1098	0.0725	0.4435	0.4840	
	0.0102	0.0904	0.8994				63.50
1952–1972	0.9749	0.0000	0.0251				
	0.0000	1.0000	0.0000	0.0000	1.0	0.0000	
	0.0000	0.0253	0.9746				37.01*
1973–1987	0.9376	0.0624	0.0000				
	0.0000	0.8557	0.1443	0.0587	0.4593	0.4820	
	0.0076	0.1299	0.8625				61.69
1952–1973	0.9729	0.0000	0.0271				
	0.0000	1.0000	0.0000	0.0000	1.0	0.0000	
	0.0000	0.0269	0.9731				43.63*
1974–1987	0.9120	0.0880	0.0000				
	0.0000	0.8518	0.1482	0.1006	0.4372	0.4622	
	0.0191	0.1210	0.8599				48.61*
1962–1973	0.9576	0.0000	0.0424				
	0.0000	1.0000	0.0000	0.0000	1.0	0.0000	
	0.0000	0.0362	0.9638				24.51*
1980–1987	0.9649	0.0351	0.0000				
	0.0000	0.7154	0.2846	0.0000	0.4982	0.5018	
	0.0000	0.2826	0.7174				16.64*
1972–1976	0.7311	0.0754	0.1935				
	0.0000	0.8709	0.1291	0.2557	0.3994	0.3449	
	0.1993	0.0936	0.7071				15.46*
1972–1977	0.9541	0.0000	0.0459				
	0.0000	0.9342	0.0658	0.0000	1.0	0.0000	
	0.0000	0.1012	0.8988				18.02*
1972–1981	0.9403	0.0597	0.0000				
	0.0000	0.9266	0.0734	0.0000	0.4617	0.5383	
	0.0000	0.0630	0.9370				41.18
1975–1987	0.8786	0.1214	0.0000				
	0.0000	0.8110	0.1890	0.1279	0.4285	0.4436	
	0.0350	0.1476	0.8174				39.18*
1976–1987	0.8389	0.1566	0.0045				
	0.0515	0.7553	0.1932	0.1361	0.4256	0.4383	
	0.0000	0.1890	0.8110				34.77*
1977–1987	0.7893	0.2107	0.0000				
	0.0743	0.7032	0.2226	0.1488	0.4219	0.4294	
	0.0000	0.2186	0.7812				30.56*

Table 4 (continued)

Period	Primary	Secondary	Tertiary	Equilibrium vector			Chi ^{2}
1978–1987	0.6727	0.3273	0.0000				
	0.1261	0.6017	0.2722	0.1610	0.4178	0.4212	
	0.0000	0.2700	0.7300				22.42*
1980–1987	0.9649	0.0351	0.0000				
	0.0000	0.7154	0.2846	0.0000	0.4982	0.5018	
	0.0000	0.2826	0.7174				16.64*
1981–1987	0.9647	0.0353	0.0000				
	0.0000	0.5573	0.4427	0.0000	0.5008	0.4992	
	0.0000	0.4441	0.5559				15.33*

Note:
1. Asterisks denote acceptable goodness-of-fit at 1% critical point.
2. Degrees of freedom are determined by $(r - 1)T$, where r is 3 and T is the number of years.

Chenery-Taylor model and the Fuchs model. The sum of squared forecast errors is even smaller if the years are grouped properly into 1972–1978 and 1979–1987, according to the stationary structure. The sum of squared errors for the last two periods combined is about one third of the errors reported for the Chenery-Taylor model and is more than ten times smaller than the results of the Fuchs model.

For the future time paths, if the 1979–1987 transition matrix is used in forecast, the equilibrium vector will be reached in about five years. The equilibrium is 14.8% for agriculture, 42.3% for secondary industry, and 42.9% for tertiary industry. For the time paths see Figure 2. Although it is not very likely that the 1967–1987 pattern will prevail in the future, it is

Table 5

Comparisons of Sum of Squared Forecast Errors

Model	Primary	Secondary	Tertiary	Total
Fuchs	0.0524	0.0302	0.0073	0.0427
Chenery-Taylor	0.0039	0.0043	0.0026	0.0108
Markov chain, 1952–1987	0.0041	0.0024	0.0014	0.0079
Markov chain, 1952–1961	0.00009	0.00004	0.00008	0.0002
1962–1971	0.00094	0.00039	0.00041	0.0017
1972–1978	0.00064	0.00016	0.00022	0.0010
1978–1987	0.00034	0.00032	0.00006	0.0007
Total	0.00201	0.00091	0.00077	0.0036

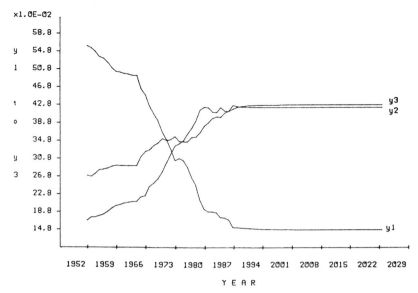

Figure 2. Forecast of employment shares based on the 1979–1987 pattern of Markov chain; y1 is primary industry, y2 is secondary industry, y3 is tertiary industry.

interesting to note that if the 1967–1987 transition matrix is used in forecast, equilibrium will be reached approximately in 30 years. This particular time paths forecast for all three sectors also show the possible de-industrialization with the peak of 43.4% for the secondary industry in five years, tapering off to the equilibrium of 42.3% (Figure 3). In all forecasts, the agriculture share of employment will not exceed 15% in equilibrium. How fast is the migration of agricultural labor to other sectors of the economy depends on the condition of the economy. If the structural change follows the industrialization pattern of 1962–1971 for a longer period, agriculture will continue to decrease its share of employment toward the bottom line of zero agriculture. This will not practically happen since the structure of the economy will continue to change. As it is found in the change of transition matrices, the absorbing nature of employment in the secondary sector did not seem to last very long. The probability of a worker staying with the secondary industry has declined from 1 in 1962–1971, 0.6059 in 1972–1978, to 0.4229 in 1979–1987. The equilibrium vectors also suggest declining employment share in the secondary industry and increasing employment share in the tertiary industry. By comparing the agricultural employment share of about 0.5% in New

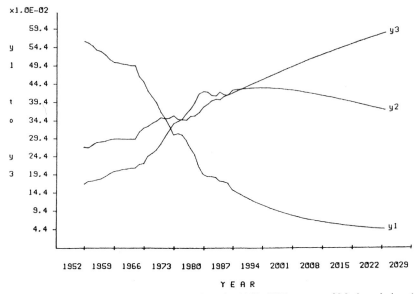

Figure 3. Forecast of employment shares based on the 1967–1987 pattern of Markov chain; y1 is primary industry, y2 is secondary industry, y3 is tertiary industry.

England states in U.S. with that of less than 15% in Taiwan, it is clear that the Taiwan economy has a good potential in development.

6. The Effect of Per Capita Income on Transition Probabilities

In the previous section, transition probabilities are assumed stationary within each period of economic growth but changing from one period to another. The goodness-of-fit tests were quite satisfactory except for the 1972–1987 period, which had to be decomposed into two subperiods in order to obtain reasonable transition probabilities with relatively small chi-square values. A better alternative is to consider the changes of transition probabilities as nonstationary for each year that can be explained by explanatory variables such as per capita income. The methodologies of estimating nonstationary transition probabilities are available in Lee and Judge [1972], and MacRae [1977]. The former shows a practical and feasible procedure of incorporating linear probability function, and the latter only presents a theoretical method of incorporating logistic function but does not provide

Table 6

Unrestricted and Restricted Least Squares Estimates of Regression
Equations that Explain Transition Probabilities

Transition Probability	Restricted	Unrestricted
$p11$	$0.5196 + 0.0005z$	$0.0481 - 0.0088z$
$p21$	0	$-0.0332 + 0.0060z$
$p31$	$0.2772 - 0.0003z$	$0.0217 - 0.0030z$
$p12$	$0.6321 - 0.0008z$	$-0.0833 + 0.0174z$
$p22$	$0.8903 - 0.0003z$	$0.0701 - 0.0111z$
$p32$	$-0.1898 + 0.0006z$	$-0.0308 - 0.0047z$
$p13$	$-0.1517 + 0.0003z$	$1.0352 + 0.9914z$
$p23$	$0.1097 + 0.0003z$	$0.9631 + 1.0051z$
$p33$	$0.9126 - 0.0003z$	$1.0091 + 1.0077z$

Note: The variable z denote per capita income in index with base
year in 1952. See Table 1.

feasible empirical results. The shortcoming of using the logistic function is
that the absolute zero and one for probability are not allowed because they
require the exogenous variables to take extreme values of infinity and
negative infinity. MacRae's maximum likelihood estimation is based on the
sum of possible multinomials involving the number of individuals who made
the transition from one Markov state i to j or $n_{ij}(t)$. Since the micro counts
of $n_{ij}(t)$ are not available, this study utilizes the method of Lee and Judge
[1972] with additional a priori constraints. The methodology is summarized in
Appendix A. Per capita income is used in explaining the changing transition
probabilities.

By following the procedures described in Appendix A, the unrestricted
least squares estimates and restricted least squares estimates are obtained.
The results of the linear probability functions are given in Table 6, and the
varying transition probabilities are given in Table 7. The unrestricted least
squares estimates of transition probabilities violate the basic postulates of
probability that they must fall within the interval of 0 and 1. For the
restricted least squares estimates, lower limit restrictions are imposed on $p11$
and $p22$, the probabilities of a worker staying in agriculture and in industry
respectively, based on the numerical results of the stationary Markov chain
reported in the previous section. In particular, $p11$ is imposed to be greater
than 0.8 and $p22$ is imposed to be greater than 0.68. The changes of
transition probabilities are explained by the per capita income. The per

Table 7

Unrestricted and Restricted Least Squares Estimates of Transition Probabilities

year	$p11$	$p21$	$p31$	$p12$	$p22$	$p32$	$p13$	$p23$	$p33$
				Unrestricted estimates					
1980	0.2198	−0.1840	0.6093	0.7358	1.2159	−0.6568	0.0444	−0.0319	1.0474
1981	−0.0139	−0.0241	0.5297	1.1979	0.9204	−0.5331	−0.1840	0.1037	1.0033
1982	−0.1965	0.1007	0.4676	1.5589	0.6896	−0.4365	−0.3624	0.2096	0.9689
1983	−0.2688	0.1502	0.4429	1.7019	0.5982	−0.3982	−0.4331	0.2516	0.9554
1984	−0.5811	0.3637	0.3366	2.3192	0.2035	−0.2330	−0.7382	0.4328	0.8964
1985	−1.0609	0.6919	0.1733	3.2679	−0.4030	0.0208	−1.2070	0.7112	0.8059
1986	−1.2743	0.8378	0.1006	3.6899	−0.6729	0.1338	−1.4156	0.8350	0.7656
1987	−1.9041	1.1269	−0.1138	4.9350	−1.4609	0.4669	−1.0309	1.2004	0.6468
				Restricted estimates					
1980	0.8000	0.0000	0.0877	0.1999	0.7466	0.1710	0.0000	0.2534	0.7414
1981	0.8143	0.0000	0.0781	0.1780	0.7392	0.1894	0.0077	0.2607	0.7326
1982	0.8255	0.0000	0.0705	0.1608	0.7335	0.2037	0.0137	0.2664	0.7258
1983	0.8299	0.0000	0.0676	0.1540	0.7313	0.2095	0.0161	0.2687	0.7231
1984	0.8490	0.0000	0.0547	0.1246	0.7215	0.2340	0.0264	0.2785	0.7114
1985	0.8783	0.0000	0.0348	0.0794	0.7064	0.2717	0.0423	0.2935	0.6935
1986	0.8914	0.0000	0.0260	0.0593	0.6997	0.2885	0.0493	0.3002	0.6855
1987	0.9299	0.0000	0.0000	0.0000	0.6800	0.3380	0.0701	0.3200	0.6620

capita income has positive effect on $p11$, $p32$, $p13$, and $p23$, while it has negative effect on $p31$, $p12$, $p22$, and $p33$, where the index 1 denotes agriculture, 2 denotes industry, and 3 denotes service. The probability of a worker moving from industry to agriculture is nil, consistent with the results of the stationary model for the same period. The largest effect of economic growth as reflected in the per capita income is on the increasing $p13$, which is the probability of a farmer changing his occupation to be in the service sector. The probability of moving from service to agriculture is decreasing, from agriculture to industry is also decreasing, but from service sector to industry sector is increasing. The other changes are best described by the following matrix of changes:

	Agriculture	Industry	Service
Agriculture	+	−	+
Industry	0	−	+
Service	−	+	−

The positive sign indicates increasing, negative sign indicates decreasing, and 0 indicates no changes. The highest effect of economic growth as reflected in per capita income on the transition probability is the declining probability of moving directly from agriculture to the service sector and increasing probability of moving from service to industry sector. Further research is needed to account for the nonmonotonic changes of probabilities by using perhaps a polynomial function of per capita income instead of a linear function. However, it requires a good computer software to estimate the huge number of parameters.

7. Summary and Conclusion

Structural change of the Taiwan economy in general and agriculture in particular has occurred in recent years. The change is quite drastic in that the employment share of agriculture has declined from 56.1% in 1952 to 15.3% in 1987. Markov chain transition probability matrix is used to describe the change. Agricultural development in Taiwan has been classified into four periods. The period 1952–1961 is the redevelopment of agriculture to facilitate the growth of industries. The estimated transition probability matrix shows the important role of agriculture in production. The period 1962–1971 is the growing period of industrialization. The transition matrix shows the absorbing nature of the industrial sector. The period after 1972 can be subclassified into the earlier period of 1972–1978 with fast paced industrial growth and momentum, and the later period of 1978–1987 with slower paced industrial growth.

The future forecast of employment among sectors depends on the pace of the growth of industries. If the pace is that of 1979–1987, agriculture will be stabilized in about five years with the equilibrium of 14.8% shares of employment. Industry and service sectors will share 42.3% and 42.9% of employment respectively. If the economic development follows the average pattern of 1972–1987, agriculture employment will continue to decline to 7.2% in equilibrium, and industry and service sectors will share 44.4% and 48.4% of employment respectively. If the pace follows the pattern of 1967–1987, agriculture employment will decline to only 4.1%, and industry and service sectors will share 17.8% and 78.1% respectively.

The structural change of the Taiwan economy was described by the changing transition matrices in four periods, each with a stationary Markov chain. The analysis is also extended to utilize the variables that characterize the growth of the economy to explain the change. This requires a use of non-stationary Markov chain in analysis. Although the micro data for transitional counts are also available for the period after 1976 in *Report on the Manpower Utilization Survey in Taiwan Area*, this information can be utilized in a logit analysis explaining the changes of transition probabilities by variables that are related to economic growth. However, the validity and consistency of the data must be examined more carefully before conducting any meaningful research. In this paper, nonstationary transition probabilities are estimated by using aggregate data. The methodology, as described in the Appendix A, is a minor revision of the Lee and Judge [1972] and Lee, Judge, and Zellner [1977] in order to incorporate additional a priori information on the probabilities. Based on the experience of the results of the stationary model reported in the previous section, additional constraints of lower limits of 0.80 and 0.68 for $p11$ and $p22$, the probabilities of a worker staying in agriculture and industry respectively, are imposed. Results show the structure of declining agriculture sector and growing sectors of industry and service. One estimate which stands out is the probability of changing from industry to agriculture which is absolute zero, both in the stationary and nonstationary model. The transition probability of moving from agriculture to industry is declining while the that of moving from agriculture to service is increasing. The tendency of moving from service to agriculture is also decreasing to zero.

The structure of the fast growing economy in Taiwan is changing in the same direction as other developed countries. The effect of economic growth, as reflected in the increasing per capita income, on the probability of staying in farming may be high for those who are farmers now, the change of occupation from industry and service is practically zero. As a result, the share of agricultural employment is declining down to about 15% and is still declining. The future structure of agriculture in Taiwan will be mostly part-time farm households with farming as recreational, depending more on income from industry and service sectors.

Appendix A: Estimating Transition Probabilities with Restrictions by Using Aggregate Data

A.1. The Stationary Model

The Markov relation under consideration is given by

$$Q = XP \tag{1}$$

where Q is a $(T \times r)$ matrix of true proportions in time t, X is a $(T \times r)$ matrix of observed proportions in time $t - 1$, and P is a $(r \times r)$ matrix of stationary transition probabilities p_{ij}, for $i, j = 1, 2, \ldots, r$. By introducing the $(T \times r)$ error matrix U in

$$Y = Q + U \tag{2}$$

the model for the $(t \times r)$ matrix of observed proportions Y is

$$Y = XP + U \tag{3}$$

The parameter matrix P has the properties, $0 \leq p_{ij} \leq 1$ and $P\eta_r = \eta_r$ where η_r is a $(r \times 1)$ vector of ones. The observation matrices have the properties that $Y\eta_r = X\eta_r = \eta_T$, where η_T is a $(T \times 1)$ vector of ones. Madansky [1959] has shown, since U is uncorrelated with X, the unrestricted least squares estimates of transition probabilities are consistent with respect to T and for a fixed T the estimates are also asymptotically consistent to the sample size N. That is, the least squares estimator

$$\bar{P} = (X'X)^{-1}X'Y \tag{4}$$

is consistent. However, it is inefficient due to heteroscedasticity. Although it has the property

$$\bar{P}\eta_r = (X'X)^{-1}X'Y\eta_r$$

$$= (X'X)^{-1}X'X\eta_r = \eta_r \tag{5}$$

the estimator $\bar{P}$ is not guaranteed to have the property

$$0 \leq \bar{p}_{ij} \leq 1 \tag{6}$$

Thus, the problem is to find an efficient and feasible estimator for P.

In order to write the model in a conventional vector form we vectorize both sides of the equation of the model

$$\text{vec}(Y) = \text{vec}(XP) + \text{vec}(U) \tag{7}$$

Simplifying, we have

$$y = (I_r \otimes X)p + u \tag{8}$$

where
   y is a $(rT \times 1)$ vector by stacking the columns of Y matrix,
   p is a $(r^2 \times 1)$ vector by stacking columns of P matrix, and
   u is a $(rT \times 1)$ vector by stacking the columns of U matrix.
The equation error u has the properties

$$E[u] = 0 \tag{9}$$

and

$$E[uu'] = \Sigma \tag{10}$$

where Σ is a $(Tr \times Tr)$ positive semidefinite matrix with elements

$$p_{ij}(t) = q_i(t)q_i(t)/N(t) \tag{11}$$

on the diagonal of the off-diagonal blocks, and

$$p_{ij}(t) = q_i(t)(1 - q_i(t))/N(t) \tag{12}$$

on the diagonal of the diagonal blocks, where $q_i(t)$ is the true value of the observed proportions $y_i(t)$. The matrix is singular since the row sums of the elements are zero. However it has rank $T(r - 1)$. Without loss of generally, we may delete the last columns of Y, P, and U to obtain the reduced model

$$Y_* = XP_* + U_* \tag{13}$$

where the asterisks denote the deletion of the last column of the corresponding matrix without asterisk. That is, Y_* is $T \times (r - 1)$ matrix, P_* is $(r \times (r - 1))$ matrix, and U_* is $T \times (r - 1)$ matrix. Vectorizing equation (13)

$$\text{vec}(Y_*) = \text{vec}(XP_*) + \text{vec}(U_*) \tag{14}$$

yields

$$y_* = (I_{r-1} \otimes X)p_* + u_* = Z_* p_* + u_* \tag{15}$$

where
   y_* is a $(T(r - 1) \times 1)$ vector by stacking the columns of Y_* matrix,
   p_* is a $(r(r - 1) \times 1)$ vector by stacking the columns of P_* matrix,
   u_* is a $(T(r - 1) \times 1)$ vector by stacking the columns of U_* matrix, and
   Z_* is a $(T(r - 1) \times r(r - 1))$ matrix, or $(I_{r-1} \otimes X)$.

The equation error vector u_* has the properties

$$E[u_*] = 0 \tag{16}$$

and

$$E[u_* u'_*] = \Sigma_* \tag{17}$$

where Σ_* is the submatrix of Σ with the last block of T rows and T columns deleted. The matrix Σ_* is nonsingular with rank $T(r-1)$.

The generalized least squares estimator is

$$\bar{P}_* = (Z'_* \Sigma^{-1}_* Z_*) Z_* \Sigma^{'-1}_* y_* \tag{18}$$

and the last column of $\bar{P}$ can be estimated as

$$\bar{p}_r = \eta_r - \bar{P}_* \eta_{r-1} \tag{19}$$

where η_{r-1} is a $((r-1) \times 1)$ vector of ones. The estimator $\bar{P} = (\bar{P}_* \bar{p}_r)$ is more efficient than the OLS estimator, but it does not guarantee that the individual elements fall in the interval 0 and 1, that is $0 \leq p_{ij} \leq 1$. To insure that the elements fall within 0 and one, we formulate the problem as to minimize

$$SS = (y_* - Z_* p_*)' \Sigma^{-1}_* (y_* - Z_* p_*) \tag{20}$$

subject to

$$Rp_* \leq \eta_r \text{ or } Rp_* + p_r = \eta_r \tag{21}$$

and

$$p_* \geq 0 \quad p_r \geq 0 \tag{22}$$

where $R = [II..I]$ is a $(r \times (r-1))$ matrix. The Lagrangian function is

$$L = (1/2)(y_* - Z_* p_*)' \Sigma^{-1}_* (y_* - Z_* p_*) - \lambda'(\eta_r - Rp_*) \tag{23}$$

Applying the Kuhn-Tucker conditions, we have

$$-Z'_* \Sigma^{-1}_* (y_* - Z_* p^\circ_*) + R'\lambda^\circ \geq 0, \quad v^{\circ\prime} p^\circ_* = 0, \quad p^\circ_* \geq 0 \tag{24}$$

$$\eta_r - Rp^\circ_* \geq 0, \quad \lambda^{\circ\prime}(\eta_r - Rp^\circ_*) = 0, \quad \lambda^\circ \geq 0 \tag{25}$$

where $v^{o\prime}$ is the left hand side of the first condition. By solving the above conditions simultaneously, the estimator p^o_* is obtained along with λ^o. The last column of P, p_r is calculated as

$$p^o_r = \eta_r - Rp^o_* \tag{26}$$

The nonnegativity constraint $p_* \geq 0$ may be generalized to include a lower limit constraint $p_* \geq d$, where d is a $(rT \times 1)$ vector of lower limited for all elements of p_*. If there is no informative prior knowledge, the vector d may be just a vector of zeroes. A possible prior knowledge which is useful in practice is that p_{ii}, the probability of an individual staying in the same Markov state is larger than any other p_{ij}. In other words, for a smooth transition of individuals among Markov states, p_{ii} is normally larger than p_{ij} for the same i. If one believes that $p_{ii} \geq d_{ij}$ for example, then some elements of d vector will have given value of d_{ij}. However, the row sums of d_{ij} must be less than one in order to prevent inconsistency in the restrictions. If additional lower limit constraint $p_* \geq d$ is imposed, the Lagrangian function is

$$L = (1/2)(y_* Z_* p_*)' \Sigma^{-1}_*(Y_* - Zp_*) - \lambda'_1(\eta_r - Rp_*)$$
$$- \lambda'_2(p_* - d) \tag{27}$$

The Kuhn-Tucker conditions are

$$-Z'_* \Sigma^{-1}_*(y_* - Z_* p^o_*) + R'\lambda^o_1 - \lambda^o_2 \geq 0, \quad v^{o\prime}p^o_* = 0, \quad p^o_* \geq 0 \tag{28}$$

$$-\eta_r + Rp^o_* \leq 0, \quad -p^{o\prime}_r\lambda^o_1 = 0, \quad \lambda^o_1 \geq 0 \tag{29}$$

and

$$-p^o_* + d \leq 0, \quad -s^{o\prime}\lambda^o = 0, \quad \lambda^o_2 \geq 0 \tag{30}$$

where $s^o = p^o_* - d$. In order to practically solve the system of Kuhn-Tucker conditions for p^o_*, p^o_r, λ^o_1, λ^o_2 and s^o, the following simplex tableau can be used:

RHS	λ_1	λ_2	p_*	p_r	s	v
η_r			R	I		
$-d$			$-I$		I	
$Z'_* \Sigma^{-1}_* y_*$	R'	$-I$	$Z'_* \Sigma^{-1}_* y_*$			$-I$

The simplex method is revised to consider the following bilinear conditions. If the i-th element of λ_1 is in the basis, do not introduce the i-th element of p_r into basis, and vice versa. If the i-th element of λ_2 is in the basis, do not introduce the i-th element of s into basis, and vice versa. If the i-th element of p_* is in the basis, do not introduce the i-th element of v into basis, and vice versa. In other words λ_1 and p_*, λ_2 and s, and p_* and v are pairs of counter part vectors, not both corresponding elements of the pairs can be in the basis at the same time for the solution to be optimal

A.2. The Nonstationary Model

The model presented previously was a stationary Markov chain. In order to study the change of economic structure, the time series data can be broken into segments. The resulting estimates can be compared to reveal the change in the economic struture. Alternatively, if the changes in economic structure are believed to be a function of some economic variables, then a nonstationary Markov model can be considered. The model can be written as

$$y_j(t) = \sum_{i=1}^{r} y_i(t-1)p_{ij}(t) + u_j(t) \quad j = 1, 2, \ldots, r \tag{31}$$

where the parameters are subject to change and are functions of some externally generated explanatory variables $Z_k(t)$,

$$p_{ij}(t) = \sum_{k=1}^{m} \beta_{ijk}Z_k(t) \quad \text{for all } i, j, t \tag{32}$$

where β_{ijk} are parameters to be estimated.
Using matrix notation we have

$$y = Zp + u \tag{33}$$

and

$$p = W\beta \tag{34}$$

where y is a $(rT \times 1)$ vector of proportions $y_j(t)$, $j = 1, 2, \ldots, r$, and $t = 1, 2, \ldots, T$, u is a $(rT \times 1)$ vector of disturbances and Z is a $(rT \times r^2T)$ block diagonal matrix of proportions $y_j(t-1)$, or $Z = (I_r \otimes X)$ and X is redefined as

$$X = \begin{bmatrix} y_1(0) & & & y_2(0) & & & \cdots & & y_r(0) & \\ & y_i(1) & & & y_2(1) & & & \cdots & & y_r(1) & \\ & & \ddots & & & \ddots & & & & & \ddots \\ & & & y_i(T-1) & & & y_2(T-2) & & \cdots & & y_r(T) \end{bmatrix}$$

(35)

p is a $(r^2 T \times 1)$ vector of variable transition probabilities $p_{ij}(t)$

$$p = \begin{bmatrix} p_1 \\ p_2 \\ \vdots \\ p_r \end{bmatrix} \quad \text{with } p_j = \begin{bmatrix} p_{1j} \\ p_{2j} \\ \vdots \\ p_{rj} \end{bmatrix} \quad \text{and } p_{ij} = \begin{bmatrix} p_{ij}(1) \\ p_{ij}(2) \\ \vdots \\ p_{ij}(T) \end{bmatrix}$$

(36)

W is a $(r^2 T \times r^2 M)$ block diagonal matrix

$$W = \begin{bmatrix} W_1 & & & \\ & W_2 & & \\ & & \ddots & \\ & & & W_{r^2} \end{bmatrix}$$

(37)

with $W_1 = W_2 \ldots = W_{r^2}$ where W_i is a $(T \times M)$ matrix of observations of predetermined variables, β is a $(r^2 M \times 1)$ vector of parameters

$$\beta = \begin{bmatrix} \beta_1 \\ \beta_2 \\ \vdots \\ \beta_r \end{bmatrix} \quad \text{with } \beta_j = \begin{bmatrix} \beta_{1j} \\ \beta_{2j} \\ \vdots \\ \beta_{rj} \end{bmatrix} \quad \text{and } \beta_{ij} = \begin{bmatrix} \beta_{ij}(1) \\ \beta_{ij}(2) \\ \vdots \\ \beta_{ij}(T) \end{bmatrix}$$

(38)

The stochastic assumptions for u are

$$E[u] = 0$$

(39)

and

$$E[uu'] = \Sigma$$

(40)

where Σ is defined as in the stationary model. By substitution of $p = W\beta$ in $y = Zp + u$, we obtain

$$y = ZW\beta + u \tag{41}$$

Since Σ is singular, we write our abbreviated model as

$$y_* = Z_* W_* \beta_* + u_* \tag{42}$$

where asterisks denote the subsets of the matrices which result when one observation vector (say, the last) is deleted. The stochastic assumptions become

$$E[u_*] = 0 \tag{43}$$

and

$$E[u_* u'_*] = \Sigma_* \tag{44}$$

the GLS estimator is

$$\hat{\beta}_* = \left(W'_* Z'_* \Sigma^{-1}_* Z_* W_* \right)^{-1} W'_* Z'_* \Sigma^{-1}_* y_* \tag{45}$$

provided that $Z_* W_*$ has full column rank. It is necessary that $rM \leqq T$. The transition probability vector is estimated as

$$\hat{p}_* = W_* \hat{B}_* \tag{46}$$

and

$$\hat{p}_r = \eta_r - R\hat{p}_* \tag{47}$$

where $R = (II \ldots I)$ a $(rT \times (r-1)T)$ matrix with $r-1$ identify matrices of size $(rT \times rT)$. From the Gauss Markov Theorem, the covariance matrix of parameters is given by

$$V(\beta_*) = \left(W'_* Z'_* \Sigma^{-1}_* Z_* W_* \right)^{-1} \tag{48}$$

and hence

$$V(p_*) = W_* \left(W'_* Z'_* \Sigma^{-1}_* Z_* W_* \right)^{-1} W'_* \tag{49}$$

and

$$V(p_r) = RW_*(W_*'Z_*'\Sigma_*^{-1}Z_*W_*)^{-1}W_*'R' \tag{50}$$

In practice, Σ_* is unknown and must be estimated, by replacing $q_j(t)$ by the observed proportions $y_j(t)$. The only problem with the GLS estimator is that there is no guarantee that $0 \leq p_{ij} \leq 1$. Therefore, the restricted least squares must be considered, and the necessary constraints are

$$Rp_* \leq \eta_r \tag{51}$$

and

$$p_* \geq 0 \tag{52}$$

or in terms of the parameter vector β_*, the constraints are

$$RW_*\beta_* \leq \eta_r \tag{53}$$

$$W_*\beta_* \geq 0 \tag{54}$$

If the nonnegative constraint $p_* \geq 0$ is generalized to include the lower limit constraint $p^* \geq d$, where d is a $(r(r-1)T \times 1)$ vector of lower limits for all elements of p_*, then the corresponding constraint in terms of β_* is

$$W_*\beta_* \geq d \tag{55}$$

The Lagrangian function is

$$L = (1/2)(y_* - Z_*W_*\beta_*)'\Sigma_*^{-1}(y_* - Z_*W_*\beta_*)$$
$$- \lambda_1'(\eta_r - RW_*\beta_*) - \lambda_2'(W_*\beta_* - d) \tag{56}$$

The Kuhn-Tucker conditions are

$$-W_*'Z_*'\Sigma_*^{-1}(y_* - Z_*W_*\tilde{\beta}_*) + W_*'R'\tilde{\lambda}_1 - W_*'\tilde{\lambda}_2 = 0 \tag{57}$$

$$\eta_r - RW_*\tilde{\beta}_* \geq 0, \quad \tilde{\lambda}_1'(\eta_r - RW_*\tilde{\beta}_*) = 0, \quad \tilde{\lambda}_1 \geq 0 \tag{58}$$

$$W_*\tilde{\beta}_* \geq d, \quad \tilde{\lambda}_2 W_*\tilde{\beta}_* = 0, \quad \tilde{\lambda}_2 \geq 0 \tag{59}$$

Solving the above equations for $\tilde{\beta}_*$ yields the restricted least squares results. In order to practically solve the system of Kuhn-Tucker conditions for $\tilde{\beta}_*$ and $\tilde{p}_*$, the following simplex tableau can be used

RHS		λ_1	λ_2	β_*^+	p_r	s	β_*^-
η_r				RW_*	I_r		
$-d$				$-W_*$		$I_{r(r-1)}$	
$W_*'Z_*'\Sigma_*^{-1}y_*$	$W_*'R'$	$-W_*$	$W_*'Z_*'\Sigma_*^{-1}Z_*W_*$				$-W_*'Z_*'\Sigma_*^{-1}Z_*W_*$

The simplex method is subject to the following bilinear conditions: If the i-th element of λ_1 is in the basis, do not introduce the i-th element of p_r into basis, and vice versa. If the i-th element of λ_2 is in the basis, do not introduce the i-th element of s into basis and vice versa. Given the solutions for $\tilde{\beta}_*^+$, $\tilde{\beta}_*^-$, p_r, and s, the solutions for β_* and p_*, are obtained as

$$\tilde{\beta}_* = \tilde{\beta}_*^+ - \tilde{\beta}_*^- \tag{60}$$

and

$$\tilde{p}_* = \tilde{s} + \tilde{d} \tag{61}$$

For the last set of parameters, $\tilde{\beta}_r$ vector can be obtained

$$\tilde{\beta}_r = \eta_r - RW_*\beta_* \tag{62}$$

A.3. Predicted Proportions and Goodness-of-fit Test

If $\tilde{P}$ is an estimate of P, then the predicted proportions can be expressed in a $(T \times r)$ matrix Y as

$$\tilde{Y} = X\tilde{P} \tag{63}$$

By the use of the asymptotic r variate normality of the multinominal distribution of the micro units $n_j(t)$ in the j-th state in time t for $j = 1, 2, \ldots, r$, the quadratic form in the exponent of this distribution

$$\sum_{i=1}^{r} \frac{\left(n(t)\tilde{y}_i(t) - N(t)y_i(t)\right)^2}{N(t)y_i(t)} \tag{64}$$

is distributed like chi-square with $r - 1$ degrees of freedom (Kendall and Stuart, 1961, pp. 335–356). This forms the basis for the chi-square goodness-of-fit test for the prediction in each time period. Suppose that the proportions are predicted for T time periods. Then according to the additive property of the chi-square distribution, the expression

$$\sum_{t=1}^{T} \sum_{i=1}^{r} \frac{N(t)\big(\bar{y}_i(t) - y_i(t)\big)^2}{y_i(t)} \tag{65}$$

is chi-square distributed with $(r - 1)T$ degrees of freedom. The predicted proportion $\bar{y}_i(t)$ is assumed to be non-zero.

References

Anderson, T.W. and Goodman, L.A. (1957), "Statistical Inference About Markov Chains," *The Annals of Mathematical Statistics*, 28, 89–110.

Bacon, R.W. and Eltis, W.A. (1976), *Briton's Economic Problem: Too Few Producers*, London, Macmillan.

Berry, A. (1978), "A Positive Interpretation of the Expansion of Urban Services in Latin America with some Columbian Evidence," *Journal of Development Studies*, Vol. 14.

Bhalla, A.S. (1970), "The Role of Services in Employment Expansion," *International Labour Review*, Vol. 101.

Bhalla, A.S. (1973), "A Disaggregative Approach to LDC's Tertiary Sector," *Journal of Development Studies*, Vol. 10.

Blackby, F. (ed.) (1978), *De-Industrialization*, London, Heinemann/NIESR.

Chang, T.T. (1982), *Long-Term Projections of Supply, Demand and Trade for Selected Agricultural Products in Taiwan*, The Research Institute of Agricultural Economics, National Taiwan University, Taipei, Taiwan, December, 246 pages.

Chenery, H.B. (1979), *Structural Change and Development Policy*, Washington: World Bank.

Chenery, H.B. and Syrquin, M. (1975), *Patterns of Development 1950–70*, London, OUP.

Chenery, H.B., and Taylor, L. (1968), "Development Patterns: Among Countries and Over Time," *The Review of Economics and Statistics*, Vol. 1, No. 4, 391–416.

CEPD, Executive Yuan, R.O.C. (1988), *Taiwan Statistical Data Book*.

DGBAS and CEPD, Executive Yuan, R.O.C., *Report on The Manpower Utilization Survey in Taiwan Area*, various issues since 1976. (Chinese)

Fox, Karl A. (1963), "The Food and Agricultural Sectors in Advanced Economies", in T. Barna (ed.), *Structural Interdependence and Economic Development*, New York, Macmillan.

Fuchs, V. (1968), *The Service Economy*, New York, NBER.

Gemmell, Norman (1982), "Economic Development and Structural Change: The Role of the Service Sector", *The Journal of Development Studies*, 19, 37–66.

Ishikawa, Shigeru (1967), *Economic Development in Asian Perspective*, Tokyo, Kinokuniya Bookstore.

Kelton, C.M. (1981), "Estimation of the Time-Independent Markov Processes with Aggregate Data: A Comparison of Techniques," *Econometrica*, 49, 517–518.

Kendall, M.G. and Stuart, A. (1961), *The Advanced Theory of Statistics*, Vol. 2, Charles Griffin and Co., Ltd., London.

Krzyzaniak, M. (1977), "Savings Behavior of Poor and Rich in Taiwan, 1964, 1966, 1968, and 1970," *The Journal of Developing Areas*, 11, 447–464.

Kuo, Sirley W.Y., Ranis, G. and Fei, John C.H. (1981), *The Taiwan Success Story: Rapid Growth with Improved Distribution in the Republic of China*, Westview Press, Boulder, Colorado, 161 pages.

Kuznets, S. (1957), "Quantitative Aspects of the Economic Growth of Nations: II. *Industrial Distribution of National Product and Labour Force*," Economic Development and Cultural Change, Vol. 5 (Supplement).

Lee, C.S. (1989), "The Effects of Free Economy on Utilization of Agricultural Labor," Symposium of The Effects of Free Economy on Agricultural Sector, May 5–6, 1989, National Taiwan University, pp. 294–318. (Chinese)

Lee, T.H. (1958), "A Study on Structural Change of Agricultural Production in Taiwan", Proceedings of Agricultural Economics Seminar, National Taiwan University, September 16–20, pp. 79–89.

Lee, T.H. (1970), *Intersectoral Capital Flows in the Economic Development of Taiwan, 1895–1960*, Cornell University Press, 197 pages.

Lee, T.H. (1974), "Agriculture: Dynamic Force for Industrialization", *Agriculture's Place in the Strategy of Development: The Taiwan Experience*, edited by T.H. Shen, JCRR Taipei, pp. 66–70.

Lee, T.C., Judge, G.G. and Zellner, A. (1968), "Maximum Likelihood and Bayesian Estimation of Transition Probabilities," *Journal of the American Statistical Association*, 63, 1162–1179.

Lee, T.C., Judge, G.G. and Zellner, A. (1977), *Estimating the Parameters of the Markov Probability Model from Aggregate Time Series Data*, Second Revised Edition, North-Holland, 260 pages.

Lee, T.C. and Judge, G.G. (1972), "Estimation of Transition Probabilities in a Nonstationary Finite Markov Chain", *Metroeconomica*, XXIV, 180–201.

Lo, Ming-Che (1989), "The Effects of Free Economy on Agricultural Structure," Symposium of The Effects of Free Economy on Agricultural Sector, May 5–6, 1989, National Taiwan University, pp. 188–206. (Chinese)

MacRae, E.C. (1977), "Estimation of Time-Varying Markov Processes with Aggregate Data", *Econometrica*, 45, pp. 183–198.

Madansky, A. (1959), "Least Squares Estimation in Finite Markov Processes," *Psychometrika*, 14, 137–44.

Shei, Shun-Yi (1979), "The Agricultural Production and Income Effects of Taiwan Trade Policy," *Academia Economic Papers* 7(2), September 1979, pp. 143–164.

Shei, Shun-Yi (1982), "Impacts of General Economic Policy on Agricultural Development in Taiwan," in Hou, C.M. and T.S. Yu eds., *Agricultural Development in China, Japan and Korea*, the Institute of Economics, Academia Sinica, Taipei, Taiwan, ROC, 667–695.

Shei, Shun-Yi (1984), "Taiwan's Economic Change—Implications for Agriculture in the 1980s," in *Economic Development in East and South-East Asia*, Bureau of Agricultural Economics, Australian Government Publishing Service, Canberra, pp. 132–148.

Shih, Chi-Tzen (1971), "Changes of Real Assets in Taiwan Farm Households", *Economic Essays*, Institute of Economics, Academia Sinica, September, 233–250, (in Chinese).

Stewart, Charles T. Jr. (1987), "Structural Change and Intergenerational Occupational Mobility," *The Journal of Developing Areas* 21, 141–158.

Sun, Chen (1974), "Trade-Offs between Agriculture and Industry", *Agriculture's Place in the Strategy of Development: The Taiwan Experience*, edited by T.H. Shen, JCRR Taipei, pp. 71–81.

Tuan, C. (1983), *Analysis of Managing Taiwan Agricultural Sector*, No. 119, Economic Research, Bank of Taiwan. (Chinese).

IV. SPATIAL EQUILIBRIUM MODELING

Readings in Econometric Theory and Practice
W. Griffiths, H. Lütkepohl and M.E. Bock (Editors)

CHAPTER 13

ALTERNATIVE SPATIAL EQUILIBRIUM FORMULATIONS:
A SYNTHESIS

T.G. MacAulay

Department of Agricultural Economics, University of Sydney, Sydney, NSW 2006, Australia

Introduction

The publication of *Spatial and Temporal Price and Allocation Models* by Takayama and Judge (1971) was a watershed in the development of spatial equilibrium modelling. This work provided an extensive foundation for the development and application of spatial equilibrium models through the use of quadratic programming. The work collected together a long sequence of research by Takayama and Judge and others which can be traced back to the early writers on the theory of general equilibrium. The contribution of Takayama and Judge was to show in an unequivocal way that an array of different spatial problems could be solved using quadratic programming. These models were based on linear supply and demand functions and constant per unit transport costs. Further, they are partial equilibrium models in the sense that they take the rest of the economy as given and do not endogenously determine income. This is both an advantage and a disadvantage. The advantage is that they are usually quite tractable and the data needed to support them is usually of higher quality than more general equilibrium type models. The disadvantage is that the boundary between endogenous and exogenous variables is quite strict.

In this chapter attention will be given to the formulation of spatial equilibrium models rather than the problems of their mathematical computation. This latter area is dealt with in subsequent chapters but appears to have progressed through the electric analog of Enke (1951), the iterative linear programming solution of Samuelson (1952), the quadratic programming solution of Takayama and Judge (1964a,b), reactive programming of Tramel and Seale (1959) and King and Ho (1972), the linear complementarity solution suggested by Takayama and Judge (1971) applying the Cottle and Dantzig (1968) approach, fixed-point algorithms, for example MacKinnon (1975) and finally to the more general variational inequality approaches of Asmuth, Eaves and Peterson (1979) and Dafermos (1980), among others, and considered by Nagurney (1990) in this book, and the recent variable dimension solution of Tobin (1988). The review in this chapter in no way makes a claim to being exhaustive of the vast literature that now exists on spatial equilibrium models, rather an attempt is made to provide a systemised view of a range of the formulations and to show how they fit within a reasonably general framework. Although computational feasibility is an important issue in such models, with modern nonlinear programming software it becomes an issue in relation to problem size rather than formulation.

A General Formulation

In economics, time, space and form transformations can be seen as completely analogous to each other provided the costs of transformation are handled correctly. Each transformation may have quite different implications but from a modelling point of view can be treated in an analogous way. This implies that multiple time periods, multiple regions and multiple products can be treated in analogous fashion. However, a problem of asymmetric coefficients arises when there are cross-coefficients between the various quantities and prices and interactions between the shipment routes and the costs of transfer. Models must be able to handle this more general case. A second principle in the development of a general formulation of the spatial equilibrium set of models is that there must be consistency in the units of measurement in the objective function of such problems but in the constraint set only each constraint need be consistent in terms of units of measurement. Third, in representing an economic system in which intervention in that system is possible such intervention will not be just on price or quantity variables but is likely to involve intervention both in terms of quantities and prices and be on a per unit of quantity and an ad valorem basis. If this is not the case for one region it may well be the case across regions, time periods or product forms. This implies including both price and quantity variables as primal variables in general models. Fifth, a general spatial model should be able to incorporate different behavioural assumptions such as perfect competition and different degrees of competition. As well, the typical assumption of a perfectly elastic supply of transportation or transformation services needs to be relaxed so transformation costs can also be competitively determined or vary with the volume shipped. Sixth, in terms of the time dimension of the objective function a number of possibilities also exist. These include the static model, intertemporal models and optimal control type models. Seventh, the specification of routes should be general in that transshipment and backloading need to be possible. Eighth, limiting forms of the model should include perfectly inelastic supply, demand and transformation cost cases as well as perfectly elastic cases. Ninth, such models should be able to take into account the problems of investment required for production and the special characteristics of capital investment. This is a tall order, and in principle, it may not be useful to represent all these possibilities in one algebraic representation, however, the recent work on spatial equilibrium models captures many of these features (for example, Rowse, 1981; Harker, 1984; Takayama and Uri, 1983; various of the papers in Harker, 1985)

Central to the formulation of spatial equilibrium models is the well-known linear programming transportation cost minimization problem. This is written as follows:

Problem LPTCM: Find $\overline{X}$ that minimizes

$$Z_P = T'X \qquad (\text{for some } T \geq 0)$$
$$\text{subject to} \tag{1}$$

$$\begin{bmatrix} G_y \\ G_x \end{bmatrix} X \geq \begin{bmatrix} \tilde{y} \\ -\tilde{x} \end{bmatrix}, \tag{2}$$
$$X \geq 0,$$

where $\tilde{y}$, $\tilde{x}$ are vectors of given demand and supply quantities for each of n regions, X is a $(n^2 \times 1)$ vector of quantities shipped between each of the n regions and T is a $(n^2 \times 1)$ vector of transport costs for those shipments. The matrices G_y and G_x $(n \times n^2)$ provide that the quantities shipped must equal or exceed the given demand quantity and that the quantities shipped cannot exceed the available supply. The form of these matrices and vectors for n regions is as follows (note that n demand and n supply regions are specified but either may have a null specification for a given number of regions):

$$G_y = \begin{bmatrix} 1 & & & & 1 & & & & 1 & & \\ & 1 & & & & 1 & & & & 1 & \\ & & \ddots & & & & \ddots & & \cdots & & \ddots \\ & & & 1 & & & & 1 & & & & 1 \end{bmatrix},$$
$$(n \times n^2)$$

$$G_x = \begin{bmatrix} -1-1\dots-1 & & & \\ & -1-1\dots-1 & & \\ & & \ddots & \\ & & & -1-1\cdots-1 \end{bmatrix},$$

$$(n \times n^2)$$

$$y = \begin{bmatrix} y_1 \\ y_2 \\ \vdots \\ y_n \end{bmatrix}, \quad x = \begin{bmatrix} x_1 \\ x_2 \\ \vdots \\ x_n \end{bmatrix}, \quad X = \begin{bmatrix} x_{11} \\ x_{12} \\ \vdots \\ x_{nn} \end{bmatrix}.$$

$$(n \times 1) \qquad\qquad (n \times 1) \qquad\qquad (n^2 \times 1)$$

The dual of the problem LPTCM is as follows:

Problem DLPTCM: Find $(\bar{\rho}_y \bar{\rho}_x)$ that maximizes

$$Z_D = [\tilde{y}' \ -\tilde{x}'_x] \begin{bmatrix} \rho_y \\ \rho_x \end{bmatrix} \tag{3}$$

subject to

$$[G'_y \ G'_x] \begin{bmatrix} \rho_y \\ \rho_x \end{bmatrix} \leq T \quad \text{(for some } T \geq 0) \tag{4}$$

$$\rho_y, \rho_x \geq 0,$$

where ρ_y, ρ_x are the market prices of the good in the demand and supply regions and as before $\tilde{y}$ and $\tilde{x}$ are given quantities demanded and supplied in each of the regions. This model may be generalised in a number of ways. First, instead of fixed supply and demand quantities provided in each region it is possible to include linear and nonlinear supply and demand functions either as a function of price or as a function of quantity (the price and quantity formulations of Takayama and Judge, 1971). Second, transport costs may vary with the volume shipped so that unit transport costs are no longer constant. Third, losses and gains may be experienced in the shipment of goods so that the coefficients in the G_y and G_x matrices are no longer unitary and could, in fact, be allowed to vary with the volume shipped. Fourth, transhipment can be introduced to the model. Fifth, the arbitrage conditions specified in inequality (4) which imply that the difference between the supply and demand prices must be less than the transformation costs can be modified to account for exchange rates, ad valorem tariffs, subsidies and taxes.

Consider first a standard spatial equilibrium model and its generalisation to nonlinear functions. Takayama and Labys (1986), Takayama and MacAulay (1989) and MacAulay, Batterham and Fisher (1989) provide such formulations among others. This problem embeds the transportation problem LPTCM and its dual. It is assumed that the supply and demand functions and the transformation cost functions could be of a reasonably general form so as to still retain a convex programming problem over the relevant domain. Note that bounds might be used to ensure that this was so. Thus, the standard static generalised primal-dual model using a net social revenue objective function in the quantity domain, GM1, is as follows (development of this model from first principles is provided in Takayama and Judge, 1971, and Martin, 1981):

Problem GM1: Find $(\bar{y}'\bar{x}'\bar{X}'\bar{\rho}_y'\bar{\rho}_x') \geq 0'$ that maximizes

$$
Z_1 = (y'x'X'\rho_y'\rho_x') \left\{ \begin{bmatrix} f(y) \\ -g(x) \\ -T(X) \\ 0 \\ 0 \end{bmatrix} - \begin{bmatrix} 0 & 0 & 0 & I & 0 \\ 0 & 0 & 0 & 0 & -I \\ 0 & 0 & 0 & -G_y' & -G_x' \\ -I & 0 & G_y & 0 & 0 \\ 0 & I & G_x & 0 & 0 \end{bmatrix} \begin{bmatrix} y \\ x \\ X \\ \rho_y \\ \rho_x \end{bmatrix} \right\}
\tag{5}
$$

subject to

$$
\begin{bmatrix} -f(y) \\ g(x) \\ T(X) \\ 0 \\ 0 \end{bmatrix} + \begin{bmatrix} 0 & 0 & 0 & I & 0 \\ 0 & 0 & 0 & 0 & -I \\ 0 & 0 & 0 & -G_y' & -G_x' \\ -I & 0 & G_y & 0 & 0 \\ 0 & I & G_x & 0 & 0 \end{bmatrix} \begin{bmatrix} y \\ x \\ X \\ \rho_y \\ \rho_x \end{bmatrix} \geq \begin{bmatrix} 0 \\ 0 \\ 0 \\ 0 \\ 0 \end{bmatrix}
\tag{6}
$$

and $(y'x'X'\rho_y'\rho_x') \geq 0'$,

where $f(y)$ is a Marshallian (indirect) market demand function vector $(n \times 1)$, $g(x)$ a Marshallian market supply function vector $(n \times 1)$, and $T(X)$

is a transport cost function vector $(n^2 \times 1)$ and

$$\rho_y = \begin{bmatrix} \rho_1 \\ \rho_2 \\ \vdots \\ \rho_n \end{bmatrix} \geqq 0 \quad \text{and} \quad \rho_x = \begin{bmatrix} \rho^1 \\ \rho^2 \\ \vdots \\ \rho^n \end{bmatrix} \geqq 0$$

are non-negative demand and supply price vectors each $(n \times 1)$.

By inspection it is clear that (5) is the net social revenue, that is, total revenue $f(y)'y$ minus total production costs $g(x)'x$ minus total transport costs $T(X)'X$. The combined set of constraints (6) are a set of perfectly competitive spatial equilibrium market conditions. These imply that the supply and demand functions must be satisfied for non-negative prices and quantities and that a set of competitive spatial pricing rules be satisfied. Thus the problem provides for solutions which maximise the net profit of society as a whole (which can be thought of as monopolistic behaviour) but are subject to a set of competitive market rules on consumption, production and allocation which must be adhered to strictly. If these rules are changed the behavioural characteristics of the problem can be changed.

Let the Lagrangian function for GM1 be ϕ_1, so that the Kuhn-Tucker necessary conditions are as follows:

$$\frac{\partial \bar{\phi}_1}{\partial P} = \begin{bmatrix} f(\bar{y}) + \left(\dfrac{\partial f(\bar{y})}{\partial y}\right)' \bar{y} \\[2ex] -g(\bar{x}) - \left(\dfrac{\partial g(\bar{x})}{\partial x}\right)' \bar{x} \\[2ex] -T(\bar{X}) - \left(\dfrac{\partial T(\bar{X})}{\partial X}\right)' \bar{X} \\[1ex] 0 \\ 0 \end{bmatrix} + \begin{bmatrix} -\left(\dfrac{\partial f(\bar{y})}{\partial y}\right)' \bar{R}_y \\[2ex] \left(\dfrac{\partial g(\bar{x})}{\partial x}\right)' \bar{R}_x \\[2ex] \left(\dfrac{\partial T(\bar{X})}{\partial X}\right)' \bar{R}_X \\[1ex] 0 \\ 0 \end{bmatrix}$$

$$+ \begin{bmatrix} 0 & 0 & 0 & -I & 0 \\ 0 & 0 & 0 & 0 & I \\ 0 & 0 & 0 & G'_y & G'_x \\ I & 0 & -G_y & 0 & 0 \\ 0 & -I & -G_x & 0 & 0 \end{bmatrix} \begin{bmatrix} \bar{R}_y \\ \bar{R}_x \\ \bar{R}_X \\ \bar{S}_y \\ \bar{S}_x \end{bmatrix} \leqq \begin{bmatrix} 0 \\ 0 \\ 0 \\ 0 \\ 0 \end{bmatrix}, \qquad (7)$$

and $\left(\dfrac{\partial \bar{\phi}_1}{\partial P} \right) \bar{P} = 0$

$$
\frac{\partial \bar{\phi}_1}{\partial D} = \begin{bmatrix} -f(\bar{y}) \\ g(\bar{x}) \\ T(\bar{X}) \\ 0 \\ 0 \end{bmatrix} + \begin{bmatrix} 0 & 0 & 0 & I & 0 \\ 0 & 0 & 0 & 0 & -I \\ 0 & 0 & 0 & -G'_y & -G'_x \\ -I & 0 & G_y & 0 & 0 \\ 0 & I & G_x & 0 & 0 \end{bmatrix} \begin{bmatrix} \bar{y} \\ \bar{x} \\ \bar{X} \\ \bar{\rho}_y \\ \bar{\rho}_x \end{bmatrix} \geqq \begin{bmatrix} 0 \\ 0 \\ 0 \\ 0 \\ 0 \end{bmatrix} \qquad (8)
$$

and $\left(\dfrac{\partial \bar{\phi}_1}{\partial D} \right) \bar{D} = 0.$

By inspection it is clear that the primal solution P is equivalent to the dual solution vector D, thus:

$$
P = \begin{bmatrix} \bar{y} \\ \bar{x} \\ \bar{X} \\ \bar{\rho}_y \\ \bar{\rho}_x \end{bmatrix} = D = \begin{bmatrix} \bar{R}_y \\ \bar{R}_x \\ \bar{R}_X \\ \bar{S}_y \\ \bar{S}_x \end{bmatrix} \geqq 0, \qquad (9)
$$

which, if such a solution can be obtained, will satisfy equations (7) and (8) (and of course the non-negativity requirement in (9)) and are solutions for Problem GM1. The question of attainability of this solution has been discussed in Takayama and MacAulay (1989). Provided the problem has a non-empty feasibility set (6) a solution exists to problem GM1. If problem GM1 has a non-negative solution and provided $f(y)'y$, $-g(x)'x$ and $-T(X)'X$ are each strictly concave functions in the small neighbourhood of the solution then it will be unique.

If, as indicated, the primal solution is the same as the dual solution then (7) and (8) will be replicates of each other. As well, the value of the objective function Z_1 will be zero at the point of the optimal solution. Thus, under a spatially competitive system all the rents are bid away. The reason for these two peculiar properties of the solution rests on: i) the fact that the quadratic matrix in (5) is skew-symmetric; and, ii) that exactly the same (except for the opposite sign) expression appears in both the second term of equation (5) (the per unit demand and supply price vectors and transport cost vector) and the left-hand-side of inequality (6).

A small example problem of the type of GM1 is provided in Appendix A.

Takayama and Woodland (1970) were able to show the equivalence of the price and quantity formulations using the concept of purified duality for concave programming models. Takayama and Judge (1970) then showed the equivalence of the two formulations for the net social monetary gain model. The equivalent price form to GM1 can thus be stated as:

Problem GM2: Find $(\bar{p}'_y \bar{p}'_x)$ unconstrained and $(\bar{\rho}'_y \bar{\rho}'_x \bar{y}'_x \bar{x}'_x \overline{X}'_x) \geqq 0'$ that maximizes

$$Z_2 = (p'_y p'_x \rho'_y \rho'_x \ y'x'X')$$

$$\times \left\{ \begin{bmatrix} F(p_y) \\ -G(p_x) \\ 0 \\ 0 \\ 0 \\ 0 \\ -T(x) \end{bmatrix} + \begin{bmatrix} & & & & I & & \\ & & & & & -I & \\ & & & & -I & & G_y \\ & & & & I & & G_x \\ -I & & I & & & & \\ & I & & -I & & & \\ & & -G'_y & -G'_x & & & \end{bmatrix} \begin{bmatrix} p_y \\ p_x \\ \rho_y \\ \rho_x \\ y \\ x \\ X \end{bmatrix} \right\} \quad (10)$$

subject to

$$\begin{bmatrix} -F(p_y) \\ G(p_x) \\ 0 \\ 0 \\ 0 \\ 0 \\ T(X) \end{bmatrix} + \begin{bmatrix} & & & & I & & \\ & & & & & -I & \\ & & & & -I & & G_y \\ & & & & I & & G_x \\ -I & & I & & & & \\ & I & & -I & & & \\ & & -G'_y & -G'_x & & & \end{bmatrix} \begin{bmatrix} p_y \\ p_x \\ \rho_y \\ \rho_x \\ y \\ x \\ X \end{bmatrix} \geqq \begin{bmatrix} 0 \\ 0 \\ 0 \\ 0 \\ 0 \\ 0 \\ 0 \end{bmatrix}$$

$$(11)$$

and p_y, p_x unconstrained

and $(\rho'_y \rho'_x y'x'X') \geqq 0'$,

where $F(p_y)$ is a Walrasian market demand function vector, $G(p_x)$ a Walrasian market supply function vector.

Note that the price form of the general spatial equilibrium model may be derived from the quantity form by using a one-to-one correspondence between price and quantities and substituting appropriately into the quantity form wherever quantity occurs (Takayama and Judge, 1971). This form must be constructed in a slightly modified fashion so that the irregular cases are taken into account in which it is possible to have supply and demand functions satisfied at negative prices. These cases are accounted for by including a set of unconstrained prices and a second set constrained to be non-negative. Note also, that with such primal-dual models it is possible to mix in the one model both price dependent and quantity dependent functions.

In the following sections various general approaches to modification of the basic competitive models will be considered. These modifications can be broken into a number of reasonably broad classifications depending on how they impact on the structure of the basic competitive model.

Ad Valorem Effects

The case of ad valorem tariffs in spatial equilibrium models has been dealt with in detail by Takayama and Judge (1971). However, it is not widely recognised that exchange rates between regions can be handled in a similar fashion. In this section a reasonably general approach to ad valorem tariffs and exchange rates will be outlined. In the early literature on spatial equilibrium models there was some debate about the way in which to include exchange rates in a spatial equilibrium system (Bjarnason, McGarry and Schmitz, 1969, and Elliot, 1972). None of these authors took advantage of the primal dual specification of the spatial model as a means of including the effects of exchange rates on trade flows (MacAulay, 1978). Essentially, in a partial equilibrium model exchange rates can be viewed as imposing an additional cost of currency exchange as goods are transferred from one country to another. This cost is in proportion to either the demand or supply price of the good. It is also a useful convenience to maintain the prices of the model in terms of the currencies of the individual countries so that the supply and demand functions remain in terms of their own currencies. Thus, using the notation of Takayama and Judge (1971), it is possible to write the arbitrage or competitive spatial pricing condition (assuming the exchange cost is based on the supply price, ρ^1, and ρ_2 is the demand price, t_{12} is the cost of transferring goods from region 1 to region 2 in currency 2 and ϵ_{12} is the exchange rate to convert currency 1 to currency 2) as:

$$\rho_2 - \rho^1 \leqq \epsilon_{12} t_{12} - (1 - \epsilon_{12})\rho^1 \quad \text{(in region 2's currency)}. \tag{12}$$

This condition can be rearranged as:

$$(1/\epsilon_{12})\rho_2 - \rho^1 \leqq t_{12}.$$ (13)

Alternatively, if the currency conversion is based on the demand price and the transport cost is in terms of currency 1 then the relationship also becomes:

$$(1/\epsilon_{12})\rho_2 - \rho^1 \leqq t_{12}.$$ (14)

In a completely analogous way tariffs can be treated as either imposed on the supply price plus transport cost or on the demand price so that ϵ_{12} can be replaced by, τ_{12}, the ad valorem tariff rate.

In terms of the objective function of the model there is a difference of treatment between tariffs and exchange rates. In the case of exchange rates and a model with prices in the currency of the country concerned the objective function must be converted to a standard currency while the ad valorem tariff only impacts on the cost of transfer of goods between regions.

Let all the costs of transport be measured in the currency of region 1 so that the set of arbitrage conditions can be written in matrix terms as:

$$[G'_y \ G'_x] R_\epsilon \begin{bmatrix} \rho_y \\ \rho_x \end{bmatrix} \leqq T$$ (15)

where R_ϵ is a $(2n \times 2n)$ matrix of exchange rate conversion factors which for a three-country case would be in the form:

$$R_\epsilon = \begin{bmatrix} 1 & & & & & \\ & 1/\epsilon_{21} & & & & \\ & & 1/\epsilon_{31} & & & \\ & & & 1 & & \\ & & & & 1/\epsilon_{21} & \\ & & & & & 1/\epsilon_{31} \end{bmatrix}.$$

In a similar way, a converter matrix such as R_ϵ can be constructed which permits specification of the tariff to be charged on the demand price (or the supply price). If different tariff rates are specified for different trade flows the specification would be:

$$[R_\tau G'_y \ G'_x] \begin{bmatrix} \rho_y \\ \rho_x \end{bmatrix} \leqq T$$ (16)

where R_τ is now an $(n^2 \times n^2)$ converter matrix. If ψ_{ij} is $1/(1 + \tau_{ij})$, where τ_{ij} is the tariff rate on the trade flow from region i to j, then in a three-region case R_τ has the form:

$$
R_\tau = \begin{bmatrix}
1 & & & & & & & & \\
 & \psi_{12} & & & & & & & \\
 & & \psi_{13} & & & & & & \\
 & & & \psi_{21} & & & & & \\
 & & & & 1 & & & & \\
 & & & & & \psi_{23} & & & \\
 & & & & & & \psi_{31} & & \\
 & & & & & & & \psi_{32} & \\
 & & & & & & & & 1
\end{bmatrix}.
$$

The objective function must be modified to take into account both types of converter matrix. This is illustrated using the quantity formulation of problem GM1 for tariffs and exchange rates:

Problem GM3: Find $(\bar{y}'\bar{x}'\bar{X}'\bar{\rho}_y'\bar{\rho}_x') \geq 0'$ that maximizes

$$
Z_1 = (y'x'X'\rho_y'\rho_x') \left\{ \begin{bmatrix} f(y) \\ -g(x) \\ -T(X) \\ 0 \\ 0 \end{bmatrix} - \begin{bmatrix} 0 & 0 & 0 & I & 0 \\ 0 & 0 & 0 & 0 & -I \\ 0 & 0 & 0 & [-R_\tau G_y' - G_x']R_\epsilon & 0 \\ -I & 0 & G_y & 0 & 0 \\ 0 & I & G_x & 0 & 0 \end{bmatrix} \begin{bmatrix} y \\ x \\ X \\ \rho_y \\ \rho_x \end{bmatrix} \right\} \tag{17}
$$

subject to

$$
\begin{bmatrix} -f(y) \\ g(x) \\ T(X) \\ 0 \\ 0 \end{bmatrix} + \begin{bmatrix} 0 & 0 & 0 & I & 0 \\ 0 & 0 & 0 & 0 & -I \\ 0 & 0 & 0 & [-R_\tau G_y' - G_x']R_\epsilon & 0 \\ -I & 0 & G_y & 0 & 0 \\ 0 & I & G_x & 0 & 0 \end{bmatrix} \begin{bmatrix} y \\ x \\ X \\ \rho_y \\ \rho_x \end{bmatrix} \geq \begin{bmatrix} 0 \\ 0 \\ 0 \\ 0 \\ 0 \end{bmatrix} \tag{18}
$$

and $(y'x'X'\rho_y'\rho_x') \geq 0'$.

Policy Intervention Functions

Governments intervene in market systems in numerous ways. When modelling trading systems, inclusion of such intervention mechanisms can be very important in obtaining realistic solutions from spatial equilibrium models. Greenberg and Murphy (1985) provide a unified framework for government price regulations in the context of a network transportation problem. To do this they classify interventions into taxes/rebates, average cost pricing and producer price floors and ceilings and apply a Gauss-Seidel solution strategy. For the general spatial equilibrium model specified in this chapter it is possible to incorporate a number of policy intervention mechanisms by modification of the transformation cost function in appropriate ways. These ways include:

(a) Fixed per unit taxes or subsidies on specific flows, including flows from production in a region to meet that region's consumption. For example, for a subsidy s_{ij} or tax a_{ij} on the flow, x_{12}, from region 1 to region 2:

$$\rho_2 - \rho^1 \leqq T(x_{12}) - s_{12} + a_{12}, \tag{19}$$

or from region's 1 supply to meet region's 1 demand:

$$\rho_1 - \rho^1 \leqq -s_{11} + a_{11}. \tag{20}$$

Taxes based on unit values are treated in a manner analogous to ad valorem tariffs. An extension of the imposition of fixed per unit taxes and subsidies is to allow the tax rate to change as the volume transported changes or the value of the quantities transported change. This will introduce a nonlinearity into the arbitrage conditions.

(b) Price ceilings and floors or physical upper and lower quota limits can easily be taken into account by placing additional inequality restrictions on the price or quantity columns (the specification of quotas has been considered by Takayama and Judge (1971)). In the primal-dual formulation allowance must be made for the fact that a quota must have the possibility of a shadow value in the price columns while a price ceiling or floor must have the possibility of an equivalent physical quota.

(c) Average cost pricing can be included in such models as follows:

$$\rho_1 - \rho^1 \leqq T(x_{12}) - \rho^1 + C(x_1) \tag{21}$$

where $C(x_1)$ is the average cost function imposed by regulation and x_1 is the supply quantity for region 1. For a solution to exist this function must be convex and monotonic (Greenberg and Murphy, 1985).

Alternative Behavioural Assumptions

A variety of different formulations have been developed to account for non-competitive market behaviour. Takayama and Judge (1971) developed models for a spatial monopoly, a precautionary monopolist and a benevolent monopolist. Maruyama and Fuller (1965) developed the notion of varying degrees of competition ranging from perfect competition to spatial monopoly by varying a parameter in the objective function of their problem while various papers in Harker (1985), especially Hashimoto (1985), and Kolstad and Burris (1986) represent early efforts at modelling oligopolistic markets in space. In a general way, the behavioural assumptions may be varied from competitive, to oligopolistic behaviour through to monopoly by varying parameters in a general specification. In this section, this approach will be developed. However, not all of the non-competitive models can be represented in this way.

Takayama and Judge (1971) proposed three monopoly models. The first was a full spatial monopoly in which the monopolist or a central authority completely controls output over all regions and there is no resale between regions nor is there monopsony in the factor markets. This model is the equivalent of the discriminating monopolist but operating in a market with space. The second case is referred to as the precautionary monopolist in which the monopolist faces arbitragers in the selling market and resale between regions is possible. The third case is of a central authority or monopolist who prices so that marginal cost is equal to price. This case is referred to as the benevolent monopolist.

Consider the case of n regions trading a homogeneous product in which the outputs for each of the regions is completely controlled by a firm or a central authority. The monopolist has plants producing in each of the n regions and purchases inputs in competitive markets and so is not at the same time a monopsonist. The transport sector can be viewed as playing a passive role and is assumed not to be under the monopolist's control. Further, there is no possibility of resale of the product between the regions. This problem has been solved by Takayama and Judge (1971) and Hashimoto (1985) for the linear demand and linear average cost function case and for more general functions by Harker (1986) who also considers the case of the monopolist controlling the transport sector as well as production.

Let the monopolist maximise profit over the set of regions (or equivalently over producing sites) then the mathematical programming problem becomes one of maximise net revenue subject to the conditions that marginal revenues be equated across regions after allowance for marginal transport costs and that marginal costs be equated across regions after allowance for marginal transport costs. This differs from the perfectly competitive model in that marginal revenues and costs replace average revenues and costs. A general monopoly problem, based on a generalisation of the primal-dual formulation of Takayama and Judge (1971, p. 213 where in their case $k_1 = 1$, $k_2 = 1$, and $k_3 = 0$), may be stated as in Problem GM4.

Problem GM4: Find $(\bar{y}'\bar{x}'\bar{X}'\bar{\rho}_x'\bar{\rho}_y' \geqq 0'$ that maximizes

$$
Z_1 = \begin{bmatrix} y \\ x \\ X \\ \rho_y \\ \rho_x \end{bmatrix}' \left\{ \begin{bmatrix} f(y) + k_1\left(\dfrac{\partial f(y)}{\partial y}\right)' y \\[2mm] -g(x) - k_2\left(\dfrac{\partial g(x)}{\partial x}\right)' x \\[2mm] -T(X) - k_3\left(\dfrac{\partial T(X)}{\partial X}\right)' X \\[2mm] 0 \\ 0 \end{bmatrix} \right.
$$

$$
\left. - \begin{bmatrix} 0 & 0 & 0 & I & 0 \\ 0 & 0 & 0 & 0 & -I \\ 0 & 0 & 0 & -G_y' & -G_x' \\ -I & 0 & G_y & 0 & 0 \\ 0 & I & G_x & 0 & 0 \end{bmatrix} \begin{bmatrix} y \\ x \\ X \\ \rho_y \\ \rho_x \end{bmatrix} \right\} \tag{22}
$$

subject to

$$
\begin{bmatrix} -f(y) - k_1\left(\dfrac{\partial f(y)}{\partial y}\right)' y \\[2mm] g(x) + k_2\left(\dfrac{\partial g(x)}{\partial x}\right)' x \\[2mm] T(X) + k_3\left(\dfrac{\partial T(X)}{\partial X}\right)' X \\[2mm] 0 \\ 0 \end{bmatrix} + \begin{bmatrix} 0 & 0 & 0 & I & 0 \\ 0 & 0 & 0 & 0 & -I \\ 0 & 0 & 0 & -G_y' & -G_x' \\ -I & 0 & G_y & 0 & 0 \\ 0 & I & G_x & 0 & 0 \end{bmatrix} \begin{bmatrix} y \\ x \\ X \\ \rho_y \\ \rho_x \end{bmatrix} \geqq \begin{bmatrix} 0 \\ 0 \\ 0 \\ 0 \\ 0 \end{bmatrix} \tag{23}
$$

and $(y'x'X'\rho_y'\rho_x') \geqq 0'$,

where $f(y)$ is a demand or average revenue function vector $(n \times 1)$, $g(x)$ is the monopolist's average cost function vector $(n \times 1)$, and $T(X)$ is an average transport cost function vector $(n^2 \times 1)$ and

$$
\rho_y = \begin{bmatrix} \rho_1 \\ \rho_2 \\ \vdots \\ \rho_n \end{bmatrix} \geq 0 \quad \text{and} \quad \rho_x = \begin{bmatrix} \rho^1 \\ \rho^2 \\ \vdots \\ \rho^n \end{bmatrix} \geq 0
$$

are non-negative marginal return and marginal cost vectors each $(n \times 1)$.

The values for k_i in inequality (23) may be varied so as to specify various types of monopoly problem. For example, $k_1 = 1$, $k_2 = 1$ and $k_3 = 0$ implies transport costs are assumed to be given and outside the control of the monopolist although they may vary with the volumes shipped between locations (see Appendix A for a sample solution of this problem). Further, if all k_i are zero then the problem collapses to the standard competitive spatial equilibrium and if all k_i are 1.0 then the problem is a full monopoly problem in which the monopolist has control over product and transport decisions. The case of the benevolent monopolist would be with $k_1 = 0$, $k_2 = 1$ and $k_3 = 0$ and the case of colluding firms acting as a monopolist but adjusting their supply according to the rule that industry marginal revenue equals individual marginal cost then $k_1 = 1$, $k_2 = 0$ and $k_3 = 0$. As Maruyama and Fuller (1965) suggest, the value of the k_i may vary from zero to 1.0 (in the case of linear functions the value on the slope coefficients would vary from 1.0 to 2.0) to give different degrees of monopoly power.

The objective function in problem GM3 is not specified as the monopolist's profit but is a primal dual objective appropriate to the form of the monopoly problem. However, an alternative objective function could be specified in terms of the monopolist's profit subject to a set of flow constraints. The solution to such a problem would have the monopolist's profit as the value of the objective function and give the same solution as GM4 with all $k_i = 1$ (this implies monopoly control over the transport sector as well when the average and marginal cost functions for transport services differ from each other). Problem GM4 will have a zero value for the objective function in all cases since it is a primal dual formulation (primal problem minus the dual problem which at the optimum must have a zero value). This alternative may be useful in the development and checking of formulations.

A further extension of this model can be made to incorporate oligopolistic behaviour (as examples, various forms of the spatial oligopoly model have been developed by Salant, 1982, Hashimoto, 1985, Kolstad and Burris, 1986, and Harker, 1986 among others). The Cournot-Nash equilibrium represents a set of solutions between the two extremes of the competitive solution and the monopoly solution in which there are a few firms operating in spatially separated markets. Further, it is assumed that each firm has a knowledge of the demand behaviour in each region and is neither a monopsonist nor controls the transportation network but takes the price of transportation services as given so that the average price of transportation services is used, as in the case of GM3, rather than the marginal values. Finally, the firms behave in a Cournot-Nash way since each firm takes into account the other firm's decisions on production when deciding its own strategy. This implies that other firm's production decisions are treated as given. The impact of this on the structure of the programming model is that the marginal conditions for each individual oligopolist must be satisfied. These marginal conditions are obtained by differentiating with respect to the profit functions of the individual oligopolists.

For the single oligopolist (region/market) exercising some market power the problem is to maximise profits while recognising as given the production decisions made in other markets. Thus

$$\text{Maximise} \quad \pi_i = f(G_y X)' X_{i \cdot} - \int g(x_i) \, \mathrm{d}x_i - T'_{i \cdot} X_{i \cdot} \tag{24}$$

$$\text{Subject to} \quad x_i \geqq G_{y_i} X$$
$$x_i \geqq 0 \quad \text{and} \quad X \geqq 0 \tag{25}$$

where i refers to the i-th region and $i \cdot$ to a partitioning of the X shipment vector according to the supply quantities from region i to all other regions (in the three-region case x_{11}, x_{12}, x_{13}). The set of price dependent demand functions is represented by $f(GX)$ where for region i the price is dependent on all the quantities shipped into region i (for region 1 in the three-region case x_{11}, x_{21}, x_{31}) while the revenue for region i is made up of the exports from region i times the price in the importing region (for region 1 in the three-region case $\rho_1 x_{11} + \rho_2 x_{12} + \rho_3 x_{13}$). The cost of producing and shipping the goods is represented by the last two terms in the objective function (24).

The Lagrangian function for this problem is:

$$L_i = f(G_y X)' X_{i \cdot} - \int g(x_i) \, \mathrm{d}x_i - T'_{i \cdot} X_{i \cdot} + \phi_i (x_i - G_{y_i} X) \tag{26}$$

The Kuhn-Tucker conditions which hold at the maximum profit become:

$$\partial L_i/\partial X_{i\cdot} = f(G_y X) + (\partial f/\partial X_{i\cdot})' X_{i\cdot} - T_{i\cdot} - \phi_i \leqq 0 \quad \text{and}$$
$$(\partial L_i/\partial X_{i\cdot})' X_{i\cdot} = 0, \tag{27}$$

$$\partial L_i/\partial x_i = -g(x_i) + \phi_i \leqq 0 \quad \text{and} \quad (\partial L_i/x_i)' x_i = 0, \tag{28}$$

$$\text{and} \quad X_{i\cdot}, x_i, \phi_i \geqq 0. \tag{29}$$

The Lagrangian multiplier ϕ_i in this instance represents the equilibrium marginal cost of production.

Condition (27) is of major interest and can be interpreted as indicating that the demand price plus the margin $(\partial f/X_{i\cdot})'X_{i\cdot}$ less the marginal cost of production must be less than the transfer cost or equal to it as long as trade takes places between the regions involved.

From these conditions the term $(\partial f/X_{i\cdot})'X_{i\cdot}$ differs from that of the standard competitive firm as shown by Hashimoto (1985) who refers to it as the oligopolist's margin. This margin is in proportion to the volume shipped. Thus, in the overall model the price and marginal cost differentials between the regions must take into account this margin (a solution to a sample problem is given in Appendix A). Taking into account the margin the new problem becomes:

Problem GM5: Find $(\bar{y}'\bar{x}'\bar{X}'\bar{\rho}'_y,\bar{\rho}'_x) \geqq 0'$ that maximizes

$$Z_1 = (y'x'X'\rho'_y\rho'_x)\left\{\begin{bmatrix} \begin{bmatrix} f(y) \\ -g(x) \\ -T(X) - k_3\left(\dfrac{\partial f(X_{i\cdot})}{\partial X_{i\cdot}}\right)' X \\ 0 \\ 0 \end{bmatrix} \right.$$

$$\left. - \begin{bmatrix} 0 & 0 & 0 & I & 0 \\ 0 & 0 & 0 & 0 & -I \\ 0 & 0 & 0 & -G'_y & -G'_x \\ -I & 0 & G_y & 0 & 0 \\ 0 & I & G_x & 0 & 0 \end{bmatrix}\begin{bmatrix} y \\ x \\ X \\ \rho_y \\ \rho_x \end{bmatrix}\right\} \tag{30}$$

subject to

$$
\left[\begin{array}{c} -f(y) \\ g(x) \\ T(X)+k_3\left(\dfrac{\partial f(X_i.)}{\partial X_i.}\right)' X \\ 0 \\ 0 \end{array}\right] + \left[\begin{array}{ccccc} 0 & 0 & 0 & I & 0 \\ 0 & 0 & 0 & 0 & -I \\ 0 & 0 & 0 & -G_y' & -G_x' \\ -I & 0 & G_y & 0 & 0 \\ 0 & I & G_x & 0 & 0 \end{array}\right]\left[\begin{array}{c} y \\ x \\ X \\ \rho_y \\ \rho_x \end{array}\right] \geqq \left[\begin{array}{c} 0 \\ 0 \\ 0 \\ 0 \\ 0 \end{array}\right] \qquad (31)
$$

and $\left(y'x'X'\rho_y'\rho_x' \right) \geqq 0'$,

where $f(y)$ is a demand or average revenue function vector $(n \times 1)$, $g(x)$ is the oligopolist's marginal cost function vector $(n \times 1)$, and $T(X)$ is an average transport cost function vector $(n^2 \times 1)$ and

$$
\rho_y = \left[\begin{array}{c} \rho_1 \\ \rho_2 \\ \vdots \\ \rho_n \end{array}\right] \geqq 0 \quad \text{and} \quad \rho_x = \left[\begin{array}{c} \rho^1 \\ \rho^2 \\ \vdots \\ \rho^n \end{array}\right] \geqq 0
$$

are non-negative price and marginal cost vectors each of dimension $(n \times 1)$. The value of the i-jth element of the vector k_3 can be written as $(1 + r_{ij})$ where, as Kolstad and Burris (1986) suggest, r_{ij} can be interpreted as an aggregate conjectural variation which represents oligopolist i's perception of how sales of all competitors combined to consumer j change with x_{ij}. If r_{ij} is zero a Cournot-Nash equilibrium is attained while if r_{ij} is -1 a Bertrand type equilibrium is attained in which price in region i is equated to marginal cost in region i (assuming transfer costs within a region are zero). It is worth noting, also, that Dafermos and Nagurney (1987) have been able to show that a reasonably general Cournot-Nash oligopoly model with spatially separated markets converges to a general spatial equilibrium model as the number of firms increases to a large number.

In a manner analogous to that for a spatial oligopoly with conjectural variations Kolstad and Burris (1986) have indicated how an oligopsony problem may be structured in a similar way to that of the oligopoly problem. In this case the oligopsonist's margin is derived by considering the marginal cost function rather than the demand function.

Recursive and Intertemporal Systems

Two broad approaches have been taken to the consideration of time in spatial equilibrium systems. The first, outlined in some detail by Takayama and Judge (1971) and illustrated by Guise and Aggrey-Mensah (1973) is of optimization over a given time horizon with the incorporation of explicit stock holding behaviour. The second is the use of recursive decision systems such as that outlined by Day (1973) and illustrated in the case of spatial equilibrium models by Martin and Zwart (1975), Pieri, Meilke and MacAulay (1977), Haack, Martin and MacAulay (1978), MacAulay (1978), Saepung (1986) and Richardson (1989). A combination of these two approaches would seem to be possible in which a rolling planning horizon is used so that the model could be designed to include various types of learning behaviour and various degrees of myopia in the planning processes included.

The recursive form of the spatial equilibrium model is solved very much in the style of a dynamic econometric model where the programming algorithm replaces the econometric simulation algorithm. This form of the problem may be written in a compact way as:

Problem GM6: Find $(\overline{w}_t') \geq 0'$ for each t that maximizes

$$Z_t = w_t' Q(w_t) w_t \tag{32}$$

subject to

$$Q(w_t) w_t \leq 0, \tag{33}$$

$$\text{and} \quad w_t \geq 0 \tag{34}$$

$$Q(w_t) = f(\overline{w}_{t-i-1}, V_{t-i}) \tag{35}$$

such that $i = 0, 1, \ldots, k$ where k is the length of lag, w_t is the set of solution variables $(y'x'X'\rho_y'\rho_x')$ for period t, $\overline{w}_{t-i-1}$ is the set of solution values obtained from previous solutions of the problem contained in equations (32) to (34) or supplied as a set of starting values, $Q(w_t)$ is the quadratic matrix of coefficients and functions as specified in the braces in equation (5) in problem GM1 (or the various other problems specified in this chapter) and V_{t-i} is a set of variables exogenous to the problem which may be current or lagged. Equation (35) is what Day and Kennedy (1970) refer to as the feedback operator and it specifies the way in which the coefficients and functions in $Q(w_t)$ are updated in each time period. Day and Kennedy (1970) refer to the problem in equations (32) to (34) as the decision operator which is solved for each time period or rolling blocks of time periods in a rolling horizon problem.

As with dynamic econometric models such recursive spatial equilibrium systems are subject to the problems of dynamic instability. Analysis of this problem is, however, more complex since such models are multi-phase in character. This means that for any given time period the model may be subject to a different set of binding constraints or first-order conditions. As well, it is possible that at any stage of the recursive simulation the model solutions may become infeasible, unbounded or involve multiple solutions.

Storage costs and discount rates become important issues in models involving time. One approach to the issue of storage in a spatial equilibrium model with a single-period horizon is to estimate demand for storage functions which are a function of the price in the particular region (Martin and Zwart, 1975; Hack, Martin and MacAulay, 1978; and MacAulay, 1978). For each region which has stocks an additional 'storage region' is defined which only has flows from supply in its associated region into closing stocks, or flows from stocks to meet the consumption in the associated demand region. The opening stock level from the previous period is used as a perfectly inelastic supply of stocks and the demand for closing stocks permits the calculation of the closing stock level. This approach has the advantage of endogenously determining the closing stock levels at the end of the simulation period using a behaviourally specified equation. It has the disadvantage of being completely myopic with respect to future periods.

In models optimizing over multiple periods in which the carrying charges are treated analogously to the transport costs the objective function must be discounted so as to be in appropriate units and the intertemporal price conditions must also be specified in comparable terms. These conditions will require that if there is a non zero quantity flow from period t to period $t + 1$ then the price difference between the two periods, discounted to period t, must be equal to the discounted storage cost (Takayama and Judge, 1971).

Investment Models

The issue of investment and its spatial consequences is complicated and still an active area of research. There are many aspects of investment which may be relevant in a spatial context. For example, if the issue is one of capital budgeting then a zero-one type method would need to be used, whereas, if investment could be considered as additions to a capital stock then a continuous variable approach might be used. Thus, investment may need to be treated in large blocks requiring integer variables or it may be viewed as continuous if there are many relatively small investments to be made.

Baker (1973) following the definition of Bierman and Smidt (1971) defined investment as a '...commitment of resources to produce returns over a "reasonably long period" of time.' Investments are therefore production activities that involve a number of time periods. Thus, it is possible to adapt the form of the multi-period spatial model to accommodate investment and depreciation of the capital stock. Investment can be viewed as using some of the output of a region to generate output in future periods.

Potential approaches to investment models are: multi-period spatial trading systems including production activities linked to investment which are an adapted form of the multi-period model discussed above and are specially suited to the linear complementarity solution algorithm because of asymmetric coefficients in the quadratic matrix (Takayama and Uri, 1983); recursive systems with investment decision rules (see Abe, 1973, for a non-spatial example); capital budgeting systems with zero-one variables; and plant location models linked to spatial trading systems (Polito, 1977; and Tobin and Friesz, 1985). In the multi-period investment model of Takayama and Uri production from a plant is specified as being restricted to be less than or equal to the depreciated initial capacity plus depreciated additional investment in that capacity through time. Most work appears to have been done on the warehouse location problem linked to spatial equilibrium systems. To solve these problems heuristic algorithms have been proposed (Roe and Shane, 1973; Polito, 1977; and Tobin and Friesz, 1985). With the development of general nonlinear programming software with integer capabilities such problems should become much more easily solved.

Other Extensions

Extensions of the formulation to take on a more general equilibrium character, yet still retain the essence of the endogenous determination of the direction of trade flows and the intermediate no trade situation, would seem to be possible. Yaron (1967) included income effects into a programming model by assuming that demand is determined by the income generated by the model in the previous period along with current prices. This problem was then solved by iterative solution. In practical terms, when policy changes are likely to impact on regional incomes and, as a result, endogenously shift the local demand function, the method suggested by Yaron provides a practical solution and turns out to be a form of recursive programming. However, examples of the inclusion of income as a current endogenous variable in the system would seem to have not yet been developed.

Other extensions to the general form of spatial equilibrium model which have been developed include the introduction of policy mechanisms such as variable import levies as used by the European community for agricultural commodities (Sampson and Snape, 1980; Crabtree, 1983; and Richardson, 1989), inclusion of the notions of user-cost in models of resource development and trade (Rowse and Copithorne, 1982), inclusion of network congestion which influences the transfer cost functions (Harker, 1983), and inclusion of endogenous policy processes (for a review of endogenous policy processes see Rausser, Lichtenberg and Lattimore, 1982). More speculative is the integration of the flow of real goods with monetary flows following the work of Moore and Nagurney (1989) and inclusion of risk effects involved in prices and the uncertainty about supply and demand response functions (Jabara and Thompson, 1980). Work on the interpretation of solutions has been assisted with the development of sensitivity analysis techniques for spatial equilibrium problems and the more general variational inequality systems (Silberberg, 1970; Dafermos and Nagurney, 1984; and Dafermos, 1988).

Concluding Comment

The central gain made by the use of spatial equilibrium models is the ability to solve problems in which the switching of the direction of trade flows occurs as the economic environment (specified in terms of the parameters of the model) changes. As is apparent, the capability to handle such switching and the intermediate no-trade position complicates the mathematics of the formulations and their solutions. Once the basic mathematics of the spatial equilibrium problem had been solved the more recent work has involved extending the the basic formulation to cover numerous real world adaptations which have been necessary to apply the basic model.

The range of possible applications of the spatial equilibrium model and its generalisations is extensive. In this chapter, various specifications have been presented which are designed to be general in character and thus facilitate the use of the various forms of the spatial equilibrium model in applied work. It is clear, that the primal-dual net revenue formulation is general in character and can accommodate many different policy interventions. When combined with recursive and rolling horizon formulations that can have policy interventions injected at various points in time these models provide a rich base for policy analysis. In using such models they should not be seen as competitive to econometric forms but as appropriate methods for the solution and simulation of spatial models which in many instances may include econometrically estimated relationships (for an example see Lee and Seaver, 1971). Spatial equilibrium models provide a solid theoretical base with which to deal with the issues imposed by the nature of spatial economic systems and when appropriately formulated with econometrically estimated response functions can have excellent simulation properties.

Appendix A

In this appendix, solutions for a sample problem based on the Problem GM1 are presented using MINOS as the solution algorithm (Murtagh and Saunders, 1986).

Example GM1 (exponential supply and demand functions, quadratic average per unit transport costs)

For this sample problem, constant elasticity demand and supply functions were combined with quadratic average per unit transport costs. The demand and supply functions used were:

$$\rho_1 = 120 y_1^{-0.7} \qquad \rho_2 = 100 y_2^{-0.5} \qquad \rho_3 = 110 y_3^{-0.6}$$
$$\rho^1 = 6.01425 x_1^{0.6} \qquad \rho^2 = 10.91089 x_2^{0.5} \qquad \rho^3 = 2.6608 x_3^{0.7}.$$

The supply functions were derived so that for a given set of demand quantities (y_i) a specific and known set of supply quantities (x_i) would result. More digits than those shown were used in the model so as to obtain an objective value as close to zero as possible.

For the transport costs a quadratic cost function was assumed to apply to the trade flows between each of the regions as follows:

$$t_{ij} = \mu_{ij} - 0.07 x_{ij} + 0.0014 x_{ij}^2,$$

where t_{ij} is the transport cost from region i to region j and x_{ij} is the shipment of the good concerned between the two regions i an j and m_{ij} is a constant which has the values as indicated in the right-hand-side of Table A.1. The tableau for the problem is provided in Table A.1.

Table A.1

Tableau for Sample Problems GM1 and GM5 (Perfectly Competitive and Oligopoly Models)

Minimize	Y1	Y2	Y3	X1	X2	X3	X11	X12	X13	X21	X22	X23	X31	X32	X33	DP1	DP2	DP3	SP1	SP2	SP3	RHS
Y1	-f(y1)																					
Y2		-f(y2)																				
Y3			-f(y3)																			
X1				g(x1)																		
X2					g(x2)																	
X3						g(x3)																
X11							0*															
X12								T(X12)*														
X13									T(X13)*													
X21										T(X21)*												
X22											0*											
X23												T(X23)*										
X31													T(X31)*									
X32														T(X32)*								
X33															0*							
OBJ								8	9	8		7.93854	9	7.93854								
RY1	1						-1	-1	-1													≤ 0
RY2		1								-1	-1	-1										≤ 0
RY3			1										-1	-1	-1							≤ 0
RX1				-1			1	1	1													≤ 0
RX2					-1					1	1	1										≤ 0
RX3						-1							1	1	1							≤ 0
RX11							0*									1			-1			≤ 0
RX12								-T(X12)*									1		-1			≤ 8
RX13									-T(X13)*									1	-1			≤ 9
RX21										-T(X21)*						1				-1		≤ 8
RX22											0*						1			-1		≤ 0
RX23												-T(X23)*						1		-1		≤ 7.93854
RX31													-T(X31)*1			1					-1	≤ 9
RX32														-T(X32)*1			1				-1	≤ 7.93854
RX33															0*			1			-1	≤ 0
RDP1	f(y1)															-1						≤ 0
RDP2		f(y2)															-1					≤ 0
RDP3			f(y3)															-1				≤ 0
RSP1				-g(x1)															1			≤ 0
RSP2					-g(x2)															1		≤ 0
RSP3						-g(x3)															1	≤ 0

Note: $f(y_i)$ and $g(x_i)$ represent the indirect demand and supply functions and $T(X_{ij}) = -0.07X_{ij} + 0.0014X_{ij}^2$ where i, $j = 1, 2, 3$ and $i \neq j$. Row names are identified with an R. The activity names DPi refer to demand prices, SPj to supply prices and Xij indicates a trade flow from region i to region j. Yi and Xi are the demand and supply quantities. The top part of the tableau is the nonlinear part of the objective function and OBJ refers to the linear objective terms. The asterisk indicates the term is modified for the oligopoly solution (see text).

The numerical solution values obtained were:

$$x_{11} = 10.0 \quad x_{12} = 0.0 \quad x_{13} = 0.0$$
$$x_{21} = 0.0 \quad x_{22} = 7.14093 \quad x_{23} = 0.0$$
$$x_{31} = 0.0 \quad x_{32} = 4.62226 \quad x_{33} = 15.17731$$

$$\rho_1 = 23.94315 \quad \rho_2 = 29.15665 \quad \rho_3 = 21.51175$$
$$\rho^1 = 23.94315 \quad \rho^2 = 28.15665 \quad \rho^3 = 21.51175$$

$$y_1 = 10.0 \quad y_2 = 11.76318 \quad y_3 = 15.17731$$
$$x_1 = 10.0 \quad x_2 = 7.14093 \quad x_3 = 19.79956$$

The objective function value for this problem was close to zero at -1.45×10^{-10}. To solve the above problem a set of arbitrary lower bounds of 1.0 were provided for the demand and supply quantities.

Example GM4 (exponential average cost and revenue functions, quadratic average per unit transport costs, with monopoly control over output and no resale among regions)

For this problem the supply and demand functions of Example GM1 will be used as the average revenue and cost functions along with the same quadratic transport cost function. The k_i values for problem GM4 were set at $k_1 = 1$, $k_2 = 1$ and $k_3 = 0$. The tableau for the problem is given in Table A.2.

The numerical solution values obtained were:

$$x_{11} = 2.75912 \quad x_{12} = 0.0 \quad x_{13} = 0.0$$
$$x_{21} = 0.0 \quad x_{22} = 2.30095 \quad x_{23} = 0.0$$
$$x_{31} = 0.0 \quad x_{32} = 1.75536 \quad x_{33} = 7.81998$$

$$MR_1 = \rho_1 = 17.6914 \quad MR_2 = \rho_2 = 24.8259 \quad MR_3 = \rho_3 = 17.0059$$
$$MC^1 = \rho^1 = 17.6914 \quad MC^2 = \rho^1 = 24.8259 \quad MC^3 = \rho^1 = 17.0059$$

$$y_1 = 2.75912 \quad y_2 = 4.05630 \quad y_3 = 4.87627$$
$$x_1 = 2.75912 \quad x_2 = 2.30095 \quad x_3 = 6.63163$$

The objective function value for this problem was close to zero at 3.85×10^{-12}. To solve the above problem a set of arbitrary lower bounds of 1.0 were

Table A.2

Tableau for Sample Problem GM4 (Monopoly Problem)

Minimize	Y1	Y2	Y3	X1	X2	X3	X11	X12	X13	X21	X22	X23	X31	X32	X33	MR1	MR2	MR3	MC1	MC2	MC3	RHS
Y1	-f'(Y1)																					
Y2		-f'(Y2)																				
Y3			-f'(Y3)																			
X1				g'(X1)																		
X2					g'(X2)																	
X3						g'(X3)																
X11							0															
X12								T(X12)														
X13									T(X13)													
X21										T(X21)												
X22											0											
X23												T(X23)										
X31													T(X31)									
X32														T(X32)								
X33															0							
OBJ								8	9	8		7.93854	9	7.93854								
RY1	1						-1			-1			-1									≤ 0
RY2		1						-1			-1			-1								≤ 0
RY3			1						-1			-1			-1							≤ 0
RX1				-1			1	1	1													≤ 0
RX2					-1					1	1	1										≤ 0
RX3						-1							1	1	1							≤ 0
RX11							0									1			-1			≤ 0
RX12								-T(X12)								1				-1		≤ 8
RX13									-T(X13)							1					-1	≤ 9
RX21										-T(X21)							1		-1			≤ 8
RX22											0						1			-1		≤ 0
RX23												-T(X23)					1				-1	≤ 7.93854
RX31													-T(X31)					1	-1			≤ 9
RX32														-T(X32)				1		-1		≤ 7.93854
RX33															0			1			-1	≤ 0
RMR1	f'(Y1)															-1						≤ 0
RMR2		f'(Y2)															-1					≤ 0
RMR3			f'(Y3)															-1				≤ 0
RMC1				-g'(X1)															1			≤ 0
RMC2					-g'(X2)															1		≤ 0
RMC3						-g'(X3)															1	≤ 0

Note: $f'(Y_i)$ and $g'(X_i)$ represent the marginal revenue and cost functions and $T(X_{ij}) = -0.07X_{ij} + 0.0014X_{ij}^2$ where $i, j = 1, 2, 3$ and $i \neq j$. Row names are identified with an R. The activity names MRi refer to marginal revenues, MCj to marginal costs and Xij indicates a trade flow from region i to region j. Yi and Xi are the demand and supply quantities. The top part of the tableau is the nonlinear part of the objective function and OBJ refers to the linear objective terms.

provided for the demand and supply quantities. To obtain the prices the quantities were inserted into the average revenue functions to obtain the following market prices:

$$p_1 = 58.9715 \quad p_2 = 49.6518 \quad p_3 = 42.5148$$

Example GM5 (Cournot-Nash oligopoly specification with exponential supply and demand functions and quadratic average per unit transport costs)
For this example the problem as specified in Example GM1 was solved as an oligopoly model. To do so, the elements in Table A.1 with an asterisk were modified to include the $T(X_{ij})$ term plus the oligopolist's margin which was derived as the derivative of the demand function for each of the three regions. For example, in the case of the constraints and for the flow x_{11} the term $84y_1^{-1.7}$ was added, for the flow x_{12} the term $50y_2^{-1.5}$ was added and for the flow x_{13} the term $66y_3^{-1.6}$ was added.

The numerical solution values obtained were:

$$x_{11} = 3.69204 \quad x_{12} = 1.99157 \quad x_{13} = 1.42702$$
$$x_{21} = 0.35330 \quad x_{22} = 4.48031 \quad x_{23} = 0.0$$
$$x_{31} = 2.20196 \quad x_{32} = 4.57073 \quad x_{33} = 6.45139$$

$$\rho_1 = 33.28104 \quad \rho_2 = 30.09291 \quad \rho_3 = 31.88081$$
$$\rho^1 = 19.51309 \quad \rho^2 = 23.98812 \quad \rho^3 = 16.21708$$

$$y_1 = 6.24730 \quad y_2 = 11.04261 \quad y_3 = 7.87842$$
$$x_1 = 7.11063 \quad x_2 = 4.83361 \quad x_3 = 13.22408$$

The objective function value for this problem was close to zero at -2.15×10^{-11}. To solve the above problem a set of arbitrary lower bounds of 1.0 were provided for the demand and supply quantities.

References

Abe, M.A. (1973), "Dynamic microeconomic models of production, investment and technological change of the U.S. and Japanese iron and steel industries," in *Studies in Economic Planning Over Space and Time*, eds. G.G. Judge, and T. Takayama, Amsterdam: North-Holland, pp. 345–367.

Asmuth, R.B., Eaves, B.C. and Peterson, E.L. (1979), "Computing economic equilibria on affine networks with Lemke's algorithm," *Mathematics of Operations Research*, 4, 209–214.

324   *T.G. MacAulay*

Baker, C.B. (1973), "Capital budgeting and financial management in linear programming models," in *Studies in Economic Planning Over Space and Time*, eds. G.G. Judge, and T. Takayama, Amsterdam: North-Holland, pp. 688–705.

Bierman, H. and Smidt, S. (1971), *The Capital Budgeting Decision*, 3rd edn, New York: Macmillan.

Bjarnason, H.F., McGarry, M.J. and Schmitz, A. (1969), "Converting price series of internationally traded commodities to a common currency prior to estimating national supply and demand functions," *American Journal of Agricultural Economics*, 51, 189–192.

Cottle, R.W. and Dantzig, G.B. (1968), "Complementary pivot theory of mathematical programming," in *Linear Algebra and its Applications*, New York: Elsevier Publishing Company.

Crabtree, J.R. (1983), "A trade and welfare analysis of UK sheepmeat exports within the European Community," *Journal of Agricultural Economics*, 34, 115–125.

Dafermos, S. (1980), "Traffic equilibrium and variational inequalities," *Transportation Science*, 14, 42–54.

Dafermos, S. (1988), "Sensitivity analysis in variational inequalities," *Mathematics of Operations Research*, 13, 421–434.

Dafermos, S. and Nagurney, A. (1983), "Sensitivity analysis for the general economic equilibrium problem," *Operations Research*, 32, 1069–1086

Dafermos, S. and Nagurney, A. (1987), "Oligopolistic and competitive behaviour of spatially separated markets," *Regional Science and Urban Economics*, 17, 245–254.

Day, R.H. (1973), "Recursive programming models: a brief introduction," in *Studies in Economic Planning Over Space and Time*, eds. G.G. Judge, and T. Takayama, Amsterdam: North-Holland, pp. 329–344.

Day, R.H. and Kennedy, P.E. (1970), "Recursive decision systems: an existence analysis," *Econometrica*, 38, 666–681.

Enke, S. (1951), "Equilibrium among spatially separated markets: solutions by electric analogue," *Econometrica*, 19, 40–47.

Elliott, D.P. (1972), "Converting national supply and demand equations to a common currency for internationally traded commodities," *American Journal of Agricultural Economics*, 54, 538.

Greenberg, H.J. and Murphy, F.H. (1985), "Computing market equilibria with price regulations using mathematical programming," *Operations Research*, 33, 935–954.

Guise, J.W.B. and Aggrey-Mensah, W. (1973), "An evaluation of policy alternatives facing Australian banana producers," in *Studies in Economic Planning Over Space and Time*, eds. G.G. Judge, and T. Takayama, Amsterdam: North-Holland, pp. 519–535.

Haack, R., Martin, L.J., and MacAulay, T.G. (1978), "A forecasting model for the Canadian and U.S. beef sectors," in *Commodity Forecasting Models for Canadian Agriculture: Volume 1*, coordinators Z.A. Hassan, and H.B. Huff, Ottawa: Policy, Planning and Economics Branch, Agriculture Canada.

Harker, P.T. (1984), "A generalized spatial price equilibrium model," *Papers of the Regional Science Association: Thirtieth North American Meetings*, 54, 25–42.

Harker, P.T. (ed) (1985), *Spatial Price Equilibrium: Advances in Theory, Computation and Application*, Berlin: Springer-Verlag.

Harker, P.T. (1986), "Alternative models of spatial competition," *Operations Research*, 34, 410–425.

Hashimoto, H. (1985), "A spatial Nash equilibrium model" in Harker, P.T. (ed), *Spatial Price Equilibrium: Advances in Theory, Computation and Application*, Berlin: Springer-Verlag, pp. 20–40.

Jabara, C.L. and Thompson, R.L. (1980), "Agricultural comparative advantage under international price uncertainty: the case of Senegal," *American Journal of Agricultural Economics*, 62, 188–198.

King, R.A. and Ho, F-S. (1972), *Reactive Programming: A Market Simulating Spatial Equilibrium Algorithm*, Economics Research Report No. 21, Raleigh, North Carolina: Department of Economics, North Carolina State University.

Kolstad, C.D. and Burris, A.E. (1986), "Imperfectly competitive equilibria in international commodity markets," *American Journal of Agricultural Economics*, 68, 27–36.

Lee, T-C. and Seaver, S.K. (1971), "A simultaneous-equation model of spatial equilibrium and its application to the broiler markets," *American Journal of Agricultural Economics*, 53, 63–70.

MacAulay, T.G. (1978), "A forecasting model for the Canadian U.S. pork sectors," in *Commodity Forecasting Models for Canadian Agriculture: Volume 2*, coordinators Z.A. Hassan, and H.B. Huff, Ottawa: Policy, Planning and Economics Branch, Agriculture Canada.

MacAulay, T.G., Batterham, R.L. and Fisher, B.S. (1989), "Solution of spatial trading systems with concave cubic programming," *Australian Journal of Agricultural Economics*, 33, 170–186.

Mackinnon, J.G. (1975), *A Technique for the Solution of Spatial Equilibrium Models*, Discussion Paper No. 199, Kingston, Ontario: Institute for Economic Research, Queen's University.

Martin, L.J. (1981), "Quadratic single and multi-commodity models of spatial equilibrium: a simplified exposition," *Canadian Journal of Agricultural Economics*, 29, 21–48.

Martin, L. and Zwart, A.C. (1975), "A spatial and temporal model of the North American pork sector for the evaluation of policy alternatives," *American Journal of Agricultural Economics*, 55, 55–67.

Maruyama, Y. and Fuller, E.I. (1965), *An Interregional Quadratic Programming Model for Varying Degrees of Competition*, Bulletin No 555, Amherst: Massachusetts Agricultural Experiment Station, University of Massachusetts.

Moore, C. and Nagurney. A. (1989), "A general equilibrium model of interregional monetary flows," *Environment and Planning*, 21, 397–404.

Murtagh, B.A. and Saunders, M.A. (1986), *MINOS 5.1 User's Guide*, Technical Report SOL 83–20R, Systems Optimization Laboratory, Stanford: Department of Operations Research, Stanford University.

Nagurney, A. (1992), "The application of variational inequality theory to the study of spatial equilibrium and disequilibrium," in *Readings in Econometric Theory and Practice: A Volume in Honor of George Judge*, eds. W.E. Griffiths, H. Lütkepohl and M.E. Bock, Amsterdam: North-Holland, pp. 327–355.

Pieri, R.G., Meilke, K.D. and MacAulay, T.G. (1977), "North-American-Japanese pork trade: an application of quadratic programming," *Canadian Journal of Agricultural Economics*, 25, 61–79.

Polito, J. (1977), Distribution systems planning in a price responsive environment, Ph. D. thesis, Purdue: Purdue University.

Rausser, G.C., Lichtenberg, E. and Lattimore, R. (1982), "Developments in theory and empirical applications of endogenous governmental behaviour," in *New Directions in Econometric Modelling and Forecasting in U.S. Agriculture*, ed. G.C. Rausser, New York: North-Holland, pp. 547–614.

Richardson, C.D. (1989), A recursive spatial equilibrium analysis of European Community beef and veal trade, M.Ec. dissertation, Armidale: University of New England.

Roe, T. and Shane, M. (1973), *A Heuristic Fixed-charge Quadratic Algorithm*, Staff Paper P73–8, Department of Agricultural and Applied Economics, St. Paul: University of Minnesota.

Rowse, J. (1981), "Solving the generalized transportation problem," *Regional Science and Urban Economics*, 11, 57–68.

Rowse, J.G. and Copithorne, L.W. (1982), "Natural resource programming models and scarcity rents," *Resources and Energy*, 4, 59–85.

Saepung, N. (1986), A recursive spatial equilibrium model of price determination in the Australian beef markets with emphasis on the export control scheme, M.Ec. dissertation, Armidale: University of New England.

Salant, S.W. (1982), "Imperfect competition in the international energy market: a computerized Nash-Cournot model," *Operations Research*, 30, 252–280.

Sampson, G.P. and Snape, R.H. (1980), "Effects of the EEC's variable import levies," *Journal of Political Economy*, 88, 1026–1039.

Samuelson, P.A. (1952), "Spatial price equilibrium and linear programming," *American Economic Review*, 42, 283–303.

Silberberg, E. (1970), "A theory of spatially separated markets," *International Economic Review*, 11, 334–348.

Takayama, T. and Judge, G.G. (1964a), "Equilibrium among spatially separated markets: a reformulation," *Econometrica*, 32, 510–524.

Takayama, T. and Judge, G.G. (1964b), "Spatial equilibrium and quadratic programming," *Journal of Farm Economics*, 64, 67–93.

Takayama, T. and Judge, G.G. (1970), "Alternative spatial equilibrium models," *Journal of Regional Science*, 10, 1–12.

Takayama, T. and Judge, G.G. (1971), *Spatial and Temporal Price and Allocation Models*, Amsterdam: North-Holland Publishing Company.

Takayama, T. and Labys, W. (1986), "Spatial equilibrium analysis," in *Handbook of Regional and Urban Economics*, ed. P. Nijkamp, Amsterdam: North-Holland Publishing Company.

Takayama, T. and MacAulay, T.G. (1991), "Recent developments in spatial (temporal) equilibrium models: non-linearity and existence and other issues," in *International Commodity Market Modelling: Advances in Methodology and Applications*, eds. O. Güvenen, W. Labys and J.-B. Lesourd, London: Chapman and Hall (in press).

Takayama, T. and Uri, N. (1983), "A note on spatial and temporal price and allocation modelling," *Regional Science and Urban Economics*, 13, 455–470.

Takayama, T. and Woodland, A.D. (1970), "Equivalence of price and quantity formulations of spatial equilibrium: purified duality in quadratic and concave programming," *Econometrica*, 38, 899–906.

Tobin, R.L. (1988), "A variable dimension solution approach for the general spatial price equilibrium problem," *Mathematical Programming*, 40, 33–51.

Tobin, R.L. and Friesz, T.L. (1985), "A new look at spatially competitive facility location models," in *Spatial Price Equilibrium: Advances in Theory, Computation and Application*, ed. P.T. Harker, Berlin: Springer-Verlag, pp. 1–19.

Tramel, T.E. and Seale, A.D. (1959), "Reactive programming of supply and demand relations – application to fresh vegetables," *Journal of Farm Economics*, 4, 1012–1022.

Yaron, D. (1967), "Incorporation of income effects into mathematical programming models," *Metroeconomica*, 19, 121–160.

Readings in Econometric Theory and Practice
W. Griffiths, H. Lütkepohl and M.E. Bock (Editors)

CHAPTER 14

THE APPLICATION OF VARIATIONAL INEQUALITY THEORY TO THE STUDY OF SPATIAL EQUILIBRIUM AND DISEQUILIBRIUM

Anna Nagurney *

*Department of General Business and Finance, School of Management,
University of Massachusetts, Amherst, MA 01003, USA*

In this paper we consider a variety of perfectly competitive asymmetric spatial price equilibrium problems and show how they can be formulated and studied as variational inequality problems. We then extend the models to handle policy interventions such as price controls in the form of price floors and ceilings and trade restrictions and demonstrate how these disequilibrium problems — in which the markets need no longer clear — can also be formulated as variational inequality problems. We then propose a decomposition algorithm for both classes of problems which decomposes these large-scale problems into three smaller and simpler variational inequality subproblems and show how their connection with network equilibrium problems can be exploited for computational purposes.

1. Introduction

The spatial price equilibrium models of Takayama and Judge have provided the basic framework for the analysis of competitive systems over space and time. Moreover, their fundamental contributions have stimulated the development of new methodologies and uncovered vistas for applications in agriculture, energy markets, mineral economics, and finance (see, e.g., Judge

* First, the author would like to thank George G. Judge whose work has been a continuing inspiration. Secondly, the author would like to express her gratitude to W. Griffiths for including her in this special volume. The author is grateful to the referee for his careful reading of the paper and his thoughtful comments and suggestions. The author acknowledges the support of NSF Grant RII-880361 and NSF Grant SES-8702831. The paper was written while the author was visiting MIT under the NSF VPW program. The hospitality and cordiality of the Operations Research Center and the Center for Transportation Studies at MIT are warmly appreciated. This research was conducted on the Cornell National Supercomputer Facility, a resource of the Center for Theory and Simulation in Science and Engineering at Cornell University, which is funded in part by the National Science Foundation, New York State, and IBM Corporation.

and Takayama (1973), Uri (1975), Takayama and Labys (1986), Newcomb, Reynolds, and Masbruch (1989), Moore and Nagurney (1989)).

In the past decade, spatial price equilibrium problems have captured the interest of scholars from a wide spectrum of disciplines, including: operations research, mathematical programming, economics, regional science, and transportation science. The attraction has come from several factors: the richness of the problems for model development, the computational challenges posed by the large-scale nature of the problems, and the evolving connections with equilibrium problems in distinct disciplines.

Historically, spatial price equilibrium models were usually reformulated as optimization problems, provided that a certain symmetry or integrability assumption held for the underlying functions. Utilizing such an approach, Samuelson (1952) and Takayama and Judge (1964, 1971) introduced a variety of spatial price equilibrium models. Convex programming algorithms could then, at least in principle, be used for the computation of the regional commodity production, consumption, and interregional (and intertemporal) trade patterns. Analogously, Beckmann, McGuire, and Winsten (1956) reformulated traffic network equilibrium models with both fixed and elastic demands as optimization problems.

It has now been realized that equilibrium problems governed by distinct equilibrium conditions and operating under distinct behavioral assumptions — for which the integrability assumption need no longer be imposed — can be modelled and studied via the theory of variational inequalities. Indeed, the theory of variational inequalities provides not only a methodology for the study of qualitative properties of existence, uniqueness, and sensitivity of equilibrium solutions, but also provides for mathematically correct algorithms for the computation of solutions to equilibrium problems for which no equivalent optimization formulation exists. Furthermore, as we shall discuss later, the marriage of variational inequalities and networks induces the creation of highly efficient algorithms which are especially suited for large-scale equilibrium problems such as spatial price equilibrium problems which have a characteristic underlying network structure.

The theory of variational inequalities had been introduced by Hartman and Stampacchia (1966) as a tool for the study of partial differential equations. The identification by Dafermos (1980) that the traffic network equilibrium conditions had the structure of a finite-dimensional variational inequality problem opened new avenues for the development of more general, asymmetric multicommodity (and multimodal) models and the design of mathematically correct and convergent algorithms. Florian and Los (1982) then formulated the spatial price equilibrium conditions as a variational inequality problem (see also, e.g., Dafermos and Nagurney (1984a), Friesz, Harker, and Tobin (1984)).

Since variational inequality problems are solved iteratively as mathematical programming problems, or decomposed into simpler variational inequality problems, which are then, in turn, solved as mathematical programming problems, the overall efficiency of a variational inequality algorithm depends upon the mathematical programming algorithm used at each iteration. For example, projection methods resolve a variational inequality problem into series of quadratic programming problems, whereas relaxation methods resolve a variational inequality problem into series of (in general) nonlinear programming problems (see, e.g., Dafermos (1983)). Although standard convex programming algorithms and packages, such as MINOS, at least in principle, can then be used to compute the solution to the embedded mathematical programming problems, several studies have shown that the use of special-purpose algorithms at each iteration of a variational inequality algorithm can induce a savings in computational expense of at least an order of magnitude. For computational comparisons of variational inequality algorithms applied to equilibrium problems, including spatial price equilibrium problems, and embedded with MINOS, the Frank-Wolfe (1956) algorithm, and special-purpose equilibration algorithms, we refer the reader to Nagurney (1984), Nagurney (1987a), and Friesz, Harker, and Tobin (1984). In the case of constrained matrix problems, it has been recently shown in Nagurney, Kim, and Robinson (1990) that the projection method, coupled with an exact equilibration algorithm, which takes advantage of the special network structure of the problem, outperformed the algorithm of Bachem and Korte (1978) by as much as two orders of magnitude, thus enabling the computation of solutions to problems with millions of variables, and at a savings of computer storage. Constrained matrix problems include the estimation of input/output matrices, social/national accounts, origin/destination traffic flows, and demographic patterns.

The desire to solve large-scale general, multicommodity spatial price equilibrium problems has motivated, hence, the development of special-purpose algorithms which take advantage of the network structure of the problems and can be used to solve the mathematical programming problems embedded within the variational inequality algorithms. The special network structure, noted by Dafermos and Nagurney (1985) (see also Dafermos (1986)), lies in that each origin/destination pair consists of paths which are disjoint. The structure has been exploited computationally by Dafermos and Nagurney (1989), Nagurney (1989a), Eydeland and Nagurney (1989), and Nagurney and Kim (1989), in the development of equilibration algorithms for classical, single commodity spatial price equilibrium problems, by observing that each restricted demand market (or supply market equilibrium subproblem) could be solved exactly in closed form. Interestingly, the special network structure can also be used to link spatial price equilibrium problems with both migration equilibrium problems (Nagurney (1990)) and constrained matrix problems (Stone (1951), Nagurney (1989a), Nagurney, Kim, and Robinson (1990)).

Other equilibrium problems which have also been studied as variational inequality problems include: imperfectly competitive oligopolistic market equilibrium problems, both aspatial (Gabay and Moulin (1980)), and spatial (Dafermos and Nagurney (1987), Harker (1986), Nagurney (1988)), market equilibrium problems with production (Dafermos and Nagurney (1984b)), Walrasian price and general economic equilibria (Border (1985), Zhao (1989)), and migration equilibria (Nagurney (1989b)). Most of these problems can be viewed as network equilibrium problems, in which, however, the nodes of the underlying abstract network representation need no longer correspond to locations in space. The principal advantage of a network formalism from a conceptual standpoint is that seemingly disparate problems can be studied in a unified fashion. On the other hand, the main advantage from a computational standpoint is that previously intractable problems can be efficiently computed.

In this paper we focus on the application of the methodology of variational inequalities, combined with network theory, to the study of spatial price equilibrium problems and — in the case of policy interventions — disequilibrium, or "constrained equilibrium" problems. We note that although our emphasis in this paper is on applications, in particular, on perfectly competitive spatial price problems, within an equilibrium/disequilibrium framework, the variational inequality problem contains, as special cases not only such problems and minimization problems, but virtually all the classical problems of mathematical programming, such as linear and nonlinear complementarity problems, fixed point problems, and minimax problems. For further discussion and additional references, see Nagurney (1987b).

The paper is organized as follows:

In Section 2 we provide the necessary background for the theory of variational inequalities and focus on the qualitative properties of existence and uniqueness.

In Section 3 we present a synthesis of asymmetric spatial price equilibrium models in quantity variables and in price variables, and give the variational inequality formulations of the governing spatial price equilibrium conditions. We also relate the models to other models in the literature.

In Section 4 we then generalize the models described in Section 3 to handle policy interventions explicitly, again within a variational inequality framework. Policy instruments which we consider include price supports and trade restrictions. Such policy instruments have been used by governments in both developed and developing regions as part of both agricultural and energy programs. These variational inequality formulations differ from those given in Section 3 in the defining functions and/or feasible sets.

We then show in Section 5 that both the equilibrium problems and the disequilibrium problems can be solved using a variational inequality decomposition algorithm which resolves the original variational inequality under consideration into three simpler variational inequality problems, in which the "dominant" subproblem has the structure of a network equilibrium problem. We also provide in Section 6 numerical results to illustrate the computational performance of the algorithm for both equilibrium and contrained equilibrium problems.

Finally, we conclude with a summary and discussion in Section 7.

2. Background

In this section we briefly review the basic theory of variational inequalities. For amplified discussions, see the book by Kinderlehrer and Stampacchia (1980), the surveys of Magnanti (1984), Dafermos (1987), Nagurney (1987b), and the thesis of Zhao (1989).

The finite dimensional variational inequality problem is to determine the vector x in a closed convex subset K of the n-dimensional Euclidean space R^n such that

$$f(x) \cdot (x' - x) \geq 0, \quad \text{for all } x' \in K \qquad VI(f, K)$$

where $f(\cdot)$ is a known function from K to R^n.

The geometric interpretation of $VI(f, K)$ is that $f(x)$ is "orthogonal" to the set K (see Figure 1). The precise statement of this connection is given by the following Theorem.

Theorem 1: *A vector $x \in K$ is a solution of $VI(f, K)$ if and only if x is a fixed point of the map*

$$G(x') = P_K(x' - \beta f(x')), \quad x' \in K, \qquad (1)$$

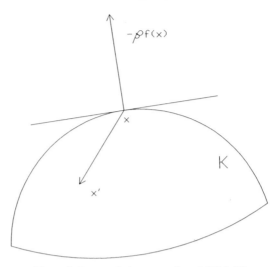

Figure 1. Geometric interpretation of $VI(f, K)$.

where β is some positive real number and P_K denotes the projection map onto the set K.

This characterization plays a crucial role in the qualitative study of existence, uniqueness, and sensitivity of solutions to variational inequalities. For instance, the combination of Theorem 1 and Brouwer's fixed point theorem yields the following well-known result.

Theorem 2: *If the convex set K is compact and the function $f: K \to R^n$ is continuous on K, then $VI(f, K)$ has at least one solution $x \in K$.*

When K is not necessarily bounded, a solution to $VI(f, K)$ exists, provided that $f(\cdot)$ is continuous and coercive, i.e.,

$$\frac{(f(\bar{x}) - f(x')) \cdot (\bar{x} - x')}{\| \bar{x} - x' \|} \to \infty, \quad \text{as } \| \bar{x} \| \to \infty \atop \bar{x} \in K \tag{2}$$

for some fixed $x' \in K$, where $\| \cdot \|$ denotes the Euclidean norm.

In the case where certain monotonicity conditions on the function f can be expected to hold, the theory of variational inequalities becomes particularly powerful. For example, when $f(\cdot)$ is strictly monotone, i.e.,

$$(f(\bar{x}) - f(x')) \cdot (\bar{x} - x') > 0 \tag{3}$$

for all $\bar{x}$, $x' \in K$, $\bar{x} \neq x'$, then $VI(f, K)$ has at most one solution.
Furthermore, when $f(\cdot)$ is strongly monotone, that is:

$$(f(\bar{x}) - f(x')) \cdot (\bar{x} - x') \geqq \alpha \| \bar{x} - x' \|^2, \quad \text{for every } \bar{x}, x' \in K \tag{4}$$

where α is a positive constant, then there exists a unique solution x to $VI(f, K)$. Necessary and sufficient conditions for (4) to hold is that the (not necessarily symmetric) Jacobian matrix $[\partial f / \partial x]$ is positive definite over the feasible set K. A sufficient condition for the coercivity condition (2) to hold is that the strong monotonicity condition (4) holds.

Finally, the function f is called monotone if the left-hand side of (4) is greater than or equal to zero for every $\bar{x}$, $x' \in K$.

The connection between variational inequality problems and minimization problems, in which monotonicity for the former plays an analogous role as convexity in the latter, is as follows:

Let $F(\cdot)$ be a continuously differentiable scalar-valued function defined on some open neighborhood of K and denote its gradient by $\nabla F(\cdot)$. If there exists an $x \in K$ such that

$$F(x) = \min_{x' \in K} F(x') \tag{5}$$

then x is a solution to the variational inequality

$$\nabla F(x) \cdot (x' - x) \geqq 0, \quad \text{for all } x' \in K. \tag{6}$$

On the other hand, if $f(\cdot)$, again on an open neighborhood of K, is the gradient of a convex continuously differentiable function $F(\cdot)$, then $VI(f, K)$ and the minimization problem (5) are equivalent; in other words, x solves $VI(f, K)$ when x minimizes $F(\cdot)$ over K. Note that $f(\cdot)$ is a gradient mapping if and only if its Jacobian matrix $[\partial f / \partial x]$ is symmetric, in which case the objective function $= \int f(y) \, dy$.

Moreover, if $F(\cdot)$ is convex, strictly convex, or uniformly convex, then its gradient mapping is, respectively, monotone, strictly monotone, or strongly monotone.

We note that the above "symmetry" or "integrability" condition had been utilized by Samuelson (1952) and Takayama and Judge (1971) to reformulate the equilibrium conditions of spatial price equilibrium models as the Kuhn-Tucker conditions of appropriately defined optimization problems. We note that now, in view of the above, a single inequality of the form $VI(f, K)$ can be used to formulate the equilibrium conditions of spatial price equilibrium problems in which the symmetry condition need no longer be assumed. Hence, multicommodity spatial price equilibrium problems, either static or intertemporal, can now be modelled and studied under more realistic conditions without the restrictive symmetry assumption. However, $VI(f, K)$ still contains such symmetric problems as special cases.

In the next two sections we will present variational inequality formulations of a series of spatial price equilibrium models in quantity variables and in price variables, in the absence and then in the presence of policy interventions in the form of trade restrictions and price controls. The motivation stems from the seminal book of Takayama and Judge (1971) and the edited volume of Judge and Takayama (1973).

We now turn to a brief overview of the numerical procedures for the computation of $VI(f, K)$.

$VI(f, K)$ can be solved via the general iterative scheme of Dafermos (1983) which contains both projection methods (Dafermos (1980, 1982), Bertsekas and Gafni (1982)), as well as other linearization methods (Pang and Chan (1981)) and relaxation/diagonalization methods (Florian and Spiess (1982)), as special cases. The computation of the solution x to $VI(f, K)$ is accomplished iteratively via the computation of the solutions to a series of simpler variational inequality subproblems, which, typically, are mathematical programming (minimization) problems, since efficient algorithms for such problems exist. Projection methods resolve the original variational inequality problem into series of quadratic programming problems, whereas, relaxation methods resolve the original variational inequality problem into, typically, series of nonlinear programming problems. Hence, the overall efficiency of a variational inequality algorithm depends on the efficiency of the algorithm selected for the computation of the embedded mathematical programming problems. Indeed, the desire to compute general multicommodity spatial price equilibrium problems within realistic time frames has spurred the development of special-purpose algorithms for single commodity spatial price equilibrium problems, which exploit the underlying problem structure. Such special-purpose algorithms, which have, in particular, exploited the underlying network structure of these mathematical programming problems, have outperformed convex programming algorithms (see, e.g., Nagurney (1987a), Nagurney (1989c,d), Dafermos and Nagurney (1989), Eydeland and Nagurney (1989), Nagurney, Kim, and Robinson (1990)).

For computational comparisons of variational inequality algorithms, see Nagurney (1984, 1987a) and the references therein.

Moreover, in the case where the feasible set K can be expressed as a Cartesian product of sets, where

$$K = \prod_{a=1}^{z} K_a \tag{7}$$

where each K_a is a subset of R^{n_a}, the reformulation of $VI(f, K)$, where K is now of the form given in (7) induces natural decompositions of the original variational inequality into subproblems of lower dimensions. Such decompositions are especially appealing in the case of large-scale multicommodity spatial price equilibrium problems. Recently, parallel and serial variational inequality decomposition algorithms have been applied to multicommodity spatial price equilibrium problems by Nagurney and Kim (1989) to compute solutions to problems with as many as 100 markets and 12 commodities using serial and parallel computers. For variational inequality decomposition algorithms applied to intertemporal spatial price equilibrium problems with discounting, gains and losses, and other modelling enhancements, see, e.g., Nagurney and Aronson (1988, 1989), Nagurney (1989d). For decomposition schemes applied to spatial oligopoly models operating under the Cournot-Nash postulate of noncooperative behavior, see Nagurney (1988). For alternative parallel and serial decomposition algorithms, see Bertsekas and Tsitsiklis (1989).

In the subsequent sections we focus on the derivation of variational inequalities over Cartesian products of sets for a variety of spatial price models and and provide a synthesis of many of the recent research results. These variational inequality formulations are not the immediately obvious ones, but are notable in that they induce efficient decomposition schemes which we then describe in Section 5.

3. Equilibrium Models

In this section we synthesize spatial price equilibrium models within a variational inequality framework. In particular, we present both quantity and price formulations.

We consider m supply markets and n demand markets involved in the production/consumption of a commodity. We denote a typical supply market by i and a typical demand market by j. We let s_i denote the supply at supply market i and we let d_j denote the demand at demand market j. We let π_i denote the supply price associated with supply market i and ρ_j the demand price associated with demand market j. We group the supplies and supply prices into vectors $s \in R^m$ and $\pi \in R^m$, respectively. Similarly, we group the demands and demand prices into vectors $d \in R^n$ and $\rho \in R^n$, respectively.

We let Q_{ij} denote the nonnegative commodity shipment between the supply and demand market pair (i, j) and we let c_{ij} denote the nonnegative transaction cost associated with trading the commodity between (i, j). We assume that the transaction cost c_{ij} includes the transportation cost. Hence, the supply and demand markets can be spatially separated. We note that the transaction cost may also include such policy intruments as tariffs, taxes, fees, duties, or subsidies. We group the commodity shipments into a vector $Q \in R^{mn}$ and the transaction costs into a vector $c \in R^{mn}$.

The well-known market equilibrium conditions, assuming perfect competition take, following Samuelson (1952) and Takayama and Judge (1971), the following form: For all pairs of supply and demand markets (i, j); $i = 1, \ldots, m$; $j = 1, \ldots, n$:

$$
\pi_i + c_{ij} \begin{cases} = \rho_j, & \text{if } Q_{ij} > 0 \\ \geq \rho_j, & \text{if } Q_{ij} = 0. \end{cases} \tag{8}
$$

The conditions (8) state that a pair of markets (i, j) will trade, provided that the supply price at supply market i plus the transaction cost between the pair of markets is equal to the demand price at demand market j. Moreover, the following feasibility conditions must hold:

$$
s_i \begin{cases} = \sum_j Q_{ij}, & \text{if } \pi_i > 0 \\ \geq \sum_j Q_{ij}, & \text{if } \pi_i = 0 \end{cases} \tag{9}
$$

and

$$
d_j \begin{cases} = \sum_i Q_{ij}, & \text{if } \rho_j > 0 \\ \leq \sum_i Q_{ij}, & \text{if } \rho_j = 0. \end{cases} \tag{10}
$$

Typically, it is assumed that both supply and demand prices are positive in equilibrium. Hence, usually the equalities are assumed to hold in both (9) and (10). Here, however, we consider the above more general situation, which is in the spirit of Takayama and Judge (1971).

Introducing now the nonnegative variables u_i and w_j, where u_i denotes the possible excess supply at supply market i and w_j denotes the possible unmet demand at demand market j, we may rewrite (9) and (10), respectively, as: For every i, $i = 1, \ldots, m$:

$$u_i \begin{cases} = 0, & \text{if } \pi_i > 0 \\ \geq 0, & \text{if } \pi_i = 0 \end{cases} \tag{11}$$

and for every j, $j = 1, \ldots, n$:

$$w_j \begin{cases} = 0, & \text{if } \rho_j > 0 \\ \geq 0, & \text{if } \rho_j = 0 \end{cases} \tag{12}$$

where

$$s_i = \sum_j Q_{ij} + u_i \quad \text{and} \quad d_j = \sum_i Q_{ij} - w_j. \tag{13}$$

We group the u_i's into a vector $u \in R^m$ and the w_j's into a vector $w \in R^n$.

We now discuss the supply price, demand price, and transaction cost structure.

We assume that the supply price associated with any supply market may depend upon the supply of the commodity at every supply market, that is,

$$\pi = \pi(s) \tag{14}$$

where π is a known smooth function. On the other hand, in the case where the supply function, rather than the supply price function is given, we assume that the supply can depend, in general, upon the supply price at every supply market, that is,

$$s = s(\pi). \tag{15}$$

Similarly, the demand price associated with any demand market may depend upon the demand of the commodity at every demand market, that is,

$$\rho = \rho(d) \tag{16}$$

where ρ is a known smooth function. Analogously, in the case where the demand function, rather than the demand price function is given, we assume that the demand can depend, in general, upon the demand price at every demand market, that is,

$$d = d(\rho). \tag{17}$$

The transaction cost, which includes the transportation cost between a pair of supply and demand markets may depend, in general, upon the shipments of the commodity between every pair of markets, that is,

$$c = c(Q) \tag{18}$$

where c is a known smooth function.

In the special case where the number of supply markets m is equal to the number of demand markets n, the transaction cost functions are assumed to be fixed and the supply price functions and demand price funcions are symmetric, i.e., $\partial \pi_i / \partial s_k = \partial \pi_k / \partial s_i$, for all $i = 1, \ldots, m$; $k = 1, \ldots, m$, and $\partial \rho_j / \partial d_l = \partial \rho_l / \partial d_j$, for all $j = 1, \ldots, n$; $l = 1, \ldots, n$, then the above model with supply price functions (14) and demand price functions (16) collapses to the quantity models introduced in Takayama and Judge (1971) for which an equivalent optimization formulation exists. Similarly, if the analogous symmetry assumption holds for the supply functions (15) and demand functions (17), then the above model contains as a special case the price models of Takayama and Judge (1971). In the case where the Jacobians of the governing functions are no longer symmetric and the functions themselves are linear, the models above collapse to the asymmetric models introduced in Takayama and Judge (1971) who proposed a primal-dual method as a solution procedure.

In the case where the equalities in (9) and (10) are assumed to hold the above model in quantity variables collapses to the spatial market model of Dafermos and Nagurney (1985) which has been solved as a variational inequality problem in Nagurney (1987a). For the relationship between this model and a general spatial oligopoly model, see Dafermos and Nagurney (1987). On the other hand, the spatial model in price variables, using (15) and (17) had been introduced by Dafermos and McKelvey (1986).

Before proceeding to state the variational inequality formulations of the spatial price equilibrium models discussed above, we first introduce some notation which is helpful in presenting the variational inequalities in compact vector form. We define the vectors $\hat{\pi} = \pi \in R^m$, and $\hat{\rho} = \rho \in R^n$, where in view of the feasibility conditions (9) and (10), we express $\hat{\pi}$ and $\hat{\rho}$ in the following manner:

$$\hat{\pi} = \hat{\pi}(Q, u) \quad \text{and} \quad \hat{\rho} = \hat{\rho}(Q, w). \tag{19}$$

We also define on the supply price side the vector $\tilde{\hat{\pi}} \in R^{mn}$ consisting of m vectors, where the i-th vector $\tilde{\hat{\pi}}_i \in R^n$, consists of n identical components $\{\hat{\pi}_i, \ldots, \hat{\pi}_i\}$. Similarly, on the demand price side we define the vector $\tilde{\hat{\rho}} \in R^{mn}$ consisting of m identical vectors where the j-th vector $\{\tilde{\hat{\rho}}_j\} \in R^n$ consists of components $\{\hat{\rho}_1, \hat{\rho}_2, \ldots, \hat{\rho}_n\}$.

We are now ready to present variational inequality formulations of a spectrum of spatial price equilibrium models in quantity variables, in price variables, and in "combined" price-quantity variables:

Assuming that we are given the supply price functions (14), the demand price functions (16), and the transaction cost functions (18), then the spatial price equilibrium conditions (8), subject to (11) and (12), take on the following equivalent variational inequality formulation:

Theorem 3: (VI 3.1): *A pattern of commodity shipments, excess supplies, and unmet demands* (Q, u, w) *satisfies equilibrium conditions* (8), (11), (12) *if and only if it satisfies the variational inequality*:

$$\left(\tilde{\hat{\pi}}(Q, u) + c(Q) - \tilde{\hat{\rho}}(Q, w) \right) \cdot (Q' - Q) + \hat{\pi}(Q, u) \cdot (u' - u)$$

$$+ \hat{\rho}(Q, w) \cdot (w' - w) \geqq 0 \tag{20}$$

for all $(Q', u', w') \in K \equiv R^{mn}_+ \times R^m_+ \times R^n_+$.

For detailed derivations of similar variational inequality formulations, see Nagurney and Zhao (1990), Dafermos (1982), Nagurney (1987a). We note that, in the case where the equalities in (9) and (10) are assumed to hold, then the governing variational inequality contains only the first term in (20), where the feasible set K is accordingly simplified.

Assuming, on the other hand, that we retain the supply price functions (14) and are given the demand functions (17), then the variational inequality formulation akin to VI 3.1, is given by:

Theorem 4: (VI 3.2): *A pattern of commodity shipments, excess supplies, and demand prices* (Q, u, ρ) *satisfies equilibrium conditions* (8), (11), (10), *if and* *only if it satisfies the variational inequality*:

$$\left(\tilde{\hat{\pi}}(Q, u) + c(Q) - \tilde{\hat{\rho}}\right) \cdot (Q' - Q) + \hat{\pi}(Q, u) \cdot (u' - u)$$

$$+ D(Q, \rho) \cdot (\rho' - \rho) \geq 0 \tag{21}$$

for all $(Q', u', \rho') \in K \equiv R_+^{mn} \times R_+^m \times R_+^n$

where $D \in R^n$ *consists of components* $D_j \equiv \Sigma_i Q_{ij} - d_j(\rho)$ *and* $\tilde{\hat{\rho}}$ *is now a vector variable.*

For details, see Nagurney and Zhao (1992).

If now, instead, we are given the demand price functions (16) and the supply functions (15), then the equivalence is given by:

Theorem 5: (VI 3.3): *A pattern of commodity shipments, supply prices, and unmet demands* (π, Q, w) *satisfies equilibrium conditions* (8), (9), (12), *if and only if it satisfies the variational inequality*:

$$\left(\tilde{\hat{\pi}} + c(Q) - \hat{\rho}(Q, w)\right) \cdot (Q' - Q) + S(\pi, Q) \cdot (\pi' - \pi)$$

$$+ \hat{\rho}(Q, w) \cdot (w' - w) \geq 0 \tag{22}$$

for all $(Q', \pi', w') \in K \equiv R_+^{mn} \times R_+^m \times R_+^n$,

where $S \in R^m$ *consists of components* $S_i \equiv s_i(\pi) - \Sigma_j Q_{ij}$, *and* $\tilde{\hat{\pi}}$ *is now a vector variable.*

Finally, if we are given both the supply functions (15), and the demand functions (17), then the variational inequality formulation becomes:

Theorem 6: (VI 3.4): *A pattern of commodity shipments, supply prices, and demand prices* (Q, π, ρ) *satisfies equilibrium conditions* (8), (9), (10), *if and only if it satisfies the variational inequality*:

$$\left(\tilde{\hat{\pi}} + c(Q) - \tilde{\hat{\rho}}\right) \cdot (Q' - Q) + S(\pi, Q) \cdot (\pi' - \pi)$$

$$+ D(Q, \rho) \cdot (\rho' - \rho) \geq 0 \tag{23}$$

for all $(Q', \pi', \rho') \in K \equiv R_+^{mn} \times R_+^m \times R_+^n$.

For a detailed derivation, see Dafermos and McKelvey (1986). For an excess demand, single price model, see Friesz, Harker, and Tobin (1984).

Observe that each of the above variational inequality formulations is of the form of $VI(f, K)$, where the vectors f and x are defined accordingly. Moreover, observe that each of the feasible sets K, for VI 3.1 through VI 3.4, is, in fact, a Cartesian product, of the form (7). In particular, each such K consists of the product of three simpler feasible sets. Hence, as intimated in Section 2, a decomposition approach is especially appealing. Indeed, as we will show in Section 5, the above problems and the disequilibrium or "constrained equilibrium" problems which will be outlined in the subsequent section can be solved using a variational inequality decomposition algorithm which will resolve each of the variational inequality problems over a Cartesian product of sets into three simpler variational inequality subproblems. The structure can then be further exploited for computational purposes by identifying the subproblems, where possible, as network equilibrium problems, and applying algorithms which take advantage of the network structure.

A qualitative analysis of the above equilibrium problems can be obtained by applying the theory described in Section 2. Illustrative and complete analyses in terms of existence and uniqueness of solutions to several of the above variational inequality problems can be found in Nagurney and Zhao (1990, 1991, 1992) and Dafermos and McKelvey (1986). Stability and sensitivity analysis results for spatial price equilibrium problems are described in Dafermos and Nagurney (1984). A general approach to sensitivity analysis for variational inequalities can be found in Dafermos (1988).

4. Disequilibrium or Constrained Equilibrium Models

In this section we focus on spatial models in the case of trade restrictions and price controls. Policy interventions in the form of tariffs, subsidies, and quotas played a prominent role in applied spatial price models studied by Takayama and Judge (1971). In particular, our goal here is to demonstrate how the equilibrium models outlined in the preceding section can be generalized within the variational inequality framework to handle policy instruments. The modifications result in changes to the governing functions and/or the feasible sets. The modelling of tariffs and subsidies can also be incorporated into the variational inequality framework by modifying the transaction cost functions appropriately. Thore (1986) had earlier introduced the concept of spatial disequilibrium but in the framework of models with separable functions. Here we, hence, demonstrate the generalization of spatial disequilibrium to the case of asymmetric functions.

We denote a minimum nonnegative supply price floor for supply market i by $\underline{\pi}_i$, and the maximum supply price ceiling by $\bar{\pi}_i$. We group the supply price floors into a vector $\underline{\pi} \in R^m$ and the supply price ceilings into a vector $\overline{\pi} \in R^m$. We denote then a minimum nonnegative demand price floor for demand market j by $\underline{\rho}_j$ and the maximum demand price ceiling by $\overline{\rho}_j$. We group the demand price floors into a vector $\underline{\rho} \in R^n$ and the demand price ceilings into a vector $\overline{\rho} \in R^n$.

We also denote a nonnegative trade floor for the commodity shipment Q_{ij} by $\underline{M}_{ij}$ and the maximum trade ceiling by $\overline{M}_{ij}$. We group the trade floors into a vector $\underline{M} \in R^{mn}$ and the trade ceilings into a vector $\overline{M} \in R^{mn}$. The market condition (8), in the presence of trade restrictions, is now extended to: For all pairs of supply and demand markets (i, j), $i = 1, \ldots, m$; $j = 1, \ldots, n$:

$$
\pi_i + c_{ij} \begin{cases} \leq \rho_j, & \text{if } Q_{ij} = \overline{M}_{ij} \\ = \rho_j, & \text{if } \underline{M}_{ij} < Q_{ij} < \overline{M}_{ij} \\ \geq \rho_j, & \text{if } Q_{ij} = \underline{M}_{ij} \end{cases} \tag{24}
$$

whereas conditions (9) and (10) now take the form:

$$
s_i \begin{cases} \leq \sum_j Q_{ij}, & \text{if } \pi_i = \overline{\pi}_i \\ = \sum_j Q_{ij}, & \text{if } \underline{\pi}_i < \pi_i < \overline{\pi}_i \\ \geq \sum_j Q_{ij}, & \text{if } \pi_i = \underline{\pi}_i \end{cases} \tag{25}
$$

and

$$
d_j \begin{cases} \geq \sum_i Q_{ij}, & \text{if } \rho_j = \overline{\rho}_j \\ = \sum_i Q_{ij}, & \text{if } \underline{\rho}_j < \rho_j < \overline{\rho}_j \\ \leq \sum_i Q_{ij}, & \text{if } \rho_j = \underline{\rho}_j. \end{cases} \tag{26}
$$

In the case where only the price floors $\underline{\pi}$ are imposed on the producers, then the analogue of condition (11) is: For every i, $i = 1, \ldots, m$:

$$
u_i \begin{cases} = 0, & \text{if } \pi_i > \underline{\pi}_i \\ \geq 0, & \text{if } \pi_i = \underline{\pi}_i. \end{cases} \tag{27}
$$

In the case where only the demand price floors are imposed on the consumers, then the analogue of condition (12) is: For every j, $j = 1, \ldots, n$:

$$w_j = \begin{cases} = 0, & \text{if } \rho_j > \underline{\rho}_j \\ \geq 0, & \text{if } \rho_j = \underline{\rho}_j. \end{cases} \tag{28}$$

We now present variational inequality formulations of the constrained equilibrium counterparts of VI 3.1 through VI 3.4. The models presented below are in increasing order of generality.

We first present the variational inequality formulation, akin to VI 3.1, satisfying conditions (24) in the presence of supply price floors only. In particular, assuming that we are given the supply price functions (14), the demand price functions (16), and the trade cost functions (17), then the market conditions (24) take on the following formulation.

Theorem 7: (VI 4.1): *A pattern of commodity shipments, excess supplies, and unmet demands (Q, u, w) satisfies conditions (24), (27), (12) if and only if it satisfies the variational inequality:*

$$\left(\hat{\tilde{\pi}}(Q, u) + c(Q) - \hat{\rho}(Q, w) \right) \cdot (Q' - Q) + \left(\hat{\pi}(Q, u) - \underline{\pi} \right) \cdot (u' - u)$$

$$+ \hat{\rho}(Q, w) \cdot (w' - w) \geq 0 \tag{29}$$

$$\text{for all } (Q', u', w') \in K \equiv K_1 \times R_+^m \times R_+^n$$

where $K_1 \equiv \{ Q' \mid \underline{M} \leq Q' \leq \overline{M} \}.$

The above model generalizes the model of Greenberg and Murphy (1985).

In the case that we retain the supply price floors $\underline{\pi}$, and include now the demand price floors $\underline{\rho}$ and ceilings $\bar{\rho}$, then the variational inequality formulation of the constrained equilibrium analogue of VI 3.2 is given by:

Theorem 8: (VI 4.2): *A pattern of commodity shipments, excess supplies, and demand prices (Q, u, ρ) satisfies conditions (24), (27), (26), if and only if it satisfies the variational inequality:*

$$\left(\hat{\tilde{\pi}}(Q, u) + c(Q) - \hat{\tilde{\rho}} \right) \cdot (Q' - Q) + \left(\hat{\pi}(Q, u) - \underline{\pi} \right) \cdot (u' - u)$$

$$+ D(Q, \rho) \cdot (\rho' - \rho) \geq 0 \tag{30}$$

$$\text{for all } (Q', u', \rho') \in K \equiv K_1 \times R_+^m \times K_3$$

where $K_3 \equiv \{ \rho' \mid \underline{\rho} \leq \rho' \leq \bar{\rho} \}.$

For a discussion of this model, see Nagurney and Zhao (1992).

On the other hand, if we now include the supply price ceilings, and retain only the demand price floors, we may rewrite VI 3.3 as

Theorem 9: (VI 4.3): *A pattern of supply prices, commodity shipments, and unmet demands* (Q, π, w) *satisfies conditions* (24), (25), (28), *if and only if it satisfies the variational inequality*:

$$\left(\bar{\bar{\pi}} + c(Q) - \bar{\rho}(Q, w)\right) \cdot (Q' - Q) + S(\pi, Q) \cdot (\pi' - \pi)$$

$$+ \left(\rho(Q, w) - \underline{\rho}\right) \cdot (w' - w) \geq 0 \tag{31}$$

for all $(Q', \pi', w') \in K \equiv K_1 \times K_2 \times R_+^n$

where $K_2 \equiv \{\pi' \mid \underline{\pi} \leq \pi' \leq \bar{\pi}\}$.

Finally, we present the most general formulation, akin to VI 3.4, in which the supply and demand functions are used, price floors and price ceilings are permitted on both the production and consumption sides and the trade restrictions remain, i.e.:

Theorem 10: (VI 4.4): *A pattern of commodity shipments, supply prices, and demand prices* (Q, π, ρ) *satisfies conditions* (24), (25), (26), *if and only if it satisfies the variational inequality problem*:

$$\left(\bar{\bar{\pi}} + c(Q) - \bar{\rho}\right) \cdot (Q' - Q) + S(\pi, Q) \cdot (\pi' - \pi)$$

$$+ D(Q, \rho) \cdot (\rho' - \rho) \geq 0 \tag{32}$$

for all $(Q', \pi', \rho') \in K \equiv K_1 \times K_2 \times K_3$.

For details, see Nagurney and Zhao (1992).

5. The Variational Inequality Decomposition Algorithm

Recall that the variational inequality formulations of the spatial price equilibrium models, VI 3.1–VI 3.4, and their constrained equilibrium analogues, VI 4.1–VI 4.4, were each defined over a Cartesian product K. Each such set, in turn, consisted of three sets. Hence, we can decompose each of the variational inequalities into three simpler variational inequality subproblems in lower dimensions. We then demonstrate that the "dominant" variational inequality subproblem will have a structure identical to a network equilibrium problem adjusted to the case of bounds on the transaction links to handle trade restrictions.

We state the algorithm for the computation of the disequilibrium problem VI 4.1 and then for VI 4.2. We also relate the statement of the algorithm for the computation of equilibrium problems VI 3.1 and VI 3.2. The statement for VI 4.3 and VI 4.4 and their equilibrium analogues should then be readily apparent. For proofs of global convergence, see Nagurney and Zhao (1990) and Nagurney and Zhao (1992).

Computation of VI 4.1

The algorithm computes a sequence (Q^0, u^0, w^0), (Q^1, u^1, w^1), ..., by solving three variational inequalities sequentially and converges to the solution of (29). The steps are:

Step 0: Start with any $(u^0, w^0) \in R^m_+ \times R^n_+$.
Step 1: $(t = 0, 1, 2, ...)$ Solve the variational inequality

$$\left[\hat{\tilde{\pi}}(Q, u^t) + c(Q) - \tilde{\hat{\rho}}(Q, w^t) \right] \cdot (Q' - Q) \geqq 0 \quad \text{for all } Q' \in K_1$$

(33)

The solution to (33) is Q^t.
Step 2: $(t = 0, 1, 2, ...,)$ Solve the variational inequality

$$\left[\hat{\pi}(Q^t, u) - \underline{\pi} \right] \cdot (u' - u) \geqq 0, \quad \text{for all } u' \in R^m_+.$$

(34)

The solution to (34) is u^{t+1}.
Step 3: $(t = 0, 1, 2, ...)$ Solve the variational inequality

$$\hat{\rho}(Q^t, w) \cdot (w' - w) \geqq 0, \quad \text{for all } w' \in R^n_+.$$

(35)

The solution to (35) is w^{t+1}.
Let $t = t + 1$, and go to Step 1.

The solution of equilibrium problem VI 3.1 can be obtained by setting $\underline{\pi}$ in (34) equal to zero and letting $K_1 = R^{mn}_+$ in (33).

Following the arguments in Nagurney and Zhao (1990), it can be shown that under the assumption that the supply price $\pi(s)$, demand price $\rho(d)$, and the transaction cost functions are strongly monotone in s, d, and Q, respectively, then each of the above subproblems (33), (34), and (35) admits a unique solution and, hence, the sequence (Q^t, u^t, w^t), $t = 1, 2, \ldots$ is well-defined. The economic meaning of such an assumption is that the supply price at a supply market depends primarily upon the supply of the commodity at that supply market, the demand price at a demand market depends primarily upon the demand for the commodity at the demand market, and the transaction cost between a pair of supply and demand markets depends primarily upon the commodity shipment between the pair of supply and demand markets. Such a condition is not unreasonable in appropriate applications.

Moreover, the algorithm is globally convergent under similar conditions to those given in Nagurney and Zhao (1990).

The effectiveness of the decomposition algorithm is based on the fact that the first variational inequality subproblem given in (33) is actually the one governing the well-known spatial price equilibrium problem in the case of equality constraints (see, e.g., Dafermos and Nagurney (1985), Nagurney (1987a)). Furthermore, this problem can be cast into a network equilibrium problem (with bounds on the transaction links) on a network with special structure (cf. Figure 2) (see also, e.g., Dafermos and Nagurney (1985), Dafermos (1986)). This problem can be efficiently solved using a Gauss-Seidel serial linearization algorithm (or a projection method) in which each restricted demand market equilibrium subproblem can be solved exactly in

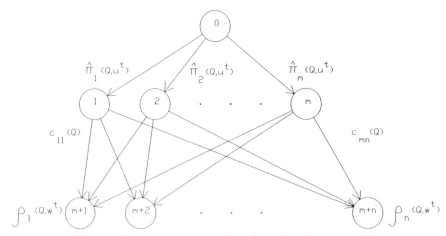

Figure 2. The network representation of variational inequality (33).

closed form via the algorithm introduced in Dafermos and Nagurney (1989) (see also, e.g., Nagurney (1987a,b, 1989a,b,c), Eydeland and Nagurney (1989), and Nagurney and Kim (1989)). Variational inequality subproblems (34) and (35) are very simple and can also be computed using a serial linearization method outlined in Nagurney (1987a).

In a similar manner, we have the

Computation of VI 4.2

The algorithm computes a sequence (Q^0, u^0, ρ^0), (Q^1, u^1, ρ^1),..., by solving three variational inequalities sequentially and converges to the solution of (30).

The steps are:

Step 0: Start with any $(u^0, \rho^0) \in R_+^m \times K_3$.

Step 1: $(t = 0, 1, 2, \ldots)$ Solve the variational inequality

$$\left[\tilde{\hat{\pi}}(Q, u^t) + c(Q) - \tilde{\hat{\rho}}^t\right] \cdot (Q' - Q) \geqq 0 \quad \text{for all } Q' \in K_1. \quad (36)$$

The solution to (36) is Q^t.

Step 2: $(t = 0, 1, 2, \ldots)$ Solve the variational inequality

$$\left[\hat{\pi}(Q^t, u) - \underline{\pi}\right] \cdot (u' - u) \geqq 0, \quad \text{for all } u' \in R_+^m. \quad (37)$$

The solution to (37) is u^{t+1}.

Step 3: $(t = 0, 1, 2, \ldots)$ Solve the variational inequality

$$D(Q^t, \rho) \cdot (\rho' - \rho) \geqq 0, \quad \text{for all } \rho' \in K_3. \quad (38)$$

The solution to (38) is ρ^{t+1}.

Let $t = t + 1$, and go to Step 1.

The solution of the equilibrium analogue, VI 3.2, follows by setting $\underline{\pi} = 0$ in (37), and letting $K_1 = R_+^{mn}$ in (36) and $K_3 = R_+^m$ in (38).

Each of the above variational inequality subproblems (36), (37), and (38) will admit unique solutions, provided that $\pi(s)$, $c(Q)$, and $d(\rho)$ are each strongly monotone in s, Q and ρ, respectively. Thus, the sequence (Q^t, u^t, ρ^t), $t = 1, 2, \ldots$ is well-defined and can be obtained by applying any appropriate algorithm for the computation of the individual variational inequalities (36), (37), and (38). In particular, variational inequality (37) is identical to variational inequality (34). Variational inequality (36), on the other hand, also

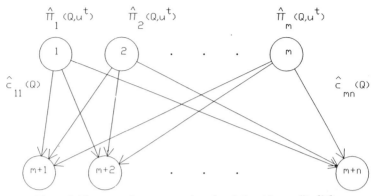

Figure 3. The network representation of variational inequality (36).

has a simple network structure which should be exploited and which will now be elaborated upon, cf. Figure 3. Specifically, variational inequality (36) is a specially-structured network equilibrium problem in which there are m origins and n potential destinations, where users at each origin seek to establish their personal cost-minimizing destinations, where the transaction cost associated between origin i and any destination j is given by:

$$\hat{c}_{ij}(Q) = c_{ij}(Q) - \rho_j^t, \quad \text{for } j = 1, \ldots, n \tag{39}$$

and the attractiveness function associated with an origin i is defined to be equal to $\hat{\pi}_i(Q, t)$. The paths available from each origin i to destinations j, $j = 1, \ldots, n$ consist of single disjoint links (i, j). Observe that the characteristic network representation of variational inequality (36) is even simpler than the one encountered in the traffic network equilibrium representation of the spatial price equilibrium problem encountered in (33). In particular, variational inequality (36) can be solved by a Gauss-Seidel serial linearization decomposition algorithm by supply markets given in Nagurney (1987a), in which the supply market equilibration algorithm introduced in Dafermos and Nagurney (1989) and further theoretically analyzed in Nagurney and Eydeland (1989) is embedded. This algorithm exploits the "disjointness" of the origin/destination paths explicitly, by solving each supply market equilibrium subproblem exactly in closed form.

A mirror image network on the demand side to the one in Figure 3 may be constructed for the dominant variational inequality subproblem encountered in the application of the decomposition algorithm to VI 4.3 and VI 3.3. On the other hand, VI 4.4 and VI 3.4, although the most general formulations, have no apparent network structure in the principal variational inequality subproblem which can be exploited. Nevertheless, the encountered principal variational inequality subproblem is simple to compute using, again, a term-by-term Gauss-Seidel scheme.

In the next section, we provide computational results for the decomposition alogrithm applied to VI 4.2 VI 3.2.

6. Numerical Experience

In this section we consider, as an illustration, the spatial market models formulated as VI 4.2 and VI 3.2 and we provide numerical experience with the variational inequality decomposition algorithm outlined in Section 5.

Since the decomposition algorithm resolves the solution of VI 4.2 and VI 3.2 into three simpler variational inequality subproblems, the decomposition algorithm allows one the opportunity to select any appropriate algorithm for the individual variational inequality subproblems. However, due to the special structure of the first and principal variational inequality subproblem (36), the application of a special-purpose algorithm is appealing. Hence, as mentioned in the preceding section, we will apply the Gauss-Seidel serial decomposition algorithm by supply markets (with the appropriate simplification since the demand prices now are fixed) in which we embed, also accordingly simplified, the supply market equilibration algorithm, proposed in Dafermos and Nagurney (1989) which solves each restricted supply market equilibrium subproblem exactly, rather than iteratively. Gauss-Seidel serial decomposition algorithms are also adapted to compute the solutions to (37) and (38). We chose to use an equilibration algorithm, rather than an algorithm such as Frank-Wolfe (1956), since computational tests contained in Nagurney (1984, 1987a, 1989c), Dafermos and Nagurney (1989), Nagurney, Kim, and Robinson (1990) strongly suggest that special-purpose algorithms are more efficient in the context of network-based equilibrium problems. Of course, if a special-purpose algorithm is not available to the practitioner, a general-purpose algorithm or package, such as MINOS, can be used to compute the embedded mathematical programming problems. For alternative algorithms and references, see Nagurney (1987b).

In our computational test, we, hence, utilized the above described algorithms for the computation of the individual variational inequality subproblems.

In order to illustrate how the decomposition algorithm performs computationally we considered spatial market problems with linear asymmetric functions, where the supply price functions are given by

$$\pi_i = \pi_i(s) = \sum_j r_{ij}s_j + t_i = \hat{\pi}_i(Q, u) = \sum_j r_{ij}\left(\sum_k Q_{jk} + u_j\right) + t_i, \qquad (40)$$

the demand functions are given by

$$d_j = d_j(\rho) = -\sum_k p_{jk}\rho_k + l_j \qquad (41)$$

and the transaction cost functions are given by

$$c_{ij} = c_{ij}(Q) = \sum_{kl} g_{ijkl}Q_{kl} + h_{ij}, \qquad (42)$$

where the not necessarily symmetric Jacobians of the supply price and transaction cost functions are positive definite, whereas the Jacobian of the demand functions is negative definite.

In this section we considered randomly generated market problems in which the supply price (40), and transaction cost functions (42) were generated uniformly in the same manner as described in Nagurney (1987a). In particular, the function term ranges were as follows: $r_{ii} \in [3, 10]$, $t_i \in [10, 25]$ and $g_{ijij} \in [1, 15]$, $h_{ij} \in [10, 25]$, $i = 1, \ldots, m$; $j = 1, \ldots, n$. The demand functions were generated so that: $-p_{jj} \in [-10, -15]$, $l_j \in [1150, 1650]$. The remaining r_{ij}, $-p_{jk}$, and g_{ijkl} terms were generated to ensure that the Jacobian matrices were strictly diagonal dominant and, hence, positive definite. We set the number of supply markets m equal to the number of demand markets n and varied the problem sizes from 45 supply markets and 45 demand markets (90 markets total) to 90 supply markets and 90 demand markets (180 markets total) in increments of 15 markets. These problems are larger than the equilibrium problems considered in Nagurney (1987a) and of the same size as the disequilibrium problems solved for the inverse demand models in Nagurney and Zhao (1990).

In Table 1 we fixed the number of cross-terms in the functions (40), (41), and (42) to 5, whereas in Table 2, we fixed the number of cross-terms to 10. We set $\underline{M} = 0$, and $\overline{M} = \infty$. The termination criterion utilized was $|\pi_i + c_{ij} - \rho_j| \leq \epsilon = 5$, if $Q_{ij} > 0$ and $\pi_i + c_{ij} - \rho_j \geq -\epsilon$ if $Q_{ij} = 0$ and $\pi_i \geq \underline{\pi}_i$, $\underline{\rho}_j \leq \rho_j \leq \bar{\rho}_j$ where ρ was set at zero and $(\pi_i - \underline{\pi}_i) \cdot u_i \leq 5$; $(\Sigma_i Q_{ij} - d_j(\rho)) \times \bar{\rho}_j \leq 5$, if $\underline{\rho}_j < \rho_j < \bar{\rho}_j$; $(\Sigma_i Q_{ij} - d_j(\rho)) \leq 0$, if $\rho_j = \bar{\rho}_j$, and $(\Sigma_i Q_{ij} - d_j(\rho)) \geq 0$, if $\underline{\rho}_j = \rho_j$. Since verification of convergence can in itself be computationally time-con-

Table 1

Computational Experience on Large-Scale Spatial Market Problems. Number of crossterms = 5, CPU time in seconds (a,b,c)

(m, n)	$\underline{\pi} = 0, \underline{\rho} = 0, \bar{\rho} = 1000$	$\underline{\pi} = 0, \underline{\rho} = 0, \bar{\rho} = 50$	$\underline{\pi} = 150, \underline{\rho} = 0, \bar{\rho} = 750$
(45, 45)	4.33(0, 0, 0)	1.64(0, 0, 33)	3.82(38, 0, 0)
(60, 60)	7.26(0, 0, 0)	3.07(0, 0, 50)	5.05(55, 0, 0)
(75, 75)	12.00(0, 0, 0)	4.88(0, 0, 61)	10.64(65, 0, 0)
(90, 90)	18.02(0, 0, 0)	5.74(0, 0, 78)	15.86((84, 0, 0)

[a] Number of supply markets, i, with supply price $\pi_i = \underline{\pi}_i$.
[b] Number of demand markets, j, with demand price $\rho_j = \underline{\rho}_j$.
[c] Number of demand markets, j, with demand price $\rho_j = \bar{\rho}_j$.

suming, especially in large-scale examples, we verified convergence for variational inequality (36) after every other iteration.

The algorithm was coded in FORTRAN and compiled using the FORTVS compiler, optimization level 3 on the IBM 4381–14 mainframe at the Cornell National Supercomputer Facility. The CPU times reported in Tables 1 and 2 are exclusive of input and output. The initial pattern was set at $Q_{ij} = 0$ for all i and j, $u_i = \max(0, \underline{\pi}_i - t_i/r_{ii})$, for all i, and $\rho_j = \max(0, \bar{\rho}_j)$ for all j.

In each of the first column examples in Tables 1 and 2, we set $\underline{\pi}_i = 0$ for all i, $\rho_j = 0$, and $\bar{\rho}_j = 1000$ for all j. (In view of the generation of functions such price floors and ceilings would generate equilibrium solutions.) Hence, the reported CPU times in these columns reflect the computational time for the decomposition algorithm to solve the market model governed by VI 3.2.

To the same problems, we then tightened the bounds on the demand side in column 2 of each table where $\underline{\pi} = 0$, $\underline{\rho} = 0$, and $\bar{\rho} = 50$. We also report the

Table 2

Computational Experience on Large-Scale Spatial Market Problems. Number of crossterms = 10, CPU time in seconds (a,b,c)

(m, n)	$\underline{\pi} = 0, \underline{\rho} = 0, \bar{\rho} = 1000$	$\underline{\pi} = 0, \underline{\rho} = 0, \bar{\rho} = 50$	$\underline{\pi} = 150, \underline{\rho} = 0, \bar{\rho} = 750$
(45, 45)	9.11(0, 0, 0)	2.72(0, 0, 34)	5.10(39, 0, 0)
(60, 60)	14.30(0, 0, 0)	4.96(0, 0, 45)	10.41(51, 0, 0)
(75, 75)	21.09(0, 0, 0)	6.29(0, 0, 59)	16.81(64, 0, 0)
(90, 90)	24.66(0, 0, 0)	11.80(0, 0, 67)	5.98(79, 0, 0)

[a] Number of supply markets, i, with supply price $\pi_i = \underline{\pi}_i$.
[b] Number of demand markets, j, with demand price $\rho_j = \underline{\rho}_j$.
[c] Number of demand markets, j, with demand price $\rho_j = \bar{\rho}_j$.

number of supply and demand markets in which the respective prices are at one of the bounds. In column 3 of each table we then raised the supply price floors to $\underline{\pi} = 150$ and loosened the demand price ceilings to $\bar{\rho} = 750$, but kept $\underline{\rho} = 0$, and report the number of supply and demand markets with prices at the bounds.

As can be seen from Tables 1 and 2, the decomposition algorithm was robust, converging for all the examples and requiring only seconds of CPU time on a readily available mainframe. The other models discussed in Sections 2 and 3 can now also be solved in a timely fashion using the variational inequality decomposition procedure. At the present time there are no alternative algorithms for the above disequilibrium models, since the models themselves are new.

The spatial price models presented and synthesized in this paper should enable the computation of a greater spectrum of problems than heretofore was possible, thus expanding the potential scope of applications for policy analyses.

7. Summary and Conclusions

In this paper we have focused on general, asymmetric, perfectly competitive spatial price equilibrium problems using as the stimulus the fundamental contributions of Takayama and Judge (1971). In particular, we have shown how variational inequality theory and networks can be utilized to formulate, study, compute, and synthesize a spectrum of spatial price problems. We first considered market models in the absence of policy instruments, and then in the presence of such interventions as price controls on the production and consumption sides and trade restrictions. The models presented were related to other models in the literature and include quantity models, price models, and combined quantity-price models.

The theory of variational inequalities, hence, can be viewed as playing the same role in the analysis of equilibrium and disequilibrium problems as mathematical programming has in optimization problems. Indeed, although we have concentrated our attention on perfectly competitive partial equilibrium models, imperfectly competitive oligopolistic market equilibrium problems operating under the Cournot-Nash behavioral postulate, Walrasian price and general economic equilibrium problems, and migration equilibrium problems, have all been formulated and studied as variational inequality problems. Moreover, since the variational inequality problem contains, as special cases: linear and nonlinear complementarity problems, fixed point problems, min/max problems, as well as minimization problems, it provides us with a powerful unifying framework, of which we can expect to see more use in economics in the future.

References

Bachem, A., and Korte, B. (1978), "Algorithm for Quadratic Optimization over Transportation Polytopes," *Zeitschrift fur Angewandte Mathematik und Mechanik*, 58, T459–T461.

Beckmann, M.J., McGuire, C.B., and Winsten, C.B. (1956), *Studies in the Economics of Transportation*, New Haven, CT: Yale University Press.

Bertsekas, D.P., and Gafni, E.M. (1983), "Projected Newton Methods and Optimization of Multicommodity Flows," *IEEE Transactions on Automatic Control*, AC-28, no. 12, 1090–1096.

Bertsekas, D.P., and Tsitsiklis, J.N. (1989), *Parallel and Distributed Computation*, Englewood Cliffs, NJ: Prentice-Hall.

Border, K.C. (1985), *Fixed Point Theory with Application to Economics and Game Theory*, Cambridge, UK: Cambridge University Press.

Dafermos, S. (1980), "Traffic Equilibrium and Variational Inequalities," *Transportation Science*, 14, 42–54.

Dafermos, S. (1982), "The General Multimodal Traffic Network Equilibrium Problem with Elastic Demand," *Networks*, 12, 57–72.

Dafermos, S. (1983), "An Iterative Scheme for Variational Inequalities," *Mathematical Programming*, 28, 57–72.

Dafermos, S. (1986), " Isomorphic Multiclass Spatial Price and Multimodal Traffic Network Equilibrium Models," *Regional Science and Urban Economics*, 16, 197–209.

Dafermos, S. (1987), "Congested Transportation Networks and Variational Inequalities," in Odoni, Bianco, and Szego (eds.), *Flow Control of Congested Networks* (NATO ASI Series, Series F: Computer and Systems Sciences), 38, Berlin: Springer-Verlag.

Dafermos, S. (1988), "Sensitivity Analysis in Variational Inequalities," *Mathematics of Operations Research*, 13, 421–434.

Dafermos, S. and McKelvey, S. (1986), "Equilibrium Analysis of Competitive Economic Systems and Variational Inequalities," Lefschetz Center for Dynamical Systems, Brown University, Providence, RI, LCDS #86–26.

Dafermos, S., and Nagurney, A. (1984a), "Sensitivity Analysis for the General Spatial Economics Equilibrium Problem," *Operations Research*, 32, 1069–1086.

Dafermos, S., and Nagurney, A. (1984b), "A Network Formulation of Market Equilibrium Problems and Variational Inequalities," *Operations Research Letters*, 3, 247–250.

Dafermos, S., and Nagurney, A. (1985), "Isomorphism Between Spatial Price and Traffic Network Equilibrium Models," LCDS #85–17, Brown University, Providence, RI.

Dafermos, S., and Nagurney, A. (1987), "Oligopolistic and Competitive Behavior of Spatially Separated Markets," *Regional Science and Urban Economics*, 17, 245–254.

Dafermos, S., and Nagurney, A. (1989), " Supply and Demand Equilibration Algorithms for a Class of Market Equilibrium Problems," *Transportation Science*, 23, 118–124.

Eydeland, A., and Nagurney, A. (1989), "Progressive Equilibration Algorithms: the Case of Linear Transaction Costs," *Computer Science in Economics and Management*, 2, 197–219.

Florian, M., and Los, M. (1982), " A New Look at Static Spatial Price Equilibrium Models," *Regional Science and Urban Economics*, 12, 579–597.

Florian, M., and Spiess, H. (1982), "The Convergence of Diagonalization Algorithms for Asymmetric Network Equilibrium Problems," *Transportation Science*, 16B, 477–483.

Frank, M., and Wolfe, P. (1956), "An Algorithm for Quadratic Programming," *Naval Research Logistics Quarterly*, 3, 95–110.

Friesz, T.L., Harker, P.T., and Tobin, R.L. (1984), "Alternative Algorithms for the General Network Spatial Price Equilibrium Problem," *Journal of Regional Science*, 24, 473–507.

Gabay, D., and Moulin, H. (1980), "On the Uniqueness and Stability of Nash-Equilibria in Noncooperative Games," in A. Bensoussan, P. Kleindorfer, and C.S. Tapiero (eds.), *Applied Stochastic Control in Economics and Management Science*, Amsterdam: North-Holland Publishing Co.

Greenberg, H.J., and Murphy, F.H. (1985), "Computing Market Equilibria with Price Regulations using Mathematical Programming," *Operations Research*, 33, 935–953.

Harker, P.T. (1986), "Alternative Models of Spatial Competition," *Operations Research*, 34, 410–425.

Hartman, P., and Stampacchia, G. (1966), "On Some Nonlinear Elliptical Differential Functional Equations," *Acta Mathematica*, 115, 271–310.

Judge, G.G., and Takayama, T., (eds.), (1973), *Studies in Economic Planning Over Space and Time*, Amsterdam: North-Holland Publishing Co.

Kinderlehrer, D., and Stampacchia, G. (1980), *An Introduction to Variational Inequalities*, New York: Academic Press.

Magnanti, T. (1984), "Models and Algorithms for Predicting Urban Traffic Equilibria," in *Transportation Planning Models*, M. Florian (ed.).

Moore, C., and Nagurney, A. (1989), "A General Equilibrium Model of Interregional Monetary Flows," *Environment and Planning A*, 21, 397–404.

Murtagh, B.A., and Saunders, M.A. (1983), "MINOS 5.1 Users" Guide, Report SOL 83–2OR, December 1983, revised January 1987, Stanford U., CA.

Nagurney, A. (1984), "Comparative Tests of Multimodal Traffic Equilibrium Methods," *Transportation Research*, 18B, 469–485.

Nagurney, A. (1987a), "Computational Comparisons of Spatial Price Equilibrium Methods," *Journal of Regional Science*, 27, 55–76.

Nagurney, A. (1987b), "Competitive Equilibrium Problems, Variational Inequality Problems, and Regional Science," *Journal of Regional Science*, 27, 503–517.

Nagurney, A. (1988), "Algorithms for Oligopolistic Market Equilibrium Problems," *Regional Science and Urban Economics*, 18, 425–445.

Nagurney, A. (1989a), " An Algorithm for the Solution of a Quadratic Programming Problem with Application to Constrained Matrix and Spatial Price Equilibrium Problems," *Environment & Planning A*, 21, 99–114.

Nagurney, A. (1989b), "Migration Equilibrium and Variational Inequalities," *Economics Letters*, 31, 109–112.

Nagurney, A. (1989c), "Import and Export Equilibration Algorithms for the Net Import Spatial Price Equilibrium Problem," *Journal of Cost Analysis*, 7, 73–88.

Nagurney, A. (1989d), "On the Solution of Large-Scale Multicommodity Market Equilibrium Problems Over Space and Time," *European Journal of Operations Research*, 42, 166–177.

Nagurney, A. (1990), " A Network Model of Migration Equilibrium with Movement Costs," *Mathematical and Computer Modelling*, 13, 79–88.

Nagurney, A., and Aronson, J.E. (1988), "A General Dynamic Spatial Price Equilibrium Model: Formulation, Solution, and Computational Results," *Journal of Computational and Applied Mathematics*, 22, 359–377.

Nagurney, A. and Aronson, J.E. (1989), "A General Dynamic Spatial Price Network Equilibrium Model with Gains and Losses," *Networks*, 19, 751–769.

Nagurney, A. and Kim, D.S. (1989), "Parallel and Serial Variational Inequality Decomposition Algorithms for Multicommodity Market Equilibrium Problems," *The International Journal of Supercomputer Applications*, 3, 34–58.

Nagurney, A., Kim, D.S., and Robinson, A.G. (1990), "Serial and Parallel Equilibration of Large-Scale Constrained Matrix Problems with Application to the Social and Economic Sciences," *The International Journal of Supercomputer Applications*, 4.1, 49–71.

Nagurney, A. and Zhao, L. (1990), "Disequilibrium and Variational Inequalities," *Journal of Computational and Applied Mathematics*, 33, 181–198.

Nagurney, A. and Zhao, L. (1991), "A Network Equilibrium Formulation of Market Disequilibrium and Variational Inequalities," *Networks*, 21, 109–132.

Nagurney, A. and Zhao, L. (1992), "Networks and Variational Inequalities in the Formulation and Computation of Spatial Equilibria and Disequilibria: The Case of Direct Demand Functions," *Transportation Science*, in press.

Newcomb, R.T., Reynolds, S.S., and Masbruch, T.A. (1989), "Changing Patterns of Investment Decision-Making in World Aluminum," *Resources and Energy*, 11, 261–297.

Pang, J.S., and Chan, D. (1981), "Iterative Methods for Variational and Complementarity Problems," *Mathematical Programming*, 24, 284–313.

Samuelson, P.A. (1952), "A Spatial Price Equilibrium and Linear Programming," *American Economic Review*, 42, 283–303.

Stone, R. (1950), "Simple Transaction Models, Information, and Computing," *The Review of Economic Studies*, XIX(2), 67–84.

Takayama, T., and Judge, G.G. (1964), "Equilibrium Among Spatially Separated Markets: A Reformulation," *Econometrica*, 32, 510–524.

Takayama, T., and Judge, G.G. (1971), *Spatial and Temporal Price and Allocation Models*, Amsterdam: North-Holland Publishing Co.

Takayama, T., and Labys, W.C. (1986), "Spatial Equilibrium Analysis: Mathematical and Programming Formulations of Agricultural, Mineral, and Emergy Models," in P. Nijkamp (ed.), *Handbook of Regional Economics*, Amsterdam: North-Holland Publishing Co..

Thore, S. (1986), "Spatial Disequilibrium," *Journal of Regional Science*, 26, 660–675.

Uri, N. (1975), *Toward an Efficient Allocation of Electric Energy*, Lexington, MA: Heath Lexington Books.

Zhao, L. (1989), Variational Inequalities in General Equilibrium: Analysis and Computation, Ph.D. thesis, Division of Applied Mathematics, Brown University, Providence, RI, also as LCDS/CCS Report #88–24 (1988), Division of Applied Mathematics, Brown University, Providence, RI.

Readings in Econometric Theory and Practice
W. Griffiths, H. Lütkepohl and M.E. Bock (Editors)

CHAPTER 15

IMPERFECT COMPETITION AND ARBITRAGE IN SPATIALLY SEPARATED MARKETS *

Terry L. Friesz

Departments of Systems Engineering and Operations Research & Applied Statistics, George Mason University, Fairfax, VA 22030, USA

David Bernstein

Department of Civil Engineering, Massachusetts Institute of Technology, Cambridge, MA 02139, USA

Recently, spatial price equilibrium models have been extended to include firms with market power. Unfortunately, however, these analyses have ignored the fact that arbitrageurs can severely limit the extent to which firms can price discriminate. In this paper we construct a model of oligopoly behavior that incorporates 'competition' from arbitrageurs. This model, which we formulate as a complementarity problem, is a natural extension of the complementarity formulation of the Samuelson-Takayama-Judge spatial price equilibrium model.

1. Introduction

The seminal papers on the equilibrium of spatially separated markets by Samuelson (1952) and Takayama and Judge (1964, 1970, 1971) have generated an enormous amount of interest. While the original formulation restricted the problem to separable, linear, supply and demand functions, fixed transportation costs and a bipartite transportation network, it has since been extended in numerous ways by many different authors [see, for example, MacKinnon (1976), Carey (1980), Florian and Los (1982), Tobin and Friesz (1983), Friesz et al. (1983), and Nagurney (1987b)]. Unfortunately, however, most of the extensions of the original model have been "mathematical" in nature (e.g., generalizing existence results, allowing more complicated trans-

---

* The authors are indebted to an anonymous referee for helpful comments on an earlier draft of this paper.

portation networks and cost functions, improving algorithms) and considerably less attention has been given to extending the underlying behavioral assumptions. This has somewhat limited the applicability of these models.

In response to this criticism, several authors have recently expanded the scope of SPE models by relaxing some of these behavioral assumptions. For example, Tobin and Friesz (1985) discuss the problem of optimally locating the production facilities of a large firm that is entering a spatially competitive market. As another example, Smith and Friesz (1985) extended the basic model to allow supply and demand levels which depend on commodity flows as well as prices in order to allow for behavior based on quantity and price signals. Finally, Harker (1985, 1986), Weskamp (1985), and Dafermos and Nagurney (1987), look at alternatives to the assumption of perfect competition and spatial monopoly employed by earlier authors.

This paper also considers a behavioral extension of the SPE model; it extends the aforementioned studies of imperfect competition within the spatial price equilibrium framework. In particular, we recognize that price discriminators can actually face "competition" from arbitrageurs and develop a suitable extension to the Samuelson-Takayama-Judge spatial price equilibrium model. We begin by motivating the problem using a textbook example of a price discriminating monopolist and demonstrating that the classic solution often cannot be sustained because it ignores arbitrageurs. We then review a more rigorous model of imperfect competition on a network, and demonstrate that this model ignores "competition" from arbitrageurs also. Following this, we present a model of oligopolistic behavior which includes arbitrageurs. Finally, we conclude with a discussion of possible extensions, including a description of several markets for which this model is appropriate. Throughout the entire discussion we will present small numerical examples that help illustrate our main points.

2. Motivation

The easiest way to demonstrate the hidden "competition" that many price discriminators face is to consider a textbook example of imperfect competition in spatially separated markets, namely the problem of the price discriminating monopolist. We set this problem on a *network* [1], $\mathscr{G}$, comprised of a set of *nodes*, $\mathscr{N}$, and *links*, $\mathscr{L}$. The cardinalities of $\mathscr{N}$ and $\mathscr{L}$ are denoted by $N = |\mathscr{N}|$ and $L = |\mathscr{L}|$ respectively. Each node, $i \in \mathscr{N}$, represents a popula-

---

[1] There is an extensive literature set within a Löschian framework. See, for example, the early work by Stevens and Rydell (1966) or the more recent work by Spulber (1984). These models assume that there is a "continuous plane" of consumers.

tion of consumers, and each link, $l \in \mathscr{L}$, represents a transport connection between an origin-destination (O-D) pair. For simplicity, we assume that $\mathscr{G}$ is a complete symmetric graph (i.e., that there is a link between every origin and destination that represents the only way to transport goods between that origin and destination). Further, we let p_i denote the (demand) *price* at node i, q_i denote the *quantity* of the single commodity (supplied) at node i, and c_{ij} denote the cost of *shipping* one unit of the commodity from node i to node j (where c_{ii} is assumed to be zero for all $i \in \mathscr{N}$).

For example, consider a single firm located at node 1, serving two separate markets located at nodes 1 and 2, and suppose that the inverse demand function in market 1 is given by

$$p_1 = 4 - q_1 \tag{1}$$

and in market 2 is given by

$$p_2 = 6 - 2q_2. \tag{2}$$

Suppose further that the total cost function for the single firm (located at node 1) is given by

$$C = 0.2(q_1 + q_2) \tag{3}$$

(i.e., zero fixed cost and constant marginal cost), and that the transportation cost between all nodes is zero (i.e., $c_{12} = c_{21} = 0$). As is well-known from elementary microeconomics, the profit-maximizing monopolist should equate its marginal revenue in each market with its marginal cost. In this case, the firm should produce 3.35 units in total, selling 1.90 units at market 1 and shipping 1.45 units to market 2. The resulting prices are 2.1 in market 1, and 3.1 in market 2.

Underlying this analysis is the assumption that the two markets are completely separated. In other words, while the monopolist can transport goods from market 1 to market 2 nobody else can, and consumers cannot travel to other markets to make purchases. However, in practice few markets, if any, are so completely separated (spatially). In fact, it is often possible for consumers to travel between markets to make purchases, and even when this is not the case, it is almost always possible for *arbitrageurs* [2] to purchase in

---

[2] Strictly speaking, an arbitrageur simultaneously purchases in one market and sells in another, thereby insuring a riskless profit. Given that the models discussed here are inherently static, our use of this term does not seem to be an abuse, and it more accurately conveys the role of these people than the term 'trader' does.

one market and resell in another. [3] If either or both of these is the case then the monopolist may be unable to sustain the profit-maximizing solution. In general, if other players can transport goods as effectively as the producing firm, then prices cannot vary between the two markets by more than the transport cost. In the above example this means that prices can't vary at all, leading to simple monopoly conditions in selling. In this example, the profit-maximizing solution that prevents arbitrageurs from "competing" is $q_1 = 1.5330$, and $q_2 = 1.7665$, with $p_1 = p_2 = 2.467$.

Of course, this observation does not begin with us [Simkin (1948) credits it to Pigou], however it does seem to have been ignored in the recently developed models of spatial oligopoly. In the remainder of this paper we explore how arbitrageurs can be incorporated into models of spatial oligopoly.

3. A Model of Oligopoly Behavior

We begin with a statement of a Cournot-Nash network oligopoly model that is similar in spirit to the models of Harker (1985,1986), Weskamp (1985), and Dafermos and Nagurney (1987). [4] Let $\Re$, $\Re_+$, and $\Re_{++}$ denote the *real numbers, nonnegative reals*, and *positive reals* respectively; let $\mathscr{Z}$ denote the *integers*; and let $\mathscr{C}^1(\mathscr{C}^2)$ denote the set of *once (twice) continuously differentiable functions*. We assume that at each node, $i \in \mathscr{N}$, there is exactly one firm, and that this firm can sell in every market, $j \in \mathscr{N}$. The quantity supplied by firm i to market j is represented by q_{ij}, and $q = (q_{ij}, i, j \in \mathscr{N})^\top$ denotes the complete vector of commodity shipments. The firm is assumed to bear the unit transportation cost which is a function, $c_{ij}(q) \in \mathscr{C}^1$, of the complete vector of commodity shipments; and the price at each market, $j \in \mathscr{N}$, is given by a decreasing *inverse demand function*, $p_j(q) \in \mathscr{C}^1$, of the form

$$p_j = p_j \left(\sum_{i \in \mathscr{N}} q_{ij} \right). \tag{4}$$

---

[3] Harker (1986) observes that, in most cases, the producing firm buys transportation services in a competitive market. Hence, other parties should also be able to purchase these services at the same price. In addition, even when the producing firm is a monopsonist in transportation services or owns its own fleet of vehicles, consumers are generally not prevented from purchasing the good in other markets.

[4] Again, there is a large body of literature that deals with oligopoly behavior within a Löschian framework. See, for example, the early work by Hoover (1937), or the more recent work by Greenhut and Greenhut (1975) and Carlton (1983).

This function represents the price that must be charged at market j in order to encourage local consumption equal to $\sum_{i \in \mathcal{N}} q_{ij}$. Further, we assume that the firm located at i has an increasing total (production) *cost function*, $C_i(q) \in \mathscr{C}^1$, given by

$$C_i = C_i\left(\sum_{j \in \mathcal{N}} q_{ij} \right). \tag{5}$$

Now, letting

$$\tilde{q}_{ij} = \sum_{k \neq i} q_{kj} \tag{6}$$

represent the quantity supplied to j by all firms other than i (which firm i assumes to be constant), observe that (4) can be rewritten as

$$p_j = p_j(q_{ij} + \tilde{q}_{ij}). \tag{7}$$

Hence, the *profit* function for firm i can be defined as

$$\pi_i = \sum_{j \in \mathcal{N}} \left\{ q_{ij}\left[p_j(q_{ij} + \tilde{q}_{ij}) - c_{ij}(q) \right] \right\} - C_i\left(\sum_{j \in \mathcal{N}} q_{ij} \right). \tag{8}$$

If we further assume that each firm is a price-taker in the transportation market, and denote the *total revenue* accruing to firm i as a result of sales to j as

$$R_{ij}(q) = q_{ij}\left[p_j(q_{ij} + \tilde{q}_{ij}) \right], \tag{9}$$

then the profit maximization problem for firm i is given by

$$\max_{q_i.} \left\{ \sum_{j \in \mathcal{N}} \left(R_{ij}(q) - c_{ij}(q)q_{ij} - C_i(q) \right) \mid q_i. \geq 0 \right\}, \tag{10}$$

where $q_{i.} = (q_{ij}, j \in \mathcal{N})^{\top}$ denotes the *supply vector* for firm i. The Karush-Kuhn-Tucker (KKT) conditions (which are both necessary and sufficient) for firm i's profit-maximization problem are given by

$$\left[C_i'(q) + c_{ij}(q) - R_{ij}'(q) \right] - \lambda_{ij} = 0 \quad \forall j \in \mathcal{N} \tag{11}$$

$$\lambda_{ij} q_{ij} = 0 \quad \forall i, j \in \mathcal{N} \tag{12}$$

$$\lambda_{ij} \geqq 0 \quad \forall j \in \mathcal{N} \tag{13}$$

$$q_{ij} \geqq 0 \quad \forall j \in \mathcal{N} \tag{14}$$

where $R_{ij}'(q) = \partial R_{ij}(q)/\partial q_{ij}$, $C_i'(q) = \partial C_i(q)/\partial q_{ij}$ $(= \partial C_i(q)/\partial q_{ik})$, and λ_{ij} is the Lagrange multiplier associated with the constraint $q_{ij} \geqq 0$.

Given this notation, we now consider the usual Cournot-Nash definition of an equilibrium:

Definition 1 *A commodity production pattern,* $q = (q_{ij}, i, j \in \mathcal{N})^\top \in \Re_+^{N \times N}$, *is said to be a Cournot-Nash equilibrium if and only if (iff)*

$$\pi_i(q) \geqq \pi_i(\bar{q}) \tag{15}$$

for all i and $\bar{q} \in \Re_+^{N \times N}$ where $\bar{q}_{kj} = q_{kj}$ for all j and $k \neq i$.

That is, we say that the market is in equilibrium iff each firm is maximizing profits given the behavior of all of the other firms.

We now also need the following definition [following Karamardian (1971)].

Definition 2 *For a given map, F: $\Re^n \to \Re^n$, the problem of finding a vector, $q \in \Re^n$, satisfying*

$$q \in \Re_+^n \quad F(q) \in \Re_+^n \quad q^\top F(q) = 0 \tag{16}$$

is referred to as the complementarity problem (CP). Each solution to a CP is referred to as a CP-solution.

Letting

$$F = \left[\left(C_i'(q) + c_{ij}(q) - R_{ij}'(q) \right), \quad i, j \in \mathcal{N} \right]^\top \tag{17}$$

we can now demonstrate the following result:

Theorem 1 *q is a Cournot-Nash equilibrium if and only if it is a CP-solution for F as defined* (17).

Proof. We begin by observing that we need only demonstrate this result for some arbitrary firm, i, since a sum of non-negative terms is zero iff each term is identically zero. Now, consider any firm i.

($\Rightarrow$) First, since $\lambda_{ij} \geq 0$ for all $j \in \mathcal{N}$, we know from that $[C_i'(q) + c_{ij}(q) - R_{ij}'(q)] \geq 0$ for all $j \in \mathcal{N}$, and from (14) we know immediately that $q_{ij} \geq 0$ for all $j \in \mathcal{N}$. Also, if $\lambda_{ij} > 0$ then by (12) and the nonnegativity of λ and q, we must have $q_{ij} = 0$. On the other hand, if $\lambda_{ij} = 0$ then by (11) it must be true that $[C_i'(q) + c_{ij}(q) - R_{ij}'(q)] = 0$. Thus, either $q_{ij} = 0$ or $[C_i'(q) + c_{ij}(q) - R_{ij}'(q)] = 0$ for all $j \in \mathcal{N}$.

($\Leftarrow$) First, observe that the positivity condition, (14), follows immediately from (16). Further, if $q_{ij} > 0$ then $[C_i'(q) + c_{ij}(q) - R_{ij}'(q)] = 0$, and hence (11) and (12) hold with $\lambda_{ij} = 0$. On the other hand, if $[C_i'(q) + c_{ij}(q) - R_{ij}'(q)] > 0$ then $q_{ij} = 0$, and hence (11) and (12) hold with $\lambda_{ij} = [C_i'(q) + c_{ij}(q) - R_{ij}'(q)] > 0$. In either case, $\lambda_{ij} \geq 0$ and hence (13) holds. $\square$

Remark This result is a straightforward extension of the results in Gabay and Moulin (1980) to problems with spatially separated firms.

4. Arbitrage Opportunities

The model described in Section 3 above might be used to describe a wide variety of markets [e.g., the market for crude oil (ignoring quality differences which are generally accounted for by fixed price differentials)]. However, this model, like the monopoly model described in Section 2 ignores the existence of arbitrageurs [e.g., traders in the "famous" New York-London arbitrage in the oil market]. Hence, we now extend this model to explicitly include arbitrageurs.

4.1. Model Formulation

First, let T_{ij} denote the quantity of the commodity shipped from i to j by arbitrageurs, [5] and let $T = (T_{ij}, i, j \in \mathcal{N})^\top$ denote the complete *arbitrage flow pattern*. [6] With this notation, we now assume that each firm is only

---

[5] We should again emphasize that we are using the term "arbitrageur" loosely. Hence, consumers that travel to a "foreign" market to make purchases are viewed as arbitrageurs, and T_{ij} includes the purchases made in market i by consumers located at market j.

[6] Observe that we could alternatively define an arbitrage flow pattern using $T = (T_{ij}, i \neq j) \in \mathfrak{R}^{N \times N - N}$. We use the above definition in order to simplify the notation somewhat.

aware of the total quantity supplied to each market by all other players. That is, each firm is unaware of the quantity that is being bought and sold specifically by arbitrageurs. Hence

$$\tilde{q}_{ij} = \sum_{k \neq i} q_{kj} + \sum_{k \in \mathcal{N}} T_{kj} - \sum_{k \in \mathcal{N}} T_{jk} \tag{18}$$

now represents the quantity 'supplied' to j by all players other than i, and the inverse demand function in each market, $j \in \mathcal{N}$, is now defined by

$$p_j \equiv p_j(q, T) = p_j\left(\sum_{i \in \mathcal{N}} q_{ij} + \sum_{i \in \mathcal{N}} T_{ij} - \sum_{i \in \mathcal{N}} T_{ji} \right), \tag{19}$$

where the argument of this function again represents the local consumption at market j.

Of course, none of these changes significantly impact the model of firm behavior introduced in the previous section. However, we must now explicitly consider the equilibrium conditions for arbitrageurs. To begin, observe that any equilibrium flow pattern must be feasible. That is, the quantity being "demanded" by arbitrageurs at any given market must be less than the "supply" to that market. More formally, in equilibrium it must be true that

$$\sum_{j \in \mathcal{N}} T_{ij} \leqq \sum_{k \in \mathcal{N}} (q_{ki} + T_{ki}) \quad \forall i \in \mathcal{N}. \tag{20}$$

In addition, several other conditions are also needed.

Observe that if $\sum_{j \in \mathcal{N}} T_{ij} < \sum_{k \in \mathcal{N}} (q_{ki} + T_{ki})$ for some $i \in \mathcal{N}$ then it must be true in equilibrium that (q, T) satisfies the conditions that $T_{ij} > 0 \Rightarrow p_j(q, T) - p_i(q, T) - c_{ij}(q, T) = 0$ and $T_{ij} = 0 \Rightarrow p_j(q, T) - p_i(q, T) - c_{ij}(q, T) \leqq 0$. In other words, whenever there is "unexhausted supply" in market i and there are no arbitrage flows to market j, then it must be true that there is no arbitrage opportunity at market j. Further, when there is "unexhausted supply" at market i and there are arbitrage flows to market j, then it must be true that the prices at i and j differ by exactly the cost of shipping between them. These conditions are identical to the standard SPE equilibrium conditions.

On the other hand, if $\sum_{j \in \mathcal{N}} T_{ij} = \sum_{k \in \mathcal{N}} (q_{ki} + T_{ki})$ for some $i \in \mathcal{N}$ then the standard SPE conditions may be inappropriate for this market. In particular, there may not be sufficient "unexhausted supply" to ensure that prices are equilibrated. Further, it must be true that arbitrageurs are only shipping to markets in which the arbitrage profits to be made are maximal. Therefore, letting $\mu_i = \max\{0,\ p_j(q, T) - p_i(q, T) - c_{ij}(q, T)\ \forall j \in \mathcal{N}\}$ denote the maximum arbitrage profit that can be earned [for a given (q, T)] making purchases at i, it follows that in equilibrium it must be true that (q, T) satisfies the conditions that $T_{ij} > 0 \Rightarrow p_j(q, T) - p_i(q, T) - c_{ij}(q, T) = \mu_i$ and $T_{ij} = 0 \Rightarrow p_j(q, T) - p_i(q, T) - c_{ij}(q, T) \leqq \mu_i$.

Combining these two sets of conditions and letting $\mu = (\mu_i,\ i \in \mathcal{N})^\top$ we now say that a (non-negative) vector, $(q, T, \mu) \in \mathfrak{R}_+^{N \times N \times 2 + N}$, is a *Cournot-Nash equilibrium in the presence of arbitrageurs* iff it satisfies the KKT conditions (11)–(14) [with $C_i'(q)$ replaced by $C_i'(q, T)$, $c_{ij}(q)$ replaced by $c_{ij}(q, T)$ and $R_{ij}'(q)$ replaced by $R_{ij}'(q, T)$], the feasibility condition (20), and the following conditions

$$\sum_{k \in \mathcal{N}} q_{ki} - \sum_{j \in \mathcal{N}} T_{ij} + \sum_{k \in \mathcal{N}} T_{ki} \geqq 0 \text{ and } T_{ij} > 0$$

$$\Rightarrow p_j(q, T) - p_i(q, T) - c_{ij}(q, T) = \mu_i \tag{21}$$

$$\sum_{k \in \mathcal{N}} q_{ki} - \sum_{j \in \mathcal{N}} T_{ij} + \sum_{k \in \mathcal{N}} T_{ki} \geqq 0 \text{ and } T_{ij} = 0$$

$$\Rightarrow p_j(q, T) - p_i(q, T) - c_{ij}(q, T) \leqq \mu_i \tag{22}$$

$$\sum_{k \in \mathcal{N}} q_{ki} - \sum_{j \in \mathcal{N}} T_{ij} + \sum_{k \in \mathcal{N}} T_{ki} > 0 \text{ and } T_{ij} > 0$$

$$\Rightarrow p_j(q, T) - p_i(q, T) - c_{ij}(q, T) = 0 \tag{23}$$

$$\sum_{k \in \mathcal{N}} q_{ki} - \sum_{j \in \mathcal{N}} T_{ij} + \sum_{k \in \mathcal{N}} T_{ki} > 0 \text{ and } T_{ij} = 0$$

$$\Rightarrow p_j(q, T) - p_i(q, T) - c_{ij}(q, T) \leqq 0 \tag{24}$$

for all $i, j \in \mathcal{N}$ (with $i \neq j$).

While these conditions are considerably more complicated than the classical SPE conditions and the Cournot-Nash conditions given above, we can nonetheless formulate this problem as a CP. Letting

$$F = \left(\left[C_i'(q, T) + c_{ij}(q, T) - R_{ij}'(q, T) \right],\ i, j \in \mathcal{N} \right)^\top, \tag{25}$$

$$G = \left(\left[p_i(q, T) + c_{ij}(q, T) - p_j(q, T) + \mu_i \right],\ i, j \in \mathcal{N} \right)^\top, \tag{26}$$

and

$$H = \left(\sum_{k \in \mathcal{N}} q_{ki} - \sum_{j \in \mathcal{N}} T_{ij} + \sum_{k \in \mathcal{N}} T_{ki}, \quad i \in \mathcal{N} \right)^{\top} \tag{27}$$

we can show that

Theorem 2   *A vector*

$$\begin{bmatrix} q \\ T \\ \mu \end{bmatrix} \in \Re^{N \times N \times 2 + N}$$

is a Cournot-Nash equilibrium in the presence of arbitrageurs iff it is a solution of the following CP:

$$\begin{bmatrix} q \\ T \\ \mu \end{bmatrix} \in \Re_+^{N \times N \times 2 + N} \begin{bmatrix} F(q, T, \mu) \\ G(q, T, \mu) \\ H(q, T, \mu) \end{bmatrix} \in \Re_+^{N \times N \times 2 + N}$$

$$[q \; T \; \mu] \begin{bmatrix} F(q, T, \mu) \\ G(q, T, \mu) \\ H(q, T, \mu) \end{bmatrix} = 0 \tag{28}$$

for F as defined in (25), G as defined in (26) and H as defined in (27).

Proof. To begin, observe that the arguments in the proof of Theorem 1 continue to hold. Also observe that the feasibility condition (20) is subsumed in the complementarity problem in (28). Hence all that remains is to demonstrate the equivalence for the arbitrage profit conditions, (21)–(24).

($\Rightarrow$) First, observe that $\mu_i H_i(q, T, \mu) = 0$ for all i with $H_i(q, T, \mu) = 0$. Also, observe from (24) that if $H_i(q, T, \mu) \geq 0$ and $T_{ij} = 0$ for all $j \in \mathcal{N}$ then $p_j(q, T) - p_i(q, T) - c_{ij}(q, T) = 0$ and it follows by definition that $\mu_i = 0$. On the other hand, observe from (23) that, if $H_i(q, T, \mu) \geq 0$ and $T_{ij} > 0$ for any j then $p_j(q, T) - p_i(q, T) - c_{ij}(q, T) = 0$ and it follows from (21) that $\mu_i = 0$. Hence, $H(q, t, \mu)^{\top} \mu = 0$.

Similarly, if $T_{ij} = 0$ it follows that $T_{ij} G_{ij}(q, T, \mu) = 0$. Further, if $T_{ij} \geq 0$ and $H_i(q, T, \mu) \geq 0$ it follows from (23) that $p_j(q, T) - p_i(q, T) - c_{ij}(q, T) = 0$ and from (21) that $\mu_i = 0$. On the other hand, if $T_{ij} \geq 0$ and $H_i(q, T, \mu) = 0$ it follows from (21) than $p_j - p_i - c_{ij} = \mu_i$. Hence, $G(q, T, \mu)^{\top} T = 0$.

Finally, it follows from the definition of μ that $\mu_i \geq 0$ and $\mu_j - [p_i(q, T) - p_i(q, T) + c_{ij}(q, T)] \geq 0$, and it follows from the definition of feasibility that $T_{ij} \geq 0$ for all $i, j \in \mathcal{N}$ and that $H_i(q, T, \mu) \geq 0$ for all $i \in \mathcal{N}$.

($\Leftarrow$) First observe that for any solution to the CP, $\mu_i \geq 0$ for all $i, j \in \mathcal{N}$ and $p_i(q, T) + c_{ij}(q, T) - p_j(q, T) + \mu_i \geq 0$ for all $i \in \mathcal{N}$. Hence, it follows that $\mu_i = \max\{0, p_j(q, T) - p_i(q, T) - c_{ij}(q, T) \,\forall j \in \mathcal{N}\}$.

Now, observe that for any solution of the CP, if $T_{ij} > 0$ then it follows that $p_i(q, T) + c_{ij}(q, T) - p_j(q, T) + \mu_i = 0$ and hence that (21) must hold. Further, if $H_i(q, T, \mu) > 0$ it follows that $\mu_i = 0$ and hence that $p_i(q, T) + c_{ij}(q, T) - p_j(q, T) = 0$ and that (23) holds.

If, on the other hand, $T_{ij} = 0$ it follows that $p_i(q, T) + c_{ij}(q, T) - p_j(q, T) + \mu_i \geq 0$ and that (22) holds. Further, if $H_i(q, T, \mu) > 0$ it follows that $\mu_i = 0$ and hence that $p_i(q, T) + c_{ij}(q, T) - p_j(q, T) \leq 0$, that (24) holds, and that $T_{ij} = 0$. $\square$

Before concluding this section, it is worth pointing out that this model can also be formulated as a "variational inequality".

Definition 3 *For a given map, $F: \mathfrak{R}^n \to \mathfrak{R}^n$, and nonempty set $X \subseteq \mathfrak{R}^n$ the problem of finding a vector, $q \in K$, satisfying*

$$F(q)^\top (x - q) \geq 0, \quad \forall x \in X \tag{29}$$

is referred to as the variational inequality problem (VIP).

Theorem 3 *A vector*

$$y^* = \begin{bmatrix} q^* \\ T^* \\ \mu^* \end{bmatrix} \in \mathfrak{R}^{N \times N \times 2 + N}$$

is a Cournot-Nash equilibrium in the presence of arbitrageurs iff it is a solution of the following VIP:

$$F(y^*)^\top (q - q^*) + G(y^*)^\top (T - T^*) + H(y^*)^\top (\mu - \mu^*) \geq 0 \tag{30}$$

for all $q \in \mathfrak{R}^{N \times N}$, $T \in \mathfrak{R}^{N \times N}$, and $\mu \in \mathfrak{R}^N$, with F as defined in (25), G as defined in (26) and H as defined in (27).

Proof. Follows immediately from Karamardian (1971, Lemma 3.1) and Theorem 2. $\square$

4.2. Existence of Equilibria

Given this formulation it is a relatively straightforward task to establish conditions which ensure the existence of an equilibrium. To begin, we now define a concept first introduced by Smith (1984).

Definition 4   *For any* $F : \mathfrak{R}_{+}^{n} \to \mathfrak{R}^{n}$, *a sequence* $\{x^{n}\}$ *on* $\mathfrak{R}_{+}^{n}$ *with* $|x^{n}| = n$ *for all* $n \in \mathscr{Z}$ *is said to be an exceptional sequence for* F *iff each* $x^{n} = (x_{i}^{n})$ *satisfies the following two conditions for some positive scalar* $\omega_{n} > 0$:

$$x_{i}^{n} > 0 \Rightarrow F_{i}(x^{n}) = -\omega_{n} x_{i}^{n}, \tag{31}$$

$$x_{i}^{n} = 0 \Rightarrow F_{i}(x^{n}) \geq 0. \tag{32}$$

In terms of this definition, we now summarize the main results of Smith (1984) in the following three lemmas:

Lemma 1   *For any continuous function* F, *either* F *has a CP-solution or there exists an exceptional sequence for* F.

Lemma 2   *Each continuous function* F *for which there are no exceptional sequences has a CP-solution.*

Lemma 3   *For any continuous function* $F: \mathfrak{R}_{+}^{n} \to \mathfrak{R}^{n}$, *if every sequence* $\{x^{n}\}$ *on* $\mathfrak{R}_{+}^{n}$ *satisfies the condition that*

$$\| x^{n} \| \to \infty \Rightarrow F(x^{n})^{\top} x^{n} \geq 0 \quad \text{for some } n \in \mathscr{Z}, \tag{33}$$

then F *has a CP-solution.*

With these results and the following assumptions:
A1 Inverse demand functions are bounded from above (i.e., demand is driven to zero at some finite price) and below. Formally, $p_{j}(0) < \infty \; \forall j \in \mathscr{N}$ and $p_{j}(\cdot) \geq 0 \; \forall j \in \mathscr{N}$.
A2 The unit cost of transporting an infinite quantity between any two nodes is infinite and all transportation costs are positive. Formally, $q_{ij} \to \infty \Rightarrow c_{ij}(q_{ij}) \to \infty$, $T_{ij} \to \infty \Rightarrow c_{ij}(T_{ij}) \to \infty \; \forall i, j \in \mathscr{N}$, and $c_{ij}(\cdot) \geq 0 \; \forall i, j \in \mathscr{N}$.
we can demonstrate the following existence result:

Theorem 4   *For any continuous, decreasing inverse demand functions satisfying* $A1$, *and continuous transportation cost functions satisfying* $A2$, *there exists a Cournot-Nash equilibrium in the presence of arbitrageurs.*

Proof. We proceed by demonstrating that there are no exceptional sequences for $[F\ G\ H]$. To do so, let us assume to the contrary that there exists an exceptional sequence $\{x^n\} = (q^n, T^n, \mu^n)$.

First, observe that $\mu_i \geq 0\ \forall i \in \mathcal{N}$ and hence that $\mu_i \nrightarrow -\infty\ \forall i \in \mathcal{N}$. Further observe that since $p_j(q, T)$ is bounded it also follows that $\mu_i \nrightarrow \infty\ \forall i \in \mathcal{N}$.

Also, observe that $T_{ij}^n > 0$ implies from (21) that $G_{ij}(q, T, \mu) < 0$. But, if we assume that $T_{ij} \to \infty$ then it follows from A2 that $c_{ij}(T_{ij}) \to \infty$, which, together with $\mu_i \geq 0$, and the boundedness of $p_i(q, T)$ and $p_j(q, T)$, implies that $G_{ij}(q, T, \mu) \geq 0$ which is a contradiction. Hence, it must be the case that $T_{ij} \nrightarrow \infty\ \forall i, j \in \mathcal{N}$.

Now, if we let $\| x^n \| \to \infty$ it must be the case that $q_i^n \to \infty$ for some $i \in \mathcal{N}$. But, since A1, A2, and (25) together imply that $F(x^n)^\top x^n \to \infty$, it follows from Lemma 3 that $\{x^n\}$ cannot be an exceptional sequence and from Lemma 2 that an equilibrium exists. □

4.3. A Small Example

The best way to see the significance of the model developed above is with a numerical example. Fortunately, since the model can be formulated as a CP, there are a wide variety if algorithms that can be used to solve these problems. For an excellent review of a variety of iterative algorithms see Pang and Chan (1982), and for an interesting approach which was developed after their review was completed see Stone (1985). For a comparison of algorithms for the standard spatial price equilibrium (SPE) problem see Friesz, Harker and Tobin (1984), Pang (1984), and Nagurney (1987a). Furthermore, the consequences of the extensions described above can be demonstrated even with a very simple example.

In particular, consider an example with two markets in which the demand function at market 1 is given by

$$p_1(q) = 4 - (q_{11} + q_{21}) \tag{34}$$

and the demand function at market 2 is given by

$$p_2(q) = 13 - 2(q_{12} + q_{22}). \tag{35}$$

The unit shipping costs are given by the constant functions, $c_{12}(q) = c_{21}(q) = 3$, and the constant marginal costs are $C_1'(q) = 0.2$ and $C_2'(q) = 2.1$. The Cournot-Nash solution to this problem is $q_{11} = 1.90$, $q_{12} = 1.45$, $q_{21} = 0$, and $q_{22} = 2$, which results in prices of $p_1 = 2.1$ and $p_2 = 6.1$. Clearly, this solution can't be sustained since arbitrageurs can profitably ship from market 1 to market 2.

If we now explicitly introduce arbitrageurs the inverse demand functions are given by

$$p_1 = 4 - (q_{11} + q_{21} + T_{21} - T_{12}) \tag{36}$$

$$p_2 = 13 - 2(q_{12} + q_{22} + T_{12} - T_{21}). \tag{37}$$

An equilibrium solution to this example is given by $q_{11} = 2.33$, $q_{12} = 1.16$, $q_{21} = 0.00$, $q_{22} = 1.71$, $T_{12} = 0.86$, and $T_{21} = 0.00$. The interpretation is that, of the 2.33 units supplied to market 1 by firm 1, 0.86 units are bought by arbitrageurs and re-sold in market 2. The total supply to market 2 is 1.16 (from firm 1) plus 1.71 (from firm 2) plus 0.86 (from arbitrageurs), with resulting prices of $p_1 = 2.53$ and $p_2 = 5.53$. This solution is substantially different from the solution obtained when arbitrageurs are ignored, and hence it is clear that arbitrageurs can have a significant impact. In particular, observe that the inclusion of arbitrageurs increases the profits of firm 1 from $7.8 to $8.1 (assuming that fixed costs are zero) but decreases the profits of firm 2 from $8.0 to $5.9 (again assuming zero fixed costs).

It is also clear that the Cournot-Nash oligopoly problem with arbitrageurs is not equivalent to the perfectly competitive SPE problem. Indeed, it is quite easy to show that, in the above example, the perfectly competitive solution is not an oligopolistic solution. To see this, assume that there are a large number of firms at both nodes and that the supply curve in each market is given by the above marginal cost curves. The solution to this standard SPE problem is $p_1 = 1.085$ and $p_2 = 4.085$. The total supply to market 1 is 5.425 and the total demand in market 1 is 2.915. The 2.511 units of excess supply in market 1 are shipped to market 2 to meet the excess demand there (supply to 2 is 1.945 and the demand there is 4.458). It is quite easy to see that this is not a Cournot-Nash oligopolistic equilibrium in the presence of arbitrageurs by comparing $R'_{11}(q, T)$ with $C'_1(q, T)$. Reinterpreting this solution in an oligopoly setting yields $q_{11} = 5.425$, $q_{12} = 0$, $q_{21} = 0$, $q_{22} = 1.945$, $T_{12} = 2.511$, and $T_{21} = 0$. Hence, $R'_{11}(q, T) = -9.4$ and $C'_1(q, T) = 0.2$ and firm 1 has an incentive to decrease q_{11}.

5. Directions for Future Research

Our model can be extended in a wide variety of ways, and applied to a large number of actual markets. We briefly discuss several of these future research topics below. Some of these topics are currently being explored, while others still remain open questions.

5.1. An Alternative Formulation

In the model presented here we have assumed that producing firms have no specific knowledge of the behavior of arbitrageurs. An alternative approach is to assume that profit-maximizing oligopolists do not allow arbitrage opportunities to persist. That is, we could assume that firms maximize profits while keeping arbitrageurs out of the market. While this would seem to yield a well-defined game, observe that, in such a formulation, the profit function for each firm is defined over only a subset of its strategy set. Hence, this type of model is often referred to as a pseudogame [see Friedman (1986)].

To see the implications of this alternate formulation, let's consider the example of the previous section and assume that firms maximize their profits subject to the following "zero-arbitrage constraints":

$$\left[4 - (q_{11} + q_{21})\right] + 3 \geq \left[13 - 2(q_{12} + q_{22})\right] \tag{38}$$

$$\left[13 - 2(q_{12} + q_{22})\right] + 3 \geq \left[4 - (q_{11} + q_{21})\right]. \tag{39}$$

A solution of this pseudogame is $q_{11} = 1.6$, $q_{12} = 1.8$, $q_{21} = 0$, and $q_{22} = 2$. The resulting prices are $p_1 = 2.4$ and $p_2 = 5.4$. This solution is quite different from the solution with arbitrageurs, both from the standpoint of the firms, and from the standpoint of the consumers.

It is well known that pseudogames can be formulated as quasi-variational inequalities [Baiocchi and Capelo (1984)], and this formulation (and the markets for which it is applicable) will be explored in a subsequent paper.

5.2. Structural Extensions

In addition to this alternate formulation, there are several obvious structural extensions to the current formulation. The first involves incorporating a more general network topology. The current approach assumes that there is one path connecting each OD-pair. However, we know that in many applications, we are interested in determining the paths used to transport the goods. A more general network can be incorporated into the current model in much the same way as it was incorporated into competitive SPE models, and this will be pursued in a subsequent paper.

In addition, our model can be readily extended to allow different transport costs for the different players. For example, in the oil market, while it is possible for arbitrageurs to transport oil, they can not generally do so as cheaply as the producing firms can. However, the inclusion of a more complete model of the transport sector and the competition between producing firms and arbitrageurs requires additional research.

Finally, some thought should be given to how to incorporate monopoly power on the demand side. This is particularly important for the modeling of input markets.

5.3. Welfare Implications

One area that we have not touched on at all in this analysis is the effect that arbitrageurs have on social welfare. We would expect that arbitrageurs would have a positive effect on social welfare (as compared to an oligopoly situation without them), however we have been unable to substantiate this hypothesis. If it is not true, it would indicate that the additional "competition" generated by arbitrageurs actually has a detrimental effect. As an indication of this, observe that in the example presented in Section 4.3 the inclusion of arbitrageurs (i.e., increased competition) causes a *decrease* in total supply from 5.35 to 5.20 whereas we normally expect increased competition to result in increased supply. Hence, we feel that this area definitely warrants further attention.

5.4. Applications

Finally, there are several applications of this model that we will be exploring in subsequent papers. The first, is the oil market (for both crude oil and refined products). The oil market is particularly interesting since it is composed of a contract market (for the large players), a spot market (for the large players and arbitrageurs), and a futures market (used predominantly by speculators and arbitrageurs, though some large players do use it to hedge). Thus, in addition to the possibility of spatial arbitrage, there is the possibility of cross-market arbitrage, and calendar arbitrage. In practice, each of these is watched quite closely by all of the players involved, and generally such opportunities exist for only a very short time. One approach we are considering is to combine the multi-period model of Nagurney and Aronson (1988) with the model described in this paper.

The other application we will be considering in a subsequent paper is the black market in narcotics. This market has a small number of firms each with market power, generally with one firm located at each demand node (generally cities, but sometimes neighborhoods in the larger cities). Each firm has a fair amount of latitude in the quantity it supplies (and hence the resulting price), but all are careful to set prices that prevent any arbitrageurs from moving narcotics from one market to another.

References

Baiocchi, C. and A. Capelo (1984) *Variational and Quasivariational Inequalities: Applications to Free-Boundary Problems*, New York, John Wiley.

Carey, M. (1980) "Stability of Competitive Regional Trade with Monotone Demand/Supply Functions", *Journal of Regional Science*, 20, 489–501.

Carlton, D.W. (1983) "A Reexamination of Delivered Pricing Systems", *Journal of Law and Economics*, 26, 51– 70.

Dafermos, S. and A. Nagurney (1987) "Oligopolistic and Competitive Behavior of Spatially Separated Markets", *Regional Science and Urban Economics*, 17, 245–254.

Florian, M. and M. Los (1982) "A New Look at Static Spatial Price Equilibrium Models", *Regional Science and Urban Economics*, 12, 579–597.

Friedman, J.W. (1986) *Game Theory with Applications to Economics*, New York, Oxford University Press.

Friesz, T.L., R.L. Tobin, T.E. Smith, and P.T. Harker (1983) "A Nonlinear Complementarity Formulation and Solution Procedure for the General Derived Demand Network Equilibrium Problem", *Journal of Regional Science*, 23, 337–359.

Friesz, T.L., P.T. Harker and R.L. Tobin (1984) "Alternative Algorithms for the General Network Spatial Price Equilibrium Problem", *Journal of Regional Science*, 24, 475–507.

Gabay, D. and H. Moulin (1980) "On the Uniqueness and Stability of Nash-equilibria in Noncooperative Games", in A. Bensoussan et al. (eds.), *Applied Stochastic Control in Econometrics and Management Science*, North-Holland, 1980.

Greenhut, J. and M. Greenhut (1975) "Spatial Price Discrimination, Competition, and Locational Effects", *Economica*, 42, 401–419.

Harker, P.T. (1985) "Investigating the Use of the Core as a Solution Concept in Spatial Price Equilibrium Games", *Lecture Notes in Economics and Mathematical Systems*, 249, 41–72.

Harker, P.T. (1986) "Alternative Models of Spatial Competition", *Operations Research*, 34, 410–425.

Hoover, E.M. (1937) "Spatial Price Discrimination", *Review of Economic Studies*, 4, 182–191.

Karamardian S. (1971) "Generalized Complementarity Problem", *Journal of Optimization Theory and Applications*, 8, 161–168.

MacKinnon, J.G. (1973) "A Technique for the Solution of Spatial Equilibrium Models", *Journal of Regional Science*, 16, 293–307.

Nagurney, A. (1987a) "Computational Comparisons of Spatial Price Equilibrium Methods", *Journal of Regional Science*, 27, 55–76.

Nagurney, A. (1987b) "Competitive Equilibrium Problems, Variational Inequalities and Regional Science", *Journal of Regional Science*, 27, 503–517.

Nagurney, A. and J. Aronson (1988) "A General Dynamic Spatial Price Equilibrium Model: Formulation, Solution, and Computational Results", *Journal of Computational and Applied Mathematics*, 22, 359–377.

Pang, J-S. (1984) "Solution of the General Multicommodity Spatial Equilibrium Problem by Variational and Complementarity Methods", *Journal of Regional Science*, 24, 403–414.

Pang J-S. and D. Chan (1982) "Iterative Methods for Variational and Complementarity Problems", *Mathematical Programming*, 24, 284–313.

Samuelson, P. (1952) "Spatial Price Equilibrium and Linear Programming", *American Economic Review*, 42, 283–303.

Simkin, C.G.F. (1948) "Some Aspects and Generalisations of the Theory of Discrimination", *Review of Economic Studies*, 15, 1–13.

Smith, T.E. (1984) "A Solution Condition for Complementarity Problems", *Applied Mathematics and Computation*, 15, 61–69.

Smith, T.E. and T.L. Friesz (1985) "Spatial Market Equilibria with Flow-Dependent Supply and Demand", *Regional Science and Urban Economics*, 15, 181–218.

Spulber, D.F. (1984) "Competition and Multiplant Monopoly with Spatial Nonlinear Pricing", *International Economic Review*, 25, 425–439.

Stevens, B.H. and C.P. Rydell (1966) "Spatial Demand Theory and Monopoly Price Theory", *Papers of the Regional Science Association*, 17, 195–204.

Stone, J.C. (1985) "Sequential Optimization and Complementarity Techniques for Computing Economic Equilibria", *Mathematical Programming Study*, 23, 173–191.

Takayama, T. and G.G. Judge (1970) "Alternative Spatial Equilibrium Models", *Journal of Regional Science*, 10, 1–12.

Takayama, T. and G.G. Judge (1964) "Equilibrium Among Spatially Separated Markets: A Reformulation", *Econometrica*, 32, 510–524.

Takayama, T. and G.G. Judge (1971) *Spatial and Temporal Price and Allocation Models*, North-Holland, Amsterdam.

Tobin, R.L. and T.L. Friesz (1983) "Formulating and Solving the Spatial Price Equilibrium Problem with Transshipment in Terms of Arc Variables", *Journal of Regional Science*, 23, 187–198.

Tobin, R.L. and T.L. Friesz (1985) "A New Look at Spatially Competitive Facility Location Models", *Lecture Notes in Economics and Mathematical Systems*, 249, 1–19.

Weskamp, A. (1985) "Existence of Spatial Cournot Equilibria", *Regional Science and Urban Economics*, 15, 219–227.

INDEX